CHRISTIAN BELIEVER

KNOWING GOD WITH HEART AND MIND

Study Manual

Writer of
CHRISTIAN BELIEVER: KNOWING GOD WITH HEART AND MIND
Study Manual
J. Ellsworth Kalas

Symbol art by Nell Fisher

Cover and internal design by Ed Wynne

For more information about
CHRISTIAN BELIEVER or CHRISTIAN BELIEVER training seminars,
call toll free 800-251-8591 or 800-672-1789.

Acknowledgments for study manual prayers

Page 65: Prayer from Zaire, from *Another Day*, edited by John Carden (Church Mission Society, 1986); p. 124. Used by permission of the Church Mission Society.

Page 75: Prayer based on the words of John Calvin, from *Contemporary Parish Prayers*, edited by Frank Colquhoun (Hodder and Stoughton, 1975). Reproduced by permission of Hodder and Stoughton Limited.

Page 115: Reprinted by permission of the publishers and the Trustees of Amherst College from THE POEMS OF EMILY DICKINSON, Thomas H. Johnson, ed., Cambridge, Mass.: The Belknap Press of Harvard University Press, Copyright © 1951, 1955, 1979, 1983 by the President and Fellows of Harvard College.

Page 125: From *The Prayers of Kierkegaard*, edited by Perry D. LeFevre, © 1956 by The University of Chicago Press; p. 99. Used by permission.

Page 205: Prayer from *Moravian Daily Texts, 1995* (The Moravian Church in America, 1995); p. 55. Used by permission of The Moravian Church in America.

Page 225: From "The Order for the Administration of the Sacrament of the Lord's Supper or Holy Communion," *The Book of Worship for Church and Home;* page 20. Copyright © 1964, 1965 by Board of Publication of The Methodist Church, Inc.

Page 235: Taken from *The Prayers of Susanna Wesley*, edited by W.L. Doughty. Copyright © 1984 by The Zondervan Corporation. Used by permission of Zondervan Publishing House.

Page 245: A Muslim's first prayer as a Christian, from *Morning, Noon and Night*, edited by John Carden (Church Mission Society, 1976); p. 53. Used by permission of the Church Mission Society.

Page 255: Poem from *Rose From Brier*, by Amy Carmichael (Christian Literature Crusade, 1933, 1973, 1992). Used by permission of Christian Literature Crusade.

Page 295: Prayer for the dead in the Orthodox tradition, from *The Lenten Tradition*, translated from the original Greek by Mother Mary and Archimandrite Kallistos Ware (Faber and Faber Ltd.). Used by permission of Faber and Faber Ltd.

Contents

As You Begin Your Study

Preparation the Key

You are beginning a thirty-week intensive study that combines study of Scripture and Christian belief. Your commitment includes at least forty-five minutes of study and prayer each day, six days a week, in preparation for the two-hour weekly group meeting. Begin and maintain disciplined daily study in order to complete the large amount of reading and writing required in preparation for group study. Careful notetaking is crucial to participation in group discussions.

Reading Package

The CHRISTIAN BELIEVER reading package consists of a study manual and a book of readings. You will use both books in your daily study.

Study Manual

The study manual guides daily study. The lesson format, designed to support disciplined daily study, provides instruction, content, and necessary space for carrying out the daily assignments. Elements in the easy-to-use lesson format are the same for all lessons. At the top of the first page of every lesson is a symbol and a group of words—the language of faith. Explanation of the symbol appears later in the lesson. The lesson title and the Scripture verse or verses that follow relate to the doctrine being studied.

Each section of the lesson has a particular function. "Life Questions" raises questions persons considering the doctrine might ask. The underlying assumption is that doctrine is the church's answer to life questions.

The "Assignment" section includes introductory paragraphs that suggest approach to the week's Scripture. Each daily assignment includes Scripture passages and readings in the book of readings. Phrases in parentheses following Scripture references make the connection between the Scripture and the lesson topic. The readings are numbered sequentially. The second and third pages of each lesson provide space for daily notetaking on Scripture and Readings.

Sequence of study is the same throughout the thirty weeks: Days 1 through 5, read and take notes on assigned Scripture and Readings. On Day 6, read "The Church Teaching and Believing" in the study manual. This commentary is fairly long and requires reflection, so it is important to come to Day 6 having completed all previous assignments for the week. "BECAUSE WE THE CHURCH BELIEVE" statements at the end of the commentary provide opportunity for reflection and decision.

Occasional blocks of information additional to the commentary appear in the margins of the pages.

"Believing and Living" consists mainly of questions that make connections between the doctrine and daily living. You will use your written responses in group discussion.

"Seeking More Understanding" suggests activities beyond the weekly assignments for individuals interested in doing additional study or research. Information gathered from such study can enrich group discussion.

We have used the New Revised Standard Version of the Bible in developing CHRISTIAN

BELIEVER, but individual study and group discussion will be enriched by many different translations. A study Bible with notes will be helpful in daily study.

Readings

The readings will introduce you to the main ideas in each doctrine. Selections fall into several categories: early Christian documents that contributed to the formulation or expression of doctrines that form the central teachings of Christian faith; writings from such founders of Protestant denominations as Martin Luther, John Calvin, and John Wesley; writings from twentieth-century thinkers on classical doctrines; selections from contemporary literature, poetry, or hymns that are expressions of or comments on doctrine; and selections that show the role of doctrine in life.

You will read approximately ten selections from this book each week. Pages 5 and 6 in the book of readings explain the nature of the readings, the organization of the book, and the steps to take in preparing for weekly group discussion. Turn to those pages right now and read them.

Scripture in CHRISTIAN BELIEVER

CHRISTIAN BELIEVER is a topical study, and the Scriptures chosen for this study throw light on the topic under study. Read Scripture through the lens of the topic. For example, if you are studying salvation, ask as you read Scripture, "What light does this Scripture throw on salvation?" The notes you take on Scripture will always be from the perspective of the topic of the lesson. Some Scripture passages are assigned more than once, but you will read them with different doctrines in mind.

Prayer

Each week group members will identify particular persons or situations needing prayer. The study manual provides space for recording those concerns. As you read and study daily, add to the list and pray faithfully about each concern. A printed prayer appears at the end of each lesson in the study manual. These prayers come from persons across the centuries and reflect the language of their times.

The Language of Faith

Faith language is both word and symbol. The Bible, book of readings, study manual, and videotapes work together through word and symbol to heighten your awareness of the language of faith. Study of CHRISTIAN BELIEVER will give you new eyes to see symbols of the Christian faith in the church and elsewhere, and new ears to hear the words of faith in sermons, songs, prayers, and in the rituals for the sacraments.

Look at the symbols at the top of this page. The fish is a symbol for both Jesus and believers. The symbol of the Trinity actually includes four symbols: three circles forming a trefoil with the crossing points becoming a triquetra with a small triangle and a larger triangle at the center. The crown symbolizes victory of Christ through the cross and victory of faithful Christians. Vines and branches weave among the symbols symbolizing the relationship between Jesus and his followers.

1

Believing

Dogma **Creeds**

Knowledge

Heart Mind

Belief

Theology **Doctrine**

Christian believer

Believing and Understanding

"But these are written so that you may come to believe that Jesus is the Messiah, the Son of God, and that through believing you may have life in his name."

—*John 20:31*

LIFE QUESTIONS

"I believe," the man cried; "help my unbelief!" (Mark 9:24). We humans are always caught in something of this dilemma. We need to believe. Believing is essential to set our intellectual and emotional roots in some kind of certainty. We can't help believing. To believe is as natural to us as eating and sleeping. We are believing creatures.

But believing also makes us nervous, because believing is powerful and therefore risky. Beliefs have consequences. Therefore, to believe is not enough; more important is having a right basis of belief. So what should I believe, and why? And what difference will my believing make—in me, and in my world? Does everything about my believing matter, or is it enough simply to say, "I believe; help my unbelief"?

ASSIGNMENT

The word *believe,* in its several forms, does not appear often in the Old Testament. But the idea is there, of course, implicit in all the stories of persons' relationships to God, sometimes for its presence and sometimes for its absence. In the New Testament believing is a dominant theme. And of course believing will be the guiding theme in this study. The Scriptures we read this week are intended to set the course for our journey—a journey of nearly a year of study but of a lifetime of living and believing.

Day 1 Genesis 12:1-9 (Abram's call); Exodus 3:1-17 (God appears to Moses) Introduction and Readings 1 and 2

Day 2 Job 42:1-6 (Job acknowledges God); Habakkuk 3:10-19 (in awe of God) Readings 3, 4, and 5

Day 3 Mark 9:14-29 (belief and faith); John 20:24-31 (doubt and belief) Readings 6 and 7

Day 4 Hebrews 11:1-6 (meaning of faith); Matthew 13:1-23 (the seed and the word) Readings 8 and 9

Day 5 Acts 17:16-34 (unknown God made known); Jude (contend for the faith) Readings 10, 11, and 12

Day 6 Read and respond to "The Church Teaching and Believing" and "Believing and Living."

Day 7 Rest and prayer

DAILY PRAYER

Pray for the persons and situations on your Prayer Concerns list and about issues or concerns emerging from your daily reading and study.

6

BELIEVING

SCRIPTURE	READINGS

DAY 1

Genesis 12:1-9; Exodus 3:1-17	Introduction and Readings 1 and 2

DAY 2

Job 42:1-6; Habakkuk 3:10-19	Readings 3, 4, and 5

DAY 3

Mark 9:14-29; John 20:24-31	Readings 6 and 7

SCRIPTURE	READINGS

DAY 4

Hebrews 11:1-6; Matthew 13:1-23	Readings 8 and 9

DAY 5

Acts 17:16-34; Jude	Readings 10, 11, and 12

DAY 6 STUDY MANUAL	PRAYER CONCERNS
"The Church Teaching and Believing" and "Believing and Living"	

THE CHURCH TEACHING AND BELIEVING

To be human is to be a believer. We differ in what we believe, and in the intensity of our beliefs, but we insist on believing in something. Life simply can't exist without some such basis. These beliefs become the set-of-sails that determine the direction of our lives and our destination. And also, of course, the nature and quality of our journey.

Occasionally persons say they don't believe in anything. But such a statement is its own declaration of faith. To say, "I believe in nothing" is to declare how one has set one's life-sails. This statement, to the degree it is really believed, will determine where life will go.

So we have no option as to whether we will believe. The issue—and it is *the* issue—is in *what* we believe. And for Christians, more specifically, in *whom* we will believe.

Christians aren't naive about this business of believing. We do a tough-minded thing. We look life in the eye and say, "I believe . . ."

However, we may not always come up to that ideal. We may recite the Apostles' Creed or the Nicene Creed in public worship, but without any profound sense of ownership, and perhaps without much understanding or conviction. Indeed, at times we may have difficulty saying how our operating creed differs from that of our secular neighbor. We surely understand that "I believe; help my unbelief" is part of life.

While it is true Christians are demonstrated better by their deeds than by their words, those deeds are ultimately determined by beliefs. And Christians are the inheritors of a magnificent body of beliefs. These beliefs have quite literally cost blood, beginning with the death of Christ at Calvary and continuing to the present day.

When the Council of Nicaea convened in A.D. 325, the gathered body included many who had suffered fearfully for their faith during the persecution under the Roman emperor Diocletian. For eight terrifying years Diocletian had wrecked churches, burned sacred books, and tortured and beheaded Christians. As thirty bishops paid honor to Constantine at the first council session, ten of the thirty were blind, their eyes having been burned out by Diocletian's forces. Every one of the thirty had bodily evidence of the years of persecution. Many of them had worked in the salt mines, others as galley slaves. The creedal words we sometimes speak in routine fashion were developed out of the strong convictions of persons whose confessions of faith often led to suffering and even death.

The importance of right believing is stated so matter-of-factly in the Gospel of Mark we generally miss it. A crowd had followed Jesus and his disciples to "a deserted place." When Jesus saw the crowd, "he had compassion for them, because they were like sheep without a shepherd" (Mark 6:34). Crowds are always a motley sight, and first-century crowds especially so. These people were marked by poverty and by an unusual number of physical ailments. Since Jesus often exercised the power to heal, we might expect he would walk through such a crowd performing miracles; the need must have been obvious. Some might argue he should have organized them into a coherent political body that would be able to seek their rights. But Jesus, moved by compassion, "began to teach them many things" (6:34). Give people a right basis of belief, and almost everything else that is good can follow. On the other hand, give us health, money, and even talent, and if we are not guided by right belief, we will not only squander these other elements, but we well may use them destructively.

Where Do We Begin?

Contemporary wisdom says to begin by looking for the latest thing; but of course we know better than that, because the latest thing is usually a fad that will be history before we have finished making the payments. Because ours is also a scientific age, we want something that is tested. Christian doctrine can stand up to that test, offering nearly two millennia of data from life itself.

The record is impressive, even if uneven. The earliest generations of Christians were said to have out-lived, out-thought, out-loved, and out-died their opponents. Significant also is the fact that Christian beliefs have been tested over an extended period of centuries, in varieties of cultures and circumstances, and with impressive results. The believers who have taken the teachings of the church most seriously have won the respect of even their enemies; we often describe those believers as "saints" or "saintly." On the other hand, a great mass of those who have called themselves believers have not been that impressive. They may have proved better than the general populace, but not dramatically so.

We must also concede that much of the evidence is what a scholar might call anecdotal; that is, based on statements and stories rather than on hard statistics. Nevertheless, the huge accumulation of such anecdotal evidence is enough to make us examine the beliefs that, generally speaking, have produced these persons.

Basically, this examination takes us back to a single document, the Bible. So our study each week begins with biblical sources. We will read daily from the Bible. The lessons will refer to ways doctrines have developed over the centuries and to the evolving of ancient and more modern creeds. We will study definitions that have come to us through ancient bodies that we call church councils. This study makes no attempt to create something new but does aim to explain these time-tested doctrines in modern language. We will be working at all times with what the New Testament describes as "the faith that was once for all entrusted to the saints" (Jude 3).

You will meet two terms that seem at times to be interchangeable but have rather distinct definitions, *theology* and *doctrine. Theology,* coming from the Latin words *theos* (God) and *logos* (speech) means literally the language about God, or talk about of God. *Doctrine,* from the Latin *doctrina* (teaching) and *docere* (to teach), is that which is officially taught by the church. Sometimes the Roman Catholic Church uses the word *dogma* to refer to a teaching considered infallible. But within general Christendom, the word *doctrine* is intended to mean teaching approved by the church. Theology may include general, speculative teaching, while doctrine refers to those teachings historically accepted as the position of the church, or of a particular denomination or church body.

The Sequence of Our Study

With what subjects shall we begin? The creeds typically begin with God. Our contemporary disposition, on the other hand, is to begin with our human condition; after all, we reason, how can we understand such subjects as God, salvation, and eternal life unless we understand ourselves and the predicament we're in.

We have chosen something of a middle ground. We assume most Christians want to know where we get our ideas about God and the other teachings of the church. So we begin with a study of the doctrine of *revelation,* and then the doctrine of the *Scriptures.* Our study of God leads us eventually to God as a *covenant-maker*—and that introduces us to the issue of the creature with whom God makes the covenant, *humankind.*

As soon as humankind enters the story, we get into the subject of *sin.* Sin, in turn, brings us to the need of *grace* and to the specific form of grace we call *salvation.* And when we speak of salvation, we are of course confronted by *Jesus Christ.* As we

The lamp, a symbol of wisdom, knowledge, and learning, provides illumination to the Christian in the search for understanding.

Constantine, Roman emperor who first granted imperial favor to Christianity, called the Council of Nicaea in 325 A.D. to settle disputes among rival factions in the church. Though unbaptized at the time, Constantine took an active part in leading the council to formulate the statement of orthodox belief about the person of Christ that became the Nicene Creed.

discuss the work of Christ as Savior, we consider a doctrine that goes all through the Scriptures, the *Atonement.*

But then comes the matter of our human response—*confession,* and particularly, the ability with which we make our response to God, which we call *faith.* And all of this study leads us into a discussion of the work of the *Holy Spirit.* Now, with God, Christ, and the Holy Spirit mentioned, we must think about the *Trinity.*

Back then to the human creature, particularly those persons who constitute the *people of God*—first the nation of Israel and then the *church.* And when we discuss the church, we come to the *sacraments,* the special mark of the church, and the broader field of *worship,* including prayer. Then we consider a more general theme, *the Christian life,* which, in turn, leads to the higher possibilities of the Christian life as defined in *sanctification.*

But Christian doctrine is never earthbound; it comes to completion in the *Christian hope.* Such completion has a flip side, however, called *judgment.* And with that, *resurrection* and then *eternal life.* Finally, we need to ask ourselves a pragmatic question—What difference do our beliefs make?—because biblical belief is practical. It affects our lives for both time and eternity.

Such is the sequence our study will follow. But the pattern is more of a weaving because all our doctrinal beliefs are somehow intertwined. What we believe about God affects what we believe about humankind, and what we believe about humankind affects our belief about the judgment or about eternal life. You will find such connecting as you study and will make any number of additional connections on your own.

A Personal Study

Be prepared for the fact this study will be personal. While the truths are objective, the approach is subjective. At all times we will be asking ourselves what a particular belief means to us, and how we ought to respond to it. This is consistent, of course, with the classical language of the Apostles' Creed: "*I* believe." This language is remarkably personal, considering we ordinarily recite this creed in a company of believers. And when we declare "*We* believe" in the Nicene Creed, we emphasize that company. But when we say "*I*," there is no escape clause, and no need to see if someone else is supporting the position. So while on one hand we are studying the beliefs of the Christian community, we respond to these beliefs in the first person singular. When we speak of God, and of matters related to God, we are making statements on which we bet our lives.

In our study together, we will leave room for differences of opinion. Such an attitude is a matter not only of Christian charity but also of common sense and humility. We respect the opinions of others, remembering they too are made in God's image. We remember also we are human creatures with limited perception. When we talk about God, Christ, the Holy Spirit,

A creed is a concise, organized statement of belief authorized by the church and initially used as a confession of faith by candidates for baptism. The word *creed* derives from the Latin meaning "I believe," the first words of most creeds and confessions of faith. In Middle English the word *symbole* was used to mean creed along with the more familiar *crede.* In Latin and Greek, the roots of our English word *symbol* mean mark or token, something identifying or representing something else. In that sense, a creed is a symbol of the belief it states.

grace, eternal life, or any other of these great topics, we are beyond our depth. Our being able to participate in such thinking and discussion is a divine compliment. We ought therefore to exercise a great deal of humility. Let us believe passionately, and affirm earnestly, but listen generously.

At the same time, remember that the creeds came out of vigorous, sometimes contentious debate. There's nothing wrong with earnest, intense discussion. Through such intellectual and spiritual engagement the lasting truths of the faith have been put into their classical form. Good discussion should deepen faith even as it clarifies understanding.

Understanding and Faith

We will discover, as we study, that understanding aids devotion. Because Christianity so often speaks of the importance of simplicity in faith, we can easily conclude knowledge is an enemy of faith. Not so. Simplicity of trust has nothing to fear from depths of knowledge. Indeed, *understanding* seems to be the main point in Jesus' explanation of the parable of the sower (Matthew 13:18-23). As he explains the parable's meaning, he says, "When anyone hears the word of the kingdom and does not understand it, the evil one comes and snatches away what is sown in the heart" (13:19). By contrast, the one who bears abundant fruit is "the one who hears the word and understands it" (13:23).

Biblical use of words like *understanding, knowledge,* and *wisdom* goes further than just intellectual apprehension. Their use includes a sense of involvement of the whole being, including the emotional and spiritual nature. But everything in Scripture encourages thoughtful study.

Another important distinction should be made. The aim of this study is not to *prove* but to understand. To prove assumes a base of truth or logic exists that passes judgment on doctrine. More than that, the desire to prove easily comes in conflict with the exercise of faith. We understand many things we cannot prove or do not even desire to prove.

In doctrine we confess from the beginning we are not able to prove what we believe. We are compelled to exercise faith. But acting on faith is not unique to Christian belief in particular or to religious belief in general. It is true of all of life. At times we will be content to say, "I don't *know,* but here's what I *believe.*" We will come to realize that such words are not a confession of defeat but a declaration of trust.

An Inherited Body of Belief

Fortunately, when it comes to doctrine, we are not reinventing the wheel. We are the inheritors and beneficiaries of a body of teaching. These doctrines have stood the test of time. Still more, they have endured the test of debate, not only by those who were the enemies of Christianity but also by those who belonged to the community of God but who differed on particular matters of doctrine. The fact that most of these beliefs have at one or more times been contested does not diminish their integrity; it adds to it. We would have reason for suspicion if matters as significant as these had never been questioned. Our inherited body of belief is substantial today not only because of the divine care of the Holy Spirit but because our predecessors in the Christian community have given such a legacy to us. No doubt doctrinal questions will continue to arise, and heresies (views outside the official teachings of the church) too. But we can say with some scholarly certainty that any "new" questions will be a repeat of questions the church has faced in centuries past.

The doctrines of the church do not exist in a vacuum. The church is meant to witness to its generation and to work toward the transformation of the surrounding secular culture. But the church is also part of that culture and is inevitably influenced by it. Sometimes, indeed, the influence has been so strong that later generations are embarrassed by the way the church reflected the culture of its time rather than reflecting the character of God.

Such cultural influences are currently at work. One need not be an alarmist to recognize this. In a far different time Paul pleaded with believers, "Do not be conformed to this world, but be transformed by the renewing of your minds, so that you may discern what is the will of God—what is good and acceptable and perfect" (Romans 12:2). We could make a rather long list of doctrines at issue today, but probably the most telling circumstance is not in doctrine itself but in the approach to truth. Where most previous generations believed in the existence of objective truth and that certain truths were held universally, we are currently in a time when truth is not seen as objective or universal. Now it is popular to say something may be true for you but not for me and certainly not for society at large. More than likely this mood is only a blip on the long line of philosophical inquiry, but it is the mood we must deal with in our time. Ambiguity about truth is a crucial part of our contemporary context of thinking.

Closely related to the idea that there is no objective, universal truth is the belief that everything is relative. Nothing is absolute. In some ways this belief is a reaction to a narrow judgmentalism unwilling to hear any argument but its own. The "relative" approach appeals to a generous-minded person who wants to see good not only in every person but also in every idea. But of course we don't accept this reasoning in everyday life. We recognize some solutions are right and others are wrong—and not only wrong but perhaps even disastrous.

Doctrine requires us to do some hard thinking. Doctrine does not authorize or condone our passing judgment on others. But it does demand we be tough on ourselves. We have to realize that to believe is also to *not* believe. Believing has a certain exclusive quality. Acknowledging this is not unkind or ungenerous; it is simply the way things are. We need to keep warm hearts without getting fuzzy minds.

So we call ourselves *believers*. We will learn, think, discuss, and reason; then, at a certain point, we will confess what we *believe*. The writer of the Second Letter to Timothy put together knowing and believing in a sentence of glad witness: "I know the one in whom I have put my trust, and I am sure that he is able to guard until that day what I have entrusted to him" (2 Timothy 1:12). Or in the language of the King James Version, "I *know* whom I have *believed*." The apostle knew the One in whom he had believed. And he believed with such intensity he was betting his life on it—even "until that day."

And that's the goal we are setting for ourselves in these months of study.

BECAUSE WE THE CHURCH BELIEVE the Christian faith has truth to be believed, I affirm my place in the company of believers.

BELIEVING AND LIVING

In a world of conflicting beliefs, it seems daring to accept some particular set of beliefs and tie our eternal welfare to them. But are beliefs really that consequential? When, either in your own experience or in history or biography, have you seen the powerful results of subscribing to certain beliefs?

_____

_____

At this point in your faith journey, how clear are you about what you believe? What beliefs are most important to you? least important to you? Try to write your own "creed" as you perceive your beliefs at this moment:

_____

_____

_____

_____

At what points are you at odds with contemporary philosophies of believing? At what points do you find you, too, think truths are not absolute and everything is relative? How do these ideas affect your believing?

_____

_____

What, if anything, makes it difficult for you to call yourself a *believer?* How might your response to this question have differed at other times in your life?

_____

_____

List ways we commonly use the word *believing* in contexts other than religion, such as believing in a person, or in an institution. Ask yourself in what ways these instances of believing are similar to, or different from, the believing you exercise in a specifically religious sense. What persons or organizations particularly ask you to believe in them? How does the exercising of such believing affect your religious faith, if at all?

_____

_____

_____

_____

SEEKING MORE UNDERSTANDING

The work of the Council of Nicaea (325) will be mentioned numerous times throughout this study. To become more familiar with the Council, do some research on why the Council was called, who the participants were, what the issues were, and what decisions or documents came out of the work of the Council. Books on church history, volumes of an encyclopedia, dictionaries of the Christian church, and the internet are all possible sources of information. Check the public library or your church library.

PRAYER

"Lord, I seek you with all my heart, with all the strength you have given me. I long to understand that which I believe.

You are my only hope; please listen to me. Do not let my weariness lessen my desire to find you, to see your face.

You created me in order to find you; you gave me strength to seek you. My strength and my weakness are in your hands: preserve my strength, and help my weakness. Where you have already opened the door, let me come in; where it is shut, open at my knocking.

Let me always remember you, love you, meditate upon you, and pray to you, until you restore me to your perfect pattern."

—*Augustine of Hippo, 354–430*

Augustine (354–430), Bishop of Hippo for thirty-five years and a "doctor of the church," was a teacher of rhetoric, consecrated bishop against his will. Born to a pagan father and Christian mother, his quest for the truth led him to join the Manichees, whose dualist interpretation of Christianity appealed to his sense of logic. After ten years he rejected their teaching and gradually redirected his thinking toward the more orthodox faith of his childhood. He loved debate and controversy, had a lifelong passion for truth and certainty, and was dedicated to the cause of the universal church. His writings on the nature of the church, the Trinity, sin, predestination, and grace have had vast influence in the history of the church.

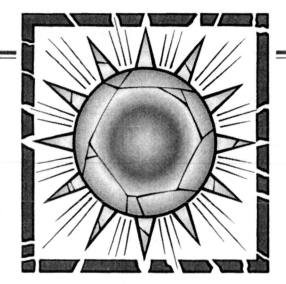

2

Revelation

Natural revelation   General revelation   Special revelation

God's self-disclosure   Bible

Mystery

Israel's history   Jesus Christ

Truths known by faith

The Self-Revealing God

"Ever since the creation of the world his [God's] eternal power and divine nature, invisible though they are, have been understood and seen through the things he has made."

—Romans 1:20

LIFE QUESTIONS

How ever in the world can a person know God, or know about God? By definition, God is out of our reach. Philosophers sometimes refer to God as "the wholly Other"; if that be so, how can we possibly hope to know God in relationship?

But the impossibility of knowing God doesn't deter us in our quest. We pursue God, and all of the ultimate questions that go with God, because we cannot do otherwise. Then we are startled to learn that God has been pleased to engage in divine self-disclosure.

How can this be? How does God reveal the divine self? And if it seems to us there has been such a disclosure, do we dare trust it, or is such an idea simply our ultimate self-delusion?

ASSIGNMENT

One could easily write a book to describe the whole Bible as the story of God's self-disclosure. When Genesis says, "In the beginning when God created the heavens and the earth" (Genesis 1:1), we are being introduced to the self-revealing God.

It is difficult to choose particular Scripture passages because the idea of revelation is woven throughout the entire Bible. The portions we will read are suggestive and helpful but far from complete. You may want to add passages that seem to you to throw light on the subject of revelation.

Day 1   Genesis 1:1–2:3 (Creation); Exodus 3:1-15 (the burning bush)
        Introduction and Readings 13, 14, and 15
Day 2   Job 38–41 (voice from the whirlwind)
        Readings 16 and 17
Day 3   Psalms 105–107 (God's deeds for Israel, confession of sin, thanksgiving)
        Readings 18, 19, and 20
Day 4   Psalm 19 (God's glory in creation); John 1:1-14 (Word became flesh)
        Readings 21, 22, and 23
Day 5   Romans 1:14-32 (knowledge of God made plain); Hebrews 1:1–2:9 (God's Son)
        Readings 24, 25, and 26
Day 6   Read and respond to "The Church Teaching and Believing" and "Believing and Living."
Day 7   Rest and prayer

DAILY PRAYER

Pray for the persons and situations on your Prayer Concerns list and about issues or concerns emerging from your daily reading and study.

Revelation

SCRIPTURE	READINGS

DAY 1

Genesis 1:1–2:3; Exodus 3:1-15	Introduction and Readings 13, 14, and 15

DAY 2

Job 38–41	Readings 16 and 17

DAY 3

Psalms 105–107	Readings 18, 19, and 20

SCRIPTURE	READINGS

DAY 4

| Psalm 19; John 1:1-14 | Readings 21, 22, and 23 |

DAY 5

| Romans 1:14-32; Hebrews 1:1–2:9 | Readings 24, 25, and 26 |

DAY 6 STUDY MANUAL	PRAYER CONCERNS
"The Church Teaching and Believing" and "Believing and Living"	

THE CHURCH TEACHING AND BELIEVING

If we're going to know about God, it will have to be by God's revealing. When Zophar, one of Job's friends, asks, "Can you find out the deep things of God? / Can you find out the limit of the Almighty?" (Job 11:7), no one has to tell us the intent of the question. God is clearly beyond our ken.

Nevertheless, the Bible also assures us that God can be found by our searching. Early in their history the people of Israel are promised that even when they have become complacent and corrupt, "you will seek the LORD your God, and you will find him if you search after him with all your heart and soul" (Deuteronomy 4:29). Israel can find God because God had already found and chosen them. Centuries later, when the people were captives in Babylon, the prophet Jeremiah reassured them on God's behalf, "When you search for me, you will find me" (Jeremiah 29:13).

Because in truth, it is God's nature to be self-revealing. Logic says that the divine would be hidden and inaccessible, but Scripture shows that God desires to be known. It well may be that the hiddenness of God has more to do with the tentativeness of our search than with divine reluctance.

A Difficult Doctrine

Let us confess, before we go further, that revelation is a difficult doctrine. Let us also confess that it is an absolutely essential one. No, we will not find the word or even the idea in the creeds. In a sense, it is prior to the creeds, because when we set out to say, "I believe," we are presupposing there is something to be believed. And where does that something come from? It comes to us by revelation.

Can we prove revelation? Not really. Not fully, at any rate. But it is important, this early in our study, to face a hard fact. Let us acknowledge that nothing we humans can know is beyond refutation. Everything we profess to know comes to us by one of four ways—our sense experience (what sight, hearing, touch, and so forth provide us), reason (or logic), authority (what trusted, qualified people say), and revelation. All of these means of knowing are open to doubt. Our sense experiences often contradict one another, and they sometimes prove untrue (as we sometimes discover in courts of law). Reason always depends on some presuppositions, and these presuppositions can't ultimately be proved. Our authorities—impressive

and learned though they may be—are as human as we are, so that their senses, motives, and reasoning can be faulty or prejudiced. Revelation is, of course, a product of experience and of interpretation of experience.

So believers should not feel apologetic about their dependence on revelation. We confess that revelation requires faith. But so does every other method of knowing.

Of course the believer doesn't depend solely on revelation. Some of the finest thinkers of human history—persons like Augustine of Hippo, Thomas Aquinas, and Blaise Pascal—have supported their faith with admirable structures of logic.

But Christianity confesses that both reason and authority rest eventually on the prior matter of revelation. It can rightly be said that all other doctrines stand or fall on this one. Thomas Aquinas (1225–1274) argued that revelation did not abolish reason but perfected it. Reason, authority, and senses may in time contribute to a person's grasp of revelation.

However, a believer should not use revelation as an excuse to stop thinking. While unaided human reason cannot lead us to God, reason can help in the search. And the God who endowed the human mind would surely honor our honest use of the mind in our quest of the divine. Belief should never mean a flight from reason, but simply a recognition of the limits of reason in a matter as profound as the knowledge and experience of God.

But what do we mean by *revelation?* The word itself comes from the Latin *revelatio,* which means simply "an uncovering." Divine revelation refers to God's self-communication or self-disclosure. Such a revelation is necessary because it has to do with matters beyond our human grasp. So revelation is not simply information, even a vast accumulation of information. I may give you pages of data about myself—the dates of events in my life, the schools I attended, the family from which I came. But none of these facts will tell you who I am. Your grasping who I am will depend on my opening myself to you, that is, on my revealing myself. If I choose to keep the integral part of myself hidden from you, you will never know me, no matter how much factual data you accumulate.

Revelation cannot finally be proved. If it were proved, it would cease to be revelation—or the proof would be superior to the revelation. But revelation can be authenticated. One ought to be skeptical, for instance, of any solitary revelation; if a revelation doesn't have some ancestry or some intellectual "family," it has no validity. While the New Testament writers knew that Jesus Christ was unique, they also were careful to quote the Law and the Prophets to prove that he had a heritage.

So too, revelation ought to make sense of the human scene. A revelation that added confusion would be a contradiction in terms. Still more, pragmatism would insist that revelation should bring good results. A revelation that corrupted life, debased it, or caused its most perceptive followers to do so would not qualify as a true revelation. It is important to keep these criteria in mind, because the idea of revelation is very appealing to a certain type of unstable personality, for example, a delusional personality. The New Testament insists that we should "test the spirits to see whether they are from God" (1 John 4:1). That admonition surely applies to any "revelation" that might be presented to us.

In any event, we should always acknowledge that any revelation we receive is limited by what we are. We are, even at best, finite creatures. This means we are limited in what we can know, or what we can receive. Our spiritual antennae can reach only so far and convey only so much truth. This limitation is complicated further by the fact that we have sinned, and sin clouds our spiritual perception. Jesus said it is "the pure in heart" who "will see God" (Matthew 5:8). Any purity we have is in some measure sullied by our own sin and by the sinfulness of the world in which we live. Thus our reception of the divine inevitably has some static.

Then there is the nature of God. While we are finite, God is infinite. That is, God is not bound by anything. Quite clearly, that which is boundless cannot be contained by that which has boundaries; or to put it another way, the unlimited cannot be squeezed into the limited. Obviously, if we could take in all of God (that is, if we fully understood God), God would cease to be God because we would have taken possession of God. Of course this idea seduces us humans, and it has led to numerous instances of tragic error. The Scriptures suggest that Moses knew a greater intimacy with God than anyone before or since. Yet when he pleaded, "Show me your glory," God answered, "But . . . you cannot see my face; for no one shall see me and live" (Exodus 33:18-20). This statement is not so much a declaration of judgment as a statement of fact: We humans simply are not equipped to comprehend the fullness of God.

And with all of this, we remember that revelation is an expression of grace, another instance of God's reaching to us when it is impossible for us to take hold of the divine. By its very nature, revelation is by divine initiative. God is revealed to us because God has chosen to make it so. Revelation is exactly opposite to the recurringly popular belief that our knowledge of God is by our effort. There is no future in the human quest except as God has made himself known.

Traditionally a circle of light has symbolized deity, divinity, holiness. So the sun, a circle of light, source of light and life, came to be used very early as a symbol for God. Its bright rays represent divine power. The sun is by nature revealing, casting light into the darkness. God is by nature self-revealing, bringing light to the mystery.

Thomas Aquinas (1225–1274)—Dominican philosopher and theologian

Blaise Pascal (1623–1662)—French scientist, polemicist, Christian apologist

Francis of Assisi (1181–1226)—abandoned a life of wealth and privilege to found the Franciscan Order, whose friars were dedicated to complete poverty, forbidden to own property, and sent out in twos to preach; known for his humility, love of nature, passionate devotion to God, and deep concern for people

The Means and Methods of Revelation

How, then, is God revealed? We might begin with nature, or with the Scriptures, but let's begin with ourselves. This is not an egocentric act; it's just that we are the closest example at hand—and significant in our own way. The book of Genesis tells us we are made in God's image and likeness (Genesis 1:26-27). Perhaps we would sense as much even if the Scriptures hadn't told us, but we would have done so in some twisted fashion. The image of God in us is distorted, but enough lines remain to give us some insight.

Especially, for instance, our sense of right and wrong. This sense varies in its details from one culture to another, but from time immemorial it has been a basic part of our human equipment. This feeling that some conduct is better than others, that some attitudes and actions are good and some evil, is evidence of light from outside ourselves. Those fraternal twins, guilt and shame—so alike, yet so unique—are also part of our divine equipment. We would not be accessible to such feelings if we did not in some measure reflect the divine.

Critics of religion often accuse believers of making a God in their own image; *anthropomorphism* is the academic word. The truth is just the opposite. We sense the reality of God within our person, and we find God revealed there. Astonishingly, we see the trace of God's image in every human creature. No matter how blurred or defaced, the human capacity for goodness, for conscience, for claiming the high ground even when it is low— all of these point to that God-image in us.

Nature is probably humanity's oldest and most recognized revelation of God. Primitive peoples worshiped sun, moon, or stars; trees; or various animals. A variety of factors entered into this worship, but basically it was a reaction to the mystery of creation and the unceasing wonder of nature.

The apostle Paul said, "What can be known about God is plain," because "ever since the creation of the world his eternal power and divine nature, invisible though they are, have been understood and seen through the things he has made" (Romans 1:19-20). So Joseph Addison, a British poet in the early eighteenth century, recast the language of Psalm 19 to say,

"The spacious firmament on high,
With all the blue ethereal sky,
And spangled heavens, a shining frame,
Their great Original proclaim."

And if some might think that their proclamation is uncertain, Addison concludes,

"In Reason's ear they all rejoice,
And utter forth a glorious voice;
Forever singing, as they shine,
' The Hand that made us is divine.' "

Paul said this revelation of God through nature was enough to show humans the way to God, so that "they are without excuse" (Romans 1:20). He goes on to say that humans, in their foolishness, "exchanged the glory of the immortal God for images resembling a mortal human being or birds or four-footed animals or reptiles" (1:23). Therefore, Paul does not think we now can reason our way to God.

So nature is one of the ways by which God is revealed. This is commonly referred to as "natural revelation." From a philosopher's point of view, it is closely related to "general revelation," the variety of revealings accessible to all persons, whatever their religious inclination. This revelation comes to "evil" people as well as "good" people, and it comes even to people who are not seeking God. General revelation also comes without regard to people's intellectual level, speaking as clearly to the simple as to the sophisticate.

Although the biblical writers spoke frequently and ecstatically of the wonders of nature, they never mistook nature for God. Indeed, they were appalled by those peoples who did. But they saw the glory of God in nature and rejoiced in it. So the psalmist expected "the sea [to] roar, and all that fills it," the floods to "clap their hands," and "the hills sing together for joy / at the presence of the LORD" (Psalm 98:7-9). But the prophet Isaiah provided perspective on how nature is to be compared with the God who created it. God is one

> "who has measured the waters in the hollow of his hand
>   and marked off the heavens with a span,
>   enclosed the dust of the earth in a measure,
>   and weighed the mountains in scales
>   and the hills in a balance" (Isaiah 40:12).

Nevertheless, it is by God's quick rehearsal of nature that Job comes to marvel more fully at the glory of God (Job 38–41), and it is through God's control of nature, in the series of plagues that come upon Egypt, that God shows divine power to both Egypt and Israel (Exodus 7–10). No doubt experiences with natural disasters and natural phenomena caused many primitive peoples to worship what they perceived to be the god of the storm, of the earthquake, or of the volcano. This perception carries through to our own time in the legal phrase "an act of God" to describe natural disasters.

But while virtually every ancient religion included elements of nature in its revelation of God, biblical religion goes a giant step further in seeing the revelation of God in *history*. The Old and New Testaments are nothing less than an astounding series of events in which God *acts*. In the Old Testament, these acts center primarily in a nation, Israel, and in the New Testament in a new people of the covenant, the church. But in both Testaments, these events happen also in the lives of specific individuals. The Bible is, in a unique sense, the quintessential history book. But it is history of a particular kind—God's self-revealing to the human race through encounters with this race.

But it is history, nevertheless—names that can often be found in other historical records, places that are still accessible to the archaeologist, and events whose reverberations are felt millennia later. And because Judaism and Christianity believe so much in the revelation of God through history, they celebrate numbers of commemorative events, such as Passover, Festival of Booths, Christmas, and Easter. The psalmists often celebrated God's revelation in history, especially in Psalms 105–107. And while the style of these psalms is that of the poet-artist, their attention to names, places, and events is that of the historian. Specifically, a historian who has seen God revealed in the unfolding of history.

Visions, dreams, and other special visitations are also seen as avenues for the revealing God. We approach this area with great caution because it is so open to abuse and misunderstanding. Nevertheless, it has been a means of revelation through the centuries, and the fact that it is difficult to deal with or that it is sometimes misused is no justification for ignoring it. The Genesis account is marked repeatedly by occasions when God speaks to persons, or visits them by way of angelic messengers. Abraham and Sarah receive a visitor who assures them of a son. Moses, a monumental figure, is apprehended by the sight of a bush that burns and is not consumed (Exodus 3) after which he enters into extended dialogues with God. So too with Samuel, David, Solomon, and Hezekiah, to name a few. And of course such phenomena are the basic stuff with which the prophets deal.

When Job was in deep distress, he complained he could not get an audience with God, but his friend Elihu argued otherwise:

"For God speaks in one way,
　　and in two, though people do not perceive it.
In a dream, in a vision of the night,
　　when deep sleep falls on mortals,
　　while they slumber on their beds,
then he opens their ears" (Job 33:14-16).

And Elihu goes still further, contending that God may speak when people are

"chastened with pain upon their beds,
　　and with continual strife in their bones" (33:19).

But the matter of visions and dreams becomes a thicket of confusion as we move out of biblical times (indeed, for many it is thicket enough even in the Scriptures). Joan of Arc is revered by believers and secularists for her visions, and so too is the Spanish nun Teresa of Avila (1515–1582). But we aren't so comfortable with the reports that come in the contemporary press of visions, or with the neighbor who says, "Now the Lord told me . . ."

Because such experiences are private, and particularly inclined to private interpretation, it is especially important that they be brought under the discipline of the Scriptures, of tradition, and of reason. This is done not to minimize their potential significance but to be sure any such significance is protected from error.

Christianity teaches that the ultimate revelation of God is in *Jesus Christ.* So the writer of Hebrews begins his awesome monograph: "Long ago God spoke to our ancestors in many and various ways by the prophets, but in these last days he has spoken to us by a Son, whom he appointed heir of all things, through whom he also created the worlds" (Hebrews 1:1-2). The writer authenticates those revelations that have gone before, but he wants us to understand that this revelation is in a class by itself, because it is "in these last days"—that is, as God's act in the eventual consummating of history—and because it comes through God's Son, one who has been "appointed heir of all things."

The book of Hebrews continues from that point to make a case for the ultimate quality of God's revelation in Christ. This is the issue of the Christian faith. We contend that God has been most clearly revealed in Jesus Christ. We do not intend by this to pass judgment on other beliefs; we simply declare, as we must, what we have come to know. Nor do we deny that God may be revealed in many other ways, places, and persons; indeed, our commitment to the Hebrew Scriptures (and our reliance upon those Scriptures) is indication enough that we recognize God at work in ways other than Jesus Christ. But Christian teaching declares that Jesus Christ is decisive and definitive, so that all other revelations are seen in light of him. We believe Christ is the ultimate revelation, the clearest picture of God and of God's purpose for all creation.

This is what the Gospel of John had in mind with its magisterial declaration, "In the beginning was the Word, and the Word was with God, and the Word was God. . . . And the Word became flesh and lived among us, and we have seen his glory, the glory as of a father's only son, full of grace and truth" (John 1:1-14). So too, with Paul's statement, "For in him [Christ] the whole fullness of deity dwells bodily" (Colossians 2:9). This idea is behind New Testament references to Jesus Christ as God's Son (Hebrews 5:5; 1 John 4:9). To a world that groped toward God sometimes anxiously, often erratically, intermittently, and uncertainly, God graciously revealed the fullness of his person by visiting us in the Son, Jesus Christ. As a result of his coming, humans never again need wonder what God is like, nor indeed, what God will do to overcome the sin that separates us from God. These most fundamental of questions are answered forever by a Baby born in Bethlehem and years later put to death outside the city of Jerusalem—and we must add, raised from the dead on the third day.

In Summation

Probably the most significant means of revelation other than Jesus Christ is the Holy Scriptures. We will consider the doctrine of Scripture in our next lesson.

From a faith/reason point of view, revelation is a profound and crucial subject; all else rests upon it. If we do not accept the principle of revelation, we will not accept the Scriptures as having anything other than cultural or intellectual importance, nor will we see Jesus Christ as more than a noble human figure. Only as we accept the idea that revelation can occur, and has occurred, will we find full meaning in the Scriptures and in Jesus Christ.

> BECAUSE WE THE CHURCH BELIEVE God has chosen to engage in a wondrous self-disclosure, I will embrace this act of grace with passion and trust.

BELIEVING AND LIVING

Revelation is not only intellectually challenging. As a matter of fact, that's the least of the issues. Revelation is also confronting—like walking out of a cave into sunlight that all but blinds us. So the huge question is, What shall we do with God's revelation? In the end, that question probably deters more persons than the intellectual issues. Blaise Pascal, one of the great minds of human history, found God revealed to him through Scripture and presence one November evening in 1654. As a result, he declared that the God of Jesus Christ "shall be my God." How do you respond to the issue of revelation, and to whatever degree of revelation you have accepted?

What do you find most difficult to understand or accept about the idea of revelation?

If nature were the only revelation of God, how would your present doctrine of God and life-purpose be changed?

What has Jesus Christ revealed to you, personally, about God that you would never otherwise have understood or appreciated?

SEEKING MORE UNDERSTANDING

Follow up on the suggestion in the Assignment section to locate additional biblical passages that throw light on the subject of revelation. One approach would be to identify and read the related biblical stories or accounts. Watch for ways God is revealed and what is revealed about God in these passages.

PRAYER

"Lord God, I find prayer hard and
    constraining.
I have little devotion,
but afterwards, with your help,
I will have devotion,
and it will become restful and easy
    for me,
though it was hard before.
Then I shall have very little labour,
or none at all.
For then, Lord God,
you will work as you please;
not always,
not even for a long time together,
but as you please.
And it will seem a joyful thing for me
to leave you to do it.
Perhaps it will be your will
to send out a ray of spiritual light,
piercing this cloud of unknowing
between you and me;
and you will show me some of your
    secrets
of which a person may not, or
    cannot, speak.
Then I shall feel my affection all
    aflame
with the fire of your love,
far more than I know how to tell."

—*The Cloud of Unknowing, 14th century*

Scripture

Word of God   **God-breathed**

God's
self-communication

Authority   **Divine inspiration**

Canon:
Old Testament   New Testament

God's Book for God's People

"All scripture is inspired by God and is useful for teaching, for reproof, for correction, and for training in righteousness, so that everyone who belongs to God may be proficient, equipped for every good work."

—2 Timothy 3:16-17

LIFE QUESTIONS

Christians are a people of the Book. The Bible is our basic document. So what kind of Book is it, and where did we get it? Why does it have such authority, and does that authority extend to my life? Is it dependable enough that I should bet my life on it? Other people have other sacred documents. Does mine have any greater claim on my life, or any authority that is superior to the others?

ASSIGNMENT

As you read the following Scripture passages, remember that what is meant by Scripture differs. When the people are called to repentance in Josiah's time by the book of the law newly found, it is probably the book of Deuteronomy, and certainly no more than part of the Pentateuch. When the psalmists thank God for the law, they are referring to those first five books of the Hebrew Scriptures. When Jesus speaks of "the law and the prophets," it is a shorthand way of describing the whole body of the Hebrew Scriptures, what we call the Old Testament. Numbers of letters were in existence by the time Second Timothy and Second

Peter were written, but we can only guess the degree of authority the first Christians invested in these documents.

As you read these passages, notice how powerfully these documents of the faith were shaping the believers, and the degree to which they were revered.

Day 1 2 Kings 22:1–23:25 (the book of the law)
Introduction and Readings 27 and 28
Day 2 Ezra 7 (God's hand on Ezra); Nehemiah 8 (reading the book of the law)
Readings 29, 30, and 31
Day 3 Psalm 119:1-24, 89-112 (honoring God's law)
Readings 32, 33, and 34
Day 4 Luke 4:14-30 (Jesus interprets Scripture); Acts 8:26-40 (Philip explains Scripture)
Readings 35 and 36
Day 5 2 Timothy 3:10-17 (inspired Scripture); 2 Peter 3 (remember God's word)
Readings 37, 38, and 39
Day 6 Read and respond to "The Church Teaching and Believing" and "Believing and Living."
Day 7 Rest and prayer

DAILY PRAYER

Pray for the persons and situations on your Prayer Concerns list and about issues or concerns emerging from your daily reading and study.

SCRIPTURE	READINGS
DAY 1	
2 Kings 22:1–23:25	Introduction and Readings 27 and 28
DAY 2	
Ezra 7; Nehemiah 8	Readings 29, 30, and 31
DAY 3	
Psalm 119:1-24, 89-112	Readings 32, 33, and 34

SCRIPTURE	READINGS
DAY 4	
Luke 4:14-30; Acts 8:26-40	Readings 35 and 36
DAY 5	
2 Timothy 3:10-17; 2 Peter 3	Readings 37, 38, and 39

DAY 6 STUDY MANUAL	PRAYER CONCERNS
"The Church Teaching and Believing" and "Believing and Living"	

THE CHURCH TEACHING AND BELIEVING

Consider a time when writing materials were rare beyond imagining. Insights about the profoundest issues of time and eternity have entered the thinking of certain persons; some of them are learned, some are not, for the lines were not so surely drawn in those days. Those who perceive this knowledge most deeply know they must share it with their community and save it for future generations. They sense that what they know has come from God, an idea they treat with caution and reverence.

So they make a written record—a laborious process. And in a nomadic world, where preserving things is difficult, they nevertheless pass these materials on to the next generation. Younger generations are not always impressed with what their forebears have left behind; we marvel these documents were preserved when so much was against this being done.

The documents accumulated. There were laws (some in great detail), records of a small but dynamic people, and stories of individuals both common and exotic. There were songs, wise sayings, and stories of human struggle. And along the way, the writings of noble and courageous individuals, not cut from the common mold, whom we call *prophets*. These documents do not seem at first to have any necessary relationship one to the other, and yet they come together—unlikely and against great odds.

We marvel at the people from whom these documents come. They were a nation but not one considered significant by the usual measures of nationhood. They had roughly a century of stable existence before breaking into two smaller kingdoms. After a time, one of those kingdoms disappeared into captivity and intermarriage with other people; and not long after, the remaining people were also taken into captivity, first by the Babylonians, then by the Persians. Even when in their homeland, they were usually under the control of some stronger political power, often one opposed to their religion, the religion of their Book.

Nevertheless, they kept their amazing documents. And somewhere along the way, in ways not fully known to us, the collection we now know as the Old Testament emerged from the many diverse documents circulating at that time.

Small in number as was the people of this Book, the Jews, in time a people still smaller in number appeared, and an equally persecuted one, the Christians. They were inheritors of the Book, partly because so many of the first of their number were themselves Jews, and partly because they recognized this Book as the ground out of which their own faith had sprung. Furthermore, they believed that the One whom they called Lord was anticipated in this Book.

Very shortly this new people became a thriving body, quickly spreading to every part of the larger Mediterranean world and beyond. And just as quickly they began collecting documents of their own. At first, these documents were letters—especially from their learned rabbi, Paul, in occasional notes written to churches he had founded or planned to visit. Then there were biographies of their Lord, Jesus Christ—biographies so urgent and insistent that some readers don't want to call them biographies. They were, of course, biographies of a particular kind, in that their dominating theme was good news, *gospel*. Then, a remarkable book written to the people in a time of severe persecution to sustain them in the knowledge that at last their Lord would triumph—the book we call Revelation.

And once again, these documents—like the Hebrew Scriptures before them—were preserved against all odds. For the first three centuries of their existence, Christians were victims of intermittent persecution. Their enemies did everything possible to wipe them out and to destroy the elements of their faith, including their documents. But somehow, even while wondering about their very lives, they managed to save the books they prized so profoundly, make still more copies, and pass them on.

And in time, out of all of the writings of that period, twenty-seven books appeared that in time the church recognized as the unique document of their faith. We now call these books the New Testament.

The rest of the story, to our own time, is full of heroism. In summary we can only marvel at the people who for centuries copied the documents by hand, who preserved them against all odds of nature and of political unrest, and those who at the peril of their lives translated the Book into the languages of the common people in their particular lands. Then came the wonder of the printing press, with this Book its first product. In our day, the languages into which it has been translated, in whole or in part, number more than two thousand—and still counting. Every month the number grows.

What Kind of Book Is It?

At first glance, it isn't a book we would expect people to preserve and propogate. The Bible is a remarkably heterogeneous collection of laws, history, saga, poetry, wise sayings, human speculations, prophecies, short stories, parables, biographies, theology, church history, letters, and apocalyptic literature. Scattered throughout are occasional lists of family lines, honored public servants, and transient heroes. Even a sympathetic reader will ask at times, "Who cares about the descendants of Naphtali? Or the offerings that representatives of the twelve tribes brought for the traveling tabernacle?"

How is it that a book of such diversity, and with so many stumbling blocks to anyone but the most dedicated reader, would spread around the world? Indeed would influence and sometimes shape the culture of entire countries? Why would people—so many people—give their lives to translate this book into the languages of different ethnic groups, or to distribute it to remote places? Essayist Annie Dillard says, "We crack open its pages at our peril," because "many educated, urbane, and flourishing experts" in every field have "entered its queer, strait gates and were lost." That is, they were taken captive by the book. What about this book gives it such extraordinary and singular power?

What Is the Bible's Authority?

The odds were against its ever coming into existence as a single book, ever being preserved, ever being translated from its original tongues (Hebrew and Greek, primarily), and ever becoming a foundation on which systems of thought are built, and institutions as well.

A practical person might say the Bible's very existence and continuing history are proof enough of its authority. The giant redwood tree needs no testimonial, no endorsement; its very existence is evidence enough. So with this book. Its authority is in its own story.

But we want more than that, and rightly so. The Old Testament, on its part, receives endorsements from the New. Jesus referred often to the Hebrew Scriptures. He said that not the smallest letter or the least stroke of a pen would disappear from the Law until it was fulfilled (Matthew 5:17-18). The Second Letter to Timothy described the Old Testament as "God-breathed" (2 Timothy 3:16). Jesus and his followers certainly looked upon the Hebrew Scriptures as inspired by God.

Clearly the New Testament writers took their role seriously. Most of them belonged to a Jewish tradition that held God's name and God's purposes in an awe that sometimes bordered on terror. They were not likely, therefore, to speak their revolu-

The scroll or roll and the open book symbolize the written Word of God. The open book indicates its message is for all people and is accessible and available throughout most of the world. The word *Bible* comes from the Greek word for books. The Old and New Testaments, the inspired Word of God, have authority for the life of the Christian faith community.

One aspect of the Protestant Reformation was the church's view of the authority of Scripture. Martin Luther and others saw the Bible as the final authority for the life of the church and of individual Christians, and they thought its teachings had been misinterpreted and weakened by church officials. Luther's writings are firmly based on Scripture, and he constantly challenged his opponents to base their arguments in Scripture as well. He translated the Bible into the language of the people and campaigned vigorously to place Scripture in the hands of the laity so they could read and interpret it for themselves.

tionary new story without profound thought. Nor would they be casual in picking up the Hebrew Scriptures, relating them to what had happened in Jesus Christ, and saying, "This happened in order that it might fulfill what the prophets said." We can hardly imagine the degree of conviction that drove these believers to recognize the tie of their new faith to their sacred book and to put this belief in writing. They were cautious about what they were doing.

When Paul discusses some issues of marriage in his letter to the Corinthians, he carefully notes that some of his counsel is his own, not the Lord's (1 Corinthians 7:10-12); that he speaks without having received a command from the Lord but as one who has experienced God's mercy (7:25); and that he writes what he identifies as his own judgment, but adds that he thinks he has "the Spirit of God" (7:40).

Paul's very tentativeness in these statements adds a special authenticity to his writing. We see the seriousness with which he approached his letters. Obviously, he recognized that those who received his letters would see them as carrying authority. Otherwise, it would not have been necessary for him to pick his way so carefully through issues where he thought he might only be giving his own, human opinion.

The author of Second Peter has the same high sense of responsibility about his writing. He writes because he thinks his death is near, and he wants to be sure his readers "may be able at any time to recall" the story (2 Peter 1:15). Why? Because "we did not follow cleverly devised myths when we made known to you the power and coming of our Lord Jesus Christ, but we had been eyewitnesses of his majesty" (1:16).

Like other New Testament writers, he makes a daring tie to the Hebrew Scriptures, even insisting they are for the purposes of this new body, the church. "We have the prophetic message more fully confirmed. . . . First of all you must understand this, that no prophecy of scripture is a matter of one's own interpretation, because no prophecy ever came by human will, but men and women moved by the Holy Spirit spoke from God" (1:19-21). With that statement, the apostolic writer declares his conviction that the Hebrew Scriptures are divinely inspired. At the same time, he rules invalid any interpretation of Scripture that is simply "one's own." Clearly, he thinks it would be blasphemy to treat the Scriptures in that way. And when he tells us Paul's letters are sometimes "hard to understand," he goes on to refer to them as "scriptures" (3:15-16), apparently putting them in the same category as the Hebrew Scriptures. And while he makes no claim for his own writing, it is reasonable to think that he spoke to his own readers with the same sense of profound responsibility. This is not, of course, a declaration of divine inspiration. However, it is an indication of a spirit disciplined enough to be accessible to such inspiration.

Luke introduces readers to his record of the life of Jesus with a statement of scholarly responsibility. He notes that "many have undertaken to set down an orderly account of the events that have been fulfilled among us," records "handed on to us by those who from the beginning were eyewitnesses and servants of the word." He has decided, after careful investigation, to write his own "orderly account" of the truth about what was being taught (Luke 1:1-4). Again, no specific statement of inspiration is made, rather, a substantial sense of sacred responsibility. Such a mood is hospitable to the Spirit of God.

The writer of the Revelation tells us his message came by way of an angel (Revelation 1:1), so he promises a blessing to those who read and hear it (1:3). When he finishes his writing, he is emphatic about the book he has delivered: "I warn everyone who hears the words of the prophecy of this book: if anyone adds to them, God will add to that person the plagues described in this book; if anyone takes away from the words of the book of this prophecy, God will take away that person's share in the tree of life and in the holy city, which are described in this book" (22:18-19). Does such a statement prove the author was writing with divine inspiration? No, not specifically. Does the intensity of his statement have any particular significance? Yes, in light of the context from which he came and the moral constraints under which he was writing.

But of course we haven't proved that the New Testament books are inspired, nor that the Old Testament books were, except as the New Testament writers, as well as our Lord, made such a witness. And in truth, we cannot prove they are inspired. Ultimately, belief in the Scriptures as the inspired Word of God is a confession of faith. As it ought to be. After all, if inspiration could be fully and finally proved, no faith would be necessary. In that case, the evidence for the Book would be a denial of the essence of the Book, since the Bible is a document that calls us to a life of faith.

Again, What Kind of Book Is the Bible?

Now we're brought back to a question we approached earlier: What kind of book is the Bible? In our previous comments, we spoke of those factors that make the Bible such an unlikely document—elements that make it unattractive to a casual reader, or even to a moderately serious one. We confessed it is an unlikely collection and not the kind of book one would expect to be an around-the-world best-seller. So what else can we say about it?

First, considering the human side of its composition, it has a continuing theme—God's relationship to our human race. One cannot imagine a more challenging subject, or one more significant to our humanity as a whole and to each of us individually. From the story of our creation in the first chapter of Genesis to the concluding invitation at the close of Revelation, it is an almost unbelievable story of God's love for and pursuit of our human race.

In the process of telling this story, the Bible gives a startling new dimension to our human worth. If we human creatures are of such significance as to be pursued by the eternal God, there is obviously more to us than meets the eye!

Perhaps then it isn't surprising that totalitarian governments of either left or right are so unwilling to have the Bible freely distributed. It well may be that the highest tribute the Bible receives is that of its enemies. Their fear is in its own way more impressive than our sometimes tepid love. People who accept the Bible at its worth inevitably come to think more highly of themselves (even after recognizing their need of redemption) and of the human race as a whole. They are therefore poor prospects for totalitarian systems.

Because the Bible, with its powerful theme of God's relationship to our human race, is a transformational book. It allows its readers to decide for themselves; but it is, as Annie Dillard has said, a book we enter at our own peril. Its record for challenging lives, transforming them, and some would say upsetting them, is quite astonishing. And all the more so when one considers it has been doing so for nearly twenty centuries, in a vast variety of cultures and circumstances. In a time such as ours, when philosophies are as faddish as dress styles and restaurant menus, it is difficult to explain a book that continues to affect persons of every intellectual and cultural station in virtually every part of the world.

Numbers of persons have described the power of the Bible in their lives by using words that say, in one form or another, the Bible "finds them." That is, the Bible has an uncanny knack for seeing us as we are, and for revealing us to ourselves. This quality gives rise to its transformational power.

The title of this lesson—"God's Book for God's People"—identifies still another characteristic of the Bible. While anyone can read the Bible, and anyone can be transformed by it, the book belongs in a special way to a community, a particular group of people. As surely as the Hebrew Scriptures belong especially to the Jewish people, the New Testament (as well as the Old) belongs to the church.

This is not an act of divine favoritism. Simply put, it was written down, compiled, and canonized within the community under the guidance of the Holy Spirit. Further, the book is understood best by those who bring themselves under its discipline. Indeed, it is partly by our bringing ourselves under the discipline of the Bible that we become Christians, and it is through such discipline we grow in the Christian faith. To many, the Bible is a remarkable piece of literature and a compendium of cultural information and benefit. But to believers it is the faith document that brings salvation.

Theologians sometimes remind us we should not confuse the words of the Bible with the Word of God. That is, our Lord Jesus Christ is the Word of God incarnate, while the Bible is a document of many words and not the Word of God in the same sense Christ is. The point is well taken, but it should not diminish our regard for the Bible. In fact, we remember that the

Bible—the Hebrew Scriptures—prepared Israel to wait for a Messiah. And when the church became convinced through his life, death, and resurrection that Jesus Christ was the messiah, it began producing other documents—the New Testament—to proclaim Jesus Christ to the world. So while the Bible is not to be confused with the Word made flesh, and is by no means to be revered in that fashion, it is nevertheless crucial to our knowledge of Jesus Christ. We would not have had a dependable memory of Jesus' coming, teaching, and significance if it were not for the Bible. Quite rightly, therefore, generations have called it "the sacred Word."

What Is Divine Inspiration?

So why should we believe the Bible? First, because it is the basic document of our faith; it has been so from the beginning. The early church acknowledged the Hebrew Scriptures as its guide, and within the first century of its existence was accepting at least some of the books that came later to be the New Testament canon, that is, the accepted body of Scripture. To be part of the Christian community is therefore to come under the governance of this book.

Also, we acknowledge with gratitude that the Bible's history—remarkable in its preservation, its power, and its continued expansion—puts us in awe. Still more, we confess it has touched our own lives in consistent and transforming ways. We believe, not only because of what we have been told but also because of what we have experienced.

And we receive it as the inspired Word of God. We use the word *inspired,* not as we would in referring to a play by Shakespeare or a sonata by Beethoven but in the sense that the Bible has a rightful claim to our loyalty. Its inspiration is unique; no other book is like it. Many other books are worthwhile; we can even say some books reflect the divine or the authors were blessed by God in their insights and in the beauty of their utterances. But only the Bible has the unique authority to declare how we must live.

We do not claim its words were dictated by the Holy Spirit, but that the Holy Spirit spoke through godly persons and their witness is to be believed. And we who live at this merging of the twentieth and twenty-first centuries are especially fortunate because we are able to look back upon a long history of the enacted power of the Word. We have pragmatic evidence not available to the early church—the church that understood the Scriptures as the Word of God.

> BECAUSE WE THE CHURCH BELIEVE the Bible is the Word of God, I shall read it daily, in order to fulfill its commands.

The *canon* is the list of Scripture considered official and authoritative. The canon of Hebrew Scriptures as established by the first and second centuries A.D. was generally accepted in the early Christian church, though some controversy arose about some Greek writings now included in the Aprocypha of Protestant Bibles. Certain Eastern Fathers questioned their authenticity, and Jerome in the West admitted only the Hebrew books. The Greek books continued to be used throughout the church until they were rejected by the sixteenth-century Reformers. The Council of Trent in its fourth session (1546) ruled those books official for the Roman Catholic Church, making official the difference in Catholic and Protestant canons.

BELIEVING AND LIVING

All Christian bodies consider the Bible a basic foundation of their faith; the Catholic and Orthodox bodies consider tradition equally important. Some groups also include reason (logic) and experience (religious experience). As you look at your own Christian life, how do you relate these several elements? In what way is the Bible more or less significant than the others?

_____

_____

What is your greatest struggle in accepting the Bible as the Word of God?

_____

_____

When has the Bible spoken to you in such a way that you have felt it is inspired of God?

_____

_____

How would you define "inspired of God" in reference to the Bible?

_____

_____

What authority does the Bible have in your life?

_____

_____

SEEKING MORE UNDERSTANDING

The details of how the Bible came to be—oral tradition; the writing, collecting, editing, and selecting of the books that make up the canon of Scripture—make a fascinating study. Some Bibles, commentaries, and Bible dictionaries include articles on the subject; and most public and church libraries and religious bookstores would have books or even videos that tell the story. Do some research and prepare a brief report for your study group.

PRAYER

"Father of mercies, in thy Word
    What endless glory shines!
Forever be thy name adored
    For these celestial lines.

O may these heavenly pages be
    My ever dear delight,
And still new beauties may I see,
    And still increasing light."
        —_Anne Steele, 1716–1778_

4

Creation Creator Creature

Creation out of nothing

Transcendence
of God

Immanence
of God

Continuous creation

Creator without beginning

Source of all things

Infinite Finite Trinity

The God of Beginnings

"In the beginning when God created the heavens and the earth, the earth was a formless void and darkness covered the face of the deep, while a wind from God swept over the face of the waters. Then God said, 'Let there be light'; and there was light."

—*Genesis 1:1-3*

LIFE QUESTIONS

To say "I believe God is the Creator of heaven and earth" is intellectually daring, but to say anything less may be foolhardy. In a scientific age, do we dare say we think God is the source of our creation? But on the other hand, if God is not, is there purpose and direction for our world?

And if God is indeed the Creator, what manner of persons ought we to be? How ought we to relate to this creation? To call creation a sacred trust may be a far more profound statement than we have realized.

ASSIGNMENT

Although our Scripture passages for the week cover a subject closely related to such sciences as biology, geology, and physics, they have more the mood of poetry than of the laboratory. You will need to read them with a particular quality of perception if you are to relate them to the intellectual world to which we belong. At the same time, you will want to maintain a quality of worship; obviously, this was the mood with which the original authors wrote, and we will understand the passages best when we read them on their own terms.

Day 1   Genesis 1–3 (Creator creates)
        Introduction and Readings 40 and 41
Day 2   Job 36:24–41:34 (the mystery of God's creation)
        Readings 42 and 43
Day 3   Psalms 8; 19; 29 (God's glory manifest in creation)
        Readings 44, 45, and 46
Day 4   Isaiah 40:12–41:20 (Creator of the universe and Lord)
        Readings 47, 48, and 49
Day 5   John 1:1-18 (the creating Word); Romans 8:1-27 (nature to be redeemed)
        Readings 50, 51, and 52
Day 6   Read and respond to "The Church Teaching and Believing" and "Believing and Living."
Day 7   Rest and prayer

DAILY PRAYER

Pray for the persons and situations on your Prayer Concerns list and about issues or concerns emerging from your daily reading and study.

SCRIPTURE	READINGS
DAY 1	
Genesis 1–3	Introduction and Readings 40 and 41
DAY 2	
Job 36:24–41:34	Readings 42 and 43
DAY 3	
Psalms 8; 19; 29	Readings 44, 45, and 46

SCRIPTURE	READINGS

DAY 4

Isaiah 40:12–41:20	Readings 47, 48, and 49

DAY 5

John 1:1-18; Romans 8:1-27	Readings 50, 51, and 52

DAY 6 STUDY MANUAL	PRAYER CONCERNS
"The Church Teaching and Believing" and "Believing and Living"	

THE CHURCH TEACHING AND BELIEVING

The ancient psalmist said, "Fools say in their hearts, 'There is no God' " (Psalm 53:1). Second place probably goes to those who try to comprehend God. It is quite audacious for the finite to try to understand the infinite, but it is a holy audacity. The saints of all ages have endorsed it; and even if they hadn't, the rest of us would continue our quest. We can't seem to help it.

Our inquiry usually begins where God is most an issue for us, in nature. This questioning was inevitable for those hundreds of generations who lived so close to nature and were so obviously at its mercy. But our urban culture is not exempt. A torrential downpour overwhelms the most effective sewer system. A tornado cuts a path of destruction through city and town. And somehow we never get so sophisticated that we do not at times feel a catch in the throat on a spring day, or when we look beyond the traffic lights to the stars of night.

No wonder, then, that the most widely recited creed, the Apostles' Creed, describes God as "maker of heaven and earth." The Nicene Creed begins in the same style, "maker of heaven and earth," but goes much farther with "of all that is, seen and unseen." Two modern creeds use the same basic language; the Korean Creed refers to God as "creator and sustainer of all things," and the statement of faith of the United Church of Canada speaks of God as the one "who has created and is creating." Some might say the creeds are beginning with what is visible and tangible before launching into matters quite beyond our physical reach. But something in us insists that the most real thing we know—nature—demands the most credible explanation we can envision—God. A cynic will say we call God the Creator in order to fill the gaps in our knowledge. Believers say, rather, that what we know about God compels us to this way of looking at nature.

The Biblical Style of Reporting

The Bible itself neither speculates nor argues; it simply declares. The language is both so majestic and so poetic that we want to hum while reading it, or better yet, call for symphonic background music. "In the beginning when God created the heavens and the earth, the earth was a formless void and darkness covered the face of the deep, while a wind from God swept over the face of the waters" (Genesis 1:1-2). The biblical writer presents us with ideas beyond our grasp. What shall we do with *beginning* when the reference is to the absolute beginning? We can talk about the beginning of a ball game or the beginning of a new semester, but what do we mean by a beginning to which all other beginnings finally refer? And how do we imagine an earth that is a formless void somewhere in the midst of a great darkness? What pictures come to mind when the wind of God sweeps over the face of the waters? And the scene becomes still more awesome when we remind ourselves that the Hebrew word for *wind* is also the word for *spirit*. And then, with it all, *God*. In the beginning, God.

The writer of Genesis is more poet than scientist. He writes in wonder and takes us into the wonder with him. In a sense, he is simply reporting the facts as he knows them, without attempting to interpret them and without seeking to prove anything. The events unfold quickly, as if they had been so long in the planning that their completion is effortless. There is no sense of divine strain.

How does this story square with science as we know it; and how do we dare, in a dogmatically scientific age, to call God "the creator of heaven and earth"? The Genesis story of Creation says almost nothing specifically about the *how* of Creation. It gives a framework of events, but the order has more to do with a sense of dramatic development than with anything else, as the Creator provides a setting and an environment for the eventual entrance of the key character, the human creature. The devout believer can therefore let the scientist do what the scientist enjoys doing—seek answers to the how.

And the scientist does this best when the door is left wide open for speculation. The business of science is to be always discovering, always revising, always seeking more knowledge. If from the point of view of science, any one thing is sure about the creation, it is that it will provide research themes as long as the generations of human creatures exist, and the devout believer can rejoice in the quest.

The Creation and Purpose in Living

The believer finds in the Genesis story—and in the continuing biblical accounts—what, from a believer's point of view, is absolutely essential. Indeed, essential to every human being who pauses momentarily to wonder about the meaning of life. Because the Genesis story says God is the source of the whole creation process; and if that be so, we can be confident there is purpose and meaning in our lives. Nothing is more essential to us than that.

Genesis is almost playful in the way it describes God's method of creation. "And God said. . . . And it was so" (Genesis 1:6-7) is the recurring motif. God spoke, and the end was accomplished.

What is Genesis trying to tell us? At least this, that God is in complete control. God need only give an order, and it happens. It is as if the voice of God activates the intelligence within the potential energies of the universe. Thus, God is not working with inert substances but with something that can respond. In this picture of God speaking and the creation responding, we have a profound insight into both the nature of God and the nature of our universe.

When Genesis shows God creating by speech, it tells us God is a communicator. Ours is a personal universe because the God who created it is a communicator; indeed, the creation itself is a result of communication. Not only is our creation intelligent; it communicates. That explains, on one hand, our capacity for loneliness, because creatures capable of communicating are of course susceptible to loneliness. But it also indicates our capacity for profound relationships, not only with one another but also with the God who made us.

Even while acknowledging that science is still looking for more definitive understanding of the Creation, we can't help being fascinated by the theories currently in the public forum, such as the evolutionary hypothesis and the Big Bang theory. They might be compared with another contemporary scientific discovery, the genetic code. We now know the genetic code determines literally thousands of personal details, including the color of our eyes, the shape of our ears, and the texture of our hair; and the code exists from before our birth. Could it be that the Creator put all the vital stuff of the universe into one small package, and that package exploded into the Big Bang that has been going ever since?

If so, and if we grasp the grandeur of a God who created such an intricate scheme, we will want to follow the pattern of the biblical writers for whom nature inspired worship.

"When I look at your heavens, the work of your fingers,
    the moon and the stars that you have established,
what are human beings that you are mindful of them,
    mortals that you care for them?" (Psalm 8:3-4).
The prophet Isaiah took comfort in the midst of trying times in the reminder that the God who created those heavens
"brings out their host and numbers them,
    calling them all by name;
because he is great in strength,
    mighty in power,
    not one is missing" (Isaiah 40:26).

Two strong symbols combine here as a symbol for God the Creator. The hand, the oldest symbol of the first Person of the Trinity, represents the creating and sustaining power of God. The surrounding clouds indicate glory, mystery, holiness. The star is referred to as the Creator's star or the star of Creation, its six points hinted at in Genesis 1:31, "God saw everything that he had made, and indeed, it was very good. And there was evening and there was morning, the sixth day."

But in their love of nature biblical writers never confused the Creator with the creation. *Pantheism* is a philosophy that occurs from time to time over the centuries and has its own expression in our day. It teaches that in some sense everything is God; so the stick, the stone, the air, the animal, the human soul—all are God, and God is in all. The Bible never considers such a view. The psalmist or the prophet may exult in the beauty of nature, but always as a work of God's hand. In fact, the biblical writers are remarkably unsentimental about nature. They don't say, "What a beautiful day!" but rather, "This is the day that the LORD has made; / let us rejoice and be glad in it," or in the translation in the footnote, "be glad in him" (Psalm 118:24).

Nor will biblical faith conform with what we call *deism*. This philosophy teaches that God is indeed the Creator but has no continuing involvement. As sometimes put in popular language, God is an "absentee landlord." Jesus pictured God as a Creator who is conscious of a sparrow's fall (Matthew 10:29) and as One who sends sun and rain indiscriminately upon the righteous and the unrighteous (Matthew 5:45). We see this understanding of God's involvement when the Korean Creed speaks of God as *sustainer* as well as creator, and when the creed of the Canadian Church speaks of God as still creating.

The term that best describes God's relation to our creation is *theism*. Unlike pantheism, theism believes God is in the world but also beyond it; and unlike deism, God, while beyond the world, is nevertheless not divorced from it. Having created the world, God continues to care for it and to relate to it.

But deism and pantheism are not simply moldy theological terms; they are active philosophies in our contemporary culture. Pantheism may even be experiencing something of a revival of expression in the Western world. Consider for a moment conversations, news items, television interviews, and book titles of recent weeks. What expressions have you seen of either deism or pantheism?

According to Thomas Aquinas, God is the only necessary being, the only being who cannot *not exist*. He reconciled the ideas of *divine transcendence* (God's being totally other, infinite, incomprehensible) and *divine immanence* (God's presence in the world) by saying that God exists at the center of every human being as the Cause and Creator of its life.

Why Did God Create?

If science has an unceasing question in the *how* of creation, believers may question the *why*. Why would God create the heavens and earth and all things in them? Ancient philosophers made the question especially difficult by reasoning that, by nature and definition, God should not need anything; and if God is complete, then why create? An African-American poet said God was lonely and made the human creature for company. But traditional theologians note that God need not feel lonely because the Trinity itself provides communion. A Jewish novelist said, probably only half-seriously, God created humans because he loves stories.

Obviously, we can't come up with a completely defensible answer. Perhaps it isn't surprising we receive so many suggestions from poets and novelists, because the question is more in the realm of imagination than of hard data. We might simply say it is the right of God to do whatever God wants to do, with no explanation necessary. But perhaps we wouldn't be worthy of the God who created us if we were content with such an answer as that.

If there is any hint in the Creation story, it might be in the recurring phrase in Genesis 1: "And God saw that it was good." Then, as a conclusion to the story, a resounding summary: "God saw everything that he had made, and indeed, it was very good" (1:31). Perhaps it is the nature of God to create, as it is the nature of a bird to sing or of grass to grow. We understand our universe is continuing to expand. God, being God, has created, is creating, and will create.

What Does the Creation Tell Us About God?

The apostle Paul contended that "ever since the creation of the world his [God's] eternal power and divine nature, invisible though they are, have been understood and seen through the things he has made" (Romans 1:20).

God spoke, and creation came into being. Probably nothing else could more significantly reveal the nature of God. The Creator is pictured, not as a kind of impersonal machine or supercomputer, or even as a remarkable artisan, but as a personality who relates to the creation. That personal quality is implied in Paul's statement about nature's revealing God's "eternal power and divine nature." Paul seems to suggest that God intends to speak to us through the creation; it is by intention, not by chance or by our effort. Indeed, Paul indicates we are at fault if we don't get the message. The promptness with which the elements respond suggests the power of the Creator, the sole sovereignity of God.

When Job takes a whirlwind trip through creation, the emphasis is on God's attention to detail. God knows the measurements of the earth's foundations (Job 38:4-5). God knows the dwelling of light, the place of darkness, and the storehouses of the snow and the hail (38:19-22). God numbers the clouds, provides for the raven's young, and watches over the calving of the deer (38:37-41; 39:1). Again, the language is that of the poet rather than that of the scientist. And yet, scientists sometimes marvel in their own way. When an eminent contemporary biologist was asked what he could infer about the Creator from a study of the Creator's work, he replied, "An inordinate fondness for beetles." No wonder, if—as some scientists estimate—there may be fifty million species of beetles on our planet!

Christ at Creation

John's Gospel introduces another dimension to the Creation story. "In the beginning was the Word, and the Word was with

God, and the Word was God. He was in the beginning with God. All things came into being through him, and without him not one thing came into being" (John 1:1-3). When John connects the preexistent Christ with the Creation, the personal nature of God's action in Creation is dramatically underlined. If the God who creates the world is also the one who reenters it to redeem it, the relationship between God and the Creation is personal beyond our grasp. Here again, God is not carefully isolated from the scene, as deism would see it; nor is God part of the problem, as pantheism would imply. Rather, God is concerned to the point of ultimate involvement and proceeds to be involved.

Creation in Trouble

The Genesis account of Creation is hardly finished before the man and woman break the tranquillity of the scene by their rebellion against God. Now there is a discordant note in nature. The man is warned that the ground is "cursed" because of him, and "thorns and thistles it shall bring forth for you" (Genesis 3:17-18). The inference is that the human creature and the rest of creation were meant to be utterly compatible, but human sin has destroyed that quality. Now nature resists us, in the measure of thorns, thistles, and sweat. And we fight nature.

As a result, nature itself has a stake in human redemption. "For the creation waits with eager longing," Paul reports, "for the revealing of the children of God." It longs to "be set free from its bondage to decay" (Romans 8:19-21). This bondage is so burdensome that "the whole creation has been groaning in labor pains until now" (8:22).

Nature's condition suggests how much of God's own nature has been invested in creation; the creation, as God's handiwork, is in distress when the tie to God is broken. It also reflects the degree to which our human conduct affects nature. The Bible presents the issue in theological terms, that human sin has upset nature in some rather mystical way. A more pragmatic observer might point to such matters as our polluting the atmosphere, our trashing the earth, and our ruining the soil, sometimes by our mining enterprises and sometimes by poor agriculture.

In any event, the Bible sees creation as marred by sin, whether in specific deeds or in cosmic violation. But the Hebrew prophets believed that the creation would someday be restored to an Edenic state, so that

"The wolf shall live with the lamb,
   the leopard shall lie down with the kid,
the calf and the lion and the fatling together,
   and a little child shall lead them. . . .
They will not hurt or destroy
   on all my holy mountain;
for the earth will be full of the knowledge of the LORD
   as the waters cover the sea" (Isaiah 11:6–9).

Any understanding of God as Creator must include this prophetic vision of nature restored, because in this vision we have the ultimate picture of God's continuing love for creation, and the farthest extension of the sustaining work of the Creator.

Faith and Knowledge

The believer is left with a serious problem. When we declare we believe in God as "creator of heaven and earth"—and even, in the language of the Nicene Creed, "of all that is, seen and unseen"—are we simply turning off our intelligence? Does such a belief border on superstition, or can one believe in the Creator and still be a respectable part of the twenty-first-century scientific age?

Perhaps we might begin by noting that science too has its limits. Our generation has become so enamored of the power of science we forget science, itself, is based on numbers of assumptions. That is, the scientist too builds on a foundation of faith. She or he assumes the universe is rational and the human mind can be depended upon to interpret it accurately. Methods and instruments of testing have to be trusted, and what works in one type of experiment or study may not work in another. What we have called the "laws" of science are not really laws in the sense of being absolutely certain; usually they are "statistical averages of high probability."

True, at a certain point the believer exercises faith in declaring God the ultimate Creator, the originator of our universe. And never is faith more significant than when it concerns factors entirely outside the realm of the physical sciences. One cannot depend on science to determine the significance of love, of trust, or of character. Nor can science help us, in the end, in determining the purpose and value of life. And these factors are linked, almost inseparably, with our view of God's relationship to our creation. It is no idle matter to declare, "I believe in God ...creator of heaven and earth."

> BECAUSE WE THE CHURCH BELIEVE God is the Creator of heaven and earth, we understand ourselves as creatures wholly dependent on God.

BELIEVING AND LIVING

When we look at creation, we can hardly help swinging between belief that compels worship and doubts that tend to despair. With a universe so vast it defies our imagination, we might easily throw up our hands and decide we can't believe anything about God and Creation; it is simply beyond us. When have you found yourself with that kind of doubt?

What questions about God as Creator are you struggling with right now?

_____

_____

What thrills you most about creation? What makes you believe most in God as the Creator?

_____

_____

If God truly is the Creator of heaven and earth, how ought a believer to relate to the physical creation? What are the practical issues of environment and ecology for a believer?

_____

_____

Write a short twenty-first-century psalm in which you worship God as the Creator. Try especially to use the language and concepts of our time.

_____

_____

SEEKING MORE UNDERSTANDING

To declare belief in God as Creator of heaven and earth is to say God is in charge. But sometimes our experiences in the world make us wonder. Spend some time considering life in the world. Read the words of the hymn "This Is My Father's World." Then reread the third stanza and stop to list as many affirmations as you can of the phrases *God is ruler yet* and *God reigns.* Summarize your affirmations in a sentence or two about God as Creator.

PRAYER

"O thou who coverest thy high places with the waters,
Who settest the sand as a bound
    to the sea
And dost uphold all things:
The sun sings thy praises,
The moon gives thee glory,
Every creature offers a hymn to thee,
His author and creator, for ever."

—*Eastern Orthodox Prayer*

5

Person   God
Omnipresence   Personal

Love   Other
Omnipotence   Holy

Lord   Eternal
Omniscience   Trinity

Immutable   I AM WHO I AM

Giving a Name to God

"God said to Moses, 'I AM WHO I AM.' . . .
This is my name forever,
and this my title for all generations."
—Exodus 3:14-15

LIFE QUESTIONS

I can't talk with you for long without asking your name. This is an act of respect; but it is also essential to me. I need something specific to relate to; your name provides that. And your name may change as I know you better.

If God exists, we have to establish a relationship, and that requires a name. So what shall we call God? What does God's name have to do with how we understand God and how we relate to God? And as we find a name, we seek still further to know the attributes of God—in part, so we can address God more adequately and fulfillingly.

ASSIGNMENT

Everything in the Bible is a revealing of the nature—and therefore, the name—of God. Some of the revelation is painful, because set alone a particular story gives a name that distorts our perception of God, at least until we have a further insight. This is how heresies develop. Heresies are not utter distruths, but fragments of truth given undue proportions. We will want therefore to study each of these Scripture passages with care, and with proper reservations, knowing that none is complete of itself but that each is valuable for what it contributes to our understanding, and then to our living.

Day 1   Exodus 3:1-15 (I AM WHO I AM); Deuteronomy 6 (the LORD alone)
Introduction and Readings 53, 54, and 55

Day 2   Job 5:8-27 (God's marvelous doings); 26 (God's power)
Readings 56, 57, and 58

Day 3   Psalm 89:1-18 (God's faithfulness); 90 (eternal God)
Readings 59 and 60

Day 4   Isaiah 44:6-20 (the Lord is God); 46 (only God saves)
Readings 61 and 62

Day 5   Luke 15:11-32 (loving God); John 14:1-14 (Jesus shows us God)
Readings 63 and 64

Day 6   Read and respond to "The Church Teaching and Believing" and "Believing and Living."

Day 7   Rest and prayer

DAILY PRAYER

Pray for the persons and situations on your Prayer Concerns list and about issues or concerns emerging from your daily reading and study.

SCRIPTURE	READINGS
DAY 1	
Exodus 3:1-15; Deuteronomy 6	Introduction and Readings 53, 54, and 55
DAY 2	
Job 5:8-27; 26	Readings 56, 57, and 58
DAY 3	
Psalm 89:1-18; 90	Readings 59 and 60

SCRIPTURE	READINGS

DAY 4

Isaiah 44:6-20; 46	Readings 61 and 62

DAY 5

Luke 15:11-32; John 14:1-14	Readings 63 and 64

DAY 6 STUDY MANUAL	PRAYER CONCERNS
"The Church Teaching and Believing" and "Believing and Living"	

THE CHURCH TEACHING AND BELIEVING

All believing requires some faith-leap; but believing in God is no more difficult than the hundreds of other faith-leaps life demands.

The faith issue comes when we begin defining the kind of God in whom we believe. If I see God in nature, I may concentrate on botany and have a God who is a source of all that is exquisite and lovely. But if I study the interactions of animal species, all red in tooth and claw, I may conclude God is quite brutal, careless of God's own creation. Or if I think long enough about the complexity of nature—or indeed, of my own genetic code—I may decide God is nothing other than the ultimate computer, with no moral or ethical quality—indeed, perhaps a computer gone mad.

So in faith, human beings have named God. What we consider the most primitive names seem to have sprung from fear and perhaps from greed. These names represented whatever gods might be as malevolent creatures who must be bought off. They come from a world of threat and terror, and of ignorance. The lightning bolt, the fire, the storm or locust invasion that might wipe out the crops—all of these made for a deity to be feared, and mollified.

Such deities appeal to our base emotions. We bargain with them and for them. In the ancient world, if a neighboring tribe defeated us, we concluded theirs was a better god than ours, and worshiped it. Such gods ask no ethical commitments of us and not even much loyalty. There is something of an unspoken understanding that if I find a more helpful or more convenient god, I have no obligation to stay with the one I have.

The Biblical View

The Bible introduced a different standard. It was demanding in the extreme. Where other cultures spoke of many gods—as many as seemed necessary or convenient—the biblical writers thundered, "Hear, O Israel: The LORD is our God, the LORD alone. You shall love the LORD your God with all your heart, and with all your soul, and with all your might" (Deuteronomy 6:4-5) and "you shall have no other gods before [besides] me" (5:7). This demand is so emphatic that God is described as being "jealous" (5:9). Not in a competitive sense; God acknowledges through Moses, "They made me jealous with what is no god"

(32:21). But for the biblical writers there is a sense of rightness that can tolerate no nonsense. To contemplate other gods insults the biblical intelligence. The writers perceive an order in the universe that must come from a single source, and to allow multiple deities diminishes the worshipers for whom God feels a divine jealousy.

But with all that the Old Testament writers tell us about God, they are cautious about giving a name. They believed a person's name revealed the truth about the individual's personality, or even fate. To know someone's name was to hold power over that person. Any giving of a name to God, or any use of that name, was therefore extremely sensitive. No wonder they lived under the command, "You shall not make wrongful use of the name of the LORD your God" (Exodus 20:7).

So when God appeared to Moses, calling him to lead the Israelites to freedom, Moses asked God for a name. God had already made an identification, "I am the God of your father, the God of Abraham, the God of Isaac, and the God of Jacob," and Moses had drawn back in awe of God (3:6). Nevertheless, if Moses were to take on such a perilous assignment, he wanted to know the quality of his authorization. The answer? "I AM WHO I AM" (3:14). The name most sacred to the Jews (referred to by the letters *YHWH*, rendered "Yahweh"), that we usually translate as "Lord," was so holy that rather early its correct pronunciation in the Hebrew was lost because the Jews avoided speaking it, lest they speak it "in vain." The most devout Jews say that in a sense God has no name (which is to say we cannot control or possess God), so modern Orthodox Jews use the term *Ha-Shem*, which means literally, "The Name."

Accessible But Not Manageable

But of course the biblical writers gave numbers of names to God as they experienced the divine. Even more, they gave adjectives to God, and those adjectives become part of the divine name. And always, these names and adjectives walk a fascinating tightrope. They portray a God who is wonderfully accessible but never maneuverable. God is always in reach, always ready to help, and magnificently patient with our human frailties and impediments, but never controlled by us. So the prophet Isaiah says that God is one

"who foils the signs of false prophets
    and makes fools of diviners,

who overthrows the learning of the wise
    and turns it into nonsense" (Isaiah 44:25, NIV).
The pagan soothsayer may think he or she can predict what God can do, somehow controlling God. Not so, Isaiah says with scorn; God "makes fools" of them. Even the wise (and the Hebrew Scriptures praise wisdom) find their learning is turned into nonsense. No one is able to "control" this God or to calculate the full divine measure.

And yet the biblical God is so accessible that the poet can write, "The LORD is my shepherd" (Psalm 23:1). The psalmist can dare to be insistent in addressing the divine: "Answer me when I call, O God" (Psalm 4:1). And Jesus explained that although two sparrows are sold for a pittance, not one falls to the ground without God's notice (Matthew 10:29).

So much of our daily relationship to God rests upon our understanding the degree to which God is accessible and the boundaries of our maneuvering.

Here I may begin to perceive the severity of God. God's goodness is not to be defined by his conformity to my wishes. God's wisdom may be in conflict with what I desire. Other persons exist and have a place in God's plan, and fulfilling my desires might hurt others or complicate God's larger plans. At such times, God may appear severe and unloving. But God is God, which means that although God has chosen to be astonishingly accessible, it is not to the point of being in our control.

The One Who Is Holy

The biblical writers are sure of one thing: God is holy. They have seen that many of the popular gods are only reflections of the persons who worship them. Not so with the biblical God. When young Isaiah experiences a revelation of God, it is while an angelic chorus sings, "Holy, holy, holy is the LORD Almighty" (Isaiah 6:3, NIV). The writer of Revelation reports the same language from a heavenly body:

    "Holy, holy, holy
    is the Lord God Almighty,
        who was, and is, and is to come" (Revelation 4:8, NIV).
The people of God are told to be holy because God is holy (Leviticus 11:44). God's name is holy (Psalm 105:3). The sabbath and other special days are holy because they are associated with God; even the first fruit from a new tree is holy because it is for rejoicing in the Lord (Leviticus 19:23-25).

The word *holy* is difficult to define because clearly the Bible perceives God as the essence of the definition. Perhaps the best word is *otherness*. That which is holy is other than all else, not a matter of being different but *other*. The measure is by another table, with dimensions not used by others because the table is not available to them.

This holiness is a moral quality. It is beyond transgression of any kind. One is left feeling that immoral conduct is inconceivable to God, not simply wrong but outside the realm of consid-

The all-seeing eye symbolizes the all-knowing, all-powerful, ever-present God. Through the eye of God we get a view of God's feeling about all creation: "God saw everything that he had made, and indeed, it was very good" (Genesis 1:31). The symbol emphasizes the personal nature of God in God's caring and watchfulness:
    "The eyes of the LORD are in every place,
      keeping watch on the evil and the good"
        (Proverbs 15:3).

eration. Thus, God feels repugnance when the chosen people are less than moral, or when they are drawn to immoral gods. And so it is that the prophets use such dramatic language in describing Israel's unfaithfulness to God (Ezekiel 23; Hosea 4). Their unfaithfulness is a violation of God's purity. Holiness is probably the primary biblical description of God. Isaiah alone uses the term "the Holy One" some thirty times. When Peter wants the religious leaders to know what they have done in rejecting Jesus, he calls Jesus "the Holy and Righteous One" (Acts 3:14). And the name given to the Spirit of God is "the Holy Spirit"—not the Loving, or the Redemptive, or the Gracious (all of them worthy terms), but the *Holy* Spirit. Quite rightly, then, we have come to refer to the Trinity as "the Holy Trinity."

God Is Love

While holiness is the attribute of God emphasized most in the Scriptures, love is the quality that appeals to us most and that we refer to most frequently. In a sense, our instinct is right, because this quality is so distinctive to biblical faith—Christianity and Judaism envision God as love. The gods of the primitive religions were angry and destructive. One has a feeling that the Israelites were often influenced by these beliefs among their neighbors; thus Jephthah would think that he should sacrifice his daughter (Judges 11). And interestingly enough, this mood continues into our day, so that while people use cozy language in referring to God, they also attribute quite brutal conduct to God. "It must have been God's will" is a common explanation for inexplicable disasters, thus making God anything but loving.

While the New Testament brings the concept of God's love to full expression, it doesn't begin there. The quality of love is present throughout the Old Testament, sometimes in extraordinarily beautiful language. So Moses explains to Israel that God "set his heart" on them, not because they were great but "because the LORD loved you" (Deuteronomy 7:7-8). The prophet Hosea, speaking for God, says:

"When Israel was a child, I loved him. . . .
I led them with cords of human kindness,
    with bands of love" (Hosea 11:1-4).

But it is the New Testament that says unequivocally, "God is love" (1 John 4:16), and "For God so loved the world that he gave his only Son" (John 3:16). And the New Testament gives us the picture of inestimable love in action in the story of the prodigal son (Luke 15). Paul declares the measure of God's love when he says, "God proves his love for us in that while we still were sinners Christ died for us" (Romans 5:8). That is, the love of God is of such dimensions that even the holiness of God accommodates to it. Considering the biblical emphasis on holiness, one could hardly make a stronger statement than that.

A full investigation of the nature of God would introduce other descriptive words: righteousness, justice, lovingkindness, mercy, and faithfulness, for instance. We have limited ourselves to holiness and love because they are the dominant representations, and because to a degree they include elements of the rest.

The Natural Attributes of God

When we speak of the love, holiness, or righteousness of God, we are using terms traditionally referred to as the moral attributes of God. Theological studies also include a classification known as the natural attributes of God. These terms—unlike the moral attributes—are not biblical terms, though they are based on biblical understanding and teaching.

Omniscience means God knows all things, and this knowledge is perfect and immediate. So Elihu describes God to Job as "the one whose knowledge is perfect" (Job 37:16). The psalmist says that God's "understanding is beyond measure" (Psalm 147:5). In the same mood, the prophet Isaiah says that God's "understanding is unsearchable" (Isaiah 40:28). No one says it better than the poet who testifies in Psalm 139,

"You know when I sit down and when I rise up;
  you discern my thoughts from far away....
Even before a word is on my tongue,
  O LORD, you know it completely" (139:2-4).

Omnipotence means God's power is unlimited. And yet, there is a limit, of a very particular kind: God's power is limited by God's own nature. God cannot do anything that would be inconsistent with the divine character. God's power is apparent from the opening verses of Genesis, as God creates all that is—without assistance, and simply by speech. Biblical writers—particularly in the Psalms—testify to God's unlimited power in creation, both in the initial act and in continuing involvement.

And in human affairs too. When Sarah doubts she and Abraham can have a child at their advanced ages, the Lord answers, "Is anything too wonderful for the LORD?" (Genesis 18:14). After Job is challenged by God, he testifies,

"I know that you can do all things,
  and that no purpose of yours can be thwarted" (Job 42:2).

Paul applies this insight by way of encouragement to God's people: "We know that all things work together for good for those who love God, who are called according to his purpose" (Romans 8:28). What God purposes, God can bring to pass.

Omnipresence means God is everywhere present at all times. This assures us God is active and available to our needs. This understanding should not be confused, however, with the pantheistic idea that claims God *is* everything. God's presence is real, but it is spiritual and not material. As someone has put it, God's center is everywhere, his circumference nowhere.

We turn again to a poet who says it so eloquently:

"Where can I go from your spirit?
  Or where can I flee from your presence?
If I ascend to heaven, you are there;
  if I make my bed in Sheol, you are there" (Psalm 139:7-8).

Jeremiah confronts the doubters of his generation with an assurance from God—indeed, a challenge: "Am I a God near by, says the LORD, and not a God far off? Who can hide in secret places so that I cannot see them? says the LORD. Do I not fill heaven and earth? says the LORD" (Jeremiah 23:23-24).

Eternal and immutable. God is before and beyond time, without beginning or ending, and immutable in the sense of being absolutely unchangeable. This brings us again to God's revelation to Moses: "I AM WHO I AM." So the psalmist testifies, "You are the same, and your years have no end" (Psalm 102:27). The letter of James puts the matter in a figure of speech, speaking of God as "the Father of lights, with whom there is no variation or shadow due to change" (James 1:17).

While the quality of eternity is beyond our full human conception, our generation may find it almost as difficult to understand the idea of unchangeableness. Because we live in a culture that we perceive to be in constant change, we are inclined to think of change as both inevitable and desirable. Perhaps it is not surprising that "process theology" has become somewhat influential in this time—a theology that God is changing and developing through interaction with the natural world and with humanity. Obviously, to perceive of God as changing is to infer that God is incomplete, or perhaps, controlled by the creation and its inhabitants. Classical theology insists on God's immutability.

But the immutability of God faces a problem in those instances where the Bible describes God as repenting of a previous plan or feeling, for example, Genesis 6:6; Jonah 3:10. In such instances God's character has not changed, but the divine dealings with humanity have changed as humanity has changed. God's purpose, however, remains the same.

The Importance of Our Beliefs About God

While God does not change, we do; and in the process, we not only come to new understandings of God but we may at times give God another name. Thus Abraham names God for *providing* (Genesis 22:13-14); Moses declares God his *banner* (Exodus 17:15) and *the God who gave you birth* (Deuteronomy 32:18). The psalmist sees God as *shepherd* (Psalm 23:1) and as *rock, fortress,* and *stronghold* (Psalm 18:2). For the prophet Jeremiah God is *our righteousness* (Jeremiah 23:6). So a contemporary believer is likely to find experiential names for God. These names will reflect the relationship; they are not unlike the kind of nicknames or names of endearment we give to family members or cherished friends.

Several of the biblical names for God are currently at issue. *King, Father,* and *Lord* all are proving troublesome to some believers or seekers. Some think terms such as *king* and *kingdom* are time and culture bound in a world that cherishes democracy and personal independence. While the terms themselves are historically conditioned, the theological issue is not.

God is, indeed, God, without benefit of election to that office. This may be offensive to our self-image, but no more so than death and several other inevitable factors of human existence. Indeed, one of the basic concepts of Christian living is that we submit ourselves to God's rule. In one sense there is a quality of humor in this idea, since we are under God's ultimate rule whether we submit ourselves or not. But in the economy of God, we are given the privilege of entering the kingdom of God's purposes by our own wise choice. Thus the King (to use a scaled-down figure of speech for God) invites us to vote ourselves into the Kingdom. But the King doesn't depend on our vote.

A second concern with these terms is more crucial. They seem to many to be sexist terms, and thus demeaning to women. Probably no responsible theologian, either now or in the past, views God as being male. But that is hardly the point for those who are troubled by the terms, because the language itself can so easily evoke male images. This is especially true with the word *Father*—particularly when the believer has unhappy or even destructive memories of an earthly father. And this is not simply a feminist issue; some who would not call themselves feminists are equally troubled by memories they associate with this term.

And yet, *Father, king,* and *Lord* are biblical terms. *Father* is endorsed by Jesus; one of Jesus' key contributions to our understanding of God was his insight on the fatherhood of God.

In one sense, our dilemma is insoluble. Our understanding of God has to be conveyed in terms accessible to us; that is, terms that are part of our human experience. But all such terms are tainted in one measure or another to one person or another. I know of no great concept that does not elicit an unhappy picture for someone, whether the term be *father, mother, home, sister, brother, child, family, friend,* or *love.*

This issue presents a predicament since we have no language to convey our understanding of God except human language, and because our figures of speech come out of human experience. The issue is especially complicated since the most significant concept in our biblical understanding of God is that God is *person*—not concept, not theory, not intelligence, but person.

So what shall we do? For one, work as earnestly as possible to free ourselves from the cultural associations that negatively affect our response to biblical language. Second, we should seek for terms, images, and figures of speech that are most hospitable to our own experiences. These ought not violate biblical revelation, nor should we make them into a new body of doctrine. But if we can find concepts that are helpful to our own understanding of God without entering some private heresy, it is all to the good.

And with it all, remember that no language and no name is ever adequate. "I AM WHO I AM," God told Moses. Always present, always accessible to us, but never within full grasp by our perception. Because God is God.

> BECAUSE WE THE CHURCH BELIEVE God is Person and therefore personal, and is known to us by name, I will address God with awe, with intimacy, and with glad humility.

BELIEVING AND LIVING

We can't go far into a relationship without addressing the other person by name. Names are essential to bonding. But a name can give a false impression, or it can limit perception. (Thus a parent may find it hard to accept a son or daughter as an adult because the name is "my child.") What names given to God call up negative images in your experience?

Which of the several natural and moral attributes of God are most important in your own understanding of God?

Think about the names you use for God. How do they reflect your understanding of God and your relationship to God?

How do you experience God as personal?

How would you address God in a time of deep personal distress? when you were profoundly moved by awe? if you were angry about your personal circumstances?

SEEKING MORE UNDERSTANDING

Think back through your life and list divine attributes and qualities that describe God as you have experienced God. Try particularly to compile lists that reflect your experience until age seven, then from eight to twenty-one, and in the adult years that have followed. In what ways do these words differ by age, and in what ways are they simply restatements of earlier experiences?

PRAYER

"The God of Abraham praise,
All praised be His name,
Who was and is, and is to be,
Always the same!
The one eternal God,
Whose timelessness is clear;
The First, the Last: beyond all thought,
Throughout the year!"

—*Daniel ben Judah, c. 1400*

6

Providence
Divine intervention
God's active presence with creation
Sustaining   Preserving
Caring
God's plan and purposes being fulfilled
Providing   Divine guidance

The God Who Is Involved

"But Joseph said to them, '...Am I in the place of God? Even though you intended to do harm to me, God intended it for good, in order to preserve a numerous people, as he is doing today.'"
—Genesis 50:19-20

LIFE QUESTIONS

When we're in trouble, we want God to be involved. At other times, we're not so sure. A God who is involved in our world is at times highly to be desired, but when God seems to intrude on our plans, or appears to be on the side of our enemies, providence becomes pesky.

God's involvement is rife with questions. Does God play favorites? Is the divine involvement of a kind that could destroy our human freedom? Where does providence end and coincidence begin? What part do we humans play in the activities of providence? Is God active in history? If God is in fact involved in human affairs, does what we do really matter, or is God always in control?

ASSIGNMENT

Our Scriptures will indicate that the biblical writers were very sure God is active in human history. The nature of God's involvement varies greatly; sometimes, in fact, the people of God are certain God has abdicated—and sometimes they wish God would. Sometimes God's role is specifi-

cally spelled out, but other times only implied.

Read with both the skepticism of a historian and the faith sensitivity of a believer. This is a difficult balancing act, but the role of a believer is never easy or simple. That's why we're called believers.

Day 1 Genesis 50:7-26 (God intended good); Psalms 105 (God's faithfulness); 106 (Israel's confession)
Introduction and Readings 65 and 66
Day 2 Psalm 139:1-18 (God present everywhere); Isaiah 45:1-19 (God's sovereign power); Hosea 11:1-11 (God's compassion)
Readings 67 and 68
Day 3 Esther 1–10 (Providence)
Reading 69
Day 4 John 15:1-17 (abide and love); Ephesians 1:1-14 (God's plan)
Readings 70, 71, and 72
Day 5 Romans 8:18–9:33 (confidence in God)
Readings 73, 74, and 75
Day 6 Read and respond to "The Church Teaching and Believing" and "Believing and Living."
Day 7 Rest and prayer

DAILY PRAYER

Pray for the persons and situations on your Prayer Concerns list and about issues or concerns emerging from your daily reading and study.

PROVIDENCE

SCRIPTURE	READINGS
DAY 1	
Genesis 50:7-26; Psalms 105; 106	Introduction and Readings 65 and 66
DAY 2	
Psalm 139:1-18; Isaiah 45:1-19; Hosea 11:1-11	Readings 67 and 68
DAY 3	
Esther 1–10	Reading 69

SCRIPTURE	READINGS

DAY 4

John 15:1-17; Ephesians 1:1-14	Readings 70, 71, and 72

DAY 5

Romans 8:18–9:33	Readings 73, 74, and 75

DAY 6 STUDY MANUAL	PRAYER CONCERNS
"The Church Teaching and Believing" and "Believing and Living"	

THE CHURCH TEACHING AND BELIEVING

For many people today, *Providence* is the name of a city in Rhode Island. For generations preceding ours, providence was a cautious but earnest acknowledgment of a God who is involved in human affairs—perhaps especially in the larger affairs of nature and politics. In the days of most common usage, *providence* was a word spoken with two dramatically different accents. For the devout, it was the word of testimony to praise God for intervening in the human journey. For the cautiously religious, whose doctrinal statements were uncertain, it was a name for God that demonstrated respect if not reverence, and tentative honor if not awe. The statesman who wanted to recognize God without making too sharp a definition found "Providence" a safe public harbor.

Like several other significant theological terms, *providence* isn't found in the Bible. But the concept is. If we didn't have such a term, the Old Testament would force us to develop it, because the Hebrew Scriptures are nothing less than a continual report of God in action—the essence of what we mean by providence.

Providence is not easy to define. Some of us would say we know it when we see it. But since our descriptions would depend on our experiences, the descriptions would vary with the intensity of those experiences and the state of our being at the time of the experiences.

But broadly speaking, the defining isn't too difficult. By providence we mean that God has specific purposes in our world—and some would say, in our individual human lives—and that God works in the events of our world to bring those purposes to pass. Occasionally the providence of God has what many would see as a miraculous quality. But more often, we think of providence as divine intervention that is recognized only after it is past, and often not recognized at all except by those who read life with a certain kind of faith.

To understand another aspect of providence, it is instructive to remember that the English word comes from the Latin *providere*, which means "to foresee." The inference is that God, seeing beforehand what is needed, engages in a provident action. Notice also that *providence* and *provide* come from a common root. Providence portrays a God who provides what is needed. But such divine activity is recognized only by those who interpret the course of history through eyes of faith—in the affairs of individuals as well as the affairs of nations. Of course providence can be read only after the fact. Some no doubt see providence playing a larger role than is probably the case. An even larger number never recognize providence, even when its name is written large.

Is providence then only in the eye of the beholder? No, but as in all matters of human experience, the measure varies with the character and perception of the observer. Then too, the believer is likely to change the measure from time to time, according to the state of his or her faith. Thus what is seen as a commonplace today may be upgraded to a minor miracle tomorrow, and the event that once was heralded as divine action is not even a matter of consideration at a later point. So it was with Israel's interpretation of the miracle at the Red Sea. They sang God's praises just after the event, "but they soon forgot his works" (Psalm 106:13).

Providence in Individual Lives

Joseph interpreted the events of his life through eyes of providence. His brothers had sold him into slavery when he was seventeen years old. In a series of events that some would see as an incredible run of luck, others as the progress of a highly talented man, but that Joseph saw as providence, Joseph became so successful as to save the nation of Egypt from starvation and to preserve his own family. After their father's death, Joseph's brothers feared Joseph would seek revenge for his long-ago crimes against him. Joseph answered, "Am I in the place of God? Even though you intended to do harm to me, God intended it for good, in order to preserve a numerous people, as he is doing today" (Genesis 50:19-20).

Joseph did not discount his brothers' responsibility; he acknowledged that they had acted in malice. But he also understood that God had used their malice to a divine end. Joseph could not take vengeance on them because to do so would be to act "in the place of God" (50:19), who was the final arbiter in all that had unfolded.

Most biblical accounts of providence are to a larger end than simply the happiness of a particular individual. This is not to minimize the importance of the individual. But the biblical story is a record of God's action in the affairs of humanity, so the providential instances are more frequently revealed in matters that reflect—ultimately—the kingship of God. That kind of development often happens, however, through events in the life of an individual. So it was with the story of Joseph. Although the providence of God developed specifically in the life of Joseph, it was "in order to preserve a numerous people" (50:20).

So too in the story of Esther. At first glance the book of Esther seems to be a story about a Jewish girl who becomes queen and of the jealousy Haman, the prime minister of Persia, feels toward Esther's cousin Mordecai. But as the story unfolds, we discover the issue is really the preservation of the Jewish people. The book of Esther is a wondrous sequence of coincidences. And the purest example of Providence, in that the name of God is never mentioned. The believer is allowed to see God at work anonymously through the series of incidents. And although Esther becomes queen through these incidents, and Mordecai's life is saved—both of which must have seemed highly providential to them—the historical issue, the primary focus, is the preservation of the nation of Israel.

From a human point of view, the doctrine of providence means God cares. The divinity is not aloof, but involved. To this end, a verse in Paul's letter to the Romans is especially significant: "We know that all things work together for good for those who love God, who are called according to his purpose" (Romans 8:28). Generations of believers have been sustained in difficult times by the faith they have found through this verse. It portrays providence at work behind the scenes, bringing together the disparate pieces of life into a pattern of purpose.

Paul's "we know" is a faith statement. A believer not only sees providence at work in situations past, but anticipates providence will manifest itself in events currently unfolding. The believer also reasons that nothing is outside the realm of providence; thus Paul announces that "all things" will work for good. This kind of trust in providence takes life conquest; believers assume they will ultimately emerge from all battles victorious.

But providence is not a statement of indiscriminate optimism. It is quite different from "Everything is going to turn out all right." The biblical writers were too realistic about evil to subscribe to such a philosophy. Their confidence was for those "who love God," and who thus were available to God's redeeming activity. And this confidence was based on their being "called according to his [God's] purpose." Once again, the issue in providential activity is the fulfilling of the purposes of God in history. This issue sees history—both corporate and personal—as having a purpose, and that purpose is God's. Because it is God's purpose, one can be confident of its being accomplished. The process of accomplishment may sometimes be complicated, even to the point a believer may wonder about the outcome. But the end is sure, because the goal is the purpose of God.

In Scripture the hand and arm are symbols of God's power; and for the first thousand years of Christianity, the hand from the clouds was the most used symbol for God. Providence says God has a hand in history, working out God's purposes for nations and individuals. Notice that God's providing hand holds the many and the one. In the words of the psalm, "Your right hand upholds me" (Psalm 63:8).

Some may be troubled that the providence of God seems so intent on larger matters as to be inattentive to individuals. The person seems to be only a means to an end. In a sense, this is true, but not necessarily negative, because it means human beings have importance beyond themselves. We are not only, in the language of John Donne, part of the mainland of life; we are also part of the continent of God's purposes.

National Providence in the Old Testament

Israel's greatest confidence as a nation was in its role as the people of God. Following from that confidence was belief in God's providential action on their behalf, as indicated already by the stories of Joseph and Esther. The prophets make much of the same theme, and the psalmists perhaps even more.

For the prophets, providence is reason for both faith and exhortation. If God is at work in the world, there is hope, but also challenge. If a nation is privy to the purposes of God, the responsibilities are immense. So Hosea says for God,

"When Israel was a child, I loved him,
    and out of Egypt I called my son" (Hosea 11:1).
Israel's exodus was not simply a national event; it was part of God's activity. And when, centuries later, what is left of Israel—the two southern tribes—is in captivity, God is still providentially at work. Now the activity is through the hand of a pagan king; but it is a hand that God has grasped, and the king, Cyrus, is now (whether he knows it or not) God's anointed.

"Thus says the LORD to his anointed, to Cyrus,
    whose right hand I have grasped
to subdue nations before him
    and strip kings of their robes" (Isaiah 45:1).
Indeed, the prophets seem always to understand that providence can be at work without its instruments knowing they are being used (10:5). The workings of providence may be so subtle that the participants think themselves in control. Their actions may be to their own ends (as when, for instance, Joseph's brothers sold him into slavery), but God uses them nevertheless. So the psalmist says, "Human wrath serves only to praise you" (Psalm 76:10). The one exercising wrath may do so with no thought of God, but God may employ it to a divine end.

Where the prophets insisted that God is and will be at work in the affairs of peoples and nations, the psalmists delight in reciting the history of their people, because that history is a record of the acts of God. "He is the LORD our God," the writer says, but "his judgments are in all the earth" (Psalm 105:7). Israel has a kind of proprietary claim, but they glory that God's judgments are not for them only, but for "all the earth." Thus,

"When they were few in number,
    of little account, and strangers in it,
wandering from nation to nation,
    from one kingdom to another people,
he allowed no one to oppress them" (105:12-14).

So faith reviews national history and sees the hand of providence. Recalling Joseph's story, the poet says,

"he [God] had sent a man ahead of them,
   Joseph, who was sold as a slave" (105:17).

And when Jacob's family lived as aliens in Egypt,

"the Lord made his people very fruitful,
   and made them stronger than their foes" (105:24).

Even the enmity of Pharaoh was providential (105:25), as were the raising up of Moses and Aaron, the plagues, the deliverance from Egypt, and the provision of food and water through their journey (105:26-42). And the end of it all?

"That they might keep his statutes
   and observe his laws" (105:45).

Israel's role is not simply to survive or even to thrive and become powerful, but to be the people who observe God's laws—and thus provide a witness to the nations of the earth.

Election

Any study of providence brings up the issue of election. If God is at work in the world, which is the essence of providence, then God is working through individuals or nations—chosen people. In its most basic form and fulfillments, the principle of election is accepted by almost all believers. The Hebrew word most often used (*bachar*) expresses the concept of deliberate selection after the weighing of alternatives. This seems reasonable enough; God, with tasks to be done, seeks ways of accomplishing those purposes.

Most believers also take for granted the story of election in the Old Testament. It begins with Abraham's being chosen as the progenitor of a family through which the nations of the earth would be blessed. God's choice was based simply on love; there was no fitness test or evaluation of talents. Some are troubled by the idea of a "chosen people"; they think it suggests favoritism. Virtually nothing of that idea appears in the Old Testament. Israel is chosen not so much to be blessed as to be a blessing. It is a compliment, but a costly one.

Especially, Israel was expected to maintain standards of holiness so it would be qualified for its role. This included not only ethical and religious matters but also separation from the contaminations of their neighbors. Some of the patterns of separation seem narrow when viewed from a nonreligious point of view (Ezra 9–10), but they were consistent with the idea of election. Israel's spiritual purity was seen as essential to their calling.

The New Testament picks up the language of chosenness for the church. So First Peter calls believers "a chosen race, a royal priesthood, a holy nation, God's own people"—and again, to a purpose: "that you may proclaim the mighty acts of him who called you out of darkness into his marvelous light" (1 Peter 2:9).

To this point, election is embraced by almost all believers. It becomes an issue, however, when it is seen as affecting the salvation or rejection of individuals. For those in the Reformed tradition (Calvinist), election also means predestination; that is, all are foreordained to either eternal life or death. The action is entirely on God's part; grace is irresistible, and the Atonement is limited to those who have been chosen. Arminian theology (Wesleyan) takes a different view. Salvation depends on the human response; grace is resistible, and the Atonement is unlimited but effective only for those who accept it.

No doubt, effective cases can be made from the Bible for both points of view. Both positions are supported by earnest and reliable advocates. Broadly speaking, the Reformed position emphasizes the otherness of God—that is, God's absolute right to deal as God wishes with God's creation—while the Arminian position emphasizes the love of God. Probably each needs the influence of the other. And certainly no one can be fair to the several themes of the Scriptures without appreciating both positions.

The Complex Ways of Providence

If God is indeed at work in our world, how does this affect human freedom? And if God is truly a participant in history, is God ultimately in control, even to a point we don't matter?

No one but God can give a final answer to such questions. Any answers we might give will always be influenced by our own experiences and by our own prior theological commitments. But both biblical teaching and human experience seem to indicate that human freedom and divine providence are companions rather than adversaries. The Scriptures show God not only welcomes human participation; he solicits it. The human contribution is often (perhaps always) awkward and sometimes counterproductive. Thus when Abraham and Sarah are to have a child, against all odds, they lose faith and seek to "help" by conceiving a son through Sarah's handmaiden Hagar.

But God is not frustrated by this misadventure. Nor does God, with divine highhandedness, bring a child on the scene another way, without Abraham and Sarah's help. In time Abraham and Sarah do, as originally announced, produce a son. They are not bypassed on one hand or coerced on the other. Their participation may be erratic (that is, human), but they are full partners in the divine enterprise.

This story of Abraham and Sarah suggests that any action of providence requires extraordinary patience and humility on God's part. As the Hebrew prophets saw it, this patience and humility extended even to the point of God's using persons who were not committed to the divine purpose. So Cyrus, King of Persia, becomes God's shepherd, who "shall carry out all my purpose" (Isaiah 44:28), and God's "anointed," whose "right hand" God has grasped (45:1). We respond well to this idea, since Cyrus is filling the role of the good guy; but we're as troubled as was the prophet Habakkuk when God said he was

Predestination is the doctrine that God knows, and has known from Creation, who will be saved. The doctrine has been interpreted many ways and has been the subject of much controversy. It is grounded solidly in Scripture. Throughout the Old Testament, God knows the destiny of individuals and nations. And Romans 8:29 says, "Those whom he foreknew he also predestined to be conformed to the image of his Son." Augustine disputed the belief that human beings could earn their salvation through good works, saying that God wills who will be saved. The doctrine of predestination has two main interpretations: (1) God *knows* who will be saved, and (2) God *wills* who will be saved. Martin Luther revived Augustine's interpretation. John Calvin taught predestination as irresistible grace. Wesleyans and Arminians accepted foreknowledge but emphasized free will. In any interpretation, the Christian depends on the grace of God for salvation.

"rousing the Chaldeans, / that fierce and impetuous nation" (Habakkuk 1:6) to do the divine will in punishing the chosen people.

Providence invites humans to invest their freedom in the purpose of God. As for God's role in history, the biblical witness insists God is ultimately in control, so that at some point the multitudes will cry out,

"Hallelujah!
For the Lord our God
   the Almighty reigns" (Revelation 19:6).

But human beings matter strategically in this plan, because God works through them for the accomplishing of the divine purpose. Knowing this should encourage both faith and thanksgiving. Faith, because we can be confident all will be well. Thanksgiving, because we are assured God is at work and has chosen to do this work with our cooperation.

Mystics and other devout believers often link providence with divine guidance, which becomes one index to the will of God. If circumstances come together in a way that seems to be significant, they are described as "providential circumstances"— that is, circumstances influenced by providence. The circumstances are then seen as shedding light on decisions or choices to be made. Deciding on the basis of "providential circumstances" is not unlike the secular practice of making decisions on the basis of "fortuitous circumstances." But this should not surprise us, because secular and sacred practices often intersect or seem similar. The devout who look for providential circumstances usually insist that any such guidance must be consistent with the teachings of Scripture.

And to what degree is providence simply a matter of coincidence? The interpretation will vary with the faith stance of the individual, and even with the personality involved. Persons of equally earnest faith may have widely varied perceptions of providence and coincidence. Some see God ablaze in every bush, while others only pause at a lightning flash. But in general we can expect that the believer will often find patterns of meaning in the accumulation of circumstances. This is reasonable, because providence is a faith issue. Indeed, it is a fairly advanced faith issue because the evidence is by no means sharply defined. Evidence for providence has to be put together by the earnest and sometimes imaginative hands of the faithful. Belief in God as providence is based on the conviction that God is good and caring. Thus the belief in God as providence is very much an issue of faith.

BECAUSE WE THE CHURCH BELIEVE God is involved in our world, we see ourselves as co-workers with God in fulfilling the divine purpose.

BELIEVING AND LIVING

If we speak thoughtfully about the providence of God, there isn't much room for the theological dabbler. There is a demanding quality about providence; first, in that our faith is stretched, then asked to define itself intelligently in the face of possible ambiguities. Still more, that we must exercise our belief by involving ourselves in ways consistent with God's involvement. In what ways is the concept of providence a challenge to your personal faith?

_____

_____

Where do you think you have seen providence at work in human history, other than in the Bible? in personal experience, either your own, or of someone you know rather well?

_____

_____

As you see it, what is the best argument for the Reformed position on election, and what is the best insight on the Arminian position on the role of human response?

_____

_____

Several of the Psalms (including Psalms 105 and 106) are written about the activity of God in history. Try to write a short psalm either about the working of God in your own life or about the working of God in your nation's history.

_____

_____

_____

SEEKING MORE UNDERSTANDING

Do further study on the theological concepts of election and predestination. Look up the words in a theological word book or a dictionary of the Christian church (check your church or public library) and summarize the main points related to each word. Bring the information you discover into your small group discussion.

PRAYER

"O thou Chief of Chiefs, we kneel before thee in obeisance and adoration. Like the bird in the branches we praise thy heavenly glory. Like the village sharpening stone, thou art always available and never exhausted. Remove we pray thee, our sins that hide thy face. Thou knowest that we are poor and unlearned; that we often work when hungry. Send rain in due season for our gardens that our food may not fail. Protect us from the cold and danger by night. Help us to keep in health that we may rejoice in strength. May our villages be filled with children. Emancipate us from the fear of the fetish and the witch doctor and from all manner of superstitions. Save the people, especially the Christian boys and girls in the villages, from the evil that surrounds them. All this we ask in the name of Jesus Christ thy Son."

—*Prayer from Zaire*

7

Covenant-maker

Covenant   God's initiative
Relationship
God's free and loving election
Divine humility   Obedience
New covenant
Mutual responsibility

God Makes Covenant With Us

"In the same way he [Jesus] took the cup also, after supper, saying, 'This cup is the new covenant in my blood.'"

—*1 Corinthians 11:25*

LIFE QUESTIONS

We are covenant-makers. The word *we* makes it necessary. If there are two of us, a covenant is needed. We want to engage with others. To do so in a way that gives both parties opportunity for fulfillment requires some sort of covenant.

But a covenant with God? That's quite another matter. Our biblical faith insists, however, that God has initiated such covenants. Not once, but repeatedly. How do I dare believe such a thing? And if I dare believe it, what obligation will be upon me? How must I then live, if God makes covenant with us?

ASSIGNMENT

Covenant is a recurring theme in the Bible; we will come upon it all through our reading. In a sense, covenant is always implicit; that's what we mean when we say the Bible is the story of God's relationship with our human race. But the theme is explicit in numbers of instances where specific covenants come into play.

Watch for the ways these covenants differ and the ways all are somewhat similar. Watch too for signs of development in covenant, and ask yourself what these developments say about God and about our human race.

Day 1   Genesis 6:11-22 (God instructs Noah); 8 (covenant with Noah)
Introduction and Readings 76 and 77
Day 2   Genesis 12:1-9 (call of Abram); 13 (promise of land and offspring)
Readings 78 and 79
Day 3   Exodus 34:1-14 (covenant renewed); Deuteronomy 5:1–7:11 (commandments to live by)
Reading 80
Day 4   Psalm 89 (covenant with David); Jeremiah 31:31-37 (new covenant)
Readings 81 and 82
Day 5   1 Corinthians 11:17-26 (cup of the new covenant); Hebrews 8–9 (covenant in Christ's blood)
Readings 83 and 84
Day 6   Read and respond to "The Church Teaching and Believing" and "Believing and Living."
Day 7   Rest and prayer

DAILY PRAYER

Pray for the persons and situations on your Prayer Concerns list and about issues or concerns emerging from your daily reading and study.

66

COVENANT-MAKER

SCRIPTURE	READINGS
DAY 1	
Genesis 6:11-22; 8	Introduction and Readings 76 and 77
DAY 2	
Genesis 12:1-9; 13	Readings 78 and 79
DAY 3	
Exodus 34:1-14; Deuteronomy 5:1–7:11	Reading 80

SCRIPTURE	READINGS

DAY 4

Psalm 89; Jeremiah 31:31-37	Readings 81 and 82

DAY 5

1 Corinthians 11:17-26; Hebrews 8–9	Readings 83 and 84

DAY 6 STUDY MANUAL	PRAYER CONCERNS
"The Church Teaching and Believing" and "Believing and Living"	

THE CHURCH TEACHING AND BELIEVING

The believer in me says our first contract was with God. We are inclined toward God. We need God. Our disposition toward God may be erratic and faltering; it may even be rebellious and resentful. Indeed, we may become so estranged we deny the existence of God. But the recluse from God is by nature a seeker of divine covenant as is the human recluse a social creature. We are what we are, deny though we may. But of course there is quite a distance, in both human and divine affairs, between the inherent need for a covenant and the entering into one.

A covenant is a formal agreement between two parties; it is longing put into commitment and into some sort of specific terms. Covenant establishes the relationship between the two parties, defining their obligations and responsibilities. Quite likely it also spells out the benefits to be found in keeping the covenant and the dangers—perhaps even penalties—in violating it.

The Early Covenants

In a real sense, the covenant was implicit in our creation. When the biblical writer describes us as made in the image of God (Genesis 1:26-27), we understand that not only are we capable of communion with God (and therefore of covenant) but we are impelled to such a relationship.

Perhaps if we had not sinned, no formal covenant would have been necessary. The covenant might have remained as instinctive as the natural clinging of infant to mother. We would have remembered our divine womb. So although God provides the man and woman with numbers of benefits, and with responsibilities, and even with a warning as to the boundaries of their role, there is no indication of a covenant. But we have broken that relationship, so now the covenant has to be a formal act.

The first formal covenant comes into being at a time when God looked upon the human race and said, "I am sorry that I have made them" (6:7). But God found "a righteous man, blameless in his generation" (6:9); and this person, Noah, "did all that God commanded him" (6:22)—an ideal partner to a covenant. When the Flood is past, and the world is ready for a new start, Noah celebrates the new beginning with an altar of dedication; and God responds with a promise:

"As long as the earth endures,
    seedtime and harvest, cold and heat,
summer and winter, day and night,
    shall not cease" (8:22).

The covenant follows. God outlines the relationship humans are to have with the rest of creation and the responsibility they are to carry; then God promises Noah and his sons and "every living creature. . . . I establish my covenant with you, that never again shall all flesh be cut off by the waters of a flood, and never again shall there be a flood to destroy the earth" (9:10-11). The sign of the covenant is the rainbow, a reminder to both God and earth's inhabitants. "When the bow is in the clouds, I will see it and remember the everlasting covenant" (9:16).

Notice some things about this covenant. First, God initiates it. This is a gracious act on God's part, because without such an initiation, we are not qualified to suggest a relationship. See also that although the covenant directly engages only God and Noah and his sons, it affects not only the rest of humankind but also all of creation. This condition is consistent with the biblical understanding that we humans determine the fate of the entire planet. Notice too the emphasis on blood: Humans shall not eat flesh with its blood, and they shall not shed "the blood of another" (9:4-6). Later covenants, continuing all the way to the new covenant celebrated in Holy Communion, are likely to have a direct or indirect reference to blood. The tie is to the idea that blood is the conduit of life and therefore the sacred symbol of ultimate seriousness. To sign in blood is to sign in life and death.

The next major covenant involves God and Abraham. As with Noah, the covenant is primarily with one person, and again with significance for the whole human race. "In you," God tells Abraham, "all the families of the earth shall be blessed" (12:3). Covenant is the consequence of God's choosing or electing to bless Abraham and through him all people.

Abraham is asked repeatedly to chance his all on this covenant. At first it is a matter of leaving country, kindred, and father's house to go into the unknown—to leave all that is secure and known for what is unknown and without promise. Some time later, when Abraham is prospering, he makes a decision that seems essentially to threaten the covenant promise of land; he allows his nephew

Lot to have first choice of the land. After the choice has been made, God speaks to Abraham and reaffirms the earlier covenant. "The LORD said to Abram, after Lot had separated from him, 'Raise your eyes now, and look from the place where you are, northward and southward and eastward and westward; for all the land that you see I will give to you and to your offspring forever. I will make your offspring like the dust of the earth; so that if one can count the dust of the earth, your offspring also can be counted'" (13:14-16). Indeed, it is a generous reaffirmation, including details not given before. Abraham responds by building an altar to the Lord, a basic covenant act (13:18).

The purpose of the biblical covenant is to create a people. Covenants may be made with individuals, but they are never to their exclusive benefit; the individuals are servants to a higher purpose and a larger body. Even so, when Moses represents Israel at Sinai, it is for the purpose of transforming a collection of former slaves into a nation, the very people of God. But neither are they simply an end in themselves. They are chosen in order to be a witness. They will transmit the covenant faith to others, indeed, to the whole world. This understanding was difficult for them to maintain; time and again they slipped into the perception that their chosenness was to their own benefit. We understand this, of course, because throughout church history we Christians have so often succumbed to the same misperception. Not often by doctrinal statement, but by pattern of life and failure of mission.

Much of the Old Testament story is a telling of God's vision for the creation of a covenant community and of the people's falling short of the divine purpose. God's call is to holy living, but Israel falters under uncertain leaders and the attraction to transient gods. After a time, God sends them prophets. The prophets speak to a variety of particular needs and issues, but always their undergirding purpose is to help Israel fulfill its covenant to be the people of God.

No one appealed to the people with more passion and pain than Jeremiah. His ministry came at a time when the political scene was most nearly hopeless. The Northern Kingdom, Israel, had already been taken captive, and Jeremiah was compelled to tell the Southern Kingdom, Judah, they were soon to follow the same route. Still worse, God approved of their coming defeat. The times were not naturally hospitable to a hopeful word.

But Jeremiah was privileged to speak the new word regarding the divine covenant. He noted that the people had broken the first covenant but that the time was coming when they would receive a new one. This covenant would be written on their hearts: "This is the covenant that I will make with the house of Israel ... says the LORD: I will put my law within them, and I will write it on their hearts; and I will be their God, and they shall be my people. No longer shall they teach one another, or say to each other, 'Know the LORD,' for they shall all know

This representation of covenant includes two symbols: the rainbow and stars. Each symbol declares God's continuing and all-inclusive covenant. God's covenant with Noah was marked by the rainbow, a sign of the covenant between God and every creature, emphasizing deliverance and the trustworthiness of God. A rainbow is an arc of a circle; a circle symbolizes the everlasting God. Countless stars symbolize God's promise of blessing to all people for all time through Abraham.

me, from the least of them to the greatest, says the LORD; for I will forgive their iniquity, and remember their sin no more" (Jeremiah 31:33-34). The covenant moves beyond the understandings of the Sinai covenant and promises restoration through a new covenant engraved on the heart. A glorious promise in a time of exile.

Christians have understood this passage to be fulfilled in the new covenant in Jesus Christ. So it is that we call the basic book of the Christian faith "the New Testament," or "Books of the New Covenant." This new covenant, ratified at Calvary, is marked by the shedding of blood. The people of God celebrate the covenant in words of the sacrament of Holy Communion: "This cup is the new covenant in my blood. Do this, as often as you drink it, in remembrance of me." And whenever they do, whether they fully realize it or not, they "proclaim the Lord's death until he comes" (1 Corinthians 11:25-26).

The Covenant God

What does the covenant tell us about God? First, the faithfulness of God. God keeps covenants. Biblical religion declares God has an eternal desire, a longing for a people. This longing is so great that it endures human vacillation. When that vacillation becomes outright rebellion, still God pursues humankind. The goal always is to have a people. And the people are to fulfill God's purpose, that all of creation should be reunited with God's will.

This desire for a people reveals a profound humility in God. By nature, God is complete; no person, thing, or experience is necessary to God's existence or fulfillment. And if there were any such necessary entity, God could compel its compliance, or create it according to fulfilling specifications. Instead, God chooses to want us but does not force us. This is divine humility.

This humility first expresses itself in God's making us as we are. The scales are tipped in God's favor only in that we are created with a longing for God. This longing is inevitable, since we come from God and since we are made in God's image and with God's breath (Spirit) within us. But we are endowed with the freedom to do what we wish with that eternal longing. Our human history demonstrates we have been infinitely imaginative in our attempts to satisfy this longing for the Divine. So although it can be said God claimed something of an advantage in giving us such a basic desire, the advantage can be turned in upon itself. We can seek to fulfill it however we will.

No wonder we have become inveterate god-makers. Some cultures form gods of wood and stone; others shape gods in their minds. Those of us who would not imagine making a graven image need to examine our souls with particular care. The cultures that make graven images do not fool themselves; they know who their gods are. Those whose gods have no

71

images may never fully realize the contours or natures of their gods.

The contemporary person whose god, whether recognized as such or not, is career, hobby, amusement, success (the pantheon is large)—that person finds no call to covenant because the god being worshiped has no persona for entering into covenant. But God chooses to enter into covenant with human beings.

By now you have no doubt sensed that the divine humility God manifests in choosing a covenant relationship is an expression of grace. The word *grace* is not used in the Old Testament in the sense in which we know it in the Christian faith. The Hebrew word *hesed,* which means loyalty or inner faithfulness, is an obvious precursor of grace. But the Bible offers no finer expression of the grace in covenant than we receive in Deuteronomy 7. After Moses reminds Israel they are God's chosen people, he went on to explain why they were chosen. It was not, he said, because they "were more numerous than any other people" that the Lord chose them, because in fact "you were the fewest of all peoples" (7:7). "It was," Moses continues, "because the LORD loved you and kept the oath that he swore to your ancestors, that the LORD has brought you out with a mighty hand, and redeemed you from the house of slavery, from the hand of Pharaoh king of Egypt" (7:8). To close the circle of Moses' logic, the lawgiver was saying, "God loved you because God loved you." This is, indeed, grace. And of course God was faithful. God had maintained loyalty to the people because of the "oath" sworn to their ancestors, that is, the covenant.

The quality of God's covenant character is revealed in another way in Psalm 89. The psalmist begins by singing of God's "steadfast love," rejoicing in the covenant God had made with David. He rejoices at length in God's faithfulness, righteousness, and justice; and then he rehearses in the same fashion the promises God had made to Israel in the covenant.

But in 89:38, the psalmist's mood changes completely. His earlier recitation of thanksgiving for times past and of the particulars of God's promise has been so that he might now say God has forsaken the covenant. And he says so, eloquently, and again at length. His question is poignant:

"Lord, where is your steadfast love of old,
  which by your faithfulness you swore to David?" (89:49).

It is an impassioned cry. A modern reader, recalling the erratic history of Israel's attention to the covenant, may wonder how the poet is reading his nation's history. How can he feel so justified in challenging God's faithfulness, in light of his own nation's obvious and frequent covenant lapses? But the Bible carries his complaint, not necessarily to say his argument is justified, but as a tacit indication that he has a right to express such an opinion.

Such is the character of the covenant-making God. Having initiated a relationship quite beyond justified human imagining,

Hesed is a Hebrew word that has no direct parallel in English. It is used 245 times in the Old Testament; and in various places and translations of the Bible it is rendered as *lovingkindness, mercy, goodness, love, steadfast love, favor.* For example, the repeated refrain of Psalm 136 uses *hesed* as an attribute of God. There the King James Version renders it as "mercy." Most other translations render it as "love" or "steadfast love" as in the New Revised Standard and New International Versions, but *The Jerusalem Bible* uses "faithful love." *The New English Bible* translates *hesed* thirty-three different ways.

God is patient not only with the lapses of the covenant partner but even with that partner's seeking to place the blame on God. These dimensions of the humility and grace of God ought to inspire songs of praise.

The Calvary Covenant

The greatest covenant revelation of God was yet to come. The prophets prepared the way. Isaiah gave us pictures of the divine heart in the suffering servant (Isaiah 52–53); Jonah revealed that God's love was broader—far broader—than our human measure had envisioned; and Hosea portrayed that love in poignant human terms.

But a covenant needs more than words. Quite specifically, it requires that the Word become flesh, to dwell among us (John 1:14). And while the Gospel of John makes no use of the word *covenant,* the idea is surely there. A concept is only a concept until it becomes a fact of human experience. It was essential that at some point the covenant should take on flesh and blood. Needless to say, the initiation must be on God's part.

Of course we are disadvantaged in grasping the wonder of this consummating covenant, because familiarity frustrates our perception. The good news is so old we don't know how good it is. To put it in simple terms, God, the covenant-maker, acknowledging that the distance between the two parties in the covenant was too great, came to the territory of the second party in the Person of his Son. The Son then took to himself the factor—sin—that had complicated and destroyed the relationship in the previous covenants.

And consistent with the covenant pattern of so much of the Old Testament, it was a blood covenant. As the New Testament writer puts it, "without the shedding of blood there is no forgiveness of sins" (Hebrews 9:22). But this blood is different, because the priest bearing the sacrifice is himself the sacrifice, and the blood employed is his blood.

The covenant is quite clear. It can be summarized in the most familiar of Bible verses: "For God so loved the world that he gave his only Son, so that everyone who believes in him may not perish but may have eternal life" (John 3:16). It is an extraordinary covenant in that the basic action of the human party is simply to believe in the integrity of God's offer. A distinctive quality of deed and life will, of course, follow from that believing. Nevertheless, the basic human contribution to the covenant is a declaration of faith in the divine participant.

This covenant is a most remarkable agreement, in that one party—God—has already signed it. The cross is God's signature to the new covenant. It is God's mark. Again, the covenant is an act of supreme divine humility.

At first glance, the new covenant seems out of style with the previous covenants. Their emphasis was on a community, a people—indeed, in the case of Israel, a nation. In the new covenant we accept Jesus Christ as our Savior by way of personal decision—though generally in the rituals of the community of faith: in baptism, confirmation, or confession of faith. Is this covenant different?

Perhaps not as much as we think. Although the earlier covenants were set in the context of community, it is clear individual participation was expected. It is also clear not every individual chose to do so. Noah's covenant is for the benefit of all humankind, yet before long new areas of paganism began to develop. Isaac carries on the covenant made with his father Abraham; but only one of his sons, Jacob, follows him. Romans 9:13, quoting Malachi, indicates Esau was refused in the process of election. Nevertheless, it is also clear Esau valued immediate, sensual fulfillment more than he valued the faith choices that led to inheritance. So, although Israel was a covenant people, an element of personal decision was still present.

On the other hand, as a new covenant people we need to pay more attention to the concept of community. For it is within the church we are brought to salvation, nurtured in our faith, and sustained as a covenant community. Our goal is not to be a heterogeneous collection of individuals but to be a community of believers—a body, as the apostle Paul said. And we have our identity, above all else, as members of the blood covenant.

> BECAUSE WE THE CHURCH BELIEVE God is a covenant-maker, I will consciously and intentionally accept God's covenant as a member of the community of faith.

BELIEVING AND LIVING

Most of us in the Western world have been nurtured with a strong sense of individualism. We are accustomed to an emphasis on the worth of the individual. How do you square this innate sense of individualism with belief in covenant, which is so closely related to the idea of community?

_____

_____

Summarize your understanding of God as a covenant-making God.

_____

_____

_____

What about the church, as you have known it, makes it most difficult for you to believe in the church as God's covenant community? What affirms your belief in the church as God's covenant community?

_____

_____

If the cross is God's signature to the new covenant, what is our signature of acceptance?

_____

_____

Is it possible to belong to the new covenant people and not know it? Explain your conclusion.

_____

_____

_____

_____

SEEKING MORE UNDERSTANDING

The lesson mentions that the book of Jonah expands our understanding of the breadth of God's love. Read all of Jonah at one time and write a few sentences describing the God you find there.

PRAYER

"Strong covenant God, save us
    from being self-centered in our
    prayers,
    and teach us to remember to pray
    for others.
May we be so bound up in love
    with those for whom we pray
    that we may feel their needs
    as acutely as our own,
    and intercede for them with
    sensitiveness,
    with understanding and with
    imagination.
This we ask in Christ's name. Amen."
—Based on words from John Calvin, 1509–1564

8

Humankind

God's image   **Sacred worth**

God-likeness

Relational   **Creature**

Imperfect image

Conscience   Personhood

Free will   *Imago dei*   **Sinner**

Created in God's Image

"So God created humankind in his image,
in the image of God he created them;
male and female he created them."

—*Genesis 1:27*

LIFE QUESTIONS

We humans are (as far as we know) the only creatures on this planet who wonder about themselves. The rabbit doesn't ask, "Why am I here?" nor does the sycamore tree say, "Am I fulfilling my purpose?" Only we humans stand at a distance from ourselves, in a figurative sense, and ask questions about our existence.

Do we ask these questions because we matter so much? If we do, how did it happen to be so? If not, how did we get such an exalted view of ourselves? How is it that we combine in our nature both baseness and magnificence? What manner of creatures are we? Why are we made as we are?

ASSIGNMENT

In a sense, nearly every page in the Bible sheds light on our human condition. Usually, however, it is by way of stories, of instances of human beings in action. Only occasionally do the biblical writers speak specifically about the kind of creatures we are.

But when they do, the insights are enough to occupy our full attention. They speak of our origins, of our present state, of how we got into the

troubles we're in, of our possibilities for a better life, and even of the exalted way God intends us to live. And with it all, of promises regarding our future beyond this planet.

As you read the assigned passages of the week, pause at times to think of particular stories of Bible characters that give additional substance to what you are reading.

Day 1 Genesis 1:26–2:7 (created in God's image)
        Introduction and Readings 85 and 86
Day 2 Job 6–7 (life hard for humans)
        Readings 87 and 88
Day 3 Psalm 8 (humans given dignity); Ecclesiastes 1 (human experience repetitious)
        Readings 89 and 90
Day 4 Romans 1:16–2:16 (God's righteous judgment)
        Readings 91 and 92
Day 5 1 Corinthians 15:35-57 (resurrection of the body); Ephesians 2:1-10 (saved by grace)
        Readings 93, 94, and 95
Day 6 Read and respond to "The Church Teaching and Believing" and "Believing and Living."
Day 7 Rest and prayer

DAILY PRAYER

Pray for the persons and situations on your Prayer Concerns list and about issues or concerns emerging from your daily reading and study.

SCRIPTURE	READINGS

DAY 1

Genesis 1:26–2:7	Introduction and Readings 85 and 86

DAY 2

Job 6–7	Readings 87 and 88

DAY 3

Psalm 8; Ecclesiastes 1	Readings 89 and 90

SCRIPTURE	READINGS
DAY 4	
Romans 1:16–2:16	Readings 91 and 92
DAY 5	
1 Corinthians 15:35-57; Ephesians 2:1-10	Readings 93, 94, and 95

DAY 6 STUDY MANUAL	PRAYER CONCERNS
"The Church Teaching and Believing" and "Believing and Living"	

THE CHURCH TEACHING AND BELIEVING

We humans are much more wonderful, more complex, and more confusing than can be realized without accepting the biblical explanation of our origins and our history.

Genesis gives two pictures of our beginnings. In the first account, God has finished creating all the "cattle and creeping things and wild animals of the earth" (Genesis 1:24). "Then God said, 'Let us make humankind in our image, according to our likeness'" (1:26).

The Genesis writer doesn't say what the phrase "So God created humankind in his image" (1:27) means. What is God's image? Clearly it isn't a physical resemblance. If we were God's physical image, then God would be quite visible. To be in God's image suggests we have personhood, which is to say we have a relational quality. It also indicates we can control our conduct. This makes us responsible for what we do. We can be educated to see issues and consequences, but our decisions will still be our own because we are responsible creatures.

One of the most awesome factors in our *imago dei* (God's image) is that we are thus capable of communing with God. Without the God image, we would have no basis of communication. If anything can be said to be instinctive with human beings, it is the inclination to worship. This inclination seems to have nothing to do with levels of intelligence, with geography, or with ethnic heritage. The inclination to worship may be exercised in vastly different ways, but it is the surest sign of kinship between the most primitive and the most sophisticated of our human race. To be in the image of God is to have an inclination toward God, to gain access to the language of divinity, the language of worship.

The writer of Ephesians adds to our understanding of the image of God. He urges believers to clothe themselves with "the new self, created according to the likeness of God in true righteousness and holiness" (Ephesians 4:24). He is not speaking of the original act of creation; rather, he is calling for a new creation. But this perception of God's image as we should pursue it is instructive; the image is one of "true righteousness and holiness."

The perception in Ephesians no doubt reflects the Genesis theme. How is it we are made in the image of God? In our capacity—and thus also, our longing—for true righteousness and holiness. Of all the extravagant claims that might be made for humans, nothing is more remarkable than this, that we have the potential to be godly. Our most deep-rooted inclination is to be like God, since we were made in God's image. But at the same time, this is our most seductive temptation. The inclination is right, but our method of pursuit may be wrong.

Genesis 2 gives a further insight into our nature: "The LORD God formed man from the dust of the ground, and breathed into his nostrils the breath of life; and the man became a living being" (Genesis 2:7). Generations of rabbis pondered from which part of the earth God gathered the dust from which the human creature was made. Some said it came from every part of the habitable earth, thus making persons of all places related. Others said the dust was taken from the site on which generations later the Temple, with its altar of atonement, would be built; thus, even though we come from the dust of the earth, sin is not a permanent part of our nature.

In any event, this picturesque and more detailed account of human creation says two elements exist in our nature. We are dust, the essence of earthliness; but the breath within us is from God. No wonder, then, that the apostle Paul would one day describe his struggle (and ours) as between something in him that "delight[s] in the law of God" and something else that is "at war" with this delight (Romans 7:21-23). The setting for Paul's struggle seems to have been established in the nature of our creation: We are both earthly and God-bent. The achievement of God's divine purposes has to be fulfilled in our primal dust—but with the help of God's breath.

The Genesis story also defines the working role of the human creatures. By God's assignment, humankind shall "have dominion over the fish of the sea, and over the birds of the air, and over the cattle, and over all the wild animals of the earth, and over every creeping thing that creeps upon the earth" (Genesis 1:26). Human beings are to be responsible caretakers. This role is consistent with our being in God's image. Since God is the Creator and the one ultimately responsible for all that happens to the planet and its inhabitants, the secondary trust would be given to the creature made in God's image. Because humans, of all the creatures, are best able to discern the purposes of God.

We mentioned earlier that to be in the image of God is to have a relational quality. Genesis pays particular attention to this demanding social factor with its story of Adam and Eve's special relationship. It describes Adam as enjoying so many benefits—an ideal setting, a position of responsibility, a sense of worth in God's plan—and yet being at something of a loss. God's analysis: "It is not good that the man should be alone" (2:18). We are meant to live in community. By our very creation, we are social creatures.

Our social nature is our glory and joy, but it is also our peril. Adam and Eve get into sin together; they become partners in rebellion just as they will later become partners in childbearing and in child-rearing. Because we are social, we are also capable of being jealous, and envious, and covetous. None of these possibilities of sin would exist were it not for our social nature. If we didn't care for others and need others, we wouldn't be in danger of perils that involve others.

But we shouldn't allow these perils to dim the glory of our social character. Because we are social creatures, we care for one another, even to the point of giving our lives for others. The noblest human deeds spring from the social side of our being. The tireless attention of a parent to an infant or of an adult child to an aged parent, the playground protectiveness of an older sibling for a younger, the sacrificial heroism of the battlefield— all are expressions of our social nature. The fact that they are so commonplace does not diminish their beauty.

And of course because we are social creatures, we are prey to the oldest human malady, loneliness. Before there was sin, there was loneliness. "It is not good," God said, "that the man should be alone" (2:18). We are social creatures, so even though other humans exist, we still have the capacity to be lonely. We look for fulfillments in human relationships that sometimes defy the ability of any human to provide. Sometimes, in fact, we expect humans to take the place of God, a role no one can fill. But this too is part of our being social, which in turn is part of our being human.

The Violation of Trust

So the biblical picture of humans presents us as created in the image of God. Further, we have been assigned the chief caretaker post for our planet. The psalmist found our creatureliness something to sing about. Having described the wonder of God's glory as revealed in the creation, he asked:

"What are human beings that you are mindful of them,
   mortals that you care for them?" (Psalm 8:4).

And then he explains some reasons he is so impressed with the attention God has given to humans: They are created "a little lower than God [or angels]," and God has "crowned them with glory and honor" (8:5). The psalmist goes on to speak of the "dominion" referred to in Genesis 1:26, listing some areas of

God, our Source, is symbolized by the circle. The figures represent two ideas: We are created male and female, and we are made to relate to one another, to the world around us, and to God. Behind this depiction is the message that the image of God is to be seen not in the way we look but in the way we relate.

80

creation under human supervision, and on the basis of all that, concludes,

"O LORD, our Sovereign,
how majestic is your name in all the earth!" (Psalm 8:9).
Suggesting, it seems, that nothing demonstrates more clearly that God deserves praise than what God has done with humankind.

But something happened. The human creature broke trust. Being made in the image of God was not enough. When the suggestion was made that humans might become equal with God, they jumped at the idea, even though it came from one with no discernible credentials (Genesis 3:1-6).

This violation of our divine trust has made all the difference. The image of God in the human creature is blurred by the rebellion against the divine. On one hand, thinking that the image in itself is not enough reflects on the One who granted it. Still worse, our ancestors (and we) assume that this equality with God that we desire is something we can attain by deception.

So it is that the human creature became known as a *sinner*. The creature made in the image of God, and infused with the breath of God, the creature a little lower than the angels, is now defined by an act of rebellion.

Literature is crowded with reflections on this present human state. Philosophers of every kind have examined the subject for as long as philosophy has existed; after all, what could be more interesting or more basic to the philosopher's concern than the state of the philosophers themselves? Poets have never tired of exploring the subject. In our own mid-to-late twentieth century, serious drama has come back repeatedly to ask about our human condition and what can be done about it.

One of the gloomiest opinions came from the writer of the Old Testament book of Ecclesiastes. His preliminary survey—a rather complete one, it seemed to him—made him conclude "All is vanity," that is, a vapor, fleeting (Ecclesiastes 1:2). Wherever he looked, whatever he tried ended in futility. Even the pursuit of wisdom, he said, was nothing but "a chasing after wind" (1:17).

Another ancient wise man, Job, found some of his greatest frustration in what might have been a testimonial to his worth. He declared in the bitterness of his struggle, "I loathe my life" (Job 7:16). Especially, he was frustrated that God would pay him so much attention:

"Will you not look away from me for a while,
let me alone until I swallow my spittle?
If I sin, what do I do to you, you watcher of humanity?
Why have you made me your target?
Why have I become a burden to you?" (7:19-20).
God is, indeed, the "watcher of humanity," and humanity indeed God's "target." Being the object of such attention is a compliment in the extreme, and Job—like millions of other

thoughtful souls—can hardly endure so much attention. But at the same time, the human creature wants this divine attention. We're made that way. As a result, sin's hold on us does not leave us hopeless.

Preachers and poets of another generation often referred to humanity as "God's masterpiece." The term may have been grandiose, but it was well chosen. Genesis implies as much by reporting the creation of humans as the climax of the creation process. It underlines that perception by saying humans are made in the image of God and the breath of God is in us. But then, most notably, Scripture doesn't give up on humanity after the human becomes a sinner. Indeed, the constantly repeated plot of the Old Testament is of human failure and God's forgiveness, human flight from God and God's unceasing pursuit. Not only is God patient beyond description; God must also see something quite worthy in this human creature.

The New Testament writers go still further with this theme. They don't deny the impact of sin; indeed, no one could be more conscious of the power of sin than Paul. He is appalled by the conduct of the human race; "Claiming to be wise," he says, "they became fools" (Romans 1:22). Their conduct is abhorrent to him. And his own human experience is equally distressing. He knows what it is to struggle with impulses he despises, impulses that make him "captive to the law of sin that dwells in my members" (7:23).

And yet, with all of that, humans can be "holy and blameless and irreproachable" before God (Colossians 1:22). We have been seated with God "in the heavenly places in Christ Jesus" (Ephesians 2:6). And this in spite of the fact that we "were once estranged and hostile in mind, doing evil deeds" (Colossians 1:21). No wonder Paul can write to quite ordinary congregations and address them as "saints"! He knows their heritage and their potential.

Nor does Paul take this lofty ground by spiritualizing us. He is always candid about the corrupt practices in which humans become involved. But he dares to say the body is "a temple of the Holy Spirit" (1 Corinthians 6:19). And these very bodies, with all their human complications, Paul urges us to give to God as a "sacrifice, holy and acceptable to God" (Romans 12:1).

Then too, the New Testament sense of our human worth justifies seeing us as persons whose bodies will be resurrected. The phrase from the Apostles' Creed, "I believe in the resurrection of the body," is one of Christianity's highest tributes to what we human creatures are. "This mortal body," Paul says, "must put on immortality" (1 Corinthians 15:53). We inherited a physical body from Adam, who "was from the earth, a man of dust" (15:47); but as surely as we "have borne the image of the man of dust, we will also bear the image of the man of heaven," that is, Christ (15:49).

The doctrine of humankind has implications for our treatment of the rest of humanity. The New Testament book of James makes such a point in an interesting way. When James is warning against misuse of the tongue, he reasons, "With it we bless the Lord and Father, and with it we curse those who are made in the likeness of God. From the same mouth come blessing and cursing. My brothers and sisters, this ought not to be so" (James 3:9-10). His logic is to the point: How dare we bless God if we curse the creature made in God's image? At this point, what we believe about humankind is as practical as tomorrow's luncheon conversation.

Every doctrine has, in its own way, a down side. If a teaching is important, it is also costly; it has consequences. If human beings are unique in all of creation, what can be expected of them, and to what end? Also, if they are made in the image of God, what are the expectations of the One whose image they bear? What judgment comes with their assignment of dominion over the earth?

The Old Testament considered that these matters were settled almost entirely on this earth: We get what we deserve, for good or ill, during our lifetime. So it is that some of the Psalms lament bitterly over times of trouble, when the trouble seems undeserved. Job argues passionately that he has been good, and his friends argue just as earnestly that he must be bad; otherwise he wouldn't be suffering misfortune. A theology entirely earthbound faces serious ethical problems because life doesn't always work out as fairly on this earth as it seems it should.

The New Testament speaks of judgment beyond this earth. This understanding was hinted at in Daniel: "Many of those who sleep in the dust of the earth shall awake, some to everlasting life, and some to shame and everlasting contempt" (Daniel 12:2). But generally we have to wait until the New Testament to see the doctrine of judgment developed in full. In some instances the emphasis is upon conduct, as in Jesus' parables of the talents and of the sheep and the goats (Matthew 25); and at other times the emphasis is on belief in Christ as Savior, as in John 3:16 and numerous passages in the letters.

But in any event, the New Testament expects we will be judged. Because we have been so lavishly endowed, we will be judged accordingly. In succinct terms, we matter enough to be candidates for heaven or hell.

The Doctrine of Humankind and the Creeds

The ancient creeds say very little about a doctrine of humankind. When the Nicene Creed and the Apostles' Creed speak of the "holy catholic church," there is an indirect reference to humanity, since the church is made up of humans, and of course the "forgiveness of sins" is a reference to humans. So too, when the Nicene Creed speaks of "the resurrection of the dead" and the Apostles' Creed of "the resurrection of the body," they refer to humankind. But in no instance do the creeds make a specific doctrinal statement about our nature or our particular place in God's plan. Perhaps because such doctrines were assumed. Or perhaps because these matters were never brought into question.

Nevertheless, the creeds leave us with some powerful testimonials about humanity, though indirect references. All the statements about the church, the communion of saints, the forgiveness of sins, the resurrection, and the life everlasting indicate the importance of humans. Obviously we are uniquely significant if God gives us so much attention of such notable kind.

The other reference, in the Nicene Creed, may be the most telling of all. In declaring the ministry and nature of Jesus Christ, it affirms that he "became truly human." Here is the supreme endorsement of humanity.

In truth, we have no idea of who we are until we know God. To view ourselves from any other perspective is to miss the wonder of our origins the magnitude of our potential, and the reality of our destination. From any other perspective we would also miss the degree of distress involved in our falling short of our divine potential.

We cannot hope to fully understand this truth unless we begin where biblical teaching begins, that is, humanity's significance rests in its relationship to God. As for our purpose in living, perhaps we cannot improve on the succinct statement of the Westminster Catechism, that the "chief end" of us humans is that we shall "glorify God and enjoy him forever."

> BECAUSE WE THE CHURCH BELIEVE human beings are made in God's image, and with a divine destiny, we will treat ourselves, other human beings, and all of creation as sacred creations.

BELIEVING AND LIVING

Why do we humans ask questions about ourselves and our reason for existence?

_____

_____

In what specific ways does the teaching that all persons are made in God's image shape your attitudes and understandings of those you relate to? even yourself?

_____

_____

If we are created for relationship, why are relationships so difficult? Why are relationships so broken? Why are families so broken?

_____

_____

How is the created world faring under the care of human beings made in God's image?

_____

_____

In your view, how should humans view their place in creation as a whole? What are the implications of your views?

_____

_____

SEEKING MORE UNDERSTANDING

For the coming week, try consciously to see each person you have contact with as made in the image of God, and try consciously to carry out your role as steward of everything else in creation. At the end of each day, make notes of your experiences. Then at the end of the week summarize your experience and your learning about God, yourself, and the created world.

PRAYER

"Lord, why should I doubt any more, when you have given me such assured pledges of your love? First, you are my creator, I your creature, you my master, I your servant. . . . I am confounded to think that God, who has done so much for me, should have so little from me. But this is my comfort, that when I come to heaven, I shall understand perfectly what he has done for me, and then I shall be able to praise him as I ought. Lord, having this hope let me purify myself as you are pure, and let me be no more afraid of death, but even desire to be dissolved and be with you, which is best of all."

—Anne Bradstreet, c. 1612–1672

9

The Fall   Sin   **Sinner**

Original sin

Rebellion against God

Forgiveness   Guilt   Reconciliation

Alienation from God   self   others

Self-centeredness   Repentance

Death   **Human sinful nature**

The Trouble We're In

"I know my transgressions,
   and my sin is ever before me.
Against you, you alone, have I sinned,
   and done what is evil in your sight,
so that you are justified in your sentence
   and blameless when you pass judgment.
Indeed, I was born guilty,
   a sinner when my mother conceived me."

—*Psalm 51:3-5*

LIFE QUESTIONS

Sin has become an almost unmentionable word in this century. Several years ago, Karl Menninger, then known as the dean of American psychiatrists, dared to challenge this attitude with a book he titled *Whatever Became of Sin?*

But most of the literate culture in the Western world is still unconvinced. *Sin* is a word that evokes snickers, or perhaps an indulgent wave of the hand. Some would say it's a word impossible to define.

Nevertheless, all of us know something is wrong with our human race. Could it be sin? What is sin? What causes us to sin? Is sin something we humans can hope to be rid of? What makes an act "sin"? What difference does it make as long as I'm not hurting anyone else by what I do?

ASSIGNMENT

Our culture has inclined us to look at sin in psychological terms; thus we have nearly eradicated the word from proper speech. We think of personality disorders, or of genetic predispositions, because we think of sin primarily in specific matters of conduct. The Scriptures, on the other hand, think of sin in theological terms. God is the issue. The issue of sin is not simply a matter of deeds done but of an attitude toward God, toward right and wrong, toward society and self.

Watch for such matters as you read Scripture. Remember that some of the most significant biblical insights on sin come in stories of human conduct as well as in laws and theological statements.

Day 1   Genesis 2:15-17 (forbidden fruit); 3:1-19 (sin and punishment)
       Introduction and Readings 96 and 97
Day 2   Leviticus 6:24-30 (sin offering); Ezekiel 18 (individual responsibility)
       Readings 98 and 99
Day 3   Psalms 32 (confession and forgiveness); 51:1-17 (prayer for forgiveness)
       Readings 100 and 101
Day 4   Matthew 5:21-30 (removing the source of sins); Romans 3:1-20 (all guilty of sin)
       Readings 102 and 103
Day 5   1 John 3:4-10 (children of God)
       Readings 104, 105, and 106
Day 6   Read and respond to "The Church Teaching and Believing" and "Believing and Living."
Day 7   Rest and prayer

DAILY PRAYER

Pray for the persons and situations on your Prayer Concerns list and about issues or concerns emerging from your daily reading and study.

SCRIPTURE	READINGS

DAY 1

Genesis 2:15-17; 3:1-19	Introduction and Readings 96 and 97

DAY 2

Leviticus 6:24-30; Ezekiel 18	Readings 98 and 99

DAY 3

Psalms 32; 51:1-17	Readings 100 and 101

SCRIPTURE	READINGS

DAY 4

Matthew 5:21-30; Romans 3:1-20	Readings 102 and 103

DAY 5

1 John 3:4-10	Readings 104, 105, and 106

DAY 6 STUDY MANUAL	PRAYER CONCERNS
"The Church Teaching and Believing" and "Believing and Living"	

THE CHURCH TEACHING AND BELIEVING

Our sophisticated generation assumes we know everything about sin. In truth we are incredibly naive about the subject. Our knowledge comes mostly in tabloid headlines and is predictably superficial.

We can't know much about sin unless we know a good deal about God, because sin is a God issue. Sin is more than a breach of courtesy or of good taste, and more than the sort of conduct that brings witnesses into courts of law. And sin is decidedly more than a psychological maladjustment, though sin may play a part in that sort of condition.

Sin makes its appearance early in the human story. The serpent, a creature "more crafty than any other wild animal that the LORD God had made" approaches with a question: "Did God say, 'You shall not eat from any tree in the garden'?" (Genesis 3:1). This question appears so innocent, but it is crucial to the nature of sin because of the suspicions it raises about God: Is God good? competent? favorably disposed toward us? Sin never begins as an outright act of rebellion. In its own way, sin is always at first a reasonable reaction. The questions it raises usually seem appropriate: Will I be happier this way? Will I get more out of life? Will I be delivered from boredom? Will I be better off—at least in the sense of pleasure—than I am now?

And as a matter of fact, after the tempter persuades Eve it is in her best interest to eat the forbidden fruit, Eve herself realizes how attractive the temptation is. She sees that the tree "was good for food, and that it was a delight to the eyes, and that the tree was to be desired to make one wise" (3:6)—a description that covers most issues that would occur to a person.

God the Issue

No doubt the Genesis writer intends the description of Eve's temptation to encompass the whole of human susceptibility. People often want to identify the first sin. The answer is quite simple, though it isn't the answer most questioners want. The first sin was disobedience, or rebellion against God. The writer quite artfully gets no more specific than that; and the writer is just as generic in describing the temptation. The temptation is not an appeal to a specific physical, intel-

lectual, or spiritual sin, but to all types of sin.

And sin is attractive. In its initial appeals, sin seems always to offer opportunity for self-betterment. Obviously we will not be drawn to adultery by the prospect of a broken home, or to theft by the promise of incarceration. Theft will give me something I want and perhaps even need; adultery will fulfill a complex of longings, some of them perhaps even rather spiritual, in the sense that the temptation assures me I will be more fulfilled.

Also, the temptations that sin offers are so tangible and so *now*. This forbidden fruit is there to be plucked, and it can be had at this very moment. The case against it is something so intangible— the plan of God. Not only is it impossible to lay our hands on the plan of God, but it is in the distant and uncertain future. When we consider how immediately fulfilling sin is (even if only momentarily), and how uncertain and far-removed is God's purpose, we conclude it is quite astonishing that anyone ever chooses goodness.

That's the point, of course. If we choose goodness, it is an act of faith in God. The forbidden fruit is here, now, appealing, and immediately gratifying. We have been told God has better things in store for us, but they are not here. We have no real evidence they exist except as we believe God. To be righteous is to believe God and to believe in the qualities God represents. To sin is to believe in whatever—immediate or longer-term—gratification sin promises. And the sin, quite simply, is in disobeying God.

That's one of the reasons sin is a God issue. It has all sorts of human ramifications, but the root issue is with God. That's why the Genesis story shows God in direct conversation with Adam and Eve after their sin. This matter is not to be discussed and settled with an angel or with some other representative of God; it must be dealt with directly with the One at issue, God.

The ancient psalmist, in words generally attributed to King David after his sin with Bathsheba, puts the matter directly:
"Against you, you alone, have I sinned,
    and done what is evil in your sight,
so that you are justified in your sentence
    and blameless when you pass judgment"
        (Psalm 51:4).
If these words were in fact written after David's sin with Bathsheba, we can list several persons

against whom David has sinned besides God: Bathsheba, her husband Uriah, David's legal wives, his children, and the kingdom that trusts him—to say nothing of the fact that David has sinned against himself, in that he has destroyed something of the image God has invested in him. But the psalmist sees it otherwise: "Against you, *you alone,* have I sinned."

And the psalmist has it right. Sin is ultimately against God because God is the source and standard. As a classical Russian novelist put it, "If God is dead, anything is permitted." When people lie, it isn't simply that they have broken faith with their fellow humans, but with the living Truth. If I tell a story that is shady or corrupting, I may offend you and even corrupt you. But my sin is against Ultimate Purity, God. If in my greed I destroy the livelihood of the poor, I sin against God, who hurts when the poor hurt. If I conduct myself toward you in a way that is impure, I may violate your standards and even your person. But my sin is against God. God is the measure of purity. Your measure or mine is fallible. But God *is* purity; so when I am impure, I sin against God.

And because sin is an act against God, it is God who will have to grant forgiveness. If my sin has hurt another person, I ought to seek that person's forgiveness. But that person's forgiveness is not determinative for me; it will not affect the state of my soul. The issue of forgiveness is with God, because sin is a God issue.

The degree to which God is the issue in sin is demonstrated most dramatically in the cross. If sin is as serious a matter as the Bible suggests, then it must be dealt with in a serious way. And how more serious than for God to become directly involved, and at last for God to become, in his Son, the point of sacrifice for sin. Thus the cross acknowledges that the sin issue is indeed a God issue. God not only overcomes sin but initiates the process of reconciliation.

Consequences of Sin

Genesis also tells of the consequences of sin. Many consequences appear even before God has pronounced judgment, as if sin is so much against the grain of the universe that no judgment need be announced. The judgment is written into all that we are and the conditions with which we live. Thus, as soon as Adam and Eve sin, they know they are naked. Their innocence is gone. They sew fig leaves together to cope with their nakedness. Their coverings are not so much to hide from each other as to hide from themselves. They must now deal with their own sense of shame. They now know the need to explain themselves, to "cover" for what they are. In doing so, they establish the endless pattern of the human race. Consider too that from now on they will spend much of their time in the unproductive activity of handling the results of their sin. This too becomes a historic pattern of our human race.

A second immediate consequence is alienation from God.

"Cursed is the ground because of you; . . . thorns and thistles it shall bring forth for you"— these words in Genesis 3:17-18 carry God's response to humankind's disobedience. The thistle symbolizes both the Fall of humankind and the entry of sin into the world.

When the man and the woman hide "from the presence of the LORD God among the trees of the garden" (Genesis 3:8), we see another tragic element come into their existence. We may infer that, prior to their sin, the humans welcome God's presence in the garden. Now "the sound of the LORD God walking in the garden at the time of the evening breeze" (3:8) is reason for terror. God is no longer their benefactor but their potential enemy. Where once, we assume, they would have come running to God, now they run from God. When God seeks them out, they explain they heard the divine sound, and they were afraid because they were naked (3:10). Nothing so encourages confidence with God as innocence, and they had lost their innocence.

The fear of alienation is great because humankind desires union with God; this is the instinct of those made in the image of God and inhabited by the divine breath. So the penitent poet cries,

"Do not cast me away from your presence,
    and do not take your holy spirit from me" (Psalm 51:11).
On the surface, the human response to God seems ambivalent. After all, humans run from God in their peculiar stretch for freedom. But even in the running, humans discover the heart calls for home even as the psyche runs from it. At times of clarity, humans realize that nothing could be worse than to be separated from God, and thus from their own true selves.

Sin not only alienates us from God; it also alienates us from one another. When God asks the man to explain how he has eaten of the fruit that had been forbidden—the man quickly blames the woman: "The woman whom you gave to be with me" (Genesis 3:12). In truth, Adam not only blames the woman for his sin; he blames God too. It is "the woman whom you gave to be with me."

But of course this is the woman who had been the fulfillment of the man's longing only a short time before. He had said of her, she "is bone of my bones / and flesh of my flesh" (2:23). Now this one who was part of his very being is seen as his enemy and the source of his troubles. Sin alienates person from person. This situation is not God's punishment for sin; it is simply part of what comes with sinning. To sin is to become susceptible to misunderstanding and division.

Even without the prospect of hell, sin is tragic beyond measure because of what it does to our human relationships. If I lie, I begin to expect falsehoods from others. The person who commits adultery becomes less trusting of morality in general, and perhaps even of a spouse in particular. This reaction is partly in self-defense, of course; if I have sinned, I want the consolation of thinking others are like me. But one way or another, sin alienates us from one another. I am suspicious of my neighbor, not necessarily because I have seen him sin but because I have sinned and so I know what my neighbor is capable of.

The judgments God announces for the man and woman are severe enough but less tragic than those built into the sin itself. The woman will have increased pain in childbearing (3:16), and she will be at particular enmity with the tempter (3:15). The man finds the ground cursed so that he will have to struggle against "thorns and thistles" and his work will now suffer the frustration of "sweat." The man and woman are reminded they are dust and will in time return to the dust from which they came (3:17-19).

Original Sin?

What about original sin? That is, that all of us are sinners because of the sinful origins of our race in Adam and Eve and their transgression—what we often refer to as "the Fall." This doctrine contends that through the first sin, humanity lost the divine righteousness and distorted the divine image. Classical theology has a Latin phrase for it—*peccatum originalis.*

This doctrine is often supported by reference to Psalm 51:5:
"Indeed, I was born guilty,
a sinner when my mother conceived me."
Of course, it is possible the ancient poet was at that moment enunciating a belief commonly taught. More likely, however, he is speaking the language of heart and of personal experience rather than the language of definitive theology. His is the cry of a person so distressed by his sin that it seems to him sin has been with him from even before his birth.

But in a sense, the doctrine of original sin needs no Scripture to prove it; human experience is evidence enough. All of us discover that a capacity for sin shows itself in our human nature very early.

Our propensity for sin also indicates the subtle nature of sin. The New Testament letter of James explains the process of temptation this way: "One is tempted by one's own desire, being lured and enticed by it; then, when that desire has conceived, it gives birth to sin, and that sin, when it is fully grown, gives birth to death" (James 1:14-15). Sin is such a powerful factor in our lives because it begins with our desires—and legitimate desires, at that. Sin is not only an acquired taste. It comes with our basic, legitimate longings. To use an old definition, sin is legitimate desire drawn beyond legitimate bounds.

No wonder sin gives us so much difficulty. It approaches us at our places of need and takes them into illegitimate territory so that hunger slips into gluttony, the need for affection becomes lust, the desire to improve oneself becomes theft, and the longing for exhilaration becomes drunkenness or drug abuse. Even the desire for spiritual fulfillment can lead to self-deification or to seeking to use God for quite ungodly purposes.

Jesus exposed something of the subtlety of sin in the Sermon on the Mount. For those who were content to define murder and adultery by physical acts, Jesus insisted on far more demanding

The doctrine of original sin seeks to explain the sinful nature of human beings. Because of the first sin of Adam, variously defined as disobedience, pride, abuse of liberty, fall from grace, every human being is born with a nature inclined to sin and needs to be redeemed or restored to original righteousness. Athanasius explained that Adam's sin was the abuse of his liberty and resulted in the loss of conformity to the image of God. Augustine and the Reformers saw original sin as corrupt human nature without free will. Thomas Aquinas saw personal sin as inevitable, showing pure human nature and a lack of divine grace. All present Christian traditions accept the doctrine of original sin and the idea that human beings are unable to save themselves.

92

SIN

rules: To say to someone "You fool" is to be "liable to the hell of fire," and to look at a woman with lust is already to commit adultery with her in the heart (Matthew 5:22-28).

No wonder, then, that Paul declares, "All, both Jews and Greeks, are under the power of sin, as it is written:

"There is no one who is righteous, not even one;
there is no one who has understanding,
there is no one who seeks God " (Romans 3:10-11).
And no wonder, indeed, that he paints a scenario of despair: "For I know that nothing good dwells within me, that is, in my flesh. I can will what is right, but I cannot do it. For I do not do the good I want, but the evil I do not want is what I do. . . . Wretched man that I am! Who will rescue me from this body of death?" (7:18-24).

Not surprisingly, we have developed some more complex definitions of sin. The Roman Catholic Church has for centuries distinguished between *venial* and *mortal* sins. Mortal sins, by this definition, are those that cause a complete break from God and thus bring eternal, spiritual death, while venial sins, though they incline one away from God, are nevertheless less severe in their effects.

More recently theologians, like the prophets of old, have spoken of *social* sin, to indicate both our sins against society and the way sin affects the whole social fabric. Some theologians speak of *systemic* sin, to describe evil that has become ingrained in our institutional structures—such evils as racism, sexism, and poverty. Others use the term *structural* sins to describe this same tendency for society's institutions to become infected with sin. Centuries ago, theologians developed a list familiarly known as "the seven deadly sins"—pride, covetousness, lust, envy, gluttony, anger, and sloth. Perhaps what is most significant about this list is that it is made up of matters that are quite beyond the conventional definitions of sin—the sort of definitions that come out of the tabloids. But the medieval writers who developed the list were quite right in defining these attitudes and practices as "deadly." It is their appearance of harmlessness that makes them dangerous.

A Way Out?

So sin is a deadly serious matter. The man was warned that in the day he ate of the forbidden fruit, he would die. The tempter advised the woman, "You will not die" (Genesis 3:4). If the death penalty was understood as a physical fact to be imposed immediately, the tempter was right. The man and the woman ate and lived to be confronted by God for what they had done, and lived, in fact, many years after that. If "you shall die" meant the entrance of death upon the human scene, where otherwise it would not have existed, this has obviously proved to be the case. And if "you shall die" meant that numbers of deadly factors now became part of the human story, this too is the case.

93

In any event, humans soon came to understand sin had a death penalty, however one might read it; and they countered with a death antidote, a system of sacrifices. This response shows itself in a variety of ways in many ancient cultures. The Bible presents a fully developed system of sacrifices. They are built on the principle that "the life of the flesh is in the blood," and therefore "it is the blood that makes atonement" (Leviticus 17:11). A New Testament writer puts the issue succinctly: "Under the law almost everything is purified with blood, and without the shedding of blood there is no forgiveness of sins" (Hebrews 9:22). Whether the philosophy appeals to us or not, its logic is simple and straightforward: Sin has brought death, and if sin is to be countered, it will be with a death, which implies the shedding of blood. Eventually this logic leads us to the cross and even the Communion table.

The biblical writers understood there must be more than ceremony. The psalmist describes the agony of his guilt:

"Then I acknowledged my sin to you,
   and I did not hide my iniquity;
I said, 'I will confess my transgressions to the LORD,'
   and you forgave the guilt of my sin" (Psalm 32:5).

And in the psalm that is probably as eloquent as anything in all of literature in its sense of sin and alienation, the penitent declares,

"The sacrifice acceptable to God is a broken spirit;
   a broken and contrite heart, O God, you will not despise"
      (51:17).

If sin is to be dealt with, it must be acknowledged and repented of, and this is a transaction to be carried through with God. Because sin is a God issue.

> BECAUSE WE THE CHURCH BELIEVE sin is an affront to God and a deceiver of all that is good, we will with all energy avoid it and will with all seriousness repent of it when we are guilty.

BELIEVING AND LIVING

Does sin have new names today? If so, what are they?

_____

_____

How would you define sin?

_____

_____

_____

How, in your own experience, has sin proved its subtlety?

_____

_____

Give some examples, as you have observed life, of the way sin is the drawing of legitimate desires beyond legitimate bounds.

_____

_____

What are the roots from which both personal sin and social sin spring? How are personal and social sin intertwined?

_____

_____

SEEKING MORE UNDERSTANDING

We generally think of Job as an exploration of faith and suffering. But another theme running through the book is the relationship between sin and suffering: If you are suffering, you must have sinned. Trace that idea through the book. Read a few chapters at a time, using these questions to guide your reading: Where does the idea arise? How is it expressed? What responses are made? What, if any, resolutions of the issue are offered?

PRAYER

"Wilt thou forgive that sin where
    I begun,
    Which is my sin, though it were
        done before?
Wilt Thou forgive that sin through
    which I run,
    And do run still, though still I do
        deplore?
        When Thou hast done, Thou
        hast not done,
            For I have more.

Wilt Thou forgive that sin by which
    I have won
    Others to sin? and made my sin
        their door?
Wilt Thou forgive that sin which I
    did shun
    A year, or two, but wallowed in a
        score?
        When Thou hast done, Thou
        hast not done
            For I have more.

I have a sin of fear, that when I have
    spun
    My last thread, I shall perish on
        the shore;
Swear by Thyself, that at my death
    Thy Son
    Shall shine as He shines now, and
        heretofore;
    And, having done that, Thou
        hast done,
            I fear no more."
                —"A Hymn to God the Father,"
                John Donne, 1572–1631

10

Grace

Gift of God   Saving grace
Free grace
Prevenient grace   Common grace
Special grace   **Undeserved favor**
Sanctifying grace   **Means of grace**
Sola gratia

The Amazing Story of Grace

"But where sin increased, grace abounded all the more, so that, just as sin exercised dominion in death, so grace might also exercise dominion through justification leading to eternal life through Jesus Christ our Lord."

—Romans 5:20-21

LIFE QUESTIONS

Grace fits our disposition when life is unmanageable, or when we think we have no particular ground of appeal. But since we don't like feeling that way, we don't often provide a setting in which grace gets a hearing.

Because although grace is lovely in its sentiments, it has several practical problems. For one, why does God choose to extend grace to us? And then, why should I want grace? Why would I want to confess I can't make it on my own?

Or from another angle, is God's grace there regardless of what I do? How can I learn to trust grace?

ASSIGNMENT

We Christians are inclined to think God didn't invent grace until the New Testament. In truth, grace has always been part of the divine nature. But the word itself doesn't appear frequently in the Old Testament. In some instances a Hebrew word, *chen,* that was translated "grace" in the King James Version is translated "favor" in other versions.

You may find, therefore, that the word *grace*

never appears in several of these Old Testament passages, but the concept of grace is present. Our Scriptures will in some instances reflect the quality of grace in the human experience, and in some cases you may wonder how to distinguish grace from love. That can be a proper confusion.

Day 1   Judges 2:10-19 (cycle of unfaithfulness); 2 Kings 20 (God's response to Hezekiah) Introduction and Readings 107 and 108
Day 2   Job 42 (Job's fortunes restored); Psalm 136 (God's steadfast love) Readings 109 and 110
Day 3   Isaiah 35 (God's people restored); Hosea 1–2 (God woos faithless Israel) Readings 111, 112, and 113
Day 4   Luke 15 (God seeks the lost); Romans 5 (justification by faith) Readings 114 and 115
Day 5   1 Corinthians 15:1-11 (Paul's experience of grace); Ephesians 1:1-14 (blessed in Christ) Readings 116, 117, and 118
Day 6   Read and respond to "The Church Teaching and Believing" and "Believing and Living."
Day 7   Rest and prayer

DAILY PRAYER

Pray for the persons and situations on your Prayer Concerns list and about issues or concerns emerging from your daily reading and study.

SCRIPTURE	READINGS
DAY 1	
Judges 2:10-19; 2 Kings 20	**Introduction and Readings 107 and 108**
DAY 2	
Job 42; Psalm 136	**Readings 109 and 110**
DAY 3	
Isaiah 35; Hosea 1–2	**Readings 111, 112, and 113**

SCRIPTURE	READINGS

DAY 4

Luke 15; Romans 5	Readings 114 and 115

DAY 5

1 Corinthians 15:1-11; Ephesians 1:1-14	Readings 116, 117, and 118

DAY 6 STUDY MANUAL	PRAYER CONCERNS
"The Church Teaching and Believing" and "Believing and Living"	

THE CHURCH TEACHING AND BELIEVING

So what happens when we have sinned and are cut off from God? If sin is as serious a matter as we have said, and if God is the issue, our human situation seems quite hopeless. If God is, as the philosopher says, the ground of being, and if sin cuts us off from that ground, then what can we do? Quite clearly, we are without bargaining power, and if there is to be a remedy, God will have to provide it.

That's where grace comes in. And that's why we call it amazing. Grace is easy to define—*unmerited favor*. But it is far more difficult to get beyond the definition to the comprehending, and harder still to get to a state of mind for the receiving. Those who have sung the most moving praise of grace are those who have been most aware of their sinfulness. The apostle Paul, who identifies himself as the chief of sinners, uses the word almost twice as often as all the other biblical writers combined. Augustine, the magisterial fifth-century theologian, writes of grace as if he still remembered the extensive immorality from which he had been converted. And John Newton, once the captain of a slave ship, gave us the phrase *amazing grace*. On the other hand, John Bunyan, who wrote *Grace Abounding to the Chief of Sinners,* a record of his own faith journey, had only a limited acquaintance with the more lurid expressions of sin. The point is this: Neither the extent nor the nature of persons' sin gives passion to their testimony of grace but the degree to which they sense their sinfulness.

Because of course grace cannot be appreciated except as one feels need of it; and that sense of need can be experienced only if a person is conscious of sin and recognizes an inability to deal with the separation sin has caused. That is, to appreciate grace, one has to feel a distinct sense of helplessness—of being in a predicament beyond one's own solving.

That isn't a popular state of mind. It violates the contemporary emphasis on self-esteem. But this response to grace is not unique to our generation; it is probably as old as the human race. We like to feel we deserve favors, so anything that speaks of unmerited favor is contrary to our nature. So we need not only *saving* grace that will redeem us but also *prevenient* grace that will help us realize our need of saving grace.

Grace in the Old Testament

The Old Testament covenants were expressions of grace. Nothing says this better than a key passage in Deuteronomy where Moses acknowledges that Israel has been chosen simply because God loved them (Deuteronomy 7:7-8); they were, so to speak, chosen because they were chosen. This is grace. It is unmerited favor.

The prophet Ezekiel puts the matter in graphic terms. Addressing Jerusalem, he tells his people, Israel, "Your father was an Amorite, and your mother a Hittite. As for your birth, on the day you were born your navel cord was not cut, nor were you washed with water to cleanse you, nor rubbed with salt, nor wrapped in cloths" (Ezekiel 16:3-4). "You were abhorred," Ezekiel says, "on the day you were born" (16:5). Nevertheless, God extended mercy to this forsaken creature—an infant without merit—clothed her, adorned her with ornaments, until she "grew exceedingly beautiful, fit to be a queen" (16:10-13).

How did Israel respond to this kindness? Hers is a continuing story of unfaithfulness. After being delivered from slavery in Egypt, Israel yearned openly and frequently for a return to the land of her captivity. Once fairly settled in the homeland that had been promised her, she again forgot her God. The book of Judges is a cycle of Israel's rebellion against God, following after gods from neighboring nations, turning desperately to God in the midst of disaster, being delivered by God (without their meriting such help), then starting the same dreary process again (Judges 2:10-19).

And so the story continues through the period of the kings, the dividing of the tribes, and the descent into captivity—Assyria for the northern tribes, and Babylon for the southern tribes. The Hebrew prophets might well be seen as visitations of grace, as they repeatedly declare the purposes of God for Israel. Often the message is poignant—as, for instance, when Hosea says, on God's behalf,
"How can I give you up, Ephraim?
How can I hand you over, O Israel?"
(Hosea 11:8).
Several Hebrew words come close to the New Testament word for grace. *Hesed* is the most notable. The word is quite beyond translation into English; so Miles Coverdale, who made the first English translation of the entire Bible, invented the word *lovingkindness* in order to convey something of the quality he saw in the Hebrew word.

The Hebrew includes also the mood of loyalty and faithfulness, and especially the concept of covenant. *Hesed* is the theme word in Psalm 136, where the poet exults in the goodness and greatness of God as exhibited in nature and in Israel's history.

Grace in the New Testament

New Testament writers faced the task of finding words for concepts that were beyond words. Old Testament writers had a somewhat simpler task, in that their language (Hebrew) and their faith came from the same matrix (meaning womb or mother). But the New Testament writers had to work with a language (Greek) already shaped and established by philosophical and religious forebears of quite a different sort. But to their advantage, it was a uniquely effective language. The Greeks not only "had a word for it"; their word was almost always a remarkably precise one.

In the case of grace, New Testament writers chose the word *charis*. This word was a prominent part of Greek social language; it was their word for thanks. In social and aesthetic contexts it conveyed such ideas as "gracious," "charming," "artful," or "exquisite." Gifts can sometimes be tainted with ulterior motives, but when "charis" was the theme, the inference was that the gift was noble and generous. No wonder, then, that the English word *charity* comes from this Greek root.

Paul begins his letters wishing grace to his congregations; Peter does the same with his two epistles, and so too does the Second Letter of John. And the writer of Revelation begins his message to the seven churches with a greeting of grace. Perhaps no word is more typical of the early days of the church, because the first believers understood that grace had broken into their lives in the coming of Jesus Christ.

For this reason they dared to make the cross their symbol. What was to others a reminder of a particularly cruel method of execution was to believers dramatic evidence of God's love. Love that would show itself not only in a divine visit but in the divine sacrifice was clearly unmerited. It was the essence of grace. In the earliest days of the church, a majority of the believers were Jews. They were familiar with the graciousness of God as shown in God's patience with Israel. But nothing could compare with this, that God would, at the divine initiative and without invitation, die for the human race. Grace had come to a manger, then to roads and villages, and at last to a cross. Grace had become something they could see.

Jesus taught grace without naming it. The story of the father with the two difficult sons (Luke 15) is a series of grace vignettes: The father accepts his younger son's request for an early distribution from the family estate—a gracious (perhaps even foolish, as grace often seems to be) act to begin with. When the son returns, destitute and defenseless, the father not only accepts him but strikes a party in his behalf; and when the older son goes off in a pout, the father patiently pleads with

Oil is a symbol of God's grace and is used in baptism, ordination, confirmation, and anointing the sick. A cruse of oil calls to mind the story of the widow whose jug of oil never ran dry no matter how much was used. Read the story in 1 Kings 17:8-16. Like the cruse of oil, the grace of our Lord and Savior is inexaustible and never-failing.

him. Grace all the way. The parable of the vineyard owner who hires workers through the day and pays the last ones hired for a full day's work is again a picture of grace—people are getting more than they deserve (Matthew 20:1-16). Indeed, the people with whom Jesus showed irritation were generally those who couldn't understand grace as applied to others.

If grace is difficult to understand, it is even more difficult to accept. Paul's angry epistle, his Letter to the Galatians, is directed to a body of people who have left grace for the Law. They have decided that grace, as demonstrated in the cross, is not enough in itself to save them; they must make their own contribution by their works. Paul answers that to seek justification through the Law and its works is to "nullify the grace of God" (Galatians 2:21).

The Several Expressions of Grace

Though grace is relatively easy to define, *unmerited favor,* it is almost impossible to draw its boundaries. Any attempt to describe generosity almost contradicts its quality. Nevertheless, if we are to comprehend something of the range of grace, we must examine some of its manifestations.

Common grace is a term used to describe the action of grace that occurs constantly and indiscriminately, but usually without being acknowledged. It refers to those blessings all human beings receive, such as life itself, physical sustenance, beauty (in nature and in all other aspects of life), pleasure, creativity, learning. The list is virtually endless.

These favors are unmerited. No one deserves a sunset or a calming breeze; no one has earned the intricate mechanism that makes up the brain and body at the time of birth. Each person in the morning traffic chaos is surrounded by common grace and inhabited by it. The preoccupied sensualist who never seems to give a thought to God is seeking to satisfy capacities given him by common grace. The logician who argues against the existence of God does so with equipment given to her, unearned, by the God she hopes to disprove.

Jesus said God "makes his sun rise on the evil and on the good, and sends rain on the righteous and on the unrighteous" (Matthew 5:45). Believers are sometimes troubled by common grace; they think God ought to be more selective in whose parade the rain falls on or on whose life the sun shines. But with such an attitude, the believer misses the point of grace; it *is* unmerited.

A believer may feel particularly upset when competing with a more talented unbeliever. Shall this person, who gives no thought to God or goodness, score more touchdowns or write better symphonies than the person whose life is dedicated to God? Possibly, if—in the generosity of a gracious God—the first person has been blessed with a large share of undeserved talent. Believers are likely to do better in whatever they do than they would have done if they had not become believers, because belief gives greater range to our talents. But the initial gifts of common grace are a fact with which we must make peace. My size thirteen feet will never fit into size four ballet slippers. I will never walk with the fluid beauty of a gymnast; common grace has distributed kindnesses in other ways.

Believers will do well to rejoice in the goodness of God, wherever it is demonstrated. Let us be glad God is wonderfully generous, not limiting sunshine to my sixty-by-one-hundred-foot tract but blazing it into the world with prodigal carelessness.

John Wesley, founder of the Methodist or Wesleyan movement, spoke especially of *free grace*. He and his brother Charles were responding particularly to what they saw as excesses in the Reformed, or Calvinist, theology of their generation. "Free grace" is a way of saying grace is given to all persons everywhere and does not depend on human goodness or merit. Grace is free to all, without exception. God has not refused salvation to anyone; grace and its attendant salvation are free to all, and the individual must decide whether to receive them.

Free grace is not the same as universal salvation, the belief that all will be saved. Free grace says simply that salvation is available to all. So while God's grace is free to all persons, it is not imposed upon us. Nor should free grace be confused with what Dietrich Bonhoeffer, the German theologian and martyr, described as *cheap grace*. That term was meant to describe a perversion of grace in which the recipient intends to assume the blessings of grace without the responsibilities of discipleship, or to expect forgiveness without repentance.

And while grace is always free, in human experience it is more accessible at certain times. We are more likely to be conscious of grace, whether in its giftedness or in a sense of need, in times of pain or emptiness. So while always free, the ease of apprehending may differ greatly, not because God is near or remote but because of the nature of our sensitivity and response.

The term *prevenient grace* means God's grace comes before any human response to God. Not only does grace save us; grace opens us to salvation and gives us the power to accept what is given. In common experience prevenient grace may also mean the apparent ordering of circumstances so one is more likely to be confronted by saving grace. Thus John Newton has caused us to sing,

"Twas grace that taught my heart to fear,
    and grace my fears relieved."
The fear, whether of eternity or of meaningless life, is itself a factor of grace that draws us to the saving grace that removes all fear.

In classical Reformed theology, this prevenient grace is seen as being *irresistible*. That is, prevenient grace works only in those who are chosen for salvation, but for them it is always effective and cannot be otherwise. The Wesleyan (or Arminian) view is that prevenient grace is extended to all persons, but they may resist it if they choose.

But both Reformed and Arminian theologies find prevenient grace a cause for gratitude. For the Reformed believer, there is gratitude for having been chosen, so that the grace has indeed been irresistible. The Arminian rejoices first in the belief that grace is free to all and that prevenient grace is extended to all, but then, experientially, that circumstances come together in such effective ways as to draw us to the grace God has given. When we are so indifferent to God or so preoccupied by self that we are not ready to be saved, prevenient grace prepares us to receive saving grace.

Saving grace is what we usually have in mind when we refer to grace. Ephesians describes this grace directly: "For by grace you have been saved through faith, and this is not your own doing; it is the gift of God—not the result of works, so that no one may boast" (Ephesians 2:8-9). Paul explains in Romans that sin came into the world through Adam's transgression but that "the free gift" came in "the one man, Jesus Christ"; so "just as one man's trespass led to condemnation for all, so one man's act of righteousness leads to justification and life for all" (Romans 5:12-18).

So here is the issue of grace. By its own actions and choices, the human race got itself into trouble from which it could not deliver itself. God provided a way when there was no way. This is saving grace. God's action was not elicited by human request or by human deserving; it was self-evoked.

And because saving grace is entirely of God's goodness, the Scriptures are emphatic that humans not credit themselves with some merit of works. "This is not your own doing," the apostle says; "it is the gift of God" (Ephesians 2:8). Historically, merit through works was a controversy in the church and particularly at issue in the Reformation. The Catholic church's system of penance encouraged the idea of salvation through works rather than entirely through grace. Thus one of the three *sola*s of the Reformation was *sola gratia*—"by grace alone"—the insistence that salvation is by God's grace alone and not by any human achievement or worth. Contemporary Catholicism has returned to this ground.

In practice, however, "grace alone" is as much a problem for Protestants as for Roman Catholics. Few ideas are harder for humans to accept than the idea they can do nothing to deserve God's favor. At the very least, they want to think they deserve it more than someone else. Paul will have none of that. "For there is no distinction, since all have sinned and fall short of the glory of God; they are now justified by his grace as a gift, through the redemption that is in Christ Jesus" (Romans 3:22-24). Because of the deadly democracy of sin, we need a grand democracy of saving grace.

One of the most dramatic expressions of grace is conveyed in the traditional form of the Apostles' Creed in the phrase, "He descended into hell." The words referred to an early belief of the church that during Christ's days in the grave, he descended

The three *sola*s of the Reformation are associated mainly with Martin Luther, though they describe the foundation of the Reformation:
* *sola fide,* "by faith alone": based on Luther's translation of Romans 3:28 as "justified by faith alone," the phrase was a statement against works-dependent righteousness.
* *sola gratia,* "by grace alone": God reaches out to human beings in their sinfulness, offering forgiveness and salvation, which come only through God's grace.
* *sola scriptura,* "by Scripture alone": As a protest against the subordination of the authority of Scripture to the authority of the church, Luther declared Scripture to be the first and only source of authority for the church and for individual Christians.

into the place of the dead, to make "a proclamation to the spirits in prison" (1 Peter 3:19). "For this is the reason the gospel was proclaimed even to the dead, so that, though they had been judged in the flesh as everyone is judged, they might live in the spirit as God does" (4:6).

The statement in the creed dealt with a question that troubled the earliest Christians, and no doubt has troubled thoughtful believers ever since: What about those people who have never heard the gospel of Jesus Christ? How will God judge such persons? The answer of the early church, as expressed in at least three of the New Testament epistles, was that Christ had gone to the abode of the dead to preach to those persons who had lived and died before his atoning death. This teaching is a wonderfully graphic way of portraying the far reaches of the grace of God; even, that is, to those who are dead. At the same time, it conveys insight into the justice of God.

Part of the work of grace is the sanctifying, or the making holy, of all of life. The several Christian bodies have different opinions as to when sanctification takes place. But the basic principle remains that sanctification, like salvation, is an act of grace. It is not a human achievement but God's gift.

The Means of Grace

When we refer to the means of grace, we are simply seeking to identify the avenues by which grace reaches us. These avenues are not virtues in themselves. To consider them so is to make grace mechanical, or even magical, as if we could convey it by some formula or instrument. Such an idea would contradict all that grace means.

Nevertheless, it is clear grace comes to us in company with certain settings and experiences. The Scriptures themselves do not specifically identify means of grace, and the lists vary among theologians.

Virtually all Christian bodies agree, however, that the sacraments are a means of grace—particularly the sacraments of Baptism and Holy Communion. These practices, instituted by both Scripture and church, clearly are ways by which grace is communicated to our lives. Perhaps the most important thing that might be said about the sacraments as means of grace is that believers ought to be made more conscious of the possibility. The sacraments can too easily be received without thought as to potential benefit. That is, Holy Communion might more often transmit grace to worshipers if they were more intentional in their seeking and expectation.

Other obvious means of grace include the reading and preaching of the Word of God. Preaching that is spiritual and thoughtful provides a setting for grace to work—for all of the activities of grace, from the prevenient to the sanctifying. Prayer and meditation are effective avenues of grace, as is music that opens the soul to God. Corporate worship provides a fruitful setting for mediating grace. So too with Christian fellowship. It is not surprising Jesus sent out his followers two by two; grace is communicated often and beautifully, and perhaps usually without our knowing it, by our fellow believers.

> BECAUSE WE THE CHURCH BELIEVE in the grace of God, I will accept grace with gratitude, and I will seek to be a mediator of grace.

BELIEVING AND LIVING

Above all else, grace is to be received, and appreciated. Any study of grace ought to have a quality of worship. But to love God with all our minds implies that we approach even the most intimate of spiritual matters thoughtfully and analytically. The spirit of grace will not be diminished by such an inquiry.

How would you trace the work of prevenient grace in your own life?

Write a personal definition of saving grace that reflects your own experience.

What is it about grace—if anything—that bothers you?

Does it seem to you that the greater the sin the greater the appreciation of grace? Why?

How can someone who has simply grown up in the faith come to understand the grandeur of grace?

SEEKING MORE UNDERSTANDING

Heighten your sensitivity to the reality of God's grace, understood as unmerited favor. Look back over your past week and list all the times and ways you experienced God's grace without being aware of it at the time. What conclusions do you draw about God's grace in your life?

PRAYER

"I was a traitor doom'd to fire,
Bound to sustain eternal pains;
Christ flew on wings of strong desire,
Assum'd my guilt, and took my chains.

Infinite grace! Almighty charms!
Stand in amaze, ye whirling skies,
Jesus the God, with naked arms,
Hangs on a cross of love, and dies.

Did pity ever stoop so low,
Dress'd in divinity and blood?
Was ever rebel courted so
In groans of an expiring God?"

—*Selected stanzas from "Desiring to Love Christ," Isaac Watts, 1674–1748*

11

Salvation

Soteriology   **Repentance**
          Lost
Redeemer   Sin   Regeneration
People of God   Israel   The church
Born of the Spirit
New birth   Adoption   Conversion

God So Loved the World

"The Son of Man came to seek out and to save the lost."

—Luke 19:10

LIFE QUESTIONS

Salvation of any kind always involves two parties, the savior and the one being saved. The effectiveness of salvation depends on a peculiar kind of cooperation by both parties. Someone who tries to save a drowning person may find that the victim doesn't cooperate, may in fact thresh about so frantically as to make saving all but impossible. Sometimes the one drowning fails to realize that the best contribution to the saving process is to relax and leave the saving to the rescuer.

Theological salvation is true to the pattern. There is a Savior, and there are victims. Frequently the victims have more confidence in their ability to save themselves than in the Savior's ability to redeem them. And in some instances the victims don't realize the peril of their state.

Why should we conclude salvation is necessary? And if it is, by what logic is God involved? Still more, what can God do? Why should God be interested in saving us, and in what way can God be involved in such a distinctively human problem?

ASSIGNMENT

The heart of the salvation issue is in the story of Jesus Christ and the cross. But the salvation theme begins in the Old Testament, especially in God's dealings with the nation of Israel.

Approach the daily Scriptures with the sense that you are reading salvation history. Observe especially the nature of divine action.

Day 1   Numbers 21:1-9 (bronze serpent); John 3:1-15 (born of water and Spirit)
Introduction and Readings 119 and 120
Day 2   Psalms 33 (the Lord our help and shield); 68 (God's power and victory)
Readings 121 and 122
Day 3   Isaiah 12 (God is salvation); 55 (invitation to life)
Readings 123 and 124
Day 4   Luke 15:1-10 (joy over repenting sinner); Acts 10 (God's impartiality)
Reading 125
Day 5   Romans 5:6-21 (reconciled through Christ); Hebrews 2 (Christ the pioneer of salvation)
Readings 126 and 127
Day 6   Read and respond to "The Church Teaching and Believing" and "Believing and Living."
Day 7   Rest and prayer

DAILY PRAYER

Pray for the persons and situations on your Prayer Concerns list and about issues or concerns emerging from your daily reading and study.

SCRIPTURE	READINGS
DAY 1	
Numbers 21:1-9; John 3:1-15	Introduction and Readings 119 and 120
DAY 2	
Psalms 33; 68	Readings 121 and 122
DAY 3	
Isaiah 12; 55	Readings 123 and 124

SCRIPTURE	READINGS
DAY 4	
Luke 15:1-10; Acts 10	Reading 125
DAY 5	
Romans 5:6-21; Hebrews 2	Readings 126 and 127

DAY 6 STUDY MANUAL	PRAYER CONCERNS
"The Church Teaching and Believing" and "Believing and Living"	

THE CHURCH TEACHING AND BELIEVING

The Greeks usually have a word for it, but sometimes the Germans do. The German word is *Heilsgeschichte—salvation history*. Salvation history is the theological term for reading the biblical story as the narrative of God's working out redemptive purposes for the world. The story's plot assumes humans are lost, that something desires they be lost and works to that end, but also assumes that God wants our planet to be saved and has gone to epic lengths to bring this salvation to pass.

The first question is this: Why should humans need to be saved? A thoroughgoing pragmatist might answer, "Isn't it obvious? Look at the state we're in." But how did we get that way? The Bible says we had a perfect start; we were made in the image of God and set up in a garden of paradise. But in the very nature of our grandeur was the possibility of a problem because we were created with the power of choice. Indeed, not only are we able to choose; we seem driven to choosing.

In the original instance, which Genesis tells about, the man and woman choose contrary to what God commands. What they do can be seen as an act of unbelief, in that they choose not to believe what God says, or as an act of negative faith, in their believing the solicitations of the serpent rather than the warnings of God. They make a choice, and a bad one.

Some people think this choice has set the human race forever on the wrong course. Others think the story in Genesis is intended to describe every human story—that each person in every generation reenacts the story from Eden. We are always being enticed by a voice that urges us to doubt the goodness of God and to violate the divine will, and each person proceeds in his or her own fashion to do just that. Inevitably we ask ourselves if perhaps someone, sometime, has come through this human process without such a rebellion against God. Paul is emphatic: "There is no one who is righteous, not even one" (Romans 3:10). He makes his point by quoting Psalms 14 and 53.

Probably, it isn't surprising we have sinned. Watch us in action and see how easily we are inclined to trouble. And consider how early this is so. See how quickly human creatures assert not simply independence but selfishness. And realize that such selfishness is almost essential. The student of human behavior says our first instinct is self-preservation, and that seems logical enough. Well, then, preserving ourselves is likely to be at the cost of someone else's desires or at their inconvenience. And almost before we know it, we have sinned. But easy as it is, and at times with seeming innocence, sinning is nevertheless a deliberate act.

Few such acts seem terribly destructive in their single instances, but they all partake of the same qualities of rebellion and self-centeredness. Taken together, our sinful acts have gotten our race in the mess it is now in; and generation after generation we continue to reinforce the pattern of self-destruction. Philosophers, optimists, and gurus of various kinds have told us cheerfully for thousands of years that we might find our way out; but we continuously prove them wrong.

The Story of a Saving Nation

Genesis tells us that after the human race was deep in distress, God set to work bringing a saving nation into existence. The choice was both unlikely and without obvious reason. The persons chosen, Abram and Sarai, were without children because Sarai was barren; so they were in no position to parent a nation. Also, we see nothing really distinctive about them. They were chosen because they were chosen. It was another instance of grace. To this couple God said, "In you all the families of the earth shall be blessed" (Genesis 12:3).

Someone has said that when this call and promise were given to Abraham, God had the last human creature on earth in mind. The idea may seem fanciful and poetic, but it is also appropriate. Salvation was announced for the entire human race ("all the families of the earth") through Abraham. Nevertheless, the course of Abraham and Sarah's pilgrimage seems to have been irregular. They left the security of a settled existence to become nomads. Meanwhile, the promised heir was slow to come. At last, in their advanced age, they became parents of Isaac, the child of promise.

Isaac's own life pattern was equally uncertain at times, but eventually he and Rebekah had sons, twins in fact. One of these sons, Jacob, was later to be known as Israel. His twelve sons then became the ancestors of the tribal community of Israel.

What happened from that time forward is at times a story of epic proportions, and at times the stuff of comic opera. When the family is no larger than a modern family reunion, they migrate to Egypt, where in time they become slaves. They remain in slavery for over four hundred years, during which time they become substantial in number—but slaves, nonetheless, and without any prospects of freedom. At last they are led to freedom by Moses; but they don't do well with their freedom, and as they fumble their way to the land that has for so long been promised to them, it is difficult to believe they can be the carriers of God's salvation.

But even while they are the carriers of the promised, far-reaching salvation, they are themselves the beneficiaries of salvation. Here is where salvation begins to have a rather broad definition. Many—in fact, probably most—Christians think of salvation as a strictly private and personal matter. The classic salvation statement may say, "For God so loved the world," but we tend to think of that world as made up entirely of individuals, all of whom will decide for themselves about accepting salvation.

This view is not incorrect, but the Bible theme is larger and perhaps more complex. Many of the Psalms, for example, seem to speak of salvation in an entirely physical sense, as the psalmist prays for deliverance in battle or gives God thanks for having been saved physically from an enemy's attack. The Israelites were especially conscious that God had saved their nation in times of war. So the psalmist wrote,

"A king is not saved by his great army;
   a warrior is not delivered by his great strength.
The war horse is a vain hope for victory,
   and by its great might it cannot save" (Psalm 33:16-17).
In another instance the psalmist recalls God's faithfulness in time of battle:
"Our God is a God of salvation,
   and to GOD, the Lord, belongs escape from death" (68:20).
These Hebrew writers didn't draw so sharp a distinction between physical and spiritual matters, or between personal and community. Their physical enemy in time of war was seen also as a spiritual enemy, and understandably so, since their enemy marched into battle carrying mementos of their gods. To lose to their enemy was to lose to their enemy's gods, and thus to bring dishonor to the Lord God. So too their sense of community was stronger than is typical of our culture; personal safety and salvation were linked to the well-being of the larger community. And personal physical or economic distress was seen as having broader spiritual ramifications; thus the prayer for salvation might seem on the surface to be a prayer for physical well-being, but to the Israelite it was also a spiritual issue.

By all normal odds, the people of Israel could so easily have been wiped out at several points in their history. And in fact, the northern tribes were eventually assimilated into other cultures. But the southern tribes, the kingdom of Judah, held on all the more passionately to their role as the vehicle of salvation for the nations. Not that they always saw their role clearly. Never-

The equilateral triangle intertwined with the cross suggests the involvement of the Trinity in the salvation of humankind—salvation offered by the Father's love, accomplished by the Son's sacrifice, and received through the work of the Holy Spirit. The arms of the cross end in trefoil design, a symbol of the Trinity, giving to the cross the name budded cross.

theless, their prophets reminded them repeatedly that they had a mission to the nations.

The nature of this mission became more focused as they came increasingly to await a messiah. Their perception of this messiah came in bits and pieces from their prophets, and as this perception grew, their teachers discovered related insights in their other sacred writings. No wonder, then, that the first followers of Jesus found evidence everywhere in the Hebrew Scriptures of the messianic expectation. In doing so, they were building on the reading, dreaming, and hoping of generations of their forebears.

The Old Testament vision of salvation reaches ecstatic levels in some of the prophetic writings, for example, Isaiah 35, 54, and 55. Usually, it is difficult to know whether the writers are talking about something close at hand, such as a return from captivity, or a more distant, idyllic scene. Some of the language, however, is so idealistic that a very special time is clearly in mind. Even nature is caught up in the gladness:
"For you shall go out in joy,
    and be led back in peace;
the mountains and the hills before you
    shall burst into song,
    and all the trees of the field shall clap their hands.
Instead of the thorn shall come up the cypress;
    instead of the brier shall come up the myrtle;
and it shall be to the LORD for a memorial,
    for an everlasting sign that shall not be cut off" (55:12-13).

These pictures of salvation from the Old Testament prophets seem to concentrate on restoration, physical welfare, and prosperity. They picture a world of good health, of nature at peace, and of national tranquility:
"The wolf shall live with the lamb,
    the leopard shall lie down with the kid" (11:6).

But it is a prophet's vision of prosperity and the good life, not a politician's. Isaiah and his prophetic colleagues see such an Edenic time as the gift of God, and nothing else. Not something brought to pass by legislative fiat or by a vote of the people but by divine favor. Thus, it is *salvation:* God's intervention beyond what humans can do for themselves.

Perhaps the most important thing to be learned about salvation from the Old Testament is that salvation is an eternal part of God's relationship to our human race. Christians are sometimes inclined to think salvation was invented at Calvary, as if God's character had improved. The Old Testament also reminds us God works through a people, in that instance the nation of Israel. (In the New Testament, we will see God at work in a new people, the church.) God still works through Judaism today as a witness to social justice and political responsibility.

Then too, as we trace salvation history from the Old Testament to the New Testament, we work toward a balance in our understanding of individual and community salvation. The Old

Testament, on one hand, seems to concentrate almost completely on community; the Day of Atonement, for example, is a day for national reckoning with sin. And on some occasions when a particular person, like Achan, sinned, the whole family was punished with him (Joshua 7). But on the other hand, the levitical system of sacrifices included provision for the sins of individuals and for personal repentance and justification. The New Testament emphasis is more directly on the salvation of individuals; and yet, when the Philippian jailer asks Paul and Silas about salvation, they answer, "Believe on the Lord Jesus, and you will be saved, you and your household" (Acts 16:31).

Salvation in the New Testament

Salvation in the New Testament still issues from the people of God, a holy community. But now this community is the church. And it soon seems clear there is a strategic emphasis on individual response. Where previously one was part of the community by birth, as an Israelite, one comes into the new community by believing. Thus the Gospel of John declares that God's love is to the whole world, but it is "everyone who believes in him [Christ]" who will "have eternal life" (John 3:16). This statement follows the dialogue between Jesus and Nicodemus, in which Nicodemus—a true member of the community of Israel—is told that he cannot get into the new community unless he is "born from above" (3:3).

Some other concepts take on new dimensions in the New Testament. Sin is more sharply defined as the problem with which we must deal, and its destructive and controlling power is specifically described, as in Paul's Letter to the Romans.

And although the Old Testament says in numbers of places, beginning with Abraham in Genesis 12, that salvation is for the whole human race, that teaching is far more explicit in the New Testament. Luke's Gospel records Jesus as saying he had come to seek and to save "the lost," without limiting that term in any way (Luke 19:10); and John 3:16 speaks of God as loving "the world," again without setting boundaries. Jesus left his followers after his resurrection with the command to "make disciples of all nations" (Matthew 28:19). When the small group of followers received the Holy Spirit on the Day of Pentecost, their new empowerment came with an implicit world-reach: They spoke "in other languages" so that visitors from many nations marveled that "in our own languages we hear them speaking about God's deeds of power" (Acts 2:4-11). And although the early followers were somewhat slow to move out, before the book of Acts closes, the witness is already on three continents.

The dominant issue in the New Testament portrayal of salvation—the issue that makes all other matters of preliminary consequence—is the role of Jesus Christ. He is named *Jesus* because the name means "savior," and he has come to "save his people from their sins" (Matthew 1:21). When religious leaders criticize Jesus for associating with sinners, Jesus tells three parables that indicate his ministry is to such (Luke 15). And when, in another setting, he chooses to have dinner with a despised member of the community, Jesus says simply, "For the Son of Man came to seek out and to save the lost" (Luke 19:10).

The Language of Salvation

Our English word *salvation* comes from the Latin root *salvare*, which means "to save." It is worth noting that *salve* and *salvage* are from the same root. In its theological sense, salvation means God's action in saving humans from the consequences of their sin and bringing them into right relationship with God. The scholarly term for the study of salvation is *soteriology*, a word that comes from the Greek term for salvation.

But *salvation* is a complex term. Human experience has made it so. In essence, salvation is quite simple: Humans are lost, and God provides a way of salvation. But the experience of salvation is shaped by the personalities of those receiving it. In a sense, the terminology of salvation is as diverse as the varieties of human experiences of salvation. But several terms have become a standard part of the language of the church.

Probably, the term most prevalent today is *new birth*, or *regeneration*. This concept comes primarily from the dialogue between Jesus and Nicodemus, in which Jesus says, "Very truly, I tell you, no one can see the kingdom of God without being born from above," or "born anew," or "born again" (John 3:3). Paul uses the same concept: "So if anyone is in Christ, there is a new creation: everything old has passed away; see, everything has become new" (2 Corinthians 5:17).

This image emphasizes that salvation is more than a matter of new resolve or personal reformation; it is a radical change— so radical that it can only be described as the making of a new person. The transforming action comes from God; it is a matter, Jesus said, of being born of the Spirit.

Because of the familiarity of this image of salvation, people often refer to some persons as "born-again Christians." The term is redundant. One cannot be a Christian without being born again, since we become Christians by God's action of transforming grace. As Jesus said, we cannot enter the kingdom of heaven except as we are born from above. The term should not be made captive to a particular type of experience or of expression.

A second term is similar—*adoption*. This too is a biblical concept. So Paul says, "For you did not receive a spirit of slavery to fall back into fear, but you have received a spirit of adoption"—a spirit that makes us say to God, "Abba! Father!" (Romans 8:15). As with the new birth, the emphasis is on our familial relationship with God and on the necessity for God's redeeming action; it is the parent that adopts the child.

Conversion is a classic synonym for salvation. The term means literally "turning around," and as such is closely related to *repentance,* always a factor in the salvation process. Conversion describes our response to God's invitation in Jesus Christ, and it makes especially vivid the sense of transformation that occurs when one is saved.

Justification is a more complex theological word. A person is said to be "just" or "justified," made right or righteous, by faith in the work of Jesus Christ. In the Protestant view, this is wholly the work of Christ without any personal acts of merit. Traditional Roman Catholic theology taught that persons are justified through participation in the sacraments of the church and by the gift of God's Spirit. Today the sacraments are given a less prominent role in salvation.

Redemption is a term with Old Testament background. The nearest of kin was empowered by law to redeem a person from debts or even from slavery. *Redeemer* comes from a Latin word meaning "to buy back"; thus Christ is seen as the Redeemer who has bought us back from the slavery of sin.

Commitment is not one of the classical words for salvation, but it may well be the one Protestantism employs most frequently. The invitation to the Christian life is often described as "a call to commitment." While significant in its own right, *commitment* is a somewhat weak term theologically, in that it carries no sense of repentance. Also, the emphasis is moved from God's action in saving to the human quality of response. But although it unduly emphasizes the human role, it offers further insight into the character of salvation.

The Reformation Controversy

Salvation was a central issue in the Protestant Reformation (sixteenth century). The Reformers were reacting against the church teaching of the time, that salvation could be gained by meritorious actions that gained favor with God. Such acts might include penance, or stipulated good works, or even drawing upon the merits of others. The Reformers insisted that salvation is by grace alone, God's free gift, without any merit or payment on the human side. The grace-works controversy also reflected many of the issues raised by Paul in his letter to the churches of Galatia, where he vigorously condemned those Jewish Christian teachers who said that a person must obey certain aspects of the Jewish law in order to be justified. Paul answered, "If justification comes through the law, then Christ died for nothing" (Galatians 2:21).

Ultimately, the issue in salvation is always the same. Someone is in need of saving, and there is a savior. The point of confusion, often in experience and sometimes even in doctrine, is usually on the need of saving. Are humans as bad off as suggested in the opening figure of speech? That is, are we drowning persons, spiritually speaking, and unable to save ourselves? Or are we merely victims of environment, heredity, and the normal difficulties of living who nevertheless can and must manage for ourselves?

The answer to that question depends partly on one's vision

for humanity. The Bible sees us as made in the image of God and a little lower than the angels. If that vision be true, we are living decidedly below expectation. And if we are to reach those expectations, we need help.

That is, we need a Savior. And Christian doctrine says God has generously made that provision.

BECAUSE WE THE CHURCH BELIEVE humans need salvation, and God has responded graciously to our need, therefore I accept God's salvation and recommend it to all.

BELIEVING AND LIVING

Our sense of the need of salvation changes with the seasons of need. The person in the grip of some deadly addiction may feel it strongly, but someone comfortable in middle-class morality may wonder what all the fuss is about. Is the image of a drowning person too dramatic for what you observe? If so, what image would you develop to describe the nature of our human need for salvation?

_____

_____

And suppose we really are in need of salvation. How do you explain God's interest in saving us, as removed as God is from this distinctly human problem?

_____

_____

_____

Judging from your own experience, which of the several terms for salvation (*regeneration, adoption, conversion, justification, redemption, commitment*) is most descriptive for you? Explain.

_____

_____

SEEKING MORE UNDERSTANDING

The word *salvation* appears more often in the Psalms than in any other Old Testament book, in fact, more often than in any other book of the Bible. The Psalms were Israel's hymnbook. To get some sense of how Israel expressed their understanding of salvation in worship, use a concordance to locate and read verses that mention salvation. Summarize your findings.

PRAYER

"Savior! I've no one else to tell—
And so I trouble *thee.*
I am the one forgot thee so—
Dost thou remember me?
Nor, for myself, I came so far—
That were the little load—
I brought thee the imperial Heart
I had not strength to hold—
The Heart I carried in my own—
'Till mine too heavy grew—
Yet—strangest—*heavier* since it
      went—
Is it too large for you?"
  —*Emily Dickinson, 1830–1886*

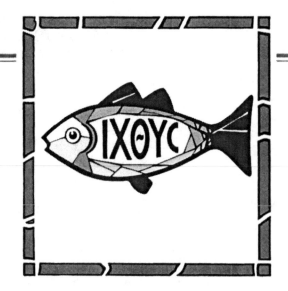

12

Jesus Christ

Incarnation   **God incarnate**

Son of Man

Human and divine

Virgin birth   Emmanuel

Messiah

Word of God (Logos)

Eternal Son of God

Fully Human Fully Divine

"Christ Jesus,
  who, though he was in the form of God,
    did not regard equality with God
    as something to be exploited,
  but emptied himself,
    taking the form of a slave,
    being born in human likeness."
                                    —*Philippians 2:5-7*

LIFE QUESTIONS

Four new books are published about Jesus every day, year after year. According to the best estimate, there are currently nearly seventy thousand books worldwide with Jesus as their subject.

Who was he, that he should continue to be the subject of so many books and the center of so much continuing controversy? How can he possibly matter to us still today, nearly two thousand years after his life and death? And why, particularly, should he matter to me? What does all this have to do with the rather strange claim that he was both human and divine?

ASSIGNMENT

Although the story of Jesus, and the teachings that developed around him, are all found in the New Testament, the first believers—including the New Testament writers—believed that the Old Testament pointed to Jesus. Our Scriptures therefore include Old Testament passages to which the New Testament writers refer. Watch for indica-

tions of both his humanity and his divinity, indications that, as the Nicene Creed says, Jesus was "true God from true God" but also "became truly human."

Day 1 Isaiah 9:1-7 (the coming king); Micah 5:2-5 (ruler from Bethlehem)
Introduction and Readings 128 and 129

Day 2 Psalm 22 (plea for God's help); Isaiah 52:13–53:12 (suffering servant); 61 (encouragement to the exiled)
Readings 130 and 131

Day 3 Matthew 1 (birth of Jesus the Messiah); 16:13–17:13 ("You are the Messiah," the Transfiguration)
Readings 132, 133, and 134

Day 4 John 1 (Word became flesh, testimony of John the Baptist and disciples)
Readings 135 and 136

Day 5 Colossians 1:15-23 (supremacy of Christ); 2:9-15 (divine nature in Christ); Hebrews 1:1–2:4 (Christ superior to angels)
Readings 137, 138, and 139

Day 6 Read and respond to "The Church Teaching and Believing" and "Believing and Living."

Day 7 Rest and prayer

DAILY PRAYER

Pray for the persons and situations on your Prayer Concerns list and about issues or concerns emerging from your daily reading and study.

JESUS CHRIST

SCRIPTURE	READINGS
DAY 1	
Isaiah 9:1-7; Micah 5:2-5	Introduction and Readings 128 and 129
DAY 2	
Psalm 22; Isaiah 52:13–53:12; 61	Readings 130 and 131
DAY 3	
Matthew 1; 16:13–17:13	Readings 132, 133, and 134

SCRIPTURE	READINGS
DAY 4	
John 1	Readings 135 and 136
DAY 5	
Colossians 1:15-23; 2:9-15; Hebrews 1:1–2:4	Readings 137, 138, and 139

DAY 6 STUDY MANUAL	PRAYER CONCERNS
"The Church Teaching and Believing" and "Believing and Living"	

THE CHURCH TEACHING AND BELIEVING

If the story of Jesus Christ is purely human, never has there been such an awesome superstructure built on so slender a point. If his story is both human and divine, as the church has traditionally taught, never has there been so demanding an issue thrust upon the human race.

As the Bible tells the story, the people of Israel had waited for many generations for a messiah. Their prophets had described him in a variety of ways, consistent primarily in the way they evoked hope. The times themselves were somewhat favorable. The Roman Empire was maintaining peace throughout the vast Mediterranean world. Travel and communication were probably the best and safest they had been in memory. Because of the widespread use of the Greek language, travelers could go almost anywhere and be understood. As for the Jewish people, they had been without a prophetic voice for several hundred years, and were perhaps as desperate as they had ever been for their promised messiah.

Only Matthew and Luke of the Gospel writers give any details of Jesus' birth. Their stories are a strange combination of the ordinary and the out-of-this-world. A young Jewish girl in the obscure village of Nazareth is visited by an angel who advises her she will bear a child, though she is a virgin; the conception will be by the Holy Spirit (Luke 1:26-28). Her fiancé is at first ready to discontinue their relationship, but he too is visited by an angel and is convinced to stand by her (Matthew 1:18-25). Because the Roman government requires all citizens to return to their ancestral villages to register for a new taxation, the man and the pregnant woman go to Bethlehem, a village the prophet Micah had predicted would be singularly used of God (Micah 5:2). While they are there, the baby is born. Because of the tax registration, there is no hotel room; so the baby is born in a cave barn. Shepherds come to visit at the time of his birth, because angels have told them of the event (Luke 2:1-20). Later, a group of wise men from the East also visit.They have come as a result of extensive studies that have convinced them a special king of the Jews was to be born (Matthew 2:1-12). This was extraordinary in its own right, since the Jews were at that time a subject people and since they hadn't been an international power in at least seven or eight centuries.

Soon thereafter the young family fled to Egypt for two years, in order to escape the wrath of a king who had been made suspicious by the visit of the wise men. The family then returned to Nazareth (Matthew 2:13-23). Except for a brief story of what happened when the family visited Jerusalem for a religious festival when the boy was twelve (Luke 2:41-52), we know nothing more about him until he was thirty years old. We assume he spent the intervening years in his quiet village, probably working out of a carpenter shop.

Then he began to teach. His teaching wasn't in the fashion of an organized classroom, nor was he authorized by some academic body. Here and there he saw persons who seemed to him to have promise, and he invited them to follow him. They did—in a way that, from our point of view, seems reckless of career, family, and future. He also healed people and sometimes worked astonishing miracles. And as one might expect of someone rising quickly to public prominence, he began to have enemies. Ironically, the enemies came from the religious leaders, the persons one would have expected to support him. Shortly he was brought to trial, convicted, and executed by crucifixion.

At the time of his death, eleven persons were known as his disciples, and a scattering of others—several faithful women, and several dozen persons who are never named. In total, apparently some one hundred twenty persons were loyal enough to still be on the scene two months later, after his resurrection from the dead and numbers of appearances to his followers.

That's the story as the Bible reports it. Secular history from the period has nothing to say except that he lived, taught, and died, which probably indicates how little attention the general public paid to him at that time. And this is the one about whom thousands of books continue to be written, whose symbol—a cross, the method of his execution—is without doubt the most widely known symbol in the world, and who is in some ways more controversial today than he has been in several generations.

Human or Divine?

So who was he? Was he simply a remarkable teacher and an admirable human being, as the secular culture and many of his own followers say? Or is he also—as the church has traditionally taught—the divine Son of God?

He was human, no doubt about that. He entered the world as several billion other babies have, through the birth canal of a woman. Like most infants, he passed through certain cultural rituals; in his case, the rituals of the Jewish people. Although some ancient books tell of extraordinary events in his childhood, the record of the Scriptures is silent, except for that visit to the Temple when he was twelve. After that, we hear nothing more until he was thirty. This silence suggests that all of those years were very ordinary, human years. The biblical record shows Jesus eating, sleeping, growing weary, and experiencing a wide variety of emotions—all typical of human behavior.

As the Gospels report it, the term Jesus used most often to refer to himself (some eighty times) was *Son of Man*. We can only speculate on all Jesus may have meant in using this term. In Hebrew the term means "human being" or "mortal." Perhaps Jesus intended to emphasize his sense of community with the human race. The logic for this interpretation seems strong.

Jesus' other references to himself give no clear indication of how he understood himself. He seems at times to fend off any attempts to glorify his role. So he "sternly" warns a healed leper not to tell anyone what has happened (Mark 1:40-45). But then he invites an issue when he forgives a paralyzed man's sins before healing him, thus putting himself (as his enemies quickly note) equal with God (2:1-12). When unclean spirits shout, "You are the Son of God," he "sternly" orders them "not to make him known" (3:11-12). So too when Peter identifies Jesus as the Messiah, Jesus orders the disciples not to tell anyone (8:29-30). But he tells the crowds he is "the bread of life" and if they eat of him they will not die (John 6:22-51). All of which is to say that, until the latter days of his life, Jesus seems quite content to let people conclude what they will about him.

Why do Christians say Jesus was divine? Many would point first to the stories of his birth in Matthew and Luke. Both say he was conceived miraculously, by the Holy Spirit (Matthew 1:18-25; Luke 1:26-38). Matthew says he is to be known as Emmanuel—"God is with us" (Matthew 1:23), and Luke calls him "Son of God" (Luke 1:35). John's language, as we shall see, is even stronger. Mark skips the birth story altogether and begins when Jesus is ready to embark on his ministry at thirty.

Some would also argue that Jesus is divine on the basis of his healings and his miracles, including even the raising of the dead. These are impressive, but they don't give basis for calling Jesus God. All through history there have been purported miracle workers, and whether the claims have been true or not, the role is not convincing.

In the mind of the early church, Jesus' resurrection was a crucial witness. As the book of Acts demonstrates, the apostles hardly seemed to make a public statement about Jesus without reference to the Resurrection. It was the definitive issue in Paul's sermon in Athens (Acts 17:29-34). He told the Corinthians what was "of first importance"—"that Christ died for our

The first Greek letter stands for *I* (Jesus); the second, *CH* (Christ); the third, *TH* (of God); the fourth, *U* (Son); and the fifth, *S* (Savior), which together, *ICHTHUS*, translates literally Jesus Christ, of God, Son, Savior. Tradition says the early church celebrated Christ's passion by roasting fish, a celebration that carried over into Roman Catholic practice of eating fish on Friday. Through the centuries the church has used the fish as a symbol of Christ, the second Person of the Trinity. Three fish in the form of a triangle symbolize the three Persons of the Trinity.

sins in accordance with the scriptures, and that he was buried, and that he was raised on the third day in accordance with the scriptures" (1 Corinthians 15:3-4). Then he proceeded to list witnesses and to offer his rabbinical logic, all to make the point that "if Christ has not been raised, your faith is futile and you are still in your sins" (15:17).

But the Resurrection itself might be only a sign of God's favor, without being proof Jesus was divine. On the Day of Pentecost, Peter tells the rest of the story: Jesus is now "exalted at the right hand of God" (Acts 2:33). We can't trace the evolution of thought in the minds of the disciples. No doubt at first they saw Jesus as a fascinating teacher who was also going to be Israel's political leader. To that degree, they probably also came to see him as the Messiah, but primarily in a political sense. When Jesus asked, "Who do people say that the Son of Man is?" (Matthew 16:13), the disciples responded with a list of persons. More than likely they had speculated at some point on one of these possibilities. Then Simon Peter spoke a conviction that probably had occurred to them only relatively recently: "You are the Messiah, the Son of the living God" (16:16).

But with Jesus crucified, resurrected, and ascended to heaven, Peter's confession has moved to an entirely new level. He sees Jesus at the right hand of God, the place of authority, and he challenges, "Therefore let the entire house of Israel know with certainty that God has made him both Lord and Messiah, this Jesus whom you crucified" (Acts 2:36).

From this point on, the New Testament writers seem to be on a search for superlatives that will adequately describe what they now perceive Jesus to be. John's Gospel, generally considered the last of the Gospels to be written, says, "He was in the beginning with God. All things came into being through him, and without him not one thing came into being" (John 1:2-3). In fact, life itself came into being through him, and "the life was the light of all people" (1:4). Thus we have a statement of what we now call "the preexistence of Christ," the doctrine that Christ existed eternally and that he was God incarnate when he came as Jesus of Nazareth. Paul uses the same kind of language. "He [Christ] is the image of the invisible God, the firstborn of all creation; for in him all things in heaven and on earth were created, things visible and invisible, whether thrones or dominions or rulers or powers—all things have been created through him and for him. He himself is before all things, and in him all things hold together" (Colossians 1:15-17). Paul makes the same sort of claim in one of his letters to Corinth (1 Corinthians 8:6). The writer of Hebrews identifies Jesus as the "Son, whom he [God] appointed heir of all things, through whom he also created the worlds" (Hebrews 1:2).

Since most of the epistles were written a little more than a generation after Jesus' crucifixion and resurrection, it seems clear the doctrine of Jesus as the preexistent, eternal Son of God was widely held throughout the church at a very early time. Indeed, Paul's eloquent statement in Philippians is thought by many scholars to have been a hymn popularly sung in the church and swept up by Paul as part of his appeal to the people at Philippi:

"Christ Jesus,
who, though he was in the form of God,
did not regard equality with God
as something to be exploited,
but emptied himself,
taking the form of a slave,
being born in human likeness" (Philippians 2:5-7).

Clearly the earliest believers understood Jesus to be more than just another person; indeed, they understood him to be from eternity, possessing "equality with God." So dramatically was this the case that some began to see Jesus as exclusively divine; thus the first major potential heresy was confronted in First John, when that writer says, "We declare to you what was from the beginning, what we have heard, what we have seen with our eyes, what we have looked at and touched with our hands" (1 John 1:1).

And from that time forward the church has struggled to maintain a balance that acknowledges Jesus Christ as both fully human and fully divine. Thus the Nicene Creed says not only that Jesus Christ is "the only Son of God" but that he is

"eternally begotten of the Father,
God from God, Light from Light,
true God from true God,
begotten, not made,
of one Being with the Father;
through him all things were made.
For us and for our salvation
he came down from heaven,
was incarnate of the Holy Spirit and the Virgin Mary
and became truly human."

Heresies, Councils, and Creeds

Generally it is agreed that the first creed was nothing more than the simple statement, "Jesus is Lord." That was a monumental statement in the first-century world, for it was a denial of Caesar and all other gods, and as such it could have meant martyrdom. Somewhat later came the symbol of the fish, *ichthus*—an acrostic in which the Greek letters stood for "Jesus Christ, Son of God, Savior." The Roman Creed, from the latter half of the second century, is much like what we know today as the Apostles' Creed and is a good bit longer than the two earlier statements. The Nicene Creed, drafted at the Council of Nicaea in 325, was further refined at the Council of Constantinople in 381.

The growing length and precision of the creeds is evidence of what was happening in the church. Inevitably questions arose, and differences of teaching. Usually those differences were

Generally, *heresy* is denying a doctrine of the church or holding any belief that does not agree with the official teaching of the church. Medieval canon law defined different levels of heresy as *material heresy* (wrong belief without blame, as when one has not been taught right belief) and *formal heresy* (persisting in wrong belief after having been taught correctly).

more in matters of emphasis than in points of contradiction, but of course what begins as a difference in emphasis easily becomes an issue of truth. So the church could not have been expected to be content for long with so simple a statement as "Jesus Christ is Lord." Someone was sure to ask for a clearer definition of "Jesus Christ." And as soon as someone has defined Jesus Christ, others would begin to ask for explanations of the words making up the earlier definition. So it is that creeds become more complete and specific, and more and longer books on doctrine come to be written.

We should not be disturbed that differences of belief arose in the church. The divine message has from the beginning been entrusted to human hands and minds. Considering the varieties of human nature, and our apparently innate capacity for thinking our opinions are right, one marvels that differences in belief have not been more frequent and more destructive. This observation is especially true of the earlier centuries of church history—indeed, until little more than a century ago, when at last words could travel faster than humans. When transportation and communication were such lengthy affairs, national and ethnic churches could easily become isolated from the larger body of Christendom and its unifying influence on beliefs.

The possibility of disagreement is further aggravated by the intensity of religious belief. By its nature, religion is a deeply felt issue. Never is it simply a package of logic. And perhaps ironically, the more earnest the religious convictions are, the more passionate the defense of even minor issues.

The major issues of classical church doctrine have tended to revolve around the nature of Jesus Christ. This is as it should be. Our very name, *Christian,* implies that Jesus Christ is the central point and issue.

The first Christological issue involved denial of the humanity of Jesus. It became known as *gnosticism,* from *gnosis,* the Greek word for "knowledge." The writer of First Timothy is apparently responding to it in his warning to Timothy: "Timothy, guard what has been entrusted to you. Avoid the profane chatter and contradictions of what is falsely called knowledge" (1 Timothy 6:20). Gnosticism was a complex of ideas that emphasized the quest for secret knowledge. A crucial element of the philosophy was the idea that matter is evil; as a part of that idea, gnostics denied the humanity of Jesus—because, of course, if matter was evil, Jesus couldn't share in it by being human.

Hardly more than a century later, a more sophisticated issue arose. We call it *modalism,* or *Sabellianism,* or *Patripassianism.* This issue, like several others that were dealt with in the church councils, had to do with the nature of the Trinity but centered particularly on the nature of Jesus Christ. Sabellius taught that God is one nature and person who has three names—Father, Son, and Holy Spirit; thus God the Father became Christ the Son, and "the Father suffered" in the Son. The term *modalism* refers to the idea that the one God was revealed in different ways at different times, and in three *modes* of appearance. The church dealt with this issue at the Council of Nicaea (A.D. 325) in the process of dealing with the larger issue of Arianism.

Arianism, named for the theologian Arius (256–336), taught that Jesus is the highest created being but that he does not share the same substance with God the Father. But the church concluded that if Jesus were only a created being, it would be wrong to worship him since he would be a creature rather than the Creator. Where modalism taught that the Son *is* the Father, Arianism taught that the Son is of "different substance" from the Father. The Council of Nicaea agreed that the Son is "of the same substance" as the Father, and so affirmed what the church perceived to be the teachings of the Scriptures.

Another issue arose, however, with Apollinarius (*c.* 310–*c.* 390). He denied the human soul of Christ, contending that the divine *Logos* (the term John's Gospel uses as *Word*) took the place of the human soul in Jesus, implying that Christ's humanity was incomplete. Almost a generation later the Nestorians insisted there were two natures and two persons in Christ, a view that was declared heretical by the Council of Ephesus in A.D. 431. Not long thereafter the Monophysites contended that the incarnate Christ has one nature; this view was condemned by the Council at Chalcedon in A.D. 451. That council affirmed that Jesus Christ is one Person in two natures—an entirely human nature and an entirely divine nature.

In all, the church had seven Ecumenical Councils, from A.D. 325 to 787; and scholars point out that all of them, in one measure or another, dealt with the doctrine of Christ's incarnation—that is, that in Jesus Christ, God came *in carnis,* in the flesh. No wonder. Nothing could be more at the heart of the Christian faith.

Because the nature of Jesus is not an end in itself. When Philip said, "Lord, show us the Father, and we will be satisfied," Jesus answered, "Whoever has seen me has seen the Father" (John 14:8-9). Jesus came as the revelation of God. To know Jesus Christ is to know God as God has chosen to be known.

And more than that. In the same conversation with his disciples, Jesus revealed himself still further by making the strong claim, "I am the way, and the truth, and the life. No one comes to the Father except through me" (14:6). We humans are, by nature, constantly seeking the way, the truth, the life. We seek for the truth because the truth invested in us at our creation is passionate to find itself. We seek the way because we know we are not meaningless vagabonds; we are made to reach a destination. We seek for life because we were made for eternal life.

Jesus says almost matter-of-factly that he is what we need. He doesn't allow us the privilege of trivializing him. We can accept him at his own recognizance, which is a grand step of faith; or we can reject his own self-description. But we really can't say he is the greatest teacher who ever lived (a quite unsupportable opinion), or that he is an utterly fine human

The debate between Arius (*c.* 260 or 280–336) and Athanasius (*c.* 296–373) about the person and nature of Christ divided the church. Arius championed the *subordinationist* teaching, meaning that Christ was not truly God but a lesser being created by God. Athanasius opposed that idea, insisting that Christ was somehow both fully human and fully divine. Their debate caused so much controversy in the church that the emperor Constantine called an ecumenical council at Nicaea in 325 to settle the dispute. The council condemned Arius's teaching and declared Athanasius's position the orthodox belief of the church.

An Ecumenical Council is a council called to decide doctrine, ritual, or discipline for the whole church. Seven major church councils are considered ecumenical, that is, binding on the whole church: First Council of Nicaea (325), First Council of Constantinople (381), Council of Ephesus (431), Council of Chalcedon (451), Second Council of Constantinople (553), Third Council of Constantinople (680–681), and Second Council of Nicaea (787). Subsequent church councils were accepted as binding only by the Western church.

being, perhaps the best the world has ever known. Because, of course, if he is not what he said he is, he is a quite irresponsible teacher and an unscrupulous human being.

So in the end, we are faced with the question Jesus posed one day to his disciples: "But who do you say that I am?" (Matthew 16:15). It is still his question today.

BECAUSE WE THE CHURCH BELIEVE Jesus Christ is fully human and fully divine, I accept him as my Lord.

BELIEVING AND LIVING

Probably our greatest problem in understanding the nature of Jesus is that we know just enough not to be shocked by the story as the Bible tells it. It isn't possible to come at the story with completely open minds, but try to some degree to imagine yourself reading the story for the first time, with no background knowledge; how do you think it would strike you? What would you conclude the nature of Jesus to be?

_____

_____

As you read the brief descriptions of gnosticism, modalism, and Arianism, what resemblance do you see to any contemporary religious philosophies?

_____

Imagine yourself one of the disciples in the scene where Jesus asks, "Who do people say that I am?" but with a contemporary gathering. What answers would you give as to how people see Jesus today?

_____

What to you is the importance of the church's claim that Jesus was both human and divine?

_____

_____

SEEKING MORE UNDERSTANDING

When the Nicene Creed defined the nature of Jesus, it was dealing with the particular belief crises of its time. Study the section of the Nicene Creed that talks about Jesus (Reading 2 in the readings book). How would you write that section of the creed in our day, reflecting the issues that seem to you to be crucial just now?

PRAYER

"Thou, who didst once wander on earth, leaving footprints which we should follow; Thou, who still from Thy heaven dost look down upon each wanderer, dost strengthen the weary, encourage the despondent, lead back the erring, comfort the striving; Thou who also at the end of days shalt return to judge whether each man individually has followed Thee: our God and our Saviour, let Thine example stand clearly before the eyes of our soul to disperse the mists; strengthen us that unfalteringly we may keep this before our eyes; that we by resembling and following Thee may later find the way to the judgment, for it behooves every man to be brought to the judgment, oh, but also through Thee to be brought to eternal happiness hereafter with Thee. Amen."
—*Søren Kierkegaard, 1813–1855*

13

Savior

Jesus Christ   **Savior of the world**

Mediator

Bearing our sins and punishment

Plan of salvation

Conquered death   **Cross**

Deliverer

The One Who Came to Save

"You are to name him Jesus, for he will save his people from their sins."

—Matthew 1:21

LIFE QUESTIONS

A British playwright put the life of Jesus in dramatic form under the title *The Man Born to Be King*. If Matthew had written the play, he would have titled it *The Man Born to Be Savior*—or perhaps even *The Man Born to Die*.

All of us will die, of course. But Jesus was born with the specific assignment to die. His purpose in being born was to die. So he said as he approached the consummation of his ministry and acknowledged the crisis just ahead. Should he avoid it? "No," he answered himself, "it is for this reason that I have come to this hour"(John 12:27).

But how do we explain this? Why did Jesus have to die? What is the relationship of his death to our salvation? How does his dying save me? What do we mean when we say Jesus is the Savior—"my" Savior and the Savior of the world?

ASSIGNMENT

Once again we read some Old Testament Scriptures as we study the doctrine of Jesus Christ. As we do so, we should remind ourselves that the first generation of Christians had no Scripture from which to preach about Jesus other than the Hebrew Scriptures. We do well therefore to try to read these Scriptures as the first-century Christians did. As we do so, we will recognize more clearly the relationship of the two Testaments. More than that, we will see—with the early church—that the message of salvation runs all through the Bible.

Day 1   Psalm 22 (prayer for deliverance from suffering); Job 19:1-27 (faith in a redeemer) Introduction and Readings 140 and 141

Day 2   Isaiah 52:13–53:12 (wounded for our transgressions) Readings 142 and 143

Day 3   Matthew 1:18-25 (he will save); Luke 19:1-10 (salvation has come) Readings 144 and 145

Day 4   John 10:1-18 (shepherd lays down his life); 11:45-57 (one man to die for the people) Readings 146 and 147

Day 5   Acts 13:26-39 (set free from sin by Jesus) Readings 148, 149, and 150

Day 6   Read and respond to "The Church Teaching and Believing" and "Believing and Living."

Day 7   Rest and prayer

DAILY PRAYER

Pray for the persons and situations on your Prayer Concerns list and about issues or concerns emerging from your daily reading and study.

SCRIPTURE	READINGS
DAY 1	
Psalm 22; Job 19:1-27	Introduction and Readings 140 and 141
DAY 2	
Isaiah 52:13–53:12	Readings 142 and 143
DAY 3	
Matthew 1:18-25; Luke 19:1-10	Readings 144 and 145

SCRIPTURE	READINGS
DAY 4	
John 10:1-18; 11:45-57	**Readings 146 and 147**
DAY 5	
Acts 13:26-39	**Readings 148, 149, and 150**

DAY 6 STUDY MANUAL	PRAYER CONCERNS
"The Church Teaching and Believing" **and "Believing and Living"**	

THE CHURCH TEACHING AND BELIEVING

Even some rather devout persons may wince at the sign over the rescue mission door or in neon at a revival center: *Jesus Saves.* It seems not quite worthy of the grandeur of the subject, a kind of cut-rate advertising slogan when the matter concerned calls for classic poetry and art.

And yet, that's what our Lord does. He *saves.* Saving is the reason for his birth; the ultimate subject of his teaching, the cause of his death; and his resurrection, finally considered, is to the purpose of authenticating his right to be the Savior. If "Jesus saves" seems so terse as to have no dignity, remember that when one needs to be saved, dignity is hardly the issue. Urgency may well be the primary issue.

So perhaps it is not surprising that when Paul begins listing the teachings he considers "as of first importance," the initial word is, "Christ died for our sins in accordance with the scriptures" (1 Corinthians 15:3). Paul was, of course, referring to the Hebrew Scriptures, the only Scriptures at the time of his writing to the people of Corinth. In other words, the story was old even when the church was young.

Job describes the need of a savior, and later his confidence that one would come. He pleads his helplessness before God and his inability to get a fair audience:

"For he [God] is not a mortal, as I am, that I
     might answer him,
   that we should come to trial together.
There is no umpire between us,
   who might lay his hand on us both"
     (Job 9:32-33).

With those words, Job declares the predicament of the human race—the need for someone to plead our cause with the Almighty. Later, in a magnificent burst of faith, he cries, "I know that my Redeemer lives" (19:25).

No one can say Job consciously had in mind a savior such as the New Testament gives us in Jesus Christ. However, Job knew what thoughtful persons have always known, that humans are overmatched by their circumstances and need an advocate qualified to speak to God on their behalf.

Systems and a Person

This lesson is a study of the Savior, not of salvation. Salvation is a doctrine; the Savior is a person. We can rightly say that in Jesus Christ, the word—*salvation*—became flesh—*Savior*—and dwelt among us.

In the Old Testament, the theme of salvation seems to begin with a system, and a rather intricate one. The books of Exodus and Leviticus say nothing specifically about a savior, but they present full-scale plans to meet the need. They describe a sacrificial system intended to win God's favor and to cleanse from sin.

From our point of view, two things stand out. One is the emphasis on blood. The New Testament picks up this theme in several places, as do Christian poetry and hymnody. But most believers are probably more comfortable with poetry celebrating this theme than with attempts to see its doctrinal logic. We notice also the highly detailed way the sacrificial system is set up. The point seems clear: The levitical system is concerned with life-and-death matters, so everything must be done with utmost care.

The longing Job expressed for a mediating individual becomes a dominant theme in the prophets. We are inclined to look at the Old Testament prophecies cautiously, lest we read too much back into them. The New Testament writers seem to have entertained no such fears, nor did the Christian theologians of the first centuries. This doesn't give us license to treat the prophecies in cavalier fashion, but it can encourage us to see them the way the first Christians did, as preparing the way for the Savior who was to come.

Some of the prophecies that seem most significant to Christian readers (including the early church) must have caused great ambivalence in the people of their own time. Because Israel was a nation, seeking a place in the company of nations, their dreams of some unique person would be of someone who would lead the nation to triumph and glory. Many prophecies spoke of such a person. One thinks of these words from Isaiah, words that Christians have made a part of every Advent and Christmas season:

"The people who walked in darkness
   have seen a great light;
those who lived in a land of deep darkness—
   on them light has shined. . . .
For a child has been born for us,
   a son given to us;
authority rests upon his shoulders;
   and he is named

Wonderful Counselor, Mighty God,
Everlasting Father, Prince of Peace" (Isaiah 9:2, 6).

But the writings of the prophets also included dark passages. If there was to be a savior, he would not be simply a vanquishing conqueror. Instead, there were haunting passages, and centuries later the first Christians would see many of these as pictures of their Lord, their Savior.

"My God, my God, why have you forsaken me? . . .
All who see me mock at me; . . .
they divide my clothes among themselves,
and for my clothing they cast lots" (Psalm 22:1, 7, 18).

Still more dramatic are some of the "suffering servant" passages, especially Isaiah 52:13–53:12. Christian believers from the very beginning looked upon these verses as a description of Jesus' death at Calvary:

"He was wounded for our transgressions,
crushed for our iniquities;
upon him was the punishment that made us whole,
and by his bruises we are healed.
All we like sheep have gone astray;
we have all turned to our own way,
and the LORD has laid on him
the iniquity of us all" (53:5-6).

The church understood these passages to describe Christ's role as Savior—one who was bearing the sins and the resultant punishment for others so they might be saved. In a world in which all "have gone astray," "the iniquity of us all" was "laid on him." The imagery of these passages is clearly taken from the Hebrew sacrificial system. We see here the same principle of laying sin upon a helpless victim, who then dies in the place of the sinner. So the prophet describes this willing sufferer as one who

"like a sheep that before its shearers is silent,
so he did not open his mouth" (53:7).

The New Testament Story

The New Testament is never uncertain about Jesus' role as Savior. When the angelic messenger told Joseph that Mary's child was "from the Holy Spirit," he also told him what to name the child, and why. "She will bear a son, and you are to name him Jesus, for he will save his people from their sins" (Matthew 1:20-21). The Jewish culture took names seriously; they believed that in both sound and meaning they were to reflect the significance of the child. He was indeed born to be the Savior, so that name was given him at his birth.

Neither is there any confusion about the issue of his saving. Many of Jesus' early followers believed he was coming to save Israel from their national enemies and to set up a political empire. The angelic description had something else in mind: "He will save his people from their sins." His role as Savior is specific and profound. Beyond politics and economics, beyond

This representation of the cross is known as the cross triumphant or the cross of victory. An orb or sphere represents the world. The Latin cross rising above the world signifies the victorious reign of the Savior over the world. The base of the cross becomes a band encircling the world, symbolizing the triumph of the gospel around the world.

even physical health and well-being, humans need to be saved from their sins. Since sin is the root problem of the human race, Jesus came to save them from this problem. Call him *Savior*.

Our understanding of Jesus as Savior is linked to the doctrine of the Incarnation. God became *incarnate*—that is, in the flesh—in Jesus in order to save the human race. John's Gospel reports that the Word made flesh came into the world and was rejected by many; "but to all who received him, who believed in his name, he gave power to become children of God" (John 1:12). Paul makes the same point in his declaration that "though he was in the form of God," he "emptied himself, . . . being born in human likeness"; and to what purpose?—"even death on a cross" (Philippians 2:6-8).

The tone in both these statements, from John and from Paul, is nothing short of exuberant. Even with John's recognition that "his [Jesus'] own people did not accept him" (John 1:11), and Paul's acknowledging that Christ Jesus "became obedient to the point of death" (Philippians 2:8), still the mood is triumphant. The Word became flesh in order to be the Savior. This accomplished, there is every reason to rejoice.

We can now understand what otherwise would seem to be the disproportionate structure of the four Gospels. Nearly a third of the content of the Gospels concentrates on the death of Jesus. Indeed, in a sense the disproportion is even greater, if one notices that—especially in Luke—the Gospels take a dramatic turn when Jesus "set his face" toward Jerusalem, the place where he will be crucified. When viewed from that angle (that is, from the point where Jerusalem and its events become the focus), fully half of the content of the Gospels is given to the death scene. How does one explain the biographical judgment of the Gospel writers?

The Gospel writers understood that Jesus had come into the world to die, so this was the point of their accounts. They did not minimize Jesus' teaching, his miracles, or his encounters with the first-century religious leaders; but these activities were preliminary to the main issue, that he should die. Any reading of the biblical record that ignores this emphasis is intellectually irresponsible.

This apparent disproportion in the Gospel accounts also turns an interesting light on the name by which these records are known. *Gospel* means, of course, "good news." A reader from outside the Christian faith might reasonably ask why these books are called "good news" when so much of their account has to do with the rejection, suffering, and death of the lead character. The same question often occurs to those who thoughtfully consider the naming of Good Friday. The word *good* is seriously inappropriate in both of these usages except as we perceive Jesus as Savior.

Nor can we go far into the earnest piety of the great Catholic, Orthodox, and Protestant saints without confronting this issue. Their emphasis on the cross, the wounds, the bleeding heart, and the sacred suffering of Jesus will seem quite grotesque unless we comprehend their understanding that these matters deliver the picture of Jesus Christ as Savior.

The Savior Experienced

The early church recognized that God's salvation plan existed from eternity, and that it took embodiment and entered the world in Jesus Christ: "This grace was given to us in Christ Jesus before the ages began, but it has now been revealed through the appearing of our Savior Christ Jesus, who abolished death and brought life and immortality to light through the gospel" (2 Timothy 1:9-10).

Jesus' own references to his role as Savior were sometimes quite practical and pointed, and at other times more mystical. When the crowds criticized him for going to the home of "one who is a sinner," Jesus replied that by his visit salvation had come to that house. "For the Son of Man came to seek out and to save the lost" (Luke 19:10). Luke provides no explanation of the meaning of "to save the lost." Literalists, limiting themselves to this one passage, might reason Jesus was speaking only of a new beginning in the life of Zacchaeus. But if the passage is put in the context of the whole New Testament understanding of Jesus Christ and his ministry, the meaning broadens. We can hardly imagine first-century believers limiting Zacchaeus's saving experience to a change in his lifestyle, although it surely began there and included that.

Jesus himself endorsed his wider role in his conversation with the criminal who died with him at Calvary. When the criminal said, in a remarkable reach of faith, "Jesus, remember me when you come into your kingdom," Jesus answered, "Truly I tell you, today you will be with me in Paradise" (Luke 23:42-43). The saving the criminal sought was obviously beyond this life, and Jesus assured him he would receive it.

But although Jesus was given the name of Savior before his birth (Matthew 1:21), and although John the Baptist identified Jesus at the outset of his ministry as "the Lamb of God who takes away the sin of the world" (John 1:29), Jesus said little about his role as Savior. He called the disciples to "follow" him in the new mission of the kingdom of God. He healed, cast out demons, raised the dead, and taught, while followers gathered about him. He exhibited a vigorous prejudice in favor of those classified as "sinners"—to the distress of the professionally religious. But he did all of this without specific reference to himself as the Savior.

The statements are more explicit, however, in the Gospel of John. There Jesus is identified with the serpent Moses lifted up in the wilderness (Numbers 21:4-9); so too "must the Son of Man be lifted up, that whoever believes in him may have eternal life" (John 3:14-15). The serpent is an image of saving; those who looked at the serpent were delivered from death. And of course the reference to the serpent being put up on a pole

In the Old Testament, God's reign was to bring order and justice, bringing the world into compliance with God's purpose. The people of Israel saw God as the ruler of their lives and the king as God's earthly representative. When the earthly kingdom no longer existed, people began to look forward to a future time when the kingdom of God would be restored. Jesus came preaching that the kingdom of God was at hand. Many of his parables concerned the Kingdom. After the Resurrection and Ascension, the early church interpreted the return of Jesus as the coming of God's rule in the world. By the third century A.D., people no longer expected Christ's return to be immediate. After Augustine, the church looked toward a supernatural Kingdom. Later interpretations of Revelation included the possibility of an actual future kingdom of God in this world in which Christ will rule.

was a graphic picture of Calvary. Nor do we stretch a point when we observe that the serpent was an image of sin, and that Paul said, "For our sake he [God] made him [Christ] to be sin who knew no sin, so that in him we might become the righteousness of God" (2 Corinthians 5:21). Four times in a brief passage in John 10, Jesus describes himself as the one who lays down his life for his sheep. And as death approaches, Jesus acknowledges his troubling of soul but says, "No, it is for this reason that I have come to this hour" (John 12:27).

Jesus' role as Savior receives its most explicit statement in what may seem a touch of irony, from the people of Samaria. After the woman of Samaria has told her friends she has met one who perhaps may be the Messiah (4:29), the townspeople persuade Jesus to remain for two days. Then they testify, "We have heard for ourselves, and we know that this is truly the Savior of the world" (4:42). Not by chance did the Gospel writer say the woman spoke of Jesus as the possible Messiah and the townspeople identified him as the Savior, thus bringing the two terms together. Also significant is the Samaritans' use of a wonderfully sweeping term—"Savior of the world." First Timothy 4:10 picks up the same far-reaching language: "the Savior of all people, especially of those who believe."

The letters add still more significance to the understanding of Jesus as Savior by linking the term to God. First Timothy begins, "Paul, an apostle of Christ Jesus by the command of God our Savior and of Christ Jesus our hope" (1:1). The letter to Titus uses the term "God our Savior" four times. Jude's benediction refers to "the only God our Savior, through Jesus Christ our Lord" (Jude 25). Thus the early church acknowledged that salvation had come through both God and Christ, and that the work specifically done at Calvary was God's action through God's Son (Romans 5:8). A powerful picture of the suffering God and of God's total involvement in the salvation process.

The Cosmic Savior

The New Testament understanding of Jesus' role as Savior is so far-reaching that the believer is challenged to enter a whole new realm of thought. By his death Jesus did become Savior to all who believe. Still more, he entered into conflict with the powers that otherwise enslave the human race. So the apostle wrote to the Colossians: "When you were dead in trespasses and the uncircumcision of your flesh, God made you alive together with him, when he forgave us all our trespasses, erasing the record that stood against us with its legal demands. He set this aside, nailing it to the cross. He disarmed the rulers and authorities and made a public example of them, triumphing over them in it" (Colossians 2:13-15).

All this dramatic statement is tied to the cross. The writer chooses even to use the language of crucifixion, saying "the record that stood against us with its legal demands" has been set aside, "nailing it to the cross." By his death, Jesus "disarmed the rulers and authorities" (2:14-15). The biblical writers perceived we are involved in a conflict with "the cosmic powers of this present darkness, against the spiritual forces of evil in the heavenly places" (Ephesians 6:12). By the work of Christ as Savior, these powers have been broken and the "rulers and authorities" have been disarmed, to the point of being humiliated—"a public example."

This perception of Jesus as Savior is consistent with the New Testament understanding of the nature of Jesus Christ. If the Christ is, as the apostle said, "the image of the invisible God, the firstborn of all creation" (Colossians 1:15), and if he "is before all things, and in him all things hold together" (1:17), then his power as Savior is quite beyond the usual boundaries of our discussion. A martyr's death is a noble thing, perhaps even to the point of bringing new levels of dedication from others; but a martyr's death, no matter how noble, cannot affect the balance of the universe or of the spiritual world. If, however, the one who has died is "the firstborn of all creation," one in whom "all things hold together," the death is nothing less than cosmic. The very structures of the universe—including structures and universes we cannot see—are shaken. Such is the nature of the death of Jesus, and the power inherent in naming him Savior.

As Jesus was being crucified, some despisers mocked him, saying, "He saved others; he cannot save himself" (Mark 15:31). Unknowingly, they paid Jesus a definitive compliment; it was *because* he was commissioned to save others that he could not save himself. Their words are also appropriate to the kind of anomaly woven all through the concept of Jesus as Savior.

The anomaly begins with the fact that the word *Savior* means nothing unless we need to be saved. But most of the time, we don't want to be saved until we realize we cannot save ourselves. So to be a savior is to be offensive to the human sense of adequacy. But Jesus came to be the Savior, and his purpose in coming was an indictment of the human race, a divine statement that human beings need help.

Still worse, his saving was by way of his dying. This fact adds to the offensiveness of the story. If Jesus had saved by teaching or by writing exquisite literature, by mounting a political structure or by the sheer nobility of his life, the saving would have been attractive and in good taste. But the method of saving was by the death of the Savior.

Jesus Christ is the issue of the Christian faith. The creeds that came from the earliest centuries of the church make this point unmistakably clear. Indeed, the creeds came into existence because of Jesus Christ, to define his place and nature. In the Nicene Creed, Jesus is the subject of twenty-one of the thirty-five lines; in the Apostles' Creed, ten of the eighteen lines.

But if Jesus Christ is the issue, he is the issue because he is the Savior. In any other role, his offense would be manageable.

Even the issues of his divinity and his humanity would lose much of their sting if he were to be seen only as teacher or moral example. But on the other hand, there would be no need for the divine/human nature if he were not coming to be Savior. Such a combination would be unnecessary for teacher, leader, or example.

He came to be the Savior. To use a common and overworked phrase, this is what it's all about.

> BECAUSE WE THE CHURCH BELIEVE Jesus Christ came to be the Savior of the world, I accept him as my Savior.

BELIEVING AND LIVING

Believers, particularly in these decades at the turn of the century, lack familiarity with the language that relates to Jesus as Savior. We speak more often of giving our lives to Christ, or of dedicating or committing ourselves. How do you relate to the term "Jesus saves," or to speaking of how he "saved" you?

_____

_____

What is your understanding of why we need to be saved? And from what are we being saved?

_____

_____

Paul wrote that "Christ crucified" is "foolishness to Gentiles," but to those who accept it, "Christ crucified" is "the power of God and the wisdom of God" (1 Corinthians 1:21-25). How do you respond to his words as you think about Jesus as Savior?

_____

_____

SEEKING MORE UNDERSTANDING

The theme of Christ as Savior has dominated much of religious art for centuries. Consider doing some research on how artists in various cultures and time periods, working in various media, have interpreted the idea of Christ as Savior. Most public libraries have collections of books of religious art, or you may have internet access to art museums and galleries. Two questions might guide your research: What do artists choose to emphasize? What is your overall impression of what the art intends to say about Christ as Savior?

PRAYER

"O Love divine, what hast thou done!
Th'incarnate God hath died for me!
The Father's co-eternal Son
Bore all my sins upon the tree!
The Son of God for me hath died:
My Lord, my Love, is crucified!

Is crucified for me and you,
To bring us rebels near to God;
Believe, believe the record true,
Ye all are bought with Jesus' blood;
Pardon for all flows from his side:
My Lord, my Love, is crucified."
—"O Love Divine, What Hast Thou Done,"
Charles Wesley, 1707–1788

14

Atonement

Sacrificial death

Cross   Blood

Day of Atonement

Lamb of God   Sins covered

Mercy seat   Paschal Lamb

Sinful human condition

Restored to Union With God

"This shall be a statute to you forever: In the seventh month, on the tenth day of the month, you shall deny yourselves, and shall do no work, neither the citizen nor the alien who resides among you. For on this day atonement shall be made for you, to cleanse you; from all your sins you shall be clean before the LORD."

—*Leviticus 16:29-30*

LIFE QUESTIONS

As any good novelist knows, some insights are too big to be grasped simply as factual data; they require an image.

So it is with atonement. The concept is too big for words; but when we turn to images, we are also in uncertain territory. In careless hands, images may seem confusing, or even unpleasant. Also, we discover different people need different images, and what conveys the concept to one is only bewildering or distracting to another.

What is the meaning of this abstract term *atonement*? And why is there no single theory of atonement? What is the real significance of atonement for our daily lives?

ASSIGNMENT

The word *atonement*, unlike some more familiar theological terms, appears in the Bible. But the concept appears more often than the word. Both word and concept are in the Old Testament as well as the New Testament. Indeed, the basic idea is established in the Hebrew Scriptures, then developed in a new and daring way in the New Testament.

As you read these passages, try to understand the thinking behind the Hebrew sacrificial system. We need to see it sympathetically if we are to be prepared for some of the atonement concepts that follow.

Day 1 Leviticus 4:13-35 (sin offerings); 16 (ritual for atonement)
Introduction and Readings 151 and 152

Day 2 Exodus 32:1-34 (broken relationship); Psalm 40 (deliverance and plea for help)
Readings 153 and 154

Day 3 Isaiah 53 (restoration through the servant's suffering); Zechariah 13 (a fountain for cleansing from sin)
Readings 155, 156, and 157

Day 4 Romans 3:21-30 (righteousness through faith in Jesus Christ); 5:6-21 (justification a free gift)
Readings 158 and 159

Day 5 Hebrews 4:14–5:10 (Jesus our high priest); 9:11-28 (Christ's sacrifice)
Readings 160 and 161

Day 6 Read and respond to "The Church Teaching and Believing" and "Believing and Living."

Day 7 Rest and prayer

DAILY PRAYER

Pray for the persons and situations on your Prayer Concerns list and about issues or concerns emerging from your daily reading and study.

	SCRIPTURE	READINGS
DAY 1		
	Leviticus 4:13-35; 16	Introduction and Readings 151 and 152
DAY 2		
	Exodus 32:1-34; Psalm 40	Readings 153 and 154
DAY 3		
	Isaiah 53; Zechariah 13	Readings 155, 156, and 157

SCRIPTURE	READINGS

DAY 4

Romans 3:21-30; 5:6-21	Readings 158 and 159

DAY 5

Hebrews 4:14–5:10; 9:11-28	Readings 160 and 161

DAY 6 STUDY MANUAL	PRAYER CONCERNS
"The Church Teaching and Believing" and "Believing and Living"	

THE CHURCH TEACHING AND BELIEVING

After Adam and Eve sinned, as reported in Genesis 3, they hurriedly put on fig leaves to hide their nakedness; and when they heard God walking in the garden, they "hid themselves from the presence of the LORD God among the trees of the garden" (Genesis 3:8). Whether the details of this story are literal or symbolic, the story is true. We know it is true, not simply because it is in the Bible but also because it is true to our own experience.

Indeed, it well may be that no human experience is more universal than this sense of separation from God. But even more significant, with the separation is a great sense of longing, so that while we humans feel cut off from God, and are therefore fearful, we also feel our need of God.

Here is where atonement comes into our story. We need somehow to be "at one" with God again; we need our relationship to be reestablished. We need this because we are human, and to be human is to long for the divine from which we have taken our image. We need it because to be cut off from the ground of our being is to lose our source, leaving us lost in the universe meant to be our home.

How widespread is this sense of separation? So widespread that in every type of culture, both primitive and advanced, systems of one kind or another have been developed for winning the divine favor. This fact is quite astonishing when we consider that the particular standards of right and wrong vary so from one culture to another. Yet whatever the standard, when it is broken, the people feel the relationship with their gods (however they define them) must somehow be resolved, often by appeasement. The modern minds of many generations discredit this insistent impulse, describing it as "primitive." They might better say it is unspoiled by rationalization. Our best human instinct knows we ought to be at one with God, and to do wrong is to break that communion. Then the problem is to reestablish the relationship.

The Day of Atonement

One of the most vivid pictures of atonement comes in the Passover story. The death angel is to take the firstborn in each family, but the homes in the Israelite community will be spared if they slaughter a lamb "without blemish" and following a careful ritual, mark their house with the blood of the lamb (Exodus 12).

But it isn't until the book of Leviticus lays out a fully-developed system of rituals, holy days, and sacrifices that the full sense of atonement is presented. The idea is clear in the detailed instructions for sin offerings. If a person "sins unintentionally"—that is, "goes astray in sin"—and "incurs guilt," the person is to bring "a female goat without blemish as your offering, for the sin that you have committed" (Leviticus 4:27-28). The ritual is carefully detailed. It is quite clearly a bloody business. And that is the point of the matter. Sin is seen as an act incurring death, so a death must occur; and since "the life of the flesh is in the blood ... it is the blood that makes atonement" (17:11). And because the blood is sacred, the Israelites were forbidden to eat the blood of any creature (17:14).

The most complete Old Testament statement about atonement is in Leviticus 16, in the ritual for the Day of Atonement. After two of Aaron's sons have died for recklessness at the altar (Leviticus 10), God warns that even Aaron should not come "just at any time into the sanctuary inside the curtain before the mercy seat" (16:2). But a special day is established— "the seventh month, on the tenth day of the month" (16:29). On that day, after the high priest has made a sin offering for himself, and has made atonement for himself and for his household, he is to take two goats and cast lots on them. One goat is a sin offering. It is slaughtered, and its blood is brought inside the holy place to sprinkle the mercy seat. Thus the priest "shall make atonement for the sanctuary, because of the uncleannesses of the people of Israel, and because of their transgressions, all their sins" (16:16).

Now the action centers on the second goat— Azazel, or the "scapegoat." The priest "shall lay both his hands on the head of the live goat, and confess over it all the iniquities of the people of Israel, and all their transgressions, all their sins, putting them on the head of the goat, and sending it away into the wilderness by means of someone designated for the task. The goat shall bear on itself all their iniquities to a barren region; and the goat shall be set free in the wilderness" (16:21-22). This procedure, with its carefully detailed rituals, was to take place once a year.

The biblical writers do not interpret the meaning of the rituals. But one thing is sure. They understood they were dealing with life-and-death matters. The careful details were intended to make that clear. A relationship had been broken—the most essential relationship human beings can know. Unless this relationship is restored, humans become less than human. Their divine nerve is cut. Let it be cut long enough, and the individual will become base. The baseness may be crude or sophisticated, but it is base nevertheless. If an unwashed body becomes in time so corrupted as to be almost unbearable, what happens with an unwashed soul? An unwashed body puts us out of the community of our fellow human beings. An unwashed soul puts us out of company with God.

So something must again make the person (and in the case of Israel, the nation) *at one* with God. The rupture is so serious that we cannot conceive of a satisfactory means of reunion. The levitical formula at least allows us to know our discussion takes place on holy ground. Thus the details that some may see as irritatingly detailed, or not quite in good taste, are in fact an attempt to put the unreachable somehow within reach.

The Lamb of God

John's Gospel says that when John the Baptist saw Jesus approaching him, he declared, "Here is the Lamb of God who takes away the sin of the world!" (John 1:29). Again, the following day, John told two of his disciples, "Look, here is the Lamb of God!" (1:36). John took the language of the Old Testament system of sacrifices and applied it dramatically to Jesus. This was an astonishing statement. He might more likely have identified Jesus as the Messiah, or in a heroic role as leader or teacher; instead, he portrays him as one who dies sacrificially.

Obviously we can't know all that was in John's mind in making such a statement. He was no doubt referring in a general way to the Jewish sacrificial system; but even more, to the Passover story. The Passover was the key event in Israel's history and the one memorialized most solemnly and joyfully each year. Now John was daring to take the key figure of that celebration, the paschal lamb, and attach it to Jesus. And more than that, to say that this Lamb of God would take away not only the sins of Israel but the sin of the whole world.

Early Christians took still another Old Testament image, this one found in Isaiah, and applied it to Jesus Christ. Isaiah 53 speaks poignantly of one who

"was wounded for our transgressions,
    crushed for our iniquities;
upon him was the punishment that made us whole,
    and by his bruises we are healed" (53:5).

The prophet goes on to speak of this person as one whose "life [is] an offering for sin" (53:10). In time, the prophet said, this sacrificial one would have

"a portion with the great . . .
because he poured out himself to death,
    and was numbered with the transgressors;

The form of the cross on which Jesus Christ was crucified is known as the Latin cross. This representation of the Latin cross is called the cross of suffering, the Passion cross, or the pointed cross. The pointed ends of the bars represent Christ's suffering and call to mind the thorns, the nails, and the spear. This cross is a symbol of Good Friday and the atonement made possible through the suffering and death of Jesus Christ.

yet he bore the sin of many,
    and made intercession for the transgressors" (53:12).
    The identity of this "suffering servant" has had many inter-
pretations. Some contemporary Jewish and Christian biblical
scholars apply Isaiah 53 to Israel as a nation, and probably
Isaiah's first hearers understood him to be talking about Israel.
But it is clear the early Christians saw this passage as descriptive of their Lord, particularly in his death at Calvary. As such,
the chapter is an especially graphic expression of atonement.
    John's Gospel makes a unique contribution to the concept of
atonement through a conversation at the council, the Sanhedrin.
As the council discussed what to do about Jesus, Caiaphas, the
high priest, said, "You know nothing at all! You do not understand that it is better for you to have one man die for the people
than to have the whole nation destroyed"—that is, destroyed by
the Romans (John 11:49-50). The Gospel writer explains that
Caiaphas didn't understand the full import of his own words,
that in truth, "he prophesied that Jesus was about to die for the
nation, and not for the nation only, but to gather into one the
dispersed children of God" (11:51-52). Apparently Caiaphas
perceived of Jesus as a political ploy; putting him to death
would curry favor with the Romans. John explains that Jesus'
death will mean much more. It will mean redemption of God's
people in the nation and the world.

Theories of Atonement
    The idea of our human estrangement from God and of God's
seeking to bring us "at one" again is quite beyond explanation.
And any images we use will prove inadequate, on one hand, or
distorting on the other. But the church has never allowed these
problems to discourage it from approaching this complex
subject. Nor should it. When faith seeks understanding, it can
expect a thorny path. The deepest concern comes when advocates
of a particular image or explanation insist theirs is one without
flaw and therefore the only one to be seriously considered.
    The New Testament itself suggests several ideas. The Letter
to the Ephesians uses the language of *redemption:* "In him
[Jesus Christ] we have redemption through his blood, the forgiveness of our trespasses, according to the riches of his grace
that he lavished on us" (Ephesians 1:7-8). This term draws
upon the Old Testament idea of the kinsman redeemer, a provision of the Jewish law whereby persons in debt beyond their
power to escape called upon their nearest kin to redeem them.
Job uses this term when in faith and despair he cries,
    "For I know that my Redeemer lives,
        and that at the last he will stand upon the earth" (Job 19:25).
The same provision is at work in the book of Ruth, when
Boaz becomes the one to redeem the family of Naomi and
her daughter-in-law Ruth (Ruth 3:1–4:12).
    The imagery is both powerful and beautiful. It suggests that
the human race is "mortgaged" beyond its own power to

redeem; even to the point where we are sold into slavery to sin. How shall we get out of our impossible predicament, since we are bankrupt? We turn to our "nearest Kin," our divine Elder Brother, who redeems us. The price of redemption? The death of our Brother. Thus the language of Ephesians, that "we have redemption through his blood."

The term John the Baptist used in hailing Jesus, "the Lamb of God who takes away the sin of the world" (John 1:29), is the core of the *expiation* theory. This concept is also pictured for us in Hebrews 9, when the writer compares the death of Christ at Calvary with the Hebrew system of sacrifices. In that system, the writer says, the high priest came with "the blood of goats and calves," but Christ came "with his own blood" (Hebrews 9:12). Christ's coming, he says, was "through the greater and perfect tent," one "not made with hands." And whereas the priests of the first covenant had to come annually, Christ came "once for all . . . thus obtaining eternal redemption" (9:11-12). Hebrews rejects the sacrificial system as incompetent to deal with the conscience: "How much more will the blood of Christ . . . purify our conscience" (9:13-14)

Expiation means appeasing or purifying through a sacred rite. It conveys a picture of our being soiled by sin and in need of cleansing. How is that cleansing to be achieved? Through Christ's blood sacrifice. A revival hymn from the nineteenth century put it in very direct form: "What can wash away my sin? Nothing but the blood of Jesus." Expiation removes sin and changes the sinner.

The *moral example* or *moral influence* theory has always had some advocates, and perhaps especially during the first half of the twentieth century. Its oldest form, associated with Peter Abelard (1079–1142/3), taught that because the death of Jesus Christ at Calvary was the greatest example of God's love, persons recognizing this love will be moved to salvation and will be influenced to live lives of love. In the twentieth century this interpretation was sometimes presented with more emphasis on the life of Christ than on his death. It reasons there is transforming power in the moral grandeur of Christ, so when persons see the beauty of his life, teachings, and death, they will be moved to live in accord with Jesus' ways. This approach appeals especially to the idealistic nature, but it is seen by others as minimizing the importance of the death of Jesus on the cross.

The term probably used most often in describing the Atonement is *substitution*. The principle is quite simple—one life given in place of another. This approach to the Atonement has some of the same insights as the redemption and expiation theories, and Scripture references that apply to those theories also fit the substitutionary image. No Old Testament image could be more appropriate, for example, than that of the Passover lamb. This lamb died in the place of the firstborn in a family, protecting that person from death. In the same way, the death of Jesus

Christ is seen as protecting us. And just as the Israelite families had to touch their doorposts with the blood of the lamb, so believers now must accept the death of Christ for themselves if it is to be effective. For although Christ's death is sufficient for the whole human race, it is efficient only for those who believe.

The New Testament letter of First Peter makes the point clear: "He himself [Jesus Christ] bore our sins in his body on the cross, so that, free from sins, we might live for righteousness" (1 Peter 2:24). Since there is no reason why he should bear our sins, his doing so is an act of pure grace. As Paul said, "For while we were still weak, at the right time Christ died for the ungodly" (Romans 5:6). He notes that one will rarely die for even a righteous person. "But God proves his love for us in that while we still were sinners Christ died for us. Much more surely then, now that we have been justified by his blood, will we be saved through him from the wrath of God" (5:7-9).

Some corollaries to the substitutionary theme have become atonement theories in their own right. One of these emphasizes *reconciliation*. It understands that sin has put a great barrier between God and humanity, one that might even be described as enmity. In fact, Paul uses a closely related term: "While we were enemies," he says, "we were reconciled to God through the death of his Son" (5:10).

Our human problem is complex. We feel guilty because we know we have fallen short of God's purposes; and feeling guilty, we easily fall prey to fear. What we fear we hate, or at least, strenuously avoid. And if someone or something makes us feel guilty, we seek to justify ourselves. The easiest way to do this is to pass our guilt to the other party; thus, we seek to blame God. Adam set an example for us by blaming Eve, then by blaming God for "the woman whom you gave to be with me" (Genesis 3:12).

So God has "reconciled us to himself through Christ" and has enlisted us in "the ministry of reconciliation; that is, in Christ God was reconciling the world to himself, not counting their trespasses against them, and entrusting the message of reconciliation to us" (2 Corinthians 5:18-19). Indeed, Paul wants us to understand that the whole universe was out of joint as a result of sin; there was a drastic dislocation. But all of that was changed by Jesus' death, so that "through him God was pleased to reconcile to himself all things, whether on earth or in heaven, by making peace through the blood of his cross" (Colossians 1:20). So it is that blood is an issue in our reconciliation; by his death on our behalf, Jesus seeks to reconcile us to God.

Perhaps you noticed another word in the earlier reading from Romans 5—*wrath*. Paul says that when we are justified by the blood of Christ, we are "saved through him from the wrath of God" (5:9). Many theologians, especially in early and medieval periods, reasoned that Christ's death appeased the wrath of God. This image suggests that sin had so marred our human race that we deserved God's wrath. But by his death, Jesus pleaded with God on our behalf. Charles Wesley grasped this idea in one of his poems:

"Five bleeding wounds he bears,
    Received on Calvary;
They pour effectual prayers,
    They strongly plead for me:
'Forgive him, O forgive,' they cry,
    'Nor let that ransomed sinner die!'"

In this view, Jesus Christ becomes our advocate with God, pleading our case; and doing so, Wesley says, by virtue of his "five bleeding wounds."

And then there is the *ransom* theory. It too partakes of the emphasis on the substitutionary death of Christ, but from a different angle. Some modern theologians say this is the oldest theory of the Atonement and thus the "classic" theory. It sees the Adversary, Satan, as having a claim on our human race as a result of our sins; specifically, we are his possession. Christ's blood is seen as ransom paid to Satan to deliver humanity from this terrible bondage. This approach is usually attributed to Origen, a third-century theologian. In part, it was an answer to the wrath of God theory, putting the emphasis instead on the goodness of God in frustrating Satan.

In a somewhat comparable mood, Christ's work of atonement has been explained as Christ's conquest of evil (*Christus victor*). Thus the apostle, referring to the battle against spiritual evil, says of Christ, "He disarmed the rulers and authorities and made a public example of them, triumphing over them in it [the cross]" (Colossians 2:15). The cross is seen as an invasion of the kingdom of evil, leaving that empire in humiliated defeat. The writer of Revelation makes an oblique reference to this idea. When the company of heaven wonder who is worthy to open the scroll sealed with seven seals, the answer is that the Lion of Judah will do so, because he "has conquered"; but when the Lion appears, it is "a Lamb standing as if it had been slaughtered" (Revelation 5:1-7). With this vision the writer of Revelation testifies that the sacrifice at Calvary is a conquering, lionlike power.

So what shall we say of this doctrine of the Atonement? We will remind ourselves that no single interpretation has ever been required by the church—perhaps because the concept is too large and too complex to be encompassed by any single image. And perhaps that is the most significant endorsement of this doctrine—that it is of such dimensions that every depiction will always leave much to be desired. After all, how can we adequately describe that our human race is at odds with its Creator and the Creator's dreams, that it is unable to deliver itself from its lostness, and that a way of redemption and of justification has been offered? Perhaps at a certain point in all our discussing and speculating we must stop and say with the unknown medieval poet, "What language shall I borrow to thank thee, dearest Friend?" and to confess that we have no satisfactory language.

BECAUSE WE THE CHURCH BELIEVE Christ has made us at one with God, I accept the divine love and will seek to extend it to others.

BELIEVING AND LIVING

The idea of atonement, like most really grand themes, is so big that it has to be put into picture-words, or images; and yet those very images can easily become troublesome. No single image appeals to everyone; and indeed, the whole concept of atonement rests upon our having a disposition of faith and gratitude. Imagine yourself trying to explain atonement to a secular young college student. What image would you develop that might be appealing or enlightening to such a person?

What is it about the whole concept of atonement that you find most difficult to accept or to comprehend?

Which of the several theories of atonement appeals most to you or best fits your understanding, and why?

When and in what settings is atonement a subject of thought, discussion, and gratitude in your congregation?

SEEKING MORE UNDERSTANDING

In studying atonement, there is something to be said for a devotional mood. Read some hymns on salvation or the cross, including such classics as "O Sacred Head, Now Wounded," "O Love Divine, What Hast Thou Done," and the American folk hymn "What Wondrous Love Is This." Take time to meditate as you read.

PRAYER

"The other gods were strong; but
  Thou wast weak;
 They rode, but Thou didst stumble
  to a throne;
But to our wounds only God's
  wounds can speak,
 And not a god has wounds, but
  Thou alone."
                —*Edward Shillito, 1872–1948*

15

Lord

Confessing   **Jesus is Lord**

Renouncing other lords

Confession of guilt and sin

Submission   Expression of belief

Confession of faith

Commitment

Jesus Christ Is Lord

"If you confess with your lips that Jesus is Lord and believe in your heart that God raised him from the dead, you will be saved."

—Romans 10:9

LIFE QUESTIONS

So God has done the divine part—a wondrous story with its own peculiar logic, a logic founded in grace and love. But that's done and settled. Now what do I do? This question is what philosophers would call the existential question; the people on the street would say here is where the rubber meets the road.

So what do I do, in the face of what God already has done? Indeed, is there anything I can do? If salvation is all by grace, what is left for me? The relationship seems so out of balance, with all of the weight on God's side. They tell me that being good won't cut it, so what can I do?

ASSIGNMENT

Most of the Scriptures for this week come from the New Testament. But in several instances, passages from the Hebrew Scriptures give depth to our understanding. You may also find yourself recalling stories from the Old Testament that illustrate human response to God's action. As such occur to you, ponder them in light of your study.

Above all, read with an attentive heart. Some elements of each of our lessons call for response of heart and will as well as for intellectual investigation. But it is especially true of this lesson, and we should keep this fact in mind as we read.

Day 1   Genesis 32:3-32 (wrestling with God); Psalm 116 (thanksgiving) Introduction and Readings 162 and 163

Day 2   Job 9:25-35 (desire for a mediator); 40:1–42:6 (Job and the Lord talk) Readings 164 and 165

Day 3   John 9:1-38 (sight and belief); 20:19-31 ("My Lord and my God") Readings 166 and 167

Day 4   Acts 8:26-40 (from belief to baptism); 16:16-34 ("Believe on the Lord Jesus Christ") Readings 168 and 169

Day 5   Romans 10:1-15 (confess Jesus as Lord); Revelation 3:14-22 (Christ knocks); 22:8-17 (Christ brings reward) Readings 170, 171, and 172

Day 6   Read and respond to "The Church Teaching and Believing" and "Believing and Living."

Day 7   Rest and prayer

DAILY PRAYER

Pray for the persons and situations on your Prayer Concerns list and about issues or concerns emerging from your daily reading and study.

SCRIPTURE	READINGS
DAY 1	
Genesis 32:3-32; Psalm 116	Introduction and Readings 162 and 163
DAY 2	
Job 9:25-35; 40:1–42:6	Readings 164 and 165
DAY 3	
John 9:1-38; 20:19-31	Readings 166 and 167

SCRIPTURE	READINGS
DAY 4	
Acts 8:26-40; 16:16-34	Readings 168 and 169
DAY 5	
Romans 10:1-15; Revelation 3:14-22; 22:8-17	Readings 170, 171, and 172

DAY 6 STUDY MANUAL	PRAYER CONCERNS
"The Church Teaching and Believing" and "Believing and Living"	

THE CHURCH TEACHING AND BELIEVING

Everybody has a lord of one sort or another. The hard part is confessing it. Most lords go unconfessed, and therefore hidden—especially, hidden from ourselves.

But the lordship part is inescapable. Call it the determining principle in your life, or your grand passion. Or don't call it anything, but ponder what calls the shots in your life. Or become honest with yourself and call it God, with a big or a small *g*. Everybody has a lord.

But if Christ is Lord, we have to confess it. The confession may come in numbers of ways—in baptism or confirmation, in revival altar call or in a moment of private, desperate reaching out to God. And the confession may be made to different persons—to pastor or priest, to teacher or dear friend, or to a wider public, as in youth or adult baptism, or walking down an aisle in public decision. The initial confession may be entirely private, spoken only to God, but eventually some acknowledgment will have to be made to a wider company. This need not necessarily be a ritualistic acknowledgment, but it must have some verbal content, and evidence of conduct too.

That is, money may be my lord, without my ever acknowledging it to myself or to anyone else; and so too with ambition, or sensuality, or self-centeredness, or any number of other things. None of these lords must necessarily be recognized for what they are, which is the reason they are such subtle lords. But Jesus becomes Lord only by confession, first of all, to my own soul; then to God; and then to others and to the life I live. Jesus never slips up on us, assuming lordship of our lives without our agreeing to it. Jesus respects our integrity and personhood. The process may be so gradual we don't recall exactly when or where we first confessed; but the state of confession is part of our self-knowledge. We may not be able to put into words all our confession means; in fact, it would be surprising if we could, because confession involves so much self-understanding. But confession of Christ as Lord will never be unconscious.

The Wrestling of the Soul

Paul said, "'The word is near you, / on your lips and in your heart' / (that is, the word of faith that we proclaim)" (Romans 10:8), because the believing occurs in our hearts and the confession is made with our lips. But the heart and the lips become a place of struggle. The problem is in the word we have to say: Jesus is Lord. Some would say this word is the hardest of all declarations to speak. The moment I say Jesus is Lord, I also confess I am not, because the kingdom of the soul can have only one Lord.

No wonder, then, that tradition says "Jesus is Lord" was the first confession of faith the church ever owned. Taken in its ultimate sense, it is all the confession we ever need. If this confession is made in full commitment, all secondary issues fall into place. But human as we are, we find it difficult to keep this confession at full commitment.

So this confession often comes with great struggle, as is quite obvious in the case of dramatic conversions. In quieter conversions, the kind that come partly through Christian education and continuing godly influences, the struggle is not usually so pronounced. But it is just as real.

One of the most vivid descriptions of this struggle comes to us in the story of Jacob (Genesis 32:22-32). The biblical writer tells us of a wrestling between Jacob and a stranger. The stranger is never named, though he gives hint enough when he says that Jacob has "striven with God and with humans" (32:28). Jacob himself knows what has happened to him; "I have seen God face to face," he says, "and yet my life is preserved" (32:30). Are his words to be taken literally? No, but they are true. Jacob has encountered God in his night of wrestling with God's representative. Jacob's moment of confessing comes when he reveals his name to the stranger. It is an act of trust. In the ancient Middle Eastern world, to reveal one's name to a stranger was to give the other person control. Many persons have seen themselves in this powerful story of soul-wrestling. At its best, such wrestling comes to a confession, and the confession is an act of trust.

Sometimes the confessing comes with less struggle; or perhaps with struggle of another kind. The psalmist recalls a time when the "snares of death encompassed" him, and in his distress he "called on the name of the LORD" (Psalm 116:3-4). It isn't clear to what degree the psalmist's needs were physical or spiritual, but the principle remains the same: He confessed his need, and he did so because of the severity of that need. Circumstances were bad enough to make confession easy.

But much of the time, confessing involves some wrestling, because something in us hates to acknowledge God's right of Lordship. We resist such soul prostration. One element of confession, of course, is admitting we are in the wrong—in classical language, that we have sinned. If that word comes thoughtfully, it doesn't usually come easily. The only ones who say it easily are the saints who have come to a wondrous openness to God, or the spiritually naive whose conception of sin is so superficial that they feel no discomfort in confessing.

Confessing Sin

In the New Testament, the same Greek verbs signify confession of sin and confession of faith. This fact is not insignificant. The same quality of inner honesty is required in both acts. One must be honest with oneself to confess sin, and confession of faith demands honesty with God and with society.

In the Christian tradition, the confession of faith almost always is preceded by a confession of sin. Usually this is explicit, but it is always implicit, in that one cannot really confess Christ as Lord without having renounced other lords; and such renouncing involves some sorrow for and rejection of a previous pattern of life. Again, confession of sin may be only implicit, but real nevertheless.

But it is difficult to confess sin, so difficult that Adam and Eve seem never to get around to it. When God confronts them in their act of disobedience, each one finds someone else to blame: Adam blames Eve, and Eve blames the tempter. But neither seems ever to have said, "I was wrong." Their son Cain follows in the same train. When he is angry that his offering has proved unacceptable, God reasons with him, promising him that if he does well, he will be accepted. But instead of confessing his shortcoming, he disposes of the person he perceives to be the source of his problem.

The Hebrew sacrificial system provided structures for confession of sin and for imposing those sins on another—specifically, on an animal. Perhaps the concreteness of this system made confession easier. Nevertheless, admitting guilt goes against the grain. It requires us to say, "I am wrong." These words don't come easily to us humans. They embarrass our dignity and reduce our sense of superiority.

So perhaps the claim that salvation is "free" is not entirely so. While it is true we pay nothing by way of purchase or reparations, we make any number of psychic payments. The returns, though, are all out of proportion to what we pay. But some things we must do. We must get ourselves off our hands; our sins, our self-absorption, our sense of independence. All such matters are at best burdensome and at worst, damning. But because they belong to us, they have a certain preciousness in our sight. At least until we see them for what they are.

In practice, the confession of sin is in transition in our time. This is so through much of Western Christianity. In Roman

The crown, a sign of royalty, symbolizes the ruling power of Christ as Lord. The scepter, a symbol of authority, ends with an orb crowned by a cross, symbolizing Christ's victory through the cross and his sovereignty over the whole world. The crown and scepter together declare that Jesus Christ is Lord and ruler forever.

Catholicism, the confessional as such is a much smaller element than it was a generation ago. Evangelical Protestantism tends often to emphasize the benefits of salvation while downplaying the importance of repentance for sin. In what is often called mainline Protestantism, the liturgical "confession of sin" is frequently omitted from the order of worship, or is treated quite cautiously.

The culture itself may have taken up the spiritual slack. Carl G. Jung said that the beginnings of psychiatry could be found in its prototype, the confessional. One wonders to what degree the massive growth of the counseling professions has taken the place of religious confession of sin. And also, the prevalence of twelve-step groups, where confession of shortcoming is an essential of growth. One might even wonder to what degree the lurid declarations on television talk shows provide a kind of antidote for confession for the viewers. They are able to project their sins on the person who is "confessing" matters much more horrendous than anything they might do.

Need is also hard to confess. The ego resists our doing so. Difficulty in confessing need is probably a special problem of our time and culture. Political and economic democracy give us a sense of self-control. We think ourselves capable of determining our own destiny. Self-reliance is a watchword. We are conditioned to believe that if we just try harder, plan better, and learn the system, we can accomplish anything. Nurtured in such a psychological culture, we find it difficult to confess our need. A confession of financial bankruptcy is repugnant to many of us; a confession of moral bankruptcy is repugnant to almost all of us.

No wonder, then, that so many conversions come at times of crisis—bereavement, divorce, potentially fatal illness, loss of employment, betrayal by a friend. No wonder that conversion is often described as a crisis experience. A crisis is almost essential to our making a confession of need.

And spiritual and nonspiritual needs intersect in complex ways. When the jailer at Philippi asked Paul and Silas, "What must I do to be saved?" (Acts 16:30), it is hard to say how much he was thinking of his eternal soul and how much of his imperiled career and general sense of disaster. This is not to minimize the spiritual. To the contrary, it is to say that the spiritual is intricately interwoven with all the rest of life, so that when the body is in pain, or a career or a personal relationship is in hazard, the spirit recognizes more clearly that it needs a savior. We are of one piece. The Holy Spirit knows this, and approaches us through whatever gate is open. Then, one way or another, we are ready to confess need.

The Bright Side of Confession

There is more to confession than the heaviness we have discussed so far. Far more. We are called not simply to confess our sins but to confess our faith. Religion that centers exclusively on confession of sin robs the soul of its sense of being beloved. Often it leads to a type of Christian living that is marked by despair, sometimes even by self-loathing.

So while confession of sin is necessary, it is only a means to an end and not an end in itself. We confess sin in order to be rid of it, and to be free of the self-deception and self-centeredness it encourages. With sin confessed, we can go on to better and more substantive matters, such as the confession of faith. In the words of Paul, "For one believes with the heart and so is justified, and one confesses with the mouth and so is saved" (Romans 10:10).

Perhaps it isn't surprising that we use the same word, in both Greek and English, for confession of sin and confession of faith. A confession declares the state of mind. When the dominant fact of life is sin, that becomes the declaration of our identity; when faith becomes the dominant quality, it in turn is our declaration of identity.

Something of the quality of the Christian gospel can be inferred from the fact that the New Testament speaks rarely of confession of sin. Its dominant theme is the confession of Christ as Lord. This doesn't diminish the significance of sin or the importance of confessing it. On only one occasion is the precise term used, when persons came to John the Baptist for baptism, "confessing their sins" (Matthew 3:6; Mark 1:5). The concept is implicit, of course, in many incidents and parables; and First John promises, "If we confess our sins, he who is faithful and just will forgive us our sins and cleanse us from all unrighteousness" (1 John 1:9). But as surely as confession of sin appears repeatedly in the Old Testament, confession of Christ is the recurring theme in the New Testament.

The Christian theologian might rightly say, "That's why we call the message 'gospel'—good news." With the death of Jesus Christ, a new quality exists in the relationship of God and humanity. Sin remains a fact, but a fact that has been dealt with in the death of Jesus Christ. The emphasis now is on the Savior.

It is interesting to see this truth come into play in the first recorded instance of a Gentile receiving Christ. When Philip meets the Ethiopian eunuch, the eunuch is reading Isaiah 53. "Starting with this scripture, he [Philip] proclaimed to him the good news about Jesus" (Acts 8:35). At the sight of water, the eunuch said, "Look, here is water! What is to prevent me from being baptized?" Philip immediately baptized him. Verse 37, which is in some ancient manuscripts but not included in our latest translations, told of Philip saying, "If you believe with all your heart, you may," and the eunuch answering, "I believe that Jesus Christ is the Son of God" (8:36-38). That idea is certainly implied in Philip's "good news about Jesus" and in his readiness to baptize the eunuch. One should not make too much of what is not said; nevertheless, it surely seems significant that in this first instance of a Gentile coming into the Kingdom, the whole emphasis is on the declaration and acceptance of the good news. The way to salvation is through believing in—or confessing—Jesus Christ as Lord.

John's Gospel says that even some of the authorities believed in Jesus, but "they did not confess it, for fear that they would be put out of the synagogue" (John 12:42). Does their experience suggest that one can believe yet not be a Christian? Specifically, is this the issue of the phrase, "confess with your lips" (Romans 10:9)? Is believing not enough? Or to put it another way, does true believing—that is, believing that carries the full content of the New Testament concept—inevitably include a verbal confession? Does the very term *believer* imply, also, *confessor?*

If so, what shall we say for Joseph of Arimathea, who is described as "a disciple of Jesus, though a secret one because of his fear of the Jews" (John 19:38)? One would reason, from the language used in John's Gospel to describe Joseph, that "confessing Christ" may be within certain circumstantial boundaries.

No doubt the phrase *confess with your lips* is intended to give a specific, verbal quality to the confession. It infers the kind of thought-through precision that words require. The biblical writers believed in the sacred power of words; they were not to be spoken idly. The heritage, in the Old Testament, that God had created by means of speech, and in the Christian tradition that Jesus Christ was the Word, lent a unique awe to the use of words. To speak a word was to institute a deed. To confess with the lips the Lordship of Jesus was to invest one's very self with the confession.

As much is implied in the other half of the formula: "and believe in your heart that God raised him from the dead" (Romans 10:9). The confession of the lips and the belief of the heart are of one piece. The word confessed is an expression of the belief cherished in the heart.

The Logic of Confession

Back now to the questions that started us on this journey. So God has done the divine part, the altogether gracious part, in providing a way of salvation. Atonement has been made, the price paid. Now what can I do—I, the human participant in this proposed covenant? While it is true that only God can initiate such a covenant, a covenant can never be a singular action. So what can I, the human, do? And the answer is, I can confess. And what does that mean?

It means I can give God the one thing that is mine to give—my commitment, my confession, my person. Confession is my act of faith. I am able to confess that Jesus is Lord, and I do this by faith. There is much evidence in the Scriptures, in human history, and in the witness of my own soul that Jesus is and ought to be Lord. But at a certain juncture in experience, I will endorse it by my believing. I will choose to *faith* it. I might confess any number of other lords; the world is full of them, as full as Athens was full of gods in Paul's day. Indeed, we seem to invent new lords every day; and in a culture as complex as

The Old Testament uses *Adonai* (Lord) as a substitute for the name of God. There God is the ruler of the nation and the people. The Lord God is the final authority. The earliest Christian creed, "Jesus is Lord," may have meant "Jesus is God" or "Jesus is Master of my life." Most modern Christians use it in the latter sense.

ours, the gods evolve with astonishing rapidity and morbidity. Furthermore, because of the kind of creatures we are, these lords hold strange appeal. When, surrounded by these myriad possibilities, I choose to confess that Jesus is Lord, I am doing the one thing I am uniquely equipped to do.

So there is a logic in confession. Grace cannot be paid for, but it can be accepted—that is, confessed. The hymn writer said,

"Nothing in my hand I bring,
    simply to the cross I cling."

But the clinging is a confession, and it is this that we are privileged, by grace, to bring to the covenant ground.

The Danger of Confession

But a hazard remains. It is possible to presume on grace. After we have accepted the grace of God, we are encouraged to "work out your own salvation with fear and trembling" (Philippians 2:12). Although God has invested great power in our ability to confess, it is not a license to exploit grace. Confession gives admission into the company of the committed. It is the community of workers. Having entered by grace, we commit to work. Because the essence of confessing that Jesus Christ is Lord is to enlist in the works of Christ. To do anything less is to deny his Lordship. Confession is a commitment to become like the one whose name we confess.

Confession is a continuing fact, both confession of sin and confession of faith. We confess sin because we fall short of the glory of God. We continue to confess our faith because with each day of living, we know more of the greatness of our Lord and see larger areas of life we wish to commit to his Lordship. It is a wondrous way. And on our side, it all begins with confession.

> BECAUSE WE THE CHURCH BELIEVE the proper human response to God's gift of grace is our confession of sin and of faith, I choose to make my full confession.

BELIEVING AND LIVING

When did you confess that Jesus is your Lord? Was it a conscious public decision, or a growing perception?

_____

_____

As you grow in Christian faith, what experiences increase your need and desire to commit more of your life to the Lordship of Christ?

_____

_____

What do you find especially difficult about the confession of sin? In what ways are the ritual prayers of confession, as in the service of Holy Communion, meaningful to you?

What, in your experience, is the difference (if any) between confession of sin and confession of need?

How public do you think the confession of faith in Christ must be? in any situation?

SEEKING MORE UNDERSTANDING

As a way of summarizing your understanding of what is involved in confessing Jesus as Lord, try writing a litany consisting of several statements, with each statement expressing one idea. Follow each statement with the confession *Jesus is Lord*. Such a litany might be read responsively during the group meeting.

PRAYER

"A broken altar, Lord, thy servant rears,
Made of a heart, and cemented with
    tears:
Whose parts are as Thy hand did frame;
No workman's tool hath touched the
    same.
      A heart alone
      Is such a stone
      As nothing but
      Thy power doth cut.
      Wherefore each part
      Of my hard heart
      Meets in this frame
      To praise Thy name.
That if I chance to hold my peace,
These stones to praise Thee may not
    cease.
Oh let thy blessed sacrifice be mine,
And sanctify this altar to be Thine."
—*George Herbert, 1593–1633*

16

Faith

Conviction of things not seen

Trust in the character of God

Gift of the Holy Spirit

Faith in God revealed in Jesus Christ

Saving faith

Assurance that God exists and responds

Faith community

Justified by faith

Faith and works

The Reach Toward God

"Without faith it is impossible to please God, for whoever would approach him must believe that he exists and that he rewards those who seek him."
—*Hebrews 11:6*

LIFE QUESTIONS

Nothing is so common as faith, and few things are more mysterious. We exercise some version of faith each time we step on an elevator, ride in an airplane, or are wheeled into an operating room. Or come to think of it, each time we pour cereal from a box into a bowl or listen to a newscast. Faith makes the world go around. Without it, all functions of life would cease.

But what is faith at this most profound of all levels, faith in God? And why does the Bible make so much of it, so that we're warned that without faith, we can't please God? How do I know I can trust God? And if faith is so important, how do we get it, and keep it, and make it still stronger?

ASSIGNMENT

We're likely to think of faith in a philosophical way, as a subject for discussion. In the Bible, it's an action word. Hebrews 11, which is popularly known as "the faith chapter," begins with a definition of faith but then goes into a series of for-instances. Our daily Scripture readings will have something of the same flavor.

As you read these passages, look for the vari-

eties of ways faith expresses itself. Notice too the different results. We so often measure faith by touchdowns, but the Bible seems just as ready to make the faith case when life is intercepted.

Day 1 Genesis 4:1-8 (Cain's and Abel's offerings); Hebrews 11:1-4 (acting on faith) Introduction and Readings 173, 174, and 175

Day 2 Genesis 12:1-9 (Abram responds to God's call); Hebrews 11:8-16 (faith to obey) Readings 176 and 177

Day 3 Exodus 2:1–3:12 (Moses called for God's purposes); Hebrews 11:23-28 (guided by faith) Readings 178 and 179

Day 4 Psalm 34 (testimony of faith); Daniel 3:1-18 (loyalty to God) Reading 180

Day 5 Romans 4 (Abraham justified by faith); Galatians 3 (righteousness by faith) Readings 181, 182, and 183

Day 6 Read and respond to "The Church Teaching and Believing" and "Believing and Living."

Day 7 Rest and prayer

DAILY PRAYER

Pray for the persons and situations on your Prayer Concerns list and about issues or concerns emerging from your daily reading and study.

SCRIPTURE	READINGS
DAY 1	
Genesis 4:1-8; Hebrews 11:1-4	**Introduction and Readings 173, 174, and 175**
DAY 2	
Genesis 12:1-9; Hebrews 11:8-16	**Readings 176 and 177**
DAY 3	
Exodus 2:1–3:12; Hebrews 11:23-28	**Readings 178 and 179**

SCRIPTURE	READINGS
DAY 4	
Psalm 34; Daniel 3:1-18	Reading 180
DAY 5	
Romans 4; Galatians 3	Readings 181, 182, and 183

DAY 6 STUDY MANUAL	PRAYER CONCERNS
"The Church Teaching and Believing" and "Believing and Living"	

THE CHURCH TEACHING AND BELIEVING

The word *faith* does not appear in the opening chapters of Genesis, but the writer of Hebrews tells us it was there all the time. That may be instructive in itself. We so often read faith through the prism of our feelings; the Bible seems to say feelings have nothing to do with it. Faith is as faith does.

Nevertheless, faith is also a state of mind. So it seems, at least, in the first case history to which the book of Hebrews refers. We're told Abel offered "a more acceptable sacrifice" than did Cain because Abel's was marked "by faith" (Hebrews 11:4). But we're not told what it was Abel did differently. The lack in Cain is hinted at by his later action. When he finds his sacrifice has fallen short, his countenance falls; and even when God chides him and appeals to him to change his ways, Cain insists instead on pursuing a negative course. Perhaps we can properly assume it was these same negative qualities that made Cain's earlier approach to God unsatisfactory.

But if so, our definition of faith, in the Abel story, owes more to the contrast than to a picture of faith at work. We really don't know what Abel did or how it was that his faith demonstrated itself. We do see, however, that Abel's faith did not lead to the kind of conclusion we "romantically" associate with faith. Abel's reward was not to live happily ever after, but to die.

Our disposition is to believe after delivery, or to expect delivery very quickly after believing, and probably as a reward for our believing. The biblical record suggests that faith may not get delivery at all, and that it will prove itself by the posture it maintains when delivery is postponed or even, apparently, denied.

A Definition of Faith

The writer of Hebrews describes faith as "the assurance of things hoped for, the conviction of things not seen" (Hebrews 11:1). But soon thereafter he explains more clearly what this means. Whoever would approach God "must believe that he exists and that he rewards those who seek him" (11:6). What is the proof God exists? Several kinds of evidence can be offered, and logic can construct some arguments. But in the end the seeker will have to make a leap of trust, a kind of tightrope walk without a safety net. And that's faith that God exists.

Trusting that God exists is venture enough in itself, but faith asks a still more significant declaration. It has to do with our estimate of the character of God. And it's a quite pragmatic measure: We must believe God "rewards those who seek him." The seeking mind does not believe God is standing at an indifferent distance, cold and detached, but that God is responsive, and therefore responsible. In actual practice, however, faith takes on a very heroic quality, because in so many instances (as in the Abel story) God's reward isn't readily apparent. In fact, after reporting some great faith examples, the New Testament writer says, "All of these died in faith without having received the promises" (11:13). Not the kind of faith-result we generally have in mind!

But the faith people of the Old Testament follow just such a pattern of "God exists and God rewards." Noah builds an ark because he believes God exists and God will reward. Abraham leaves home and kindred, striking out toward the wilderness, because he believes that God exists and that God will reward. Against all odds, he and Sarah expect to have a family—because God exists and God rewards. And when that promised family line, Isaac, is mature and ready to fulfill the promise, Abraham goes to Mount Moriah in faith that God exists and God rewards. An astonishing series of stories—and they define faith. Because faith is as faith does.

So if it is true, as we said earlier, that faith is also a state of mind, it is a hearty state—and it is a mind that demonstrates itself in life and action. Faith is never a bemused onlooker. Faith is in the fray. So Job said defiantly from his ash heap, "Though he [God] kill me, yet I will trust in him" (Job 13:15). The three young Israelites, facing imminent destruction in the king's furnace, declare their belief that God will deliver them. "But if not," they continue, "we will not serve your gods" (Daniel 3:18). Their faith was demonstrating itself not simply in their expectation that God would work a miracle on their behalf but also in their resolve to be true even if no miracle happened.

All this brings us back to the matter of believing God exists and God rewards seekers. The belief in the first part of the equation—God exists—is so strong that the believer is content to leave the peculiar working out of God's reward entirely in divine hands. Shadrach, Meshach, and Abednego prefer, of course, to be spared the furnace; but their faith will not be shaken if deliverance does not come. Their faith will not even change its posture. All along their trust has been in the character of God, and that trust is related only incidentally to what happens to them. If they are not delivered, it must mean this is God's will and therefore it is good. Why? Because God can do no ill; it would not be consistent with the divine character.

Obviously, then, obedience is a primary factor in faith. To say we believe God, yet disobey him, would be quite irrational. And that brings us back to the story of Adam and Eve and their sin. Their sin was an act of disobedience. God had told them not to eat of the tree of knowledge, and they insisted on doing so. And why did they disobey? Quite simply, because they did not believe. Perhaps they didn't believe they would die as God had warned, choosing rather to believe the tempter. Or perhaps they didn't believe God had their best interests at heart in making the tree off limits. That is, they may have had a low estimate of God, not believing that God is a rewarder.

Faith and Salvation

To a believer, the supreme faith issue is the relationship of faith to eternal salvation. In a general sense, the issue is defined in Hebrews 11:6: "Without faith it is impossible to please God." If we can't please God without faith, then we can hardly hope to have salvation without it. But the biblical writers state the point more specifically. The writer of Ephesians declares, "For by grace you have been saved through faith, and this is not your own doing; it is the gift of God—not the result of works, so that no one may boast" (Ephesians 2:8-9).

Here and in other places in the New Testament letters—especially in the book of Galatians—faith and works are set in opposition. Galatians, in fact, is a kind of battle cry. Paul challenges that community of believers, "You foolish Galatians! Who has bewitched you?" (Galatians 3:1). "A person is justified not by the works of the law but through faith in Jesus Christ." In fact, "no one will be justified by the works of the law" (2:16). Paul is very clear. Christ died for our sins, and only by faith in this sacrifice can a person be saved.

A certain logic is involved. If the essence of sin as portrayed in Genesis is an act of disobedience to God—that is, of faith in other than God—then the way to counteract that pattern is by accepting God's provision. We lost Eden by not believing in God's character; we will gain a better Eden by believing in the divine character as revealed in Jesus' death at Calvary.

What do you think Jesus' death reveals about God's character?

But if it be true that faith is as faith does, and that faith shows itself by our actions, then how are faith and works so different?

A shield is a symbol of protection. The shield of faith signifies trust in God. It is one part of the whole armor of God described in Ephesians 6:10-20 as protection against the evil powers that would destroy us.

In this: Faith trusts in the character of God and acts upon that trust, while works rely upon their own merit. Might this have been the issue in the Cain and Abel story? Both men brought offerings to God. Could it be that Abel made his offering, trusting in God to accept it, while Cain brought his, trusting in the merit of the offering itself? Is this what is meant when the writer of Hebrews says, "By faith Abel offered to God a more acceptable sacrifice than Cain's" (Hebrews 11:4)? Is it that Abel's faith was in the character of God, while Cain's was in the character of his offering, or of his own worth? And does this idea bring us back to the basic issue, that in order to please God we must believe "that he exists and that he rewards those who seek him" (11:6)?

Everyone has faith, and everyone exercises faith. And, in fact, everyone places faith in something or other for salvation. But the only kind of faith to which the Bible will give that name is faith directed to God. Faith directed to other than God is called unbelief. Why? Because faith directed elsewhere is by that very fact an act of rebellion against God, a repeating of the turning away from God that occurred in the story in Genesis 3.

Saving Faith

As Hebrews 11 presents the faith pilgrimage of the Old Testament, the prevailing thrust was the larger purposes of God's kingdom. This was expressed particularly as God's salvation unfolded through the nation of Israel. Yes, individuals struggled with and affirmed faith, but in most instances the faith issue in their lives had to do with their role in God's greater purpose. We get a more personal view in the book of Job and in some of the psalms, but the recurring theme is the bringing to pass of God's purpose.

In the New Testament the emphasis shifts to individual salvation. God's kingdom is still the goal. But whereas in the Old Testament people were born into the kingdom body, Israel, by family heritage, in the New Testament people are born into the kingdom body, the church, by the personal act of faith. Thus the church is probably best defined as the community of those who declare faith in Jesus Christ, identifying him as their Lord and Savior. It is, indeed, a faith community.

Thus Jesus Christ becomes the issue in any Christian discussion of faith. This fact is not understood by a large percentage of professing Christians. Ask them to define a Christian, and more than likely they will say, "Someone who believes in God." This definition is not simply imprecise; it misses the point almost entirely. A Christian does, of course, believe in God; but a Christian believes in God specifically as revealed in Jesus Christ, and by faith in Christ as God's way of salvation.

This belief was both the theme and the stigma of the early church. If the first Christians had only been willing to define God more broadly, or to include Jesus as one of the pantheon of gods, there would have been no martyrs. Those Christians offended the generally broad-minded first-century world by claiming a unique place for Jesus Christ and by insisting on the critical importance of having faith in him.

Nor were they cautious about declaring this position. Their singular insistence began on the day the church was born, Pentecost. When the crowds asked what they should do, Peter replied, "Repent, and be baptized every one of you in the name of Jesus Christ so that your sins may be forgiven" (Acts 2:38). The name of Jesus Christ—that is, his essential person—had now become the issue.

When, soon thereafter, Peter and John were brought before the religious council, Peter erased any remaining doubt about what was at stake: "There is salvation in no one else, for there is no other name under heaven given among mortals by which we must be saved" (4:12). When Peter first attempted to explain salvation to Gentiles, he not only centered upon faith in Christ, but he supported his insistence by a general reference to the Hebrew Scriptures: "All the prophets testify about him [Jesus Christ] that everyone who believes in him receives forgiveness of sins through his name" (10:43). Forgiveness comes through an act of faith—believing in Jesus Christ.

Perhaps, then, it is no wonder the book of Acts always refers to baptism in Jesus' name. The risen Lord himself had told his disciples they should baptize "in the name of the Father and of the Son and of the Holy Spirit" (Matthew 28:19); but when baptism is referred to in Acts, only the name of Jesus is mentioned. Some have built a doctrine around this fact. It seems likely, however, that the accounts in Acts simply reflect the strategic issue of salvation as the earliest believers perceived it. They understood they were saved by believing in Jesus Christ; thus when they referred to baptism, it was to his name they pointed since he was the particular, unique object of their faith—and also, the crucial issue. Saving faith was faith in Jesus Christ and his saving work.

The exclusiveness of this message is generally offensive in our broad-minded times. It was offensive in the first century also, so much so that from time to time the believers were persecuted and martyred for their conviction. To say faith must be placed in Jesus Christ seems judgmental—as it is. But it is a judgment we pass on ourselves, not on others. If we believe salvation is in Jesus Christ, we must of course accept him. Also, we must share this extraordinary knowledge. That is the judgment we pass on ourselves. As for what God will do about those who do not have saving faith in Jesus Christ, we will leave that judgment to God, for it is clearly God's business. And just as surely, what we do about our own believing, and the sharing of that believing, is our business.

Paul makes saving faith conveniently accessible. It is not a matter of ascending into heaven or descending into an abyss to lay claim, because "The word is near you, / on your lips and in your heart" (Romans 10:8). And lest we be confused about this "word," he explains that it is "the word of faith that we proclaim." The faith process is so simple it seems almost to be a ritual: "If you confess with your lips that Jesus is Lord and believe in your heart that God raised him from the dead, you will be saved. For one believes with the heart and so is justified, and one confesses with the mouth and so is saved" (10:9-10).

Then Paul seems to sense that a question still remains: Just how do we get the ability to believe in our hearts? Our daily experience so often goes against that kind of believing. Particularly, Paul asks how people can call on one in whom they have not believed, or of whom they have not heard. So the news must be proclaimed, because "faith comes from what is heard, and what is heard comes through the word of Christ" (10:17). The faith process begins with the hearing of the God-sent word.

The struggle for human attention goes on interminably. We are always submitting ourselves to the influence of one voice or another. Out of all those voices—good, bad, and neutral—only one voice is calculated to build faith—the voice that announces "the word of Christ."

Is faith, then, a means by which we control God? Popular belief sometimes seems to suggest as much. Faith is presented as a sure way to get healing, perhaps, or a particular answer to prayer. It is presented as if God found faith irresistible. But teaching that presents faith as controlling God places faith in faith rather than placing faith in God. Faith in God understands God has the right of final decision. That is, it allows God to be God. People who place absolute power in faith are inclined also to believe what they seek is right. Thus their faith is twice misplaced; their faith is in faith, and faith in their own judgment. Needless to say, such an interpretation of faith misses the quality of faith that characterizes much of Hebrews 11, since there faith demonstrates itself more often by endurance than by earthly victory.

How Do We Come to Believe?

If faith is so essential to effective living, and even to our salvation, how do we get faith? At first observation, it might seem faith is divinely ordered, so that some people have it and some do not. Or perhaps it has to do with personality types. Are some people naturally skeptical and others trusting? some negative and others positive? If so, Cain could not be blamed for lacking the faith that made Abel's offering more acceptable. On the other hand, if faith were a matter simply of human disposition, God was mistaken in urging Cain to change his ways (Genesis 4:6-7).

Probably all humans possess generic faith, because faith is essential to life. A person utterly bereft of faith retreats from life; and we conclude such a person is mentally ill, because generic faith is a normal state of mind. The issue is the object of our faith: Will we believe in health or in sickness? in goodness or in evil?

If we grant that faith is essential, we face another question:

Why do some persons find it more difficult to believe in health, goodness, love, and purity than do others? No doubt heredity (genes, if you prefer) is a factor. No doubt too, environment plays a part.

Probably the most significant biblical answer (and one that has sound logical basis as well) is given in Romans 10. Paul is speaking primarily of the faith that brings salvation, but the principle applies equally well to all of life. "So faith comes from what is heard, and what is heard comes through the word of Christ" (Romans 10:17). The secret of faith is in what we hear, with what we take in with both ears and eyes. Faith in Christ and in the purposes of God is built by the nourishment given to mind and soul. Those who choose to dwell on whatever is true, honorable, just, pure, pleasing, and commendable (Philippians 4:8) will, in time, possess great faith.

Fortunately, this can happen even in adverse circumstances and settings, as long as persons maintain an inward faith diet. Right daily decisions strengthen faith, and faith grows as it is exercised and reinforced, but only if the believer tends to what is "heard." It is significant that Abel, Noah, and Abraham were all altar builders. They consciously tended to their souls.

The New Testament speaks also of faith as a gift of the Holy Spirit (1 Corinthians 12:9) and as a fruit of the Spirit (Galatians 5:22). These are special, extended expressions of faith. The faith that is a gift of the Spirit is intended to minister to the community of believers. We see it in those persons who are a source of strength and encouragement to fellow believers and often to persons in general. Faith as a fruit of the Spirit functions more at the level of faithfulness, the translation used in the New Revised Standard Version. Faithfulness is the fruit that develops in a life that earnestly holds to God.

"And now faith, hope, and love abide," Paul said, and concluded, "and the greatest of these is love" (1 Corinthians 13:13). But he was not minimizing faith when he said so. By faith, as Paul said in numbers of other places, we apprehend the grace of God that saves us. This same faith helps us to continue to grow in Christ.

BECAUSE WE THE CHURCH BELIEVE faith is essential to our salvation and to godly living, I will pursue faith in all of my thinking, speaking, and doing.

BELIEVING AND LIVING

Perhaps the greatest problem we face in understanding faith is in our preconceptions. We think of faith as a miracle-working force, or something to be employed at times of notable crisis. Although such expressions of faith are praised and sought after, in a sense they are nearly secularizations of faith, because by our attention to them we lose sight of the primary issue of faith as an element in our salvation and in our growth as believers.

Hebrews 11:13 speaks of the faithful who died without having received the promises but who greeted them from a distance. Faith might be described as having the long view. When in your life, or in your observation of another's life, have you seen faith demonstrated in the "long view," or in its quality of loyal perseverance?

_____

_____

Our lesson says faith is as faith does. How, then, are faith and works related?

_____

_____

What books, sermons, or habits have nourished your faith? What persons? What factors might contribute to deterioration of faith?

_____

_____

_____

Consider the "narrowness" implied when we say salvation is by faith in Christ. How is such narrowness justified? How would you explain it to someone who holds a different view?

_____

_____

SEEKING MORE UNDERSTANDING

Consider beginning a journal of your faith journey. Take plenty of time before you start writing to think back over your life to the time when faith began to be important for you. Make notes as you meditate. Then begin to record your journey in writing. Pay attention to people, events, and situations that influenced your faith. Record the high and low times, the times of doubt and of deep faith. Bring the journey into the present. Add to the journal at regular intervals.

PRAYER

"O God, too near to be found, too simple to be conceived, too good to be believed; help us to trust, not in our knowledge of Thee, but in Thy knowledge of us; to be certain of Thee, not because we feel our thoughts of Thee are true, but because we know how far Thou dost transcend them. Turn us back from our voyages of thought to that which sent us forth. Teach us to trust not to cleverness or learning, but to that inward faith which can never be denied. Lead us out of confusion to simplicity. Call us back from wandering without to find Thee at home within. Amen."

—*W.E. Orchard, early 20th century*

Holy Spirit

Presence   **Paraclete**
Breath   **Advocate**   Wind

God at work in the present
Spirit
Spirit of Christ   **Spirit of God**
Holy Spirit fully God

God With Us

*"Do not cast me away from your presence,
and do not take your holy spirit from me."*
—Psalm 51:11

LIFE QUESTIONS

Of all the intangibles in religion, nothing is more intangible than the Holy Spirit. And yet, as the Christian faith sees it, nothing is more significantly and intimately related to our daily lives.

What is the Holy Spirit? Is this just a Christian name for the kind of psychic experiences almost anyone might profess to have? Is the Holy Spirit really part of God? And if so, how long has the Holy Spirit been around? And most of all, what difference does the Holy Spirit make to me or to anyone else in the way we live our lives?

ASSIGNMENT

Christians are inclined to think that the Holy Spirit didn't enter the world until the Day of Pentecost. In truth, the Holy Spirit is mentioned scores of times in the Old Testament, usually as "the spirit of the LORD." And because the Hebrew word for spirit is also the word for breath or wind, sometimes translators use the words interchangeably. So it is that in our first Scripture of the week, some translators speak of the Spirit of God moving on the waters, and others of a wind from God.

As you read these passages, see how many ways the Spirit of God is present in the biblical story, and how surprisingly diverse those ways are. And note that the Spirit's activity goes from the beginning to the end of the biblical record.

Day 1   Genesis 1:1-2 (the Spirit at Creation); 6:1-8 (God's intention for creation threatened); Numbers 11:16-30 (elders given the spirit) Introduction and Reading 184

Day 2   Judges 14 (spirit of Lord on Samson); 1 Samuel 10:1-13 (Saul possessed by the Spirit) Reading 185

Day 3   1 Samuel 16 (Spirit on David); Psalm 139:1-12 (God's Spirit everywhere) Readings 186 and 187

Day 4   Isaiah 61:1-6 (anointed for mission); Ezekiel 11:1-13 (directed to prophesy) Readings 188 and 189

Day 5   Matthew 1:18-25 (conceived from the Holy Spirit); John 14:15-31 (promise of Holy Spirit); Revelation 22:7-17 (invitation of the Spirit) Reading 190

Day 6   Read and respond to "The Church Teaching and Believing" and "Believing and Living."

Day 7   Rest and prayer

DAILY PRAYER

Pray for the persons and situations on your Prayer Concerns list and about issues or concerns emerging from your daily reading and study.

SCRIPTURE	READINGS
DAY 1	
Genesis 1:1-2; 6:1-8; Numbers 11:16-30	Introduction and Reading 184
DAY 2	
Judges 14; 1 Samuel 10:1-13	Reading 185
DAY 3	
1 Samuel 16; Psalm 139:1-12	Readings 186 and 187

SCRIPTURE	READINGS

DAY 4

Isaiah 61:1-6; Ezekiel 11:1-13	Readings 188 and 189

DAY 5

Matthew 1:18-25; John 14:15-31; Revelation 22:7-17	Reading 190

DAY 6 STUDY MANUAL	PRAYER CONCERNS
"The Church Teaching and Believing" and "Believing and Living"	

THE CHURCH TEACHING AND BELIEVING

When a devout theologian and devotional writer began a book on the Holy Spirit over a century ago, he referred to the Spirit as the unknown member of the Trinity. Yet a modern novelist and literary critic who is also a Christian says when she speaks with agnostic literary friends about her faith, it is the Holy Spirit they understand best. And a notable modern believer recalls that during her years as an atheist and a poet, she would be shaken by the Spirit dozens of times a day, yet never recognize the action as the Spirit of God. What is this strange personality that is such a mystery to us, yet so evidently a factor in our lives?

As a matter of fact, if average persons on the street were to define God, quite likely the definition would sound more like the Holy Spirit than either of the other two Persons in the Trinity. Especially in our day, when popular theological definitions tend to be sketchy, the vagueness we associate with "spirit" is all the more appealing.

But while references in the Bible to God's Spirit may be many and varied, they are not meant to be vague. And while the work of the Holy Spirit is no doubt more wide-ranging than we can ever imagine, it is not capricious or without purpose.

The Spirit in Genesis

The Spirit of God is referred to in the opening paragraph of Genesis; but because the same Hebrew word means "spirit," "wind," and "breath," the translators have sometimes chosen one of the alternative terms. A Jewish scholar, in a recent translation of the Pentateuch, uses the vigorous term, "rushing-spirit of God." That catches the feel of the wind without losing the personal quality of the Spirit. On the other hand, the word *breath* has the intimate quality suggested in the process of creation, as God spoke the creation into existence.

And if any particular word should be used in referring to the Spirit, perhaps *intimate* is the word. Because God is wholly other, we have difficulty perceiving the divine nature and even more difficulty approaching the divine. The Spirit makes it easier for us to understand that God is near—immediate, that is, an unmediated presence—so near that "in him we live and move and have our being" (Acts 17:28). Thus the Spirit of God may be at work in our lives even when we do not know it or are not responsive.

Such seems the case in the next reference to the Spirit in Genesis. The writer describes a time when wickedness was increasing, and God said, "My spirit shall not abide in mortals forever, for they are flesh" (Genesis 6:3). These words seem to refer to the fact that God's Spirit was invested in humans at Creation, when God breathed "the breath of life" into human nostrils (2:7). Apparently the people weren't conscious they were inhabited by such sacred breath. In this regard, they were much like us. God's presence may sustain us, protect us, and solicit us without our recognizing the source.

Or perhaps they, like us, were ready to settle for inexact definitions. One wonders what was in Pharaoh's mind when he chose Joseph to be his first in command. When Joseph had set out to interpret the dreams that the court advisers could not, he had quickly explained to Pharaoh that he could not interpret the dreams but that God would. And when he proceeded with the interpretation, he continued to identify God as the primary agent of action. Thus Pharaoh saw Joseph as "one in whom is the spirit of God" (41:38). I doubt Pharaoh knew much at this point about the God of Joseph, except that this God obviously possessed important power. But it was clear the Spirit of this God was in Joseph. However limited Pharaoh's knowledge of God, he sensed the presence of God's Spirit in a particular person.

So it is that in Genesis the Spirit of God is seen at work in the creation process, as a sustaining and perhaps correcting influence in the lives of persons who were indifferent to God, and as a presence so real in the life of a godly young man that a pagan ruler recognizes it.

The Spirit at Work

We see the continuing work of the Spirit in various ways. When persons are needed to design the articles for the Tabernacle, God calls Bezalel for the task, and fills him "with divine spirit, with ability, intelligence, and knowledge in every kind of craft, to devise artistic designs, to work in gold, silver, and bronze, in cutting stones for setting, and in carving wood, in every kind of craft" (Exodus 31:3-5). Bezalel's skills are not simply good craftsmanship; they are a result of his being filled with God's Spirit.

Does this instance suggest that all creative skills are evidences of God's Spirit at work? Possibly.

Does this mean every use of these skills is therefore divinely ordained? Not at all. Scripture indicates again and again that humans can use good gifts for evil purposes. But in spite of human waywardness, the Holy Spirit continues to invest creative gifts in human beings—one of the most significant expressions of common grace.

A tidy reader may be troubled by the manifestations of God's Spirit in the book of Judges. This book reports on a period of Israel's history when almost everything was going wrong, or perhaps, to put it more correctly, when the people of Israel were so often going wrong. Again and again, therefore, as circumstances grew desperate, the people sought help from God. The answers to their prayers came through a series of rather unlikely leaders. Several of them seem to have one thing in common: They were anointed by the Spirit of the Lord. So Othniel prevails over his enemies (Judges 3:10), Gideon enlists an army after the Spirit has taken possession of him (6:34), and Jephthah, after suffering rebuffs from anticipated allies, gains new strength when "the spirit of the LORD came upon" him (11:29).

But Samson is the most fascinating case. Dedicated to God's purposes before his birth, he grew under God's blessing; and then, "The spirit of the LORD began to stir him in Mahaneh-dan, between Zorah and Eshtaol" (13:25). The writer records the place much the way any of us might recall the details of a transforming experience. The Spirit of the Lord continued to visit him at special and—to us—peculiar times. When a young lion attacked him, "the spirit of the LORD rushed on him," and he was able to overwhelm the beast (14:6). When he got himself into a predicament at his wedding feast, again "the spirit of the LORD rushed on him"; and this time he used his strength to kill thirty men (14:19). Then, when he was securely bound by Israel's traditional enemy, the Philistines, "the spirit of the LORD rushed on him," and he broke the restraints as if they were nothing (15:14). In Judges the Spirit is often understood as a sudden onrush of power.

At least one thing is clear and significant in these incidents from the book of Judges: The Spirit uses the talents we have, and particularly the talents we make available. Othniel was a leader, Gideon and Jephthah were military men (though Gideon didn't at first realize it), and Samson was an exuberant bundle of strength. So the Spirit used what they were.

One thinks, on the other hand, of Moses. When he was called, he objected that he could not speak. Whether this was true, or simply his sense of personal insecurity, the Spirit did not make him into a gifted orator. Instead, God sent Moses' brother Aaron to help. The Spirit uses what we have and what we make available. And according to the biblical record, the Spirit uses what is needed in a given situation. Our possible offense at some of the stories from Judges may spring from our inability to relate to the circumstances and the ethos of the times and thereby recognize that the Spirit was using what was available.

According to the four Gospel accounts of Jesus' baptism—Matthew 3:13-17; Mark 1:9-11; Luke 3:21-22; John 1:32-34—the Spirit descended in the form of a dove. Depictions of the Holy Spirit as a dove always show the dove with a circle of light around its head, indicating a person of the Trinity. Each report of the baptism included the presence of the three Persons of the Trinity and the testimony of God's approval of the Son.

Early translators of the Bible used the Latin word *spiritus* to translate the Hebrew *ruach* and the Greek *pneuma*, both meaning "wind" and "breath." The Latin word translated directly into English as *spirit*.

Religious truths and experiences often are communicated through symbols. Such symbols were found for the Spirit. The oil of anointing is the one most often used in the Old Testament. Olive oil was a basic commodity in Middle Eastern life; it was food, lubricant, medicine, and illumination. As such it conveys the all-pervasiveness of God's Spirit, touching matters both essential and enriching.

So oil was used in all sorts of ceremonies where Israel desired to recognize the need and the presence of the Spirit in some given calling or task. Moses was instructed to make a special aromatic oil to anoint the tent of meeting, the ark, and numbers of sacred objects in the tent. With the same oil he was to anoint Aaron and his sons as part of their consecration to their task. Because of its sacred symbolism, this oil was not to be used "in any ordinary anointing of the body," and they were to "make no other like it in composition; it is holy, and it shall be holy to you" (Exodus 30:32).

Anointing oil appears repeatedly in the Old Testament story. Samuel uses it to anoint Saul as king (1 Samuel 10:1). The public ceremony of installation came later, but the matter was settled once the prophet poured the oil on Saul's head. So too a few years later when Samuel anointed David to succeed Saul. Several years would pass before David would actually come to the throne, but the anointing had been done; the Spirit's presence had been invoked. No doubt it is significant that as soon as the writer has told of David's anointing, and that "the spirit of the LORD came mightily upon David from that day forward," he goes on to report that "the spirit of the LORD departed from Saul" (16:13-14). In truth, Saul's reign was over, because the Spirit was gone from him; the actual end would come later.

The role of anointing oil has been claimed, even if only vaguely, by all who love Psalm 23. "You anoint my head with oil" (23:5). A reader can only speculate what the ancient poet had in mind. If the writer was David, was he thinking back on Samuel's anointing him? Or if the psalmist was some unknown person, was he or she reflecting on the kind of grandeur that had come into life with the touch of God's Spirit?

Oil as symbol of the Spirit carried over into the Christian practice of anointing and prayer for the sick. So James advised that if any are sick, "They should call for the elders of the church and have them pray over them, anointing them with oil in the name of the Lord" (James 5:14). The use of oil is not incidental; it is meant to carry the authority of the Spirit, just as it has for centuries in Jewish practice. Interesting too, oil is still used in baptism in some traditions, in the ordination of clergy, and in Great Britain in the ceremony of installing a monarch.

God With Us

One way or another, the essence of the doctrine of the Spirit in the Old Testament is the near presence of God. When the psalmist cries,

"Where can I go from your spirit?

Or where can I flee from your presence?" (Psalm 139:7), he is declaring both doctrine and experience. The Spirit of God has no boundaries, no limitations. The psalmist has found it to be so, and he senses that wherever he might go—to heaven or Sheol, even—God's Spirit will be there.

But the Spirit's activity in the Old Testament is generally selective rather than democratic. The prophet Joel foresaw a day of which God would say,

"I will pour out my spirit on all flesh;

your sons and your daughters shall prophesy,

your old men shall dream dreams,

and your young men shall see visions.

Even on the male and female slaves,

in those days, I will pour out my spirit" (Joel 2:28-29). The wonder of this prophecy was its contrast to the customary experience. The anointing of the Spirit was usually received by priests, prophets, or national leaders. It was not something for "all flesh," nor was it enjoyed by "the male and female slaves." The Spirit came to a rather special few, for special purposes, generally having to do with the wider welfare of the people of God.

But when the narrative of God's salvation is picked up in the New Testament, already there is a hint of the greater day Joel had envisioned. Having given us the genealogy of Jesus, Matthew writes, "Now the birth of Jesus the Messiah took place in this way," and goes on to say that Mary "was found to be with child from the Holy Spirit" (Matthew 1:18). She is not a priest, a prophet, or a potential ruler. She is about to take one of the most democratic of roles, that of mother. But the Holy Spirit has come upon her. The Spirit's coming is not only a miracle of conception; it is a preliminary announcement of a new order. The Spirit has begun a broader, graciously inclusive work.

This mood is expressed in another way when Jesus comes to the synagogue in his home town. Having read the passage from Isaiah 61, "The Spirit of the Lord is upon me" (Luke 4:18), he announces to the congregation, "Today this scripture has been fulfilled in your hearing" (4:21). Jesus' statement is not only a declaration that the prophecy has been fulfilled in him; it is also an announcement of the wider action of God's Spirit. The Spirit is, in fact, being set loose in the world.

In Jesus' discourse with his disciples on the night before his crucifixion, he assures them that though he is going away, they will not be forsaken, because "I will ask the Father, and he will give you another Advocate, to be with you forever. This is the Spirit of truth, whom the world cannot receive, because it neither sees him nor knows him" (John 14:16-17). The disciples must surely have felt this was a poor exchange, to lose the clear presence of Jesus for the comparatively immaterial Advocate. But Jesus insisted they would be better off: "I tell you the truth: it is to your advantage that I go away, for if I do not go away,

Paraclete, a Greek word that means "called to the side of," is a name for the Holy Spirit. In various versions of the New Testament it is translated "advocate," "comforter," "helper," and "counselor." Origen differentiated its meaning by translating it "intercessor" for Christ and "counselor" for the Holy Spirit.

the Advocate will not come to you" (16:7). The Spirit is promised, more than ever, to be "God with us."

Nevertheless, the Spirit is never portrayed as being so present as to be under human control. The ancient poet, burdened by his sense of sin, pleads especially,

"Do not cast me away from your presence,
and do not take your holy spirit from me" (Psalm 51:11).

The psalmist knows it is possible that God's Spirit could be taken from him, and he fears the possibility. Whether the writer is David or some other ancient believer, he knows he dare not presume upon the Spirit of God. In our relationship with God, as in all other relationships, familiarity can breed, if not contempt, at least casualness. Precisely because the Spirit is intimate, close, immediate.

Jesus added new emphasis to this theme when he said, "Therefore I tell you, people will be forgiven for every sin and blasphemy, but blasphemy against the Spirit will not be forgiven. Whoever speaks a word against the Son of Man will be forgiven, but whoever speaks against the Holy Spirit will not be forgiven, either in this age or in the age to come" (Matthew 12:31-32). Perhaps because of the very intimacy of the Spirit, sin against the Spirit is incomparably serious. To abuse the Spirit is to reject God when God is approaching us in openness.

Conscience and the Holy Spirit

Is the Holy Spirit, then, closely tied to the concept of conscience? The Spirit is usually understood as the member of the Trinity who convicts of sin and who draws the sinner back to God. Is conscience a manifestation of the Holy Spirit?

Conscience is referred to some twenty to thirty times in the New Testament (depending on the translation used). So Paul, in explaining how persons without the Old Testament knowledge of God might still "do instinctively what the law requires" (Romans 2:14), continues, "They show that what the law requires is written on their hearts, to which their own conscience also bears witness" (2:15). When he wants to emphasize that he is speaking the truth, he says, "My conscience confirms it by the Holy Spirit" (9:1). Peter's first letter urges, "Keep your conscience clear, so that, when you are maligned, those who abuse you for your good conduct in Christ may be put to shame" (1 Peter 3:16).

Clearly the New Testament writers saw conscience as an ally of God's Spirit. Nevertheless, conscience is not to be understood as synonymous with the Spirit. The conscience is conditioned by association and experience. Conscience is the product of our reading, our hearing, and a vast variety of passing influences. For a person living in a highly permissive culture, the conscience can become so broad as to be nearly meaningless. For such a person to say, "My conscience doesn't bother me," reveals nothing more than the culture that has shaped that conscience. On the other hand, the conscience of someone condi-

tioned by severe restrictions will outdo God in its requirements. Such a person will need John's reminder that when our
hearts condemn us, "God is greater than our hearts, and he
knows everything" (1 John 3:20).

The conscience can be favorably shaped by many of the
same elements that convey grace or faith to our lives. The
Scriptures, godly reading and music, preaching and worship,
nurturing friendships—all these can strengthen the conscience
and make it a more effective instrument of the Holy Spirit.
Without a doubt, the conscience is meant to fulfill such a function. But like all elements of possible good in our culture, conscience is subject to our use and misuse.

The Controversy of the Spirit

If the Holy Spirit is, as we said earlier, the unknown member
of the Trinity, it may also be the most controversial. For example, let us look at the issue that troubles Eastern and Western
Christendom, a large matter resting on a small word, the Latin
que (and). The Nicene Creed, as adopted by the First Council
of Constantinople in A.D. 381, declared that the Holy Spirit
"proceeds from the Father." Augustine (A.D. 354–430) became
more specific, saying that the Holy Spirit proceeds from the
Father "principally," and "commonly from both," Father and
Son. The Third Council of Toledo (A.D. 589) condemned "those
who do not believe . . . that the Holy Spirit proceeds from the
Father and the Son." So the controversy continued back and
forth, until in A.D. 1012 an emperor persuaded the pope to add
the phrase "and the Son" to the creed used in the Roman
church. This position was officially rejected by the Eastern
(Orthodox) Church in A.D. 1054 and has been a point of division between the two major bodies of Christendom ever since.
Protestants generally subscribe to the Roman view.

The Eastern Church meant to maintain the equality of the
Holy Spirit with the Father. They feared that a doctrine that said
the Spirit proceeds also from the Son would suggest that the
Spirit originates from the Father only secondarily, and that the
Spirit is therefore inferior to the Father. They were also seeking
to protect the Father's originating role as perfect and complete.
Again, they feared that adding *filioque* ("and the Son") would
make the Father's role imperfect and partial. On the other hand,
the Western view clarifies that Jesus Christ is the content of the
Holy Spirit; that is, that the Holy Spirit is the Spirit of Christ at
work in the world, and that this is achieved by the Father and
the Son.

In the midst of such controversy we dare not lose the basic
concepts of the work and presence of the Holy Spirit in our
world. And particularly the possibilities of the work of the Holy
Spirit in our own lives. From the beginning of the biblical
canon, when God's act of creation involves the "rushing-spirit
of God," to its end, with its gracious invitation, "The Spirit and
the bride say, 'Come'" (Revelation 22:17), the Holy Spirit is a

wondrous reality. Sometimes subtle, often unpredictable, but always present, it is the Spirit that reveals to us most of what we know about God—and therefore, what we know of reality.

> BECAUSE WE THE CHURCH BELIEVE God is present with us in the Holy Spirit, I will live with a sense of the wondrous nearness of God.

BELIEVING AND LIVING

Mystery intrigues us, but it also unsettles us. No wonder we have such ambivalence about the Holy Spirit. Here is mystery indeed—as intangible as the wind or the breath of God, yet as real and demanding as an incoming tide. When have you experienced the Holy Spirit in your life?

_____

_____

How would you explain the Holy Spirit as presence to someone who is seeking a sense of God in daily living?

_____

_____

Describe your sense of the ministry of the Spirit in the Old Testament, and in the New Testament.

_____

_____

How do you understand the statement that Israel was the people of God while the church is the community of the Spirit?

_____

_____

What do you find most difficult to understand or accept about the Holy Spirit? What do you find reassuring?

_____

_____

SEEKING MORE UNDERSTANDING

In the biblical narrative the activity of the Spirit in and through the lives of women is more often implied than detailed. Look at some of their stories through the eyes of faith that the Spirit of God was present to them and at work in them: Sarah, Hagar, Pharaoh's daughter, Deborah, Hannah, Esther, Huldah, Mary, Elizabeth. What do you see?

PRAYER

"O thou who camest from above,
   the pure celestial fire to impart,
kindle a flame of sacred love
   upon the mean altar of my heart.

There let it for thy glory burn
   with inextinguishable blaze,
and trembling to its source return,
   in humble prayer and fervent praise.

Jesus, confirm my heart's desire
   to work and speak and think for thee;
still let me guard the holy fire,
   and still stir up thy gift in me.

Ready for all thy perfect will,
   my acts of faith and love repeat,
till death thy endless mercies seal,
   and make my sacrifice complete."
—"O Thou Who Camest From Above,"
Charles Wesley, 1707–1788

18

Comforter

Empowering

**God present
in power**

Pentecost

Agent of
change

Convicting
power

**Gifts
of the
Spirit**

God's Spirit
bearing witness
with our spirit

**Fruit
of the
Spirit**

Guaranteeing the truth of Christ

Cleansing and purifying power

Power to Live and to Serve

*"You will receive power when the Holy
Spirit has come upon you; and you will be my
witnesses."*

—Acts 1:8

LIFE QUESTIONS

Jesus promised that when the Holy Spirit came,
his followers would receive power. The book of
Acts reports that the Holy Spirit did indeed come.
And when we read what happened in those early
days of the church, we're impressed that it was a
lively time.

But what is the power of the Holy Spirit? And
who may have it? Why isn't the church in general,
and why aren't individual Christians in particular,
more surely possessed of such power? And what
shall we say about some of the rather exotic hap-
penings attributed to the Holy Spirit? Is God at
work in these remarkable ways?

ASSIGNMENT

Our study of the Holy Spirit now moves to the
New Testament, first, in the life of Jesus, and then
more especially in the life of the early church.
From there we move quite naturally to the role of
the Holy Spirit in the world today, and particularly
in our own lives.

As you read these passages, watch for application to the present day, and to our own lives. How
do the stories in Acts and the counsel in the letters
fit our time and our lives? How might the church
and individual believers become more effective
witnesses to the faith?

Day 1   John 3:1-8 (born of the Spirit); 16:1-15
(the Spirit of truth)
Introduction and Readings 191 and 192

Day 2   Acts 1:1-11 (promise of Holy Spirit baptism); 2 (filled with the Holy Spirit)
Readings 193 and 194

Day 3   Acts 10 (Holy Spirit given the Gentiles);
19:1-7 (Ephesians receive the Holy Spirit)
Readings 195 and 196

Day 4   1 Corinthians 12 (one Spirit, many gifts);
14 (all things for building up)
Reading 197

Day 5   Ephesians 4:1-16 (one body and one
Spirit); 1 John 4:1-6 (test the spirits)
Readings 198 and 199

Day 6   Read and respond to "The Church Teaching
and Believing" and "Believing and Living."

Day 7   Rest and prayer

DAILY PRAYER

Pray for the persons and situations on your
Prayer Concerns list and about issues or concerns
emerging from your daily reading and study.

SCRIPTURE	READINGS

DAY 1

John 3:1-8; 16:1-15	Introduction and Readings 191 and 192

DAY 2

Acts 1:1-11; 2	Readings 193 and 194

DAY 3

Acts 10; 19:1-7	Readings 195 and 196

SCRIPTURE	READINGS

DAY 4

1 Corinthians 12; 14	Reading 197

DAY 5

Ephesians 4:1-16; 1 John 4:1-6	Readings 198 and 199

DAY 6 STUDY MANUAL	PRAYER CONCERNS
"The Church Teaching and Believing" and "Believing and Living"	

THE CHURCH TEACHING AND BELIEVING

If Jesus hoped to make an impact on the pagan and somewhat sophisticated first-century world, he might have been expected to start with a more impressive core group. From all outward appearances, not one of the first disciples was a potential leader. Certainly none of them belonged to the power structures of their time, nor were any of them trained to influence the wider society into which they were about to go.

And yet, they did what assessments of their abilities would have said they couldn't do. The first generation of believers was still relatively new when a mob in a major European city spoke of the Christians as "these people who have been turning the world upside down" (Acts 17:6). Even after discounting the statement as inflated mob language, it is still impressive. With so little going for them, and with no apparent strategy other than the general order to go into all the world, beginning with Jerusalem, how did these first believers accomplish so much? What was their secret?

New Life, New Birth

One of the most intriguing conversations in the New Testament engages Jesus and Nicodemus, a leading Pharisee. Jesus advises Nicodemus he cannot see the kingdom of God without being born again, or born from above. When Nicodemus seeks further information, Jesus explains he must be "born of water and Spirit. What is born of the flesh is flesh, and what is born of the Spirit is spirit" (John 3:5-6).

Here is further evidence of the new democracy of the Spirit's work. Jesus' insistence that a person must be born of the Spirit in order to enter God's kingdom indicates this is an experience available to all. The Spirit is not restricted to special persons or to persons with special ministries. But the Spirit is strategically involved in new life, and at an individual level. Perhaps this conversation indicates as clearly as anything before the Day of Pentecost that the Spirit, in the New Testament, is a potentially active agent for all the human race.

On the night before the Crucifixion, Jesus spoke at length about the larger role of the Holy Spirit. "You know him," Jesus said, "because he abides with you, and he will be in you" (14:17). He spelled out some of the details of the Spirit's role a bit later (16:8-11). And particularly Jesus said of the Spirit, "He will glorify me, because he will take what is mine and declare it to you" (16:14).

Power for a Purpose

The work of the Holy Spirit is, above all else, to glorify Christ. Jesus told the disciples they will receive power when the Holy Spirit comes on them, but it is power to a particular end, so they can become witnesses of Christ wherever they go (Acts 1:8). This seems never to have been lost on the disciples. They were advocates for Jesus, not for the Holy Spirit. As miracles followed their ministry in the opening chapters of Acts, the disciples constantly noted that what had happened had been "in the name of Jesus." Clearly enough, the Holy Spirit was to them always a means to an end, and not an end in itself. The Holy Spirit was in the world in this larger role in order to reveal Christ and to bring glory to him, not to draw attention to the Spirit or to the work of the Spirit.

But it is also clear the followers of Jesus would not be able to do their work as witnesses for their Lord except as the Holy Spirit gave them power. Theirs was a task beyond simple human ability; not even the best of talent could convict persons of sin, and it surely could not transmit the Spirit of Christ to others. And for that matter, the disciples did not represent the best human ability. They were quite ordinary men and women. That only makes clearer that the effectiveness of their remarkable ministries was from outside themselves. Jesus had told the disciples they must abide in him, "because apart from me you can do nothing" (John 15:5). Now, with the power of the Holy Spirit, they were able to abide in him and to do greater works than they had ever imagined.

Pentecost

Soon after Jesus' ascension, the disciples and others of the most devout gathered in Jerusalem, in an upstairs room, to pray and take care of the business of their little group. While there, on the day of Pentecost, they experienced the extraordinary visitation of the Spirit. "And suddenly from heaven there came a sound like the rush of a violent wind, and it filled the entire house where they were sitting. Divided tongues, as of fire, appeared among them, and a tongue rested on each of them. All of them were filled with the Holy Spirit and began to speak in other languages, as the Spirit gave them ability" (Acts 2:2-4).

Each of the elements of this event has obvious significance. The "violent wind" reminds us again of the Creation story, and of the way both the Hebrew and the Greek use *wind* and *spirit* interchangeably. Perhaps too, this "wind" suggests a new creative activity coming into the world through this fresh action of God's Spirit. The tongues of fire remind us of the cleansing nature of fire, recalling especially the experience of the prophet Isaiah. When he saw the holiness of God, he recognized he was "a man of unclean lips" in the midst of "a people of unclean lips" (Isaiah 6:5). His cleansing came when a seraph touched his mouth with a coal of fire. The tongues of fire suggest just such a dramatic remedy for the sin that perverts humanity's power of communication. The new power of the Holy Spirit is, among other things, a cleansing and a purifying of the communication process.

But above all, it is an extension of the power of communication. And the democracy of the Spirit is especially notable. The experience had come to "all of them" (Acts 2:4), and now they were speaking in tongues that could be understood by the multitudes who were milling about outside their meeting place. They were "devout Jews," but they were "from every nation under heaven" (2:5). Their astonishment is that "we hear, each of us, in our own native language" (2:8). A new geography has come to the human experience, and particularly to the religious experience. Religion, which heretofore had been very much a national matter, with a single holy place and generally a holy language, was now expressing itself in every imaginable tongue. A new day had indeed come.

Peter confirmed, in his sermon to the assembled crowd, that this was a new day, for a larger world. He referred to Joel's prophecy about God's pouring out the Spirit "upon all flesh" (2:17). He made it also a warning of judgment still to come. But then Peter turned the focus on Jesus. In doing so, he demonstrated what Jesus had said the Holy Spirit would do—glorify Christ (John 16:14). Nevertheless, as Peter concluded his sermon with a call to repentance, it was with the promise that his hearers too would "receive the gift of the Holy Spirit" (Acts 2:38). And then again, the gracious, far-reaching word: "For the promise is for you, for your children, and for all who are far away, everyone whom the Lord our God calls to him" (2:39). The Holy Spirit is available to all, and Peter gladly announced that fact.

Holy Spirit Action

The Holy Spirit is the constant agent of action in the book of Acts. When Peter and John were called before the council, they were not intimidated. Peter, "filled with the Holy Spirit," answered his questioners (Acts 4:8). Facing persecution by the authorities, the company of believers prayed together, and then they were "all filled with the Holy Spirit," so they could speak "the word of God with boldness" (4:31). When Ananias lied to

In the Old Testament, fire is seen as a symbol of God's presence and power—God in the burning bush calling Moses (Exodus 3:1-6), God in the pillar of fire guiding the Israelites (13:21). So the tongues of fire at Pentecost symbolizing the arrival of the empowering Holy Spirit would have been quickly recognized as the presence and power of God. That power for believers is depicted as a seven-tongued flame representing the seven gifts of the Holy Spirit—prophecy, ministry, teaching, exhorting, giving, leading, and compassion (Romans 12:6-8).

Peter about his gift, Peter asked how he would dare "to lie to the Holy Spirit" (5:3). In another instance of public showdown, Peter said that the believers were witnesses to what Jesus did, "and so is the Holy Spirit whom God has given to those who obey him" (5:32). Whatever the issues or concerns, the Holy Spirit is the constant factor.

The activity of the Holy Spirit became the clinching point of persuasion when Peter preached to the household of Cornelius. Peter had been convinced by a vision and by the Spirit (10:19) that he must go to Cornelius's home, even though Cornelius was a Gentile. But while Peter was still preaching, he and his companions were "astounded that the gift of the Holy Spirit had been poured out even on the Gentiles" (10:45). No further evidence was needed; Peter asked simply, "Can anyone withhold the water for baptizing these people who have received the Holy Spirit just as we have?" (10:47).

And yet it is interesting to see that the knowledge of the Holy Spirit wasn't universal in some segments of the early church. When Paul came to Ephesus, he asked believers there if they had received the Holy Spirit. Their answer, rather surprisingly, was, "No, we have not even heard that there is a Holy Spirit" (19:2). It appears they had become believers on the knowledge of Jesus that had come through John's baptism of repentance.

Jesus had promised that when the Holy Spirit came to the disciples, in what obviously was to be a new and more far-reaching way, "he will prove the world wrong about sin and righteousness and judgment: about sin, because they do not believe in me; about righteousness, because I am going to the Father and you will see me no longer; about judgment, because the ruler of this world has been condemned" (John 16:8-11). Sin, righteousness, and judgment—these are matters about which humans aren't easily convinced. They have to do with our estimate of ourselves and our inclination to think ourselves in the right. We aren't ready to be told that we are not right, that we sin, and that judgment is coming. We are especially unprepared to consider our sin has to do with our not believing in Christ, or that judgment has to do with something so beyond our grasp as the condemnation of "the ruler of this world."

Especially if conviction leads to change. We humans enjoy a remarkable dichotomy. We can acknowledge something intellectually, recognizing its logic, yet have no real moral compulsion to change. We need some persuasion beyond logic if we are to act upon the rightness we know. This compelling persuasion is the work of the Holy Spirit. The disciples needed such resources if they were to encounter their culture in a new way.

At that point the disciples were the fragile link between the person and teaching of Jesus and the world at large. The Spirit was the guarantor of that link. It remains so to the present day.

Without doubt, the first disciples operated with power from beyond themselves. As Acts says, "they were uneducated and ordinary men" (Acts 4:13)—and that phrase is attached to the best of them, Peter and John. They dared to challenge ensconced power; and when their audacity was challenged, they prayed for "all boldness," and the Holy Spirit granted it (4:29-31). Jesus had promised, "Very truly, I tell you, the one who believes in me will also do the works that I do and, in fact, will do greater works than these, because I am going to the Father" (John 14:12). They seemed quite simply to take Jesus at his word, until they were cutting an increasingly wide swath through the paganism and bewilderment of the first-century world. These people who had forsaken Jesus at the trial and Crucifixion seemed now to be indifferent to potential martyrdom.

We can think of only two explanations—the Resurrection and the infilling of the Holy Spirit. But the Resurrection alone would not have brought these results. Matthew reports, with admirable honesty, that when the eleven remaining disciples saw Jesus in a Resurrection appearance, "they worshiped him; but some doubted" (Matthew 28:17). Even on the day of Jesus' ascension, their questions still centered on the coming of Israel's kingdom. Surely the new presence of the Holy Spirit made the difference, and made the resurrection of their Lord an operative reality in their lives.

Fruit and Gifts

Two particular manifestations of the Holy Spirit deserve attention. *Fruit* is mentioned quite frequently in both the Old Testament and New Testament, but not often specifically as fruit of the Spirit. Paul uses this term in the letter to the Galatians, as he compares the life of the flesh with the life of the Spirit. "By contrast, the fruit of the Spirit is love, joy, peace, patience, kindness, generosity, faithfulness, gentleness, and self-control. There is no law against such things" (Galatians 5:22-23). These nine qualities are often held up as the essence of godly or Christlike living.

The term *fruit of the Spirit* indicates the early church had much more in mind than simply genteel behavior or carefully developed character. These are qualities of life and conduct made possible by the presence of the Holy Spirit. To be true to the figure of speech, they are nothing other than an outgrowth of the presence of the Spirit in a life. While the several qualities exist in our general culture (an evidence, we might say, of common grace), the fruit of the Spirit is different not only in degree but in its origin, nature, and expression. While believers ought surely to seek the fruit of the Spirit, they should also know that such fruit is a natural, predictable product of the presence of the Holy Spirit in our lives.

The *gifts of the Spirit* are discussed at much greater length, no doubt because they were more controversial. And also, no doubt because they were an object of greater fascination in the church, just as they are today. Biblical scholars have compiled various lists of the gifts of the Spirit. The most familiar of the gifts, and the ones most often discussed, are in 1 Corinthians

12–14—wisdom, knowledge, faith, healing, working miracles, prophecy, discernment of spirits, tongues, and interpretation of tongues. Considering these gifts, Paul says they "are activated by one and the same Spirit, who allots to each one individually just as the Spirit chooses" (12:11).

The gifts listed in Romans 12:6-8 include prophecy, but introduce several others—ministry, teaching, exhorting, giving, leading, and compassion. A list in Ephesians emphasizes what we might call offices in the church—"some would be apostles, some prophets, some evangelists, some pastors and teachers, to equip the saints for the work of ministry, for building up the body of Christ" (Ephesians 4:11-12). Peter makes no attempt to identify particular gifts but urges, "Like good stewards of the manifold grace of God, serve one another with whatever gift each of you has received. Whoever speaks must do so as one speaking the very words of God; whoever serves must do so with the strength that God supplies, so that God may be glorified in all things through Jesus Christ" (1 Peter 4:10-11).

When we compare the fruit of the Spirit with the gifts of the Spirit, we notice immediately that where the fruit of the Spirit have to do with interior character, and usually are not easily identified, the gifts of the Spirit are almost always matters of public ministry. Scholars as well as general readers will confess it is hard to distinguish among these gifts. We can't delineate with certainty the differences among prophecy, ministry, teaching, and exhorting, or how these might overlap with the other list of apostles, prophets, evangelists, pastors, and teachers.

In Paul's day there was some controversy over who was an apostle. But the greater issue had to do with the comparative importance of the gifts listed in Paul's letter to the Corinthians.

In at least some of the early churches, gifts of the Spirit were manifested in almost every gathering. "When you come together, each one has a hymn, a lesson, a revelation, a tongue, or an interpretation" (1 Corinthians 14:26). These expressions were so frequent Paul set down regulations for their use. For speaking in tongues, for example, "let there be only two or at most three, and each in turn; and let one interpret" (14:27).

And although these were gifts of the Spirit, they were under the control of the user and they were to be regulated by the community. Thus the person who was inclined to speak in tongues was not to do so unless someone was present with the gift of interpretation (14:28). And after prophets had spoken, others were to "weigh what is said" (14:29). This suggests that though a prophet might think his or her message was of God, it was nevertheless to come under the judgment of the community. We see here a healthy recognition that though the Holy Spirit may bestow a gift, the gift is still being expressed through very human channels; as such it is susceptible to error, and must therefore be brought under the discipline of the larger community, the community of the Holy Spirit.

The most urgent controversy in some parts of the early

church (and for certain, in Corinth) was the use of the gift of tongues—what is termed *glossolalia* in our day. Those who exercised this gift were inclined to think it the most important gift. A not surprising thought; it was one of the most noticeable gifts, and one that apparently could be exercised almost at will. Gifts of healing and miracles might be more impressive when in action, but they didn't always happen. As for gifts like wisdom and knowledge, who could say for sure when they were at work? The gift of tongues, however, was another matter. Add the fact that they usually had an ecstatic quality, and we can see why this gift was so attractive.

Glossolalia is a key element in the contemporary pentecostal movement (often referred to as the charismatic renewal movement). Other elements are also present, but glossolalia is the distinguishing characteristic. It is found in almost all Christian bodies, both Catholic and Protestant, and occasionally in the Orthodox church as well. It is not an organized movement but an experiential one.

Some see this pentecostal movement as the hope of the church. Others oppose it vigorously—often on the ground that all such markedly supernatural manifestations of the Holy Spirit ceased after the first or second century of church history, after they had fulfilled a particular purpose. At best, the pentecostal movement brings obvious qualities of joy and enthusiasm to the church; at worst, qualities of self-righteousness and sometimes, doctrinal casualness. At its best, pentecostalism is no doubt an activity of the Holy Spirit, even if sometimes exploited or abused. A tough-minded observer might note, of course, that the work of the Holy Spirit has always, in some measure, been exploited and abused, beginning with incidents in the New Testament—further evidence God works through human beings, and that is never a tidy process.

The New Testament makes one thing clear about the gifts of the Spirit and of the larger work of the Holy Spirit. In his discussion of the gifts Paul says, "Let all things be done for building up" (1 Corinthians 14:26). The same idea is expressed in a different listing of the gifts of the Spirit; these gifts, the writer reminds, are "to equip the saints for the work of ministry, for building up the body of Christ" (Ephesians 4:12).

And never is it said better than when Paul interrupts his discussion of gifts to say, "I will show you a still more excellent way" (1 Corinthians 12:31), after which he points us to love, without which we "gain nothing" (13:3). We can hardly imagine the Holy Spirit working in any other way.

Glossolalia, from the Greek *glosso* (tongue) and *lalia* (talking), describes speaking in tongues in worship services, ecstatic speech sometimes called "prayer language." The word was coined in the nineteenth century to designate a practice common in New Testament times and described in 1 Corinthians 14:6, 32. *Glossolalia* has survived in the church in pentecostalism and in the charismatic renewal movement.

BECAUSE WE THE CHURCH BELIEVE the Holy Spirit gives power to live and to serve, I will expect and be open to the power of the Holy Spirit in my daily living.

BELIEVING AND LIVING

Think of someone you would judge to be a truly Spirit-filled person? Why do you say that of this individual?

_____

_____

Think about your church. What hesitancy about the Holy Spirit are you aware of in the congregation as a whole and in individual members? When and in what ways does your congregation seek and claim the power of the Holy Spirit?

_____

_____

How have you experienced Holy Spirit power?

_____

_____

What gifts of the Spirit do you think you have seen in operation? What has impressed you most about these gifts?

_____

_____

In one column, list the fruit of the Spirit from Galatians 5:22-23. In another column, list ten or twelve Christians you especially admire. Now match the two columns, recognizing that you may have several persons for some fruit and none for others. What conclusions do you draw?

Fruit of the Spirit	Admired Christians

What fruit and gifts of the Spirit do you see in yourself?

_____

_____

SEEKING MORE UNDERSTANDING

The book of Acts is generally referred to as the Acts of the Apostles. But in fact the action in Acts is that of the Holy Spirit. Find a time to read the whole book at once with the specific purpose of watching the Holy Spirit at work. Take note of Holy Spirit presence and power.

PRAYER

"O Almighty God, who on the day of Pentecost didst send the Holy Ghost the comforter to abide in thy Church unto the end: Bestow upon us and upon all thy faithful people his manifold gifts of grace, that with minds enlightened by his truth and hearts purified by his presence, we may day by day be strengthened with power in the inward man; through Jesus Christ our Lord, who with thee and the same Spirit liveth and reigneth, one God world without end."

—*Scottish Prayer Book*

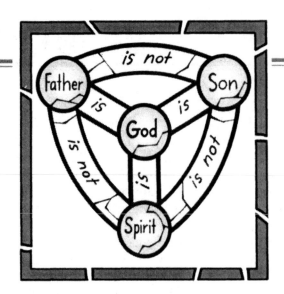

19

Godhead   **Trinity**   Equality

Father   Son   Holy Spirit

Distinction   Unity

**Same essence   Eternal loving
or substance   relationship**

Indivisible in will and action

One God three Persons

The Mystery and Message of the Trinity

"Go therefore and make disciples of all nations,
baptizing them in the name of the Father and of
the Son and of the Holy Spirit."

—*Matthew 28:19*

LIFE QUESTIONS

The doctrine of the Trinity may be the one particular doctrine people are most likely to want explained. It is also the one about which the pastor or teacher most dreads to be questioned. After all, how does one explain that there is only one God, yet insist that God is "in three Persons, blessed Trinity"? The question is far too abstract for most of us. What sense can I make of the doctrine of the Trinity, and what does the Trinity have to do with my relationship with God? What difference does the Trinity make to my daily living?

ASSIGNMENT

Most Christian theologians think that the doctrine of the Trinity is inferred in the Old Testament, but the language carrying the concept of Trinity—Father, Son, Holy Spirit—is found only in the New Testament. Therefore, our Scripture comes almost entirely from the New Testament. As we read these passages, we will see that they do not explicitly spell out the doctrine; they simply provide the several pieces from which the early church constructed a coherent whole.

Day 1 Genesis 1:26-31 (creation of humankind);
        Deuteronomy 6:1-9 (God, the Lord alone)
        Readings 200 and 201

Day 2 Isaiah 63:1-14 (recalling God's mercy);
        Mark 1:1-14 (Jesus' baptism)
        Readings 202 and 203

Day 3 John 14 (Holy Spirit promised); 15:26–16:15
        (Jesus announces his departure)
        Readings 204 and 205

Day 4 Acts 2:22-39 (Peter's Pentecost sermon);
        Romans 1:1-7 (Paul's witness)
        Readings 206, 207, and 208

Day 5 1 John 5:1-12 (the Spirit's witness); Revelation 22:8-21 (Alpha and Omega)
        Readings 209 and 210

Day 6 Read and respond to "The Church Teaching and Believing" and "Believing and Living."

Day 7 Rest and prayer

DAILY PRAYER

Pray for the persons and situations on your Prayer Concerns list and about issues or concerns emerging from your daily reading and study.

SCRIPTURE	READINGS
DAY 1	
Genesis 1:26-31; Deuteronomy 6:1-9	Readings 200 and 201
DAY 2	
Isaiah 63:1-14; Mark 1:1-14	Readings 202 and 203
DAY 3	
John 14; 15:26–16:15	Readings 204 and 205

SCRIPTURE	READINGS
DAY 4
Acts 2:22-39; Romans 1:1-7	**Readings 206, 207, and 208**
DAY 5
1 John 5:1-12; Revelation 22:8-21	**Readings 209 and 210**

DAY 6 **STUDY MANUAL**	**PRAYER CONCERNS**
"The Church Teaching and Believing" and "Believing and Living"	

THE CHURCH TEACHING AND BELIEVING

The word *Trinity* is not in the Apostles' Creed, the Nicene Creed, or in the Bible. But in any part of the world where the Christian faith is significantly present, it is a rare city that doesn't have a church, a hospital, a school, or some agency of mercy named "Trinity" or "Holy Trinity." *Trinity* is a word that differentiates Christianity from the other two great monotheistic religions, Judaism and Islam. Trinity is also a doctrine that represents a division within historic Christianity, not only in those bodies that explicitly define themselves as Unitarian but also in persons who belong to Trinitarian communions but whose beliefs are not clearly defined.

So although the word *Trinity* is not in the creeds or the Scriptures, the doctrine itself is an ancient and nearly inviolable part of the Christian faith. Thus when Luther's people presented a confession of faith to the Diet of the Holy Roman Empire at Augsburg in 1530, the doctrine of the Trinity was the first article. It was a tacit acknowledgment that if Protestantism were to be taken seriously, it must be orthodox in this primary matter. While the sixteenth-century Protestant reformers (Martin Luther, Ulrich Zwingli, John Calvin, and others) dissociated themselves from many teachings that must have held sentimental value for them and that they had once considered primary—such as teachings on the sacraments and the Virgin Mary—they never wavered on the issue of the Trinity. When the Church of England separated from Rome, it drew up Thirty-Nine Articles that would constitute its faith statement. The first of these is "Of Faith in the Holy Trinity." When John Wesley, in his eighty-first year, shortened those thirty-nine articles to twenty-five for use by the rising Methodist movement, he too began with the Trinity, with a statement identical to the original in all its important parts. Only in the last three centuries has this doctrine been challenged in any serious way.

The History of the Doctrine

The doctrine of the Trinity, perhaps more than any other doctrine, is a case of formation following experience. Consider that the first body of Christians were Jews by belief. Consider that for Jews the definitive statement of their believing was the *Shema:* "Hear, O Israel: The LORD is our God, the LORD is one" (Deuteronomy 6:4). This was the grand deposit of their faith, that which made them different from neighboring nations, and that which they were called to extend to all other peoples. It was out of their belief that God is one that all other belief and conduct flowed.

But now there was Jesus Christ. He had showed himself to be God. He had done so naturally, as an acknowledgment of fact, without arrogance or pretense; and against all their prior inclination, they had found it to be so—particularly after his resurrection and their infilling with the Holy Spirit.

And the Holy Spirit was a further complication. Clearly, now, God was with them in a unique way. Jesus had said that after his own departure "the Advocate, the Holy Spirit, whom the Father will send in my name, will teach you everything, and remind you of all that I have said to you" (John 14:26). Then, as the risen Jesus left them, he told them to make disciples of all nations, "baptizing them in the name of the Father and of the Son and of the Holy Spirit" (Matthew 28:19).

So here they were, with a body of experiences and teachings. All of them were trustworthy; none could justifiably be denied or laid aside. Their problem was to put together in a viable whole the pieces that were irrefutable. Perhaps we should not be surprised that the doctrine of the Trinity is difficult to enunciate. *Trinity* is, in a real sense, our word for what we know to be true but can't fully explain.

The Biblical Heritage

But the church did not go at its task in a theological vacuum. The idea of complexity in the unity of God existed in some form from early times. In the Creation story, the writer of Genesis reports, "God said, 'Let *us* make humankind in *our* image, according to our likeness,'" then goes on to say,

"So God created humankind in his image,
in the image of God he created them;
male and female he created them" (Genesis
1:26-27).

So the writer goes from a plural to a singular reference without pause or explanation. Some scholars have suggested that the "us" and "our" referred to the heavenly company; but as even Jewish scholars acknowledge, no other reference to angels appears in the story. And for that matter, such an explanation only complicates the problem, because it would suggest that the angelic company was equal with God in order that the creation could be in "our" image.

Other instances of such plural language are found in the Old Testament (for example, Genesis 11:7; Isaiah 6:8), but such cases may or may not prove anything. So too with what are called *theophanies*—appearances or visitations by God in some visible form. "Three men" visit Abraham and Sarah at the oaks of Mamre, but as the conversation develops, "the LORD" becomes the speaker in the group (Genesis 18). Was this a visitation by the Holy Spirit?

As the biblical story unfolds, the Spirit becomes a rather frequent though unpredictable factor in events. The phrase "the spirit of the LORD" or "the spirit of God" appears again and again through the Old Testament. This participation by God through the Spirit is entirely similar to what in the New Testament we come to see as the work of the Holy Spirit. It is similar enough so that when the Christian community experienced the Holy Spirit at Pentecost, Peter explained to the crowd that this was nothing other than what the prophet Joel had promised:

"In the last days it will be, God declares,
that I will pour out my Spirit upon all flesh" (Acts 2:17).

Jesus, God, and the Holy Spirit become intertwined and interactive. When Jesus is baptized by John, the Spirit descends on Jesus like a dove, and a voice from heaven says, "You are my Son, the Beloved; with you I am well pleased" (Mark 1:10-11). This is a Trinitarian event; all three parties are so identified—God, the Spirit, and the Son. The writer of the Gospel doesn't bother to explain this complex happening. But since the Gospel of Mark probably was written a little more than three decades after Jesus' crucifixion and resurrection, no explanation was necessary; the experience of the Trinity was already a common possession of the church and accepted as a fact. Explanations would come later, as needed.

John's Gospel gives the most detailed account of the relationship between Jesus and the Holy Spirit, and he uses Trinitarian language: "I will ask the Father, and he will give you another Advocate, to be with you forever" (John 14:16). And again, "But the Advocate, the Holy Spirit, whom the Father will send in my name, will teach you everything, and remind you of all that I have said to you" (14:26). The language suggests the roles of the Godhead: God will send the Spirit but will do so in Jesus' name, and so that the Spirit can carry on the work Jesus had begun. Indeed, because of the Holy Spirit, not only will Jesus' work be carried on; it will be greatly enlarged. "I tell you the truth: it is to your advantage that I go away, for if I do not go away, the Advocate will not come to you; but if I go, I will send him to you" (16:7). The Spirit will be able to guide them "into all the truth," including matters they were not yet ready to receive (16:12-13).

The apostolic understanding of the relationship between God and Jesus Christ is clear in the language the apostles used in

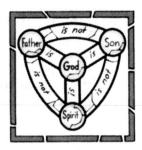

Here the mystery of the Trinity is expressed in graphic form. The drawing is not so much a symbol as a diagram in which the words can be read in any direction and yet make sense. This design, often referred to as the Shield of the Trinity, was created in the sixteenth century and used widely in stained-glass windows and wood carvings.

writing to the churches. Paul's standard greeting is "Grace to you and peace from God our Father and the Lord Jesus Christ" (Romans 1:7; 1 Corinthians 1:3; 2 Corinthians 1:2). James identifies his ministry with God and Christ together: "James, a servant of God and of the Lord Jesus Christ" (James 1:1). And Peter includes the full Trinity in his greeting, as he describes his scattered flock as those "who have been chosen and destined by God the Father and sanctified by the Spirit to be obedient to Jesus Christ and to be sprinkled with his blood" (1 Peter 1:2).

All of which is to say that the Trinity was a fact in the life of the early church. Their language showed that Trinitarian references were commonplace and called for no explanation. Their experience was a doctrine waiting to be spelled out. Interestingly, the clearest expressions of their belief came in the language of their liturgy. One was in what must have been the baptismal formula: "baptizing them in the name of the Father and of the Son and of the Holy Spirit" (Matthew 28:19). Another, the conclusion of Paul's second letter to Corinth, has become a benedictory formula in common use: "The grace of the Lord Jesus Christ, the love of God, and the communion of the Holy Spirit be with all of you" (2 Corinthians 13:14).

Controversies and Conclusions

It became essential that definitive statements should at last be made. Without them, heresies would develop. In fact, it was the appearance of aberrant views that gradually brought about refined statements regarding the nature of the Trinity. The views of Arius regarding the relationship of the Son and the Holy Spirit to the Father forced the church to make a clear and unified statement. Athanasius (296–373), Bishop of Alexandria, was the leader in shaping the position the church formalized at Nicaea (325) and Constantinople (381).

Augustine (354–430), Bishop of Hippo and the premier theologian of early Christendom, wrote most helpfully about the Trinity. He taught that God, Christ, and the Holy Spirit are in union with one another, and that their operation is inseparable because it springs from a single, indivisible will and action. He described their distinctiveness in relationship with one another—the Father's begetting, the Son's begottenness, and the Spirit's proceeding from both. The Orthodox (Eastern) Church holds, however, to an earlier reading of the First Council of Constantinople (381) that the Spirit proceeds from the Father and not from the Father and the Son. This continues to be a major point of difference between the Eastern and Western churches.

How to Explain the Trinity?

Several Greek, Latin, and English terms are part of any thorough discussion of the Trinity. Precision in language is essential to thoughtful discussions, and the early theologians labored to get such precision. *Ousia,* the Greek word for "being," or "substance" (Latin, *substantia*), was a key term at the Council of

What is often called the "Athanasian Creed," probably dating from the latter part of the fifth century, states rather clearly the position of the West—that is, the Catholic Church and the Protestant bodies that followed: "The Godhead of the Father, of the Son, and of the Holy Ghost is all one: the Glory equal, the Majesty coeternal. ... And in this Trinity none is afore, or after another; none is greater, or less than another; But the whole three Persons are coeternal, and coequal."

Nicaea to say that Jesus was of the same essence or substance with God. A later council made the same statement for the Holy Spirit. *Hypostasis,* the Greek word for "substance" or "self-subsistence," was used to describe the three Persons in the Godhead.

In the East, one *ousia* in three *hypostases* became the classic formula for the Trinity. In the West, the formula became *one substance in three Persons.* Two other Greek words that at first look identical to the casual eye were crucial in this discussion, primarily in relation to the nature of God and Christ. *Homoiousios,* which means "of *like* substance," was a term used by those who said Jesus Christ was like God but not of the same substance with God. *Homoousios,* on the other hand, means "of the *same* substance." This term was the one finally adopted by the councils at Nicaea and Constantinople to affirm that Jesus Christ was of the same essence or substance as the Father.

But words in whatever language fall short in helping the average person, or even the sophisticated scholar, grasp the full meaning and mood of the Trinity. As a result, over the centuries believers—scholars as well as beginners—have resorted to picture language, and often to literal pictures. Augustine found his best analogy in the human being, based on the fact that the Scriptures had said, "Let us make humankind in our image." He recognized the failure of any analogy to carry the full idea of Trinity but liked the image of the mind as that which remembers, knows, and loves God, and found in that analogy an image of the Trinity. According to tradition, St. Patrick (fifth century) explained the Trinity to the Irish by way of the three-leaf clover—three separate identities in one source. Tertullian, who wrote so effectively in the early years of the third century, drew some analogies from nature—for instance, the sun, the rays proceeding from the sun, and the sunbeam reflected by some object on earth.

What contemporary analogies of the Trinity have you read or heard?

_____

_____

So God is Father, Son, and Holy Spirit; but the Father is not the Son, nor the Son the Spirit, nor the Spirit the Father. No analogy is fully satisfactory, but each adds a measure of insight to a complex subject.

How Does This Doctrine Matter?

What difference does this doctrine make? We can see the practical implications of the doctrine of God, of sin, and of salvation. But the Trinity?

Whether or not our desire for "practical" benefits in believing is justified, specific benefits do exist. The doctrine of the Trinity is relevant to our lives first in what it reveals to us about

God. Theologians writing devotionally have always found in the Trinity a deeper perception of the love of God. In the Trinity, there is fullness of exchange—a relational wholeness.

God's very existence in Trinity is personal, communal, and loving. God exists as a loving relationship engaging the Father, Son, and Holy Spirit. Without the concept of the Trinity, we might easily reason that Jesus Christ is love but God is judgment; indeed, many Christians—not grasping the doctrine of the Trinity—no doubt do just that. But love is the essence of the Trinity, and it is as much present in the Spirit and in the Creator-Father as in Christ who came to earth. When Jesus dies at Calvary, the love expressed is as much that of the Father and the Spirit as it is of our Lord Christ. The Trinity is indivisible, both in Person and in work; and it is indivisible in its love because the very character of the unity of the Trinity is love.

This teaching has profound implications for understanding human personality, especially our intricacy and worth. Our contemporary culture is almost fiercely individualistic. In this regard, remember the distinction between the person and the individual: To be a person is to be who you are, but to be an individual is to assert your independence of others. We are never more personal than when we relate to others, either in revealing our own person or in inquiring into the person of others. But to be individualistic is to move away from personhood by exalting the solitary.

In this highly individualistic culture, we need a true understanding of personhood. We might even say, a "sanctified understanding," because to see persons rightly is to see them holy. And wholly too. Both of these images of the person come to us in the Trinity. The Trinity reveals the divine nature not in individualism (which would, of course, give us three gods) but in relationship and community. When we sing, "God in three persons, blessed Trinity," we declare that one cannot really be a person except in community. The independence that asserts itself in the contemporary mantra, "What I do with myself is my own business," is a flight from personhood because it denies relationship to others. The Holy Trinity teaches us so, because the Holy Trinity gives us an eternal paradigm for personhood.

Modern Issues of Trinity

The doctrine of the Trinity held a virtually unassailable position for many centuries. Theologically, it was the distinctively Christian statement—more than love, which appears in some form in many religious beliefs; more than sacrifice, which is taught by several; and more than monotheism, which Christianity shares with Judaism and Islam. The Trinity was unique and central to the Christian understanding of God and thus to Christianity's understanding of everything else.

Nevertheless, during the religious ferment of the sixteenth century Faustus Socinus (1539–1604) developed a theology that became a basis for the Unitarian movement. The key issue for Unitarians was denial of the divinity of Jesus Christ; but they also insisted on the unity of God—that is, God alone is divine, and the Son and the Holy Spirit are not equally and eternally God. Thus their name, "Unitarian," in contrast with "Trinitarian." The Unitarian distinction has become somewhat blurred since their union in 1961 with the universalists. The Universalist Church did not deny Trinitarianism, so it is possible today that a person belonging to a Unitarian Universalist Church accepts, personally, the Trinity and the deity of Christ.

A relatively small but highly visible body, Jehovah's Witnesses, also rejects the doctrine of the Trinity. Much like the Arians of the fourth century, they teach that Jesus Christ is the beginning of God's creation and that the Holy Spirit is God's hidden power in the world.

No doubt more significant, but much more difficult to identify or quantify, is the movement within contemporary Christianity that, in practice, denies the Trinity. This tendency expresses itself in several forms—in a questioning of the deity of Jesus Christ, in a vagueness about the Holy Spirit, and in a general uncertainty about the supernatural aspect of the Christian faith. All these trends, in their own way, deny or distort the historic doctrine of the Trinity.

The most lively discussion of the Trinity has to do with issues related to Trinitarian language raised by feminist scholars in the church. Of course the language eventually shapes the doctrine. Trinitarian language is an issue mainly in Europe and North America, though the issue is gaining a hearing in other parts of the world.

The issue is that the traditional formula, "Father, Son, and Holy Spirit," is perceived as male language. The most popular substitution is probably "Creator, Redeemer, and Sanctifier." Some object to this formula on the theological ground that the terms describe three functions in one God rather than three Persons, and that in doing so, this language is guilty of the heresy of modalism (three modes of appearance rather than one God in three Persons), which appeared in the second and third centuries. While the issue might seem to some to be more culturally than spiritually based, it is no more so than numbers of other issues that have arisen over the centuries. It remains a matter for thoughtful, charitable, prayerful consideration. The community of God is richer when the people of God are thinking prayerfully.

> BECAUSE WE THE CHURCH BELIEVE that the one God is revealed in three Persons, I pray that the Trinity will be more fully at work in, and glorified by, my life.

BELIEVING AND LIVING

There's a "venerable limerick" that says,
"We surmise that God's a community,
  Three persons in a single unity.
  But how it can be,
We simply can't see,
We can only revere the mystery."

In what ways has the Trinity become for you a "mystery" that inspires reverence and aids worship?

_____

_____

How would you explain the Trinity to an inquiring youth or adult?

_____

_____

When you pray, what Person of the Trinity do you customarily address? Why?

_____

_____

What does the Trinity teach us about community and relationships?

_____

_____

What about the doctrine of the Trinity troubles you? What blesses you?

_____

_____

SEEKING MORE UNDERSTANDING

For centuries Christians have learned and sung their faith through the words of hymns. Find a hymnal and locate hymns on the Trinity. Read all the stanzas of several hymns to discover what each hymn has to say about God the Father, God the Son, and God the Holy Spirit. Here are some examples of hymns on the Trinity: "O Trinity, O Blessed Light"; "Holy, Holy, Holy! Lord God Almighty"; "All Glory Be to God on High"; "Come, Thou Almighty King"; "God Hath Spoken by the Prophets"; "Eternal Father, Strong to Save."

PRAYER

"God, you are Trinity:
Trinity is our maker,
Trinity is our protector,
Trinity is our everlasting lover,
Trinity is our endless joy and
    our bliss,
by our Lord Jesus Christ,
and in our Lord Jesus Christ:
    Blessed be our Lord!"
    —Julian of Norwich, 1342–after 1416

20

Church   Belonging   Assembly
Called out
A worshiping   Called to bless
people   *Ekklesia*   others
Priesthood of believers
Congregation   A holy people
Synagogue
Jesus Christ head of the church

God's Called-Out People

"I am the LORD, I have called you in righteousness,
    I have taken you by the hand and kept you;
I have given you as a covenant to the people,
    a light to the nations."

—*Isaiah 42:6*

LIFE QUESTIONS

Some of us are naturally independent. We believe in God and in Christ, and consider ourselves Christians, but we don't care to belong to anything. We think we can live a good life without being part of any organization. In fact, maybe it's easier to be a better person if we don't have to trouble ourselves with the procedures of a group.

So why should we become part of a church? Isn't the church just a human way of keeping people under control, and of being sure the institutional side of religion is carried on from generation to generation? Where does God come into all of this? And how would belonging to a church make me a better Christian?

ASSIGNMENT

As Christians, we think of the church as having been born on the Day of Pentecost; and if we're going to discuss the church, we figure on starting there. But the idea of a people of God existed long before Pentecost. Our roots go back a long way.

Our Scripture assignments therefore begin with passages from the Pentateuch that show the people of Israel in action and include some Psalms that show Israel as a worshiping people and as a people rehearsing their salvation history. The New Testament passages include one from the book of Revelation that reflects the tie between Israel and the church as the early church perceived it.

Day 1 Numbers 2:1-17 (assembled in God's presence); Deuteronomy 32:1-47 (Moses' song a witness)
Introduction and Readings 211 and 212

Day 2 Psalms 84 (joy of worship in the Temple); 105 (Israel recalls God's actions)
Readings 213 and 214

Day 3 Psalm 106 (praise and confession); Isaiah 5:1-7, 24-30 (judgment on the vineyard)
Readings 215 and 216

Day 4 Matthew 16:13-20 (church built on the rock); Acts 15:1-31 (Gentiles admitted to the church)
Readings 217 and 218

Day 5 Revelation 21:1-14 (the church Christ's bride)
Readings 219, 220, and 221

Day 6 Read and respond to "The Church Teaching and Believing" and "Believing and Living."

Day 7 Rest and prayer

DAILY PRAYER

Pray for the persons and situations on your Prayer Concerns list and about issues or concerns emerging from your daily reading and study.

BELONGING

SCRIPTURE	READINGS
DAY 1	
Numbers 2:1-17; Deuteronomy 32:1-47	Introduction and Readings 211 and 212
DAY 2	
Psalms 84; 105	Readings 213 and 214
DAY 3	
Psalm 106; Isaiah 5:1-7, 24-30	Readings 215 and 216

SCRIPTURE	READINGS
DAY 4	
Matthew 16:13-20; Acts 15:1-31	**Readings 217 and 218**
DAY 5	
Revelation 21:1-14	**Readings 219, 220, and 221**

DAY 6 STUDY MANUAL	PRAYER CONCERNS
"The Church Teaching and Believing" and "Believing and Living"	

THE CHURCH TEACHING AND BELIEVING

We have heard it said that religion is what a person does with aloneness. In a sense, yes; but religion that remains private is far removed from biblical religion. The Bible pictures God bringing together a holy community. Often it begins with a single person, and others may be added to the company one by one, or family by family. But always to the end of establishing a holy people.

And *holy* is the key word. Not in the sense in which we usually think of the word—as a people of particular virtue—but in its basic biblical sense, as a people set apart and different.

That mood is established at the beginning of the story, when Abram is called to leave his country, kindred, and father's house to go to a land God would show him. One might rightly wonder why it was necessary for Abram and Sarai to leave all that was familiar; couldn't they as easily establish God's new community right where they were? Indeed, might it not be simpler to do so in a place that was familiar and where they were known? Perhaps, but they were to be a holy people, a people called out; and they were setting a pattern for all that would follow.

The promise God gave to Abram defines, in a sense, the continuing role of the divine community. "I will make of you a great nation, and I will bless you, and make your name great, so that you will be a blessing" (Genesis 12:2). They are to be a *nation,* a people belonging to one another. And they are a nation for a purpose—to bring blessing to others. This characteristic will always mark God's people, whether in the Old Testament or the New Testament, and even to the present day. God's people are not simply to be blessed or favored; they are the channel through which blessing will come to the rest of creation. Theirs is an astonishing calling, and we should not be surprised they often fail to fulfill it.

A Special Nation

If the story of Israel's development is read simply as a typical national saga, it is notable primarily for its ups and downs and its frequent periods of struggle and humiliation. They have only a brief period, primarily in the reigns of David and Solomon, when they seem to hold any significant place among the nations of their time. Much of the rest of the time they struggle to maintain their independence. Other nations—most of them long since only footnotes in history—torment them and often take their cities captive.

But the sacred history of all these years is not primarily a story of their changing political fortunes. For the writers of the books of Samuel, Kings, and Chronicles, the point is religious—the quality of their relationship with God. Their kings are rated as good or bad, not for the buildings they erect, and not even for their military prowess, but for their loyalty to the Lord God. The issue is always whether they "did what was right in the sight of the LORD."

This concern is linked, of course, to the overarching call of Israel to be God's chosen people. So, in the Old Testament, if a king is outstanding in all other ways but fails to lead the people in godly paths, he has failed. The ultimate test—the only issue—is that Israel should be the people of God. So the only issue for their leaders is whether they further that purpose.

Israel's sense of being a called people marked them—even literally, physically so in the matter of circumcision, and in their substantial body of laws. Israel was not the first ancient people to have some system of law, but Israel's laws were singular in their focus on holiness and in their complexity. Their primary body of law, what we know as the Ten Commandments, began, "I am the LORD your God, who brought you out of the land of Egypt, out of the house of slavery; you shall have no other gods before me" (Exodus 20:2-3). The first law is not a prohibition of murder, theft, lying, or adultery, but a commandment to keep God, the God of the Exodus, first. All else rests on this. And the whole body of the Law is justified by the fact that it comes from the One who had brought them "out of the land of Egypt, out of the house of slavery." Israel is to be a community brought into existence by God. Their birth has been a gracious one; they were slaves, but God has chosen to deliver them, with no special merit on their part. Salvation from Egypt is grace before Law.

This sense of God's involvement in all the details of their community life, and therefore of their Law, is a recurring motif in the Pentateuch, the five books with which the Old Testament begins. Leviticus 19, for example, seems like a catchall of laws, intersected repeatedly with the declaration, "I am the LORD your God." God is the point of reference in the whole complex of laws—and thus (because of the inclusiveness of the laws) in all the myriad details of daily living.

Israel's sense of being a separate, called-out people has dimensions that may offend a modern reader. They are instructed at times to wipe out their enemies, lest they be contaminated by their evil practices. After the Southern Kingdom, Judah, had returned from several generations in captivity, the issue was especially sensitive. The Jews "had married women of Ashdod, Ammon, and Moab; and half of their children spoke the language of Ashdod, and they could not speak the language of Judah, but spoke the language of various peoples" (Nehemiah 13:23-24). The language of Ashdod will inevitably lead to the religion of Ashdod, because no influence on culture and belief is more powerful than language. Nehemiah recognized the future of the community was at peril, and he went to fierce lengths to protect the purity of the people. He would not let them forget they were a called-out people.

Perhaps the most visible statement of Israel's role as a worshiping community is the position given to the Tabernacle, or tent of meeting. In their journey through the wilderness, the twelve tribes marched in established positions but camped "facing the tent of meeting on every side" (Numbers 2:2). "The tent of meeting," the writer continues, "with the camp of the Levites, shall set out in the center of the camps" (2:17). The house of worship was in a protected position, like a jewel set in the midst of the tribes. At the same time, it stood symbolically as the heart of who they were. Israel was never simply a political entity; it was always intended to be a community of God.

The psalmists said as much when they recounted the history of Israel in song.

"He is the LORD our God;
    his judgments are in all the earth" (Psalm 105:7).
As you continue in the psalm, you recognize these judgments are to the end of God's keeping "the covenant that he made with Abraham" (105:9) and are unfolded in a series of historical events. The psalmist believes it is not by chance Joseph went into Egypt as a slave; God "had sent a man ahead of them, Joseph" (105:17). And though they were aliens in Egypt, "the LORD made his people very fruitful" (105:24). Even so, God provided for their escape from Egypt, and gave them food and water as they journeyed, until at last they would be given "the lands of the nations" (105:44). And why? All of this, "that they might keep his statutes / and observe his laws" (105:45).

God's care of Israel continued even though the people forgot God's works and "did not wait for his counsel" (106:13), worshiped "the image of an ox that eats grass" (106:20), and "angered the LORD at the waters of Meribah" (106:32). The psalmist was writing when Israel is again in captivity, at a later point in their history, this time in Babylon. Obviously he found

Wheat is a symbol of the church on earth. The head of wheat with its individual grains bound together reminds us of the church with its many members in one body. Another symbolic use of wheat is based on the parable in Matthew 13:24-30. Wheat and weeds together represent the church as it is—believers and unbelievers—and as it will continue to be until Judgment Day.

The Psalms in the Old Testament are a collection of songs used in worship and prayer in the Temple in Jerusalem. Traditionally attributed to David, some undoubtedly date from his time. Jews in exile in Babylon, recalling these "songs of Zion," began to collect and write them down to ensure the survival of their worship traditions.

comfort in recalling God's care at an earlier time. But he dared
to expect God would still bless Israel:

"Save us, O LORD our God,
 and gather us from among the nations,
that we may give thanks to your holy name
 and glory in your praise" (106:47).

At the moment of writing, Israel was in captivity. But they were
still a called people, and their mission was still to bring praise
to God.

Community in the New Testament

The role of God's community as a called-out people takes on
new dimensions in the New Testament. Those who heard the
message at Pentecost were probably all Jews by faith, but they
were Jews who had come from many nations. The mix of languages at Pentecost is an obvious symbol of the vast variety
intended to make up the new community of faith.

From the point of view of grace, this is a beautiful prospect.
But it presents huge new problems for community cohesiveness. Those who have been many peoples—or no people—will
now become a people. If we are so often disappointed the people of God are not more unified, we should also be astonished
they find unity as often as they do. All the laws of human inclination are against it.

The sense of being "called out" is inherent in the very name
the New Testament uses for "church," the Greek word *ekklesia*.
It means literally "to call out of," and also "assembly." Ancient
Greeks used the term to refer to their assembling citizens for a
community political meeting. For the church, *ekklesia* became
the common word for the people who were to be God's people
in the world. The New Testament uses a wide variety of figures
of speech in referring to God's people—the flock of God, a
field, a vineyard, a building, a family, a house, a holy temple—
but the operative name from almost the beginning was the
church. The early Christians saw themselves as a called-out
people, because it was clear they were different from the culture around them. Indeed, the culture said so by frequently per-
secuting them.

This persecution may have done for the New Testament
church what bondage in Egypt did for the family of Israel. It
intensified the sense of otherness, of belonging to an isolated
people. And just as the family of Israel multiplied during their
generations of bondage, the early believers grew exponentially
under the frequent instances of isolation and persecution. Not
surprising then, they saw themselves as in the world but not of
the world. This self-perception was both positive and negative.
It helped to congeal them into a loyal body, but it also inclined
them to a sense of isolation from their culture. Such isolation
easily led to a feeling of superiority, and sometimes to a neglect
of their ministry to the world to which they were called. In such
instances, while the early believers fulfilled that part of their

description as a called-out people, they failed to realize the purpose for which they were called, that they might be a blessing.

The Relationship Between Israel and the Church

We can never properly understand the new community of the church without recognizing its tie to the earlier (and continuing) community of Israel. The first Christian believers were either Jews or Gentile converts to Judaism. No doubt they were seen by others as a sect within Judaism; they saw themselves not as a sect within the larger group but as the fulfillment of what Judaism was meant to be. On the Day of Pentecost Peter addressed the assembled crowd as "Fellow Israelites" (Acts 2:29) and concluded his sermon by saying, "Therefore let the entire house of Israel know with certainty that God has made him [Jesus Christ] both Lord and Messiah, this Jesus whom you crucified" (2:36).

The crucial issue in the fledgling church concerned the rite of admission for Gentile converts. The original assumption was that they must first fulfill the ritual requirements of Judaism. But when Peter preached to the household of the Roman centurion Cornelius, the Holy Spirit fell upon them, and "the circumcised believers who had come with Peter were astounded that the gift of the Holy Spirit had been poured out even on the Gentiles" (10:45). Peter concluded immediately that they must admit the Gentiles, by baptism, into the community of the church. Peter's decision was a monumental one, and it called forth a policy by the leaders in Jerusalem (11:1-18) that would be refined later as more and more Gentiles began coming into the church (15:1-29).

But the growing presence of Gentiles, including even uncircumcised ones, did not weaken the tie to the heart of Judaism. Wherever Paul went to preach, he began in that community's synagogue. We may assume the other apostles followed the same pattern. Only after they found themselves unwelcome in synagogues did they minister elsewhere, either outdoors or in the homes of believers. Their pattern of worship followed closely what they had known in the synagogue; thus the apostle urged, "With gratitude in your hearts sing psalms, hymns, and spiritual songs to God" (Colossians 3:16). The Psalms, traditionally part of Judaism's worship, were already part of the tradition in the new community of faith.

So too with the Scriptures. No one in the new Christian community wondered about a faith document; they had one already. When the apostle reminded Timothy, "All scripture is inspired by God and is useful for teaching, for reproof, for correction, and for training in righteousness" (2 Timothy 3:16), he was referring to the Hebrew Scriptures since no other Scriptures existed at the time. The new believers took these Scriptures as their own. Continuing in the line of Israel, they were relying on the documents that had blessed Israel.

But they went beyond Israel as they read and used these

202

Scriptures. They read the Old Testament through the lens of their experience of Jesus Christ. The followers of Jesus understood everything that happened to Jesus as in accord with what the Hebrew Scriptures had said. Not only did they understand Jesus as fulfilling what the prophets had spoken (Matthew 1:22-23; 2:5-6); they found symbolic pictures of Jesus in Old Testament events and practices (Hebrews 4:14–5:10; 9:1-22). The Christian community saw themselves not only as a continuation of Israel but as the people God had always meant Israel to become.

But in its complexity this new community is far removed from ancient Israel. Israel was one nation; the new community was to be from "every tribe and language and people and nation" (Revelation 5:9). Israel had a central place of worship where the people were to gather at regular intervals; the new community was likely to meet—at first—in homes, on a riverbank, or almost any place accessible and reasonably safe. Israel had a grand deposit of tradition; the new community held to the sacred book they had inherited from Israel, the Jesus traditions, and the symbol of their Lord's death and remembrance of that death in a feast of bread and wine. Israel, at least at times, had a political leader to symbolize their national entity; the new community hailed Jesus Christ as its Lord, but he was not physically present, so they had to celebrate his reality by faith.

These differences tell us the odds were strongly against the survival of the new community, the church. And the early history of the church, as reported in the book of Acts and in the lettters, underscores the obstacles. We read of meetings of the leadership of the church, but the language is comparatively vague. It appears James, the brother of Jesus, replaced Peter as the leader. The most articulate representative, Paul, indicates at times he was a bit of an outsider, struggling to make his point of view heard.

Early conflicts arose over such practical matters as potential ill feelings between Hebrew-speaking and Greek-speaking Jews regarding distribution of food (Acts 6) and such theological issues as how much of the Jewish Law should be observed (10; 15). The church was troubled by hypocrisy (5:1-11), astonishing instances of immorality (1 Corinthians 5), and division between leaders (Galatians 2). Furthermore, in the first several centuries of the church's existence, communication was slow and difficult, so the scattered Christian communities had problems keeping in contact with one another.

Nevertheless, the church held together. Not easily, not without pain, and not without occasional breaks in the fabric. But it continues to the present day. The secret in its survival is the community's ultimate allegiance to its Lord. Colossians describes Jesus Christ as "the head of the body, the church" (Colossians 1:18). The sense of the term is spiritual and mystical, and it is a powerful figure indeed. The Christian community saw itself in union with its Lord; he was the head and they the body. This concept of an organic relationship was both astonishing and empowering. Thus the Christian community continues to survive, sometimes almost in spite of itself.

The relationship between the old and the new communities is celebrated in the book of Revelation. Clearly, Revelation is directed to the new community, by way of the letters to the seven churches. But as the message of the book begins to unfold, it speaks of "twenty-four thrones, and seated on the thrones are twenty-four elders, dressed in white robes, with golden crowns on their heads" (Revelation 4:4). Numbers are important in the Scriptures, especially in the Old Testament but carrying over into the New Testament. A first-century reader needed no explanation to understand twenty-four elders as representing the twelve tribes of Israel and the twelve apostles of Jesus. This numeric symbolism is spelled out near the end of Revelation, when we are told the twelve gates of the holy city are inscribed with "the names of the twelve tribes of the Israelites," and that the wall of the city has twelve foundations, on which "are the twelve names of the twelve apostles of the Lamb" (21:12-14). No wonder, then, the first believers were intent on choosing a replacement for Judas (Acts 1:15-26); there must be twelve, so the symmetry with the twelve tribes can be maintained.

Similarly, the one who is able to open the scroll of judgment is "the Lion of the tribe of Judah, the Root of David." And when he is revealed, he is "a Lamb standing as if it had been slaughtered" (Revelation 5:5-6). So the tie is made between Old Testament symbolism and New Testament fulfillment; the two communities of God are one. When a celestial multitude sings, it is "the song of Moses, the servant of God, and the song of the Lamb" (15:3)—again, a joining of the community of Israel, as Moses knew it, and the Christian community, founded by the Lamb.

A called-out people! Stretching over several millennia, one of them a nation by ethnic right and the other a new community by virtue of its tie to a common Lord, they have held fitfully to a divine assignment. They have a purpose, ever since Abraham, whom both claim as their faith-father: They are to be a blessing to the nations of humankind. Human as the two communities have been and are, we are well surprised by the degree to which they have fulfilled their calling.

> BECAUSE WE THE CHURCH BELIEVE we are a people called out by God for mission in the world, I will gladly join that mission.

BELIEVING AND LIVING

In a society where so many worthwhile organizations ask for our allegiance and our support, the church asks for these responses in a unique measure. It insists its claim is not one among many, but in a class by itself. To what degree do you accept this claim on your life?

_____

_____

In today's culture, what distinguishes the church that takes seriously its role as a set-apart people?

_____

_____

In what ways do you experience the tie of the Christian faith to Israel of the Old Testament? How might that tie become more significant for you?

_____

_____

From your observation, do most church members you know think of themselves as being called to a special purpose? Do you? If so, why? If not, why not?

_____

_____

SEEKING MORE UNDERSTANDING

If you have an interest in church history, consider doing some research on occasions in history when the church lived up to its description as a called-out people. Choose a century or a millennium and limit yourself to five to ten examples. Write a brief summary of your findings to share with your group.

PRAYER

"From our ancestors and from preceding generations, Lord, we have knowledge of you. They provided the background information about your mercy and goodness. Then, as we grew, we used our own energy and effort to learn to know you better. Now we look to future generations who will use our collective religious experience to keep the chain unbroken. We want your goodness and merciful deeds to be heard and known forever and ever. Help us to be faithful storytellers, griots, narrators, and teachers, Lord. Amen."

—*Moravian Daily Texts, 1995*

21

Bride
of Christ
Body of Christ
Apostolic
New
creation
One   **Holy**   **Catholic**
Communion of Saints
Holy and without blemish
Household of God
**Visible
and invisible**
**Professing
community**

The Body of Christ in the World

"Christ loved the church and gave himself up for her, in order to make her holy by cleansing her with the washing of water by the word, so as to present the church to himself in splendor, without a spot or wrinkle or anything of the kind—yes, so that she may be holy and without blemish."

—Ephesians 5:25-27

LIFE QUESTIONS

The church is so often a disappointing institution. Perhaps most institutions are, because they set goals beyond their ability to fulfill. But none more so than the church. The church makes such great claims, but in practice often seems no better than many secular institutions.

So what right has the church to claim to be the body of Christ in our world? And why should I be expected to affiliate with some local congregation? After all, who can say these groups who say they are church are worthy of the name? Why can't I just go it alone, a solitary believer obligated to no one but myself? What is the church, anyway?

ASSIGNMENT

The word *church* appears in the Bible only a few times until we get to Acts and the letters. Then we find it used in two quite different ways—sometimes in a mystical sense, referring to some larger, undefined body, and other times referring to a particular congregation. We need to keep these two views in wholesome tension as we read.

Day 1   Psalm 122 (the house of the Lord); Isaiah 52:1-12 (home to Zion)
Introduction and Readings 222 and 223

Day 2   Matthew 13:24-30 (weeds and wheat together); 18:15-22 (discipline among followers)
Reading 224

Day 3   1 Corinthians 12:12-31 (one body, many members); Ephesians 1:3-23 (chosen by God)
Readings 225 and 226

Day 4   Ephesians 2:11-22 (one body); Colossians 1:15-29 (Christ the head)
Readings 227 and 228

Day 5   1 Timothy 3 (instructions for household of God); 1 Peter 2:1-10 (a priesthood); Revelation 2 (messages to the church)
Readings 229 and 230

Day 6   Read and respond to "The Church Teaching and Believing" and "Believing and Living."

Day 7   Rest and prayer

DAILY PRAYER

Pray for the persons and situations on your Prayer Concerns list and about issues or concerns emerging from your daily reading and study.

BODY OF CHRIST

SCRIPTURE	READINGS
DAY 1	
Psalm 122; Isaiah 52:1-12	Introduction and Readings 222 and 223
DAY 2	
Matthew 13:24-30; 18:15-22	Reading 224
DAY 3	
1 Corinthians 12:12-31; Ephesians 1:3-23	Readings 225 and 226

SCRIPTURE	READINGS

DAY 4

Ephesians 2:11-22; Colossians 1:15-29	Readings 227 and 228

DAY 5

1 Timothy 3; 1 Peter 2:1-10; Revelation 2	Readings 229 and 230

DAY 6 STUDY MANUAL	PRAYER CONCERNS
"The Church Teaching and Believing" and "Believing and Living"	

THE CHURCH TEACHING AND BELIEVING

The title of this section in our weekly study makes a point. Believers are the church; and believers belong to the church. We come to the application of each study with the declaration, "Because we the church believe...." So what is this institution that dares to lay such claim on our lives?

By definition, the church is the community of persons who profess faith in Jesus Christ. It has its origins in the plan and purposes of God. So those who become part of it sense, at best, they have been called to this affiliation. It is not so much a matter of their having chosen to join the church as it is the church (the ultimate, mystical body, not just the building down the street) has chosen them. This conviction makes the church quite different from any other institution we might join. The origins of the church are divine. The church is God's people. But recognizing this is no reason for pride. God did not choose the church because it is good; if it is good, it is because God has chosen it.

The Church: Of God

Any discussion of the church must acknowledge it is both of God and human. This is inevitable, because although the church is God's people, these people are themselves human and live out their mission on the earth. The New Testament moves without apology or word of transition between references to its final "splendor, without a spot or wrinkle or anything of the kind" (Ephesians 5:27) to details about daily structure and functioning, and then, at times, to recommendations regarding evidences of pettiness and inadequacy.

Nowhere in the New Testament is there a record of a meeting for the founding of the church. Traditionally we speak of the Day of Pentecost as the birthday of the church; but we have no evidence of motions made or passed, committees appointed, or membership roll signed. The Spirit of God settled upon some one hundred twenty persons; and before the day was over, "three thousand persons were added" to the fellowship (Acts 2:41). Their baptism was apparently their only ritual of joining. The church had no headquarters beyond their temporary meeting place. The founding of the church was of God. No doubt as the participants in that day looked back upon it later, they could only marvel at what had happened, and at how little they had had to do with it.

The New Testament uses several figures of speech to describe the church. The strongest figure is probably the one that describes the church as "the body of Christ" (1 Corinthians 12:27). Christ is seen as the head of this body (Colossians 1:18). The figure suggests, on one hand, that the members of the church are wonderfully related to and dependent on one another (1 Corinthians 12:14-26), as are the parts of a human body. But more significantly, this figure identifies who we are, and the identity is quite overwhelming. We are more than a group of persons held together by common convictions or ethnic or historic connection; we are the physical presence of Christ in the world.

In a quite different image, the church is described as the bride of Christ (Ephesians 5:25-32; Revelation 21:2, 9). This picture requires that the church be "holy and without blemish" (Ephesians 5:27). Christ's love for the church is such that he "gave himself up for her, in order to make her holy" (5:25-26). Thus the goodness seen in the church, when the church is at its best, is a holiness won by the sacrifice of Christ.

The church is also seen as people who are "a new creation" (2 Corinthians 5:17) and as God's temple, built on the foundation of Jesus Christ (1 Corinthians 3:10-17). Again, the church is "the household of God" (1 Peter 4:12-19). We find in all these images a sense of God's immediate and effective involvement with the church. The church is not an orphan or a self-propelling entity.

The Church: Human

But all this beautiful imagery has to be lived out in a physical world. In New Testament days, the reference was to "the church in their house" (Romans 16:5) or "in your house" (Philemon 2). When congregations were very small, and in times when meetings had to be secret to escape detection and persecution, they gathered in the homes of members. So Paul said, "Gaius ... is host to me and to the whole church" (Romans 16:23). But these gatherings were seen always as part of the whole body of the church, not as independent, local units of a larger whole.

Eventually some sort of organizational structure became essential for these local manifestations of the church, and the larger body as well. The offices were entirely ministry-oriented: "to equip the saints for the work of ministry, for building up the body of Christ, until all of us come to the unity of the faith and of the knowledge of the Son of God, to maturity, to the measure of the full stature of Christ" (Ephesians 4:12-13). The callings that were to make this possible were apostles, prophets, evangelists, pastors, and teachers (4:11). First Timothy also describes the qualifications for bishops and deacons (1 Timothy 3:1-13).

To give contemporary meaning to each of these first-century offices would be nearly impossible. Scholars cannot fully agree about what may have been meant by the words *apostle, prophet,* and *evangelist,* or even by *pastor* and *teacher.* When we observe how the role of pastor has changed in our country in the last half-century, we recognize how difficult it is to define first-century use of such words.

But several matters are clear. First, the church had recognizable structure and defined positions or roles within that structure. Second, these offices were to a purpose, and the purpose was a clearly spiritual one. Persons in these offices were not mere functionaries. Third, the qualifications for these offices had everything to do with character, example, and spiritual maturity. The Bible says little about the sort of things that would be included in a modern job description. Probably because those factors, in the mind of the early church, were provided for by the gifts and endowments of the Spirit.

This early church "inspired" (evoked), received, and preserved the books of the New Testament. We use the word *inspired* somewhat playfully in noting that the earliest documents of the New Testament, the letters, came into existence largely because of the problems and failures of the first congregations and first believers. As the people raised questions, the apostles responded with these letters. Likewise, perhaps, it was because of the hunger of early believers for a permanent record of Jesus' life and teachings that anointed writers sought the help of the Holy Spirit in recording the Gospels. By the acceptance and endorsement of those early congregations, some few documents came to be known as the canon of the New Testament, while numbers of other books dropped by the wayside. And by the courageous earnestness of the church, during times of persecution, the books were preserved so that we have them today.

That early church, like the church today, was fully human. Those who find the church disappointing today would have been no less disappointed in the first or second century. Nevertheless, in good times and in bad, whether prospering or foundering, the church survived; and in surviving, it maintained the body of Scripture and struggled its way through church councils to a lasting and authoritative formulation of the faith.

The Church Described More Fully

With the passing of the centuries, several terms have become widely accepted as defining the church. The creed coming out of Nicaea (325) and Constantinople (381) described the church as *one, holy, catholic,* and *apostolic.*

The beehive is a modern symbol of the church as a body or community of those who work together to achieve its unique purpose or mission. Like bees and beehive, the church is characterized by order, activity, and devotion to cause, with each member of the community contributing skills and abilities to the work of the community.

The understanding of the church as *one* finds its roots in the prayer of our Lord "that they may be one, as we are one" (John 17:22) and in these words from Ephesians: "There is one body and one Spirit, just as you were called to the one hope of your calling, one Lord, one faith, one baptism, one God and Father of all" (Ephesians 4:4-6). The very glory of the church, that it has crossed ethnic and language barriers, is also its hazard. For the church to be one in a world that has so many national and cultural differences is difficult. So too the very vigor of faith complicates the oneness of belief. Ironically, having unity of faith may be easier where the faith itself is somewhat asleep; liveliness and earnestness encourage differences.

Some Christians reason that oneness must include unanimity in doctrinal belief. The Roman Catholic Church primarily sees oneness in itself. Reformed teaching insists on unity through hearing the word of God in Jesus Christ. Many theologians consider unity achieved when those of differing opinions nevertheless maintain the bonds of love and of mutual commitment to Jesus Christ as Lord.

The church is holy because the Holy Spirit works through it to accomplish God's purposes in human life. Other definitions have been offered from time to time in church, particularly that the holiness of the church is demonstrated by the holiness of its members or of its leadership. But the holiness of the church comes from outside itself or its achievements. *Holy* is one of the two descriptive words for the church included in the Apostles' Creed: "I believe in the holy catholic church."

For many Protestants, *catholic* is a controversial word in its place in the Apostles' Creed, so much so that they substitute either *Christian* or *universal*. At the time of the Reformation, Martin Luther wanted to substitute the words "I believe in a holy Christian people" for "the holy catholic church" in the sentences of the Apostles' Creed. As used in the creed, and as broadly believed, the word *catholic* refers to the universal nature of the Christian church and not to Roman Catholicism. In its earliest usage, the word *catholic* was a kind of redeclaration of the Great Commission (Matthew 28:19). The church was dedicated to spread the good news of Christ throughout the whole world and to bring the knowledge of Christ to all persons. Its universality is impressive.

The church is *apostolic* in that the succession of believers reaches from the original apostles to the present time. The Catholic and Anglican churches hold that this apostolic line is preserved through the consecration of bishops from the first apostles to the present time. Most Protestants, following especially the lead of John Calvin (1509–1564), contend that true apostolicity comes through loyalty and obedience to the Lord of the church, Jesus Christ. The apostolic tie is of the Spirit, rather than of a particular historical lineage.

Apostolic also refers to the apostolic faith maintained in the church. When we consider the frequent periods of persecution and the difficulties of maintaining the faith through those and other perils, the unbroken continuity of the church is quite impressive. The church can rightly rejoice in being apostolic.

While most Protestant bodies would agree in principle that the church is one, holy, catholic, and apostolic, they generally emphasize different measures. The classic Protestant position is that the church exists wherever the Word of God is rightly preached and the sacraments rightly administered. (The emphasis on the sacraments would not be endorsed, of course, by Quakers and the Salvation Army, who do not celebrate any sacraments.) In many communions, ordination is the authorization to preach the Word and administer the sacraments.

This emphasis on preaching and sacraments recognizes that for most persons preaching and the sacraments are the most vital means of grace. And this emphasis is, by extension, a declaration that the church is God's appointed channel of grace to the world. From a secular point of view, both preaching and the sacraments can be seen as human ventures. Preaching may not seem distinguishable from generic speech-making, and the sacraments hardly more than typical organizational rites of passage. Believers contend, however, that the Holy Spirit invests these otherwise common functions when they are rightly done. As such, they are distinctive to the church; these inspired functions are characterizing features of the church. And more than that, the church cannot exist without hearing the Word of God and without some measure of sacramental celebration, even if called by another name.

But above all else, the church is the community that gladly acknowledges that Jesus Christ is Lord. As we learned earlier, the earliest creed of the church was "Jesus is Lord." Here is the doorway to the church. We will eventually believe a great deal more, but we cannot believe less and be part of the church. The church is Christ's kingdom, his people, his servants and kin. Thus it is never *my* church, *our* church, or our denomination's church. Jesus Christ is Lord of the church—singularly, exclusively, passionately, triumphantly.

Because the members of the church come from so many nations and tongues, expressions of the faith will always have variety that enriches but also may lead to dispute. Because humans are so different, points of emphasis will be almost as numerous as the persons making up the church. By our nature, we are susceptible to exulting the part over the whole. All of these differences, however, can be lived with if only the church's true north can be maintained: *Jesus Christ is Lord.* Each time believers return sincerely to that confession, other issues are put in perspective.

The Church Visible and Invisible

Augustine (354–430) first described the church as both *visible and invisible,* but that perception has always been apparent. The church is, on one hand, an earthly body, organized and visible.

But the church is also invisible in that no human agency can finally say who is or is not a member. That final judgment belongs to God.

Our human disposition is to establish standards on God's behalf. This has been true since the beginning. The apostle John complained to Jesus, "Master, we saw someone casting out demons in your name, and we tried to stop him, because he does not follow with us" (Luke 9:49). Jesus answered, "Do not stop him; for whoever is not against you is for you" (9:50). John wanted a visible church; Jesus said the boundaries are not always as clear as we might want them to be. As theologians over the centuries have said, no doubt there are sheep outside the fold as we have defined it, and just as surely there are wolves within our visible, earthly fold.

To say the "invisible church" is made up of the genuine believers, both in heaven and on the earth, is not to discredit the visible church. It is, rather, a confession that we are not the final arbiters and that our earthly facilities of judgment are imperfect. We accept persons into the visible church on the basis of their confession of faith. We have no right to estimate the degree of their sincerity or the validity of their experience. If we act with charity, it is inevitable we will include some in the visible church who do not qualify for the invisible. If we are to err, this is the way to go. Since the final judgment will be made by God, it is better we err on the side of charity than on the side of narrowness of spirit (Matthew 13:24-30).

The invisible church is made up of all who have truly acknowledged Jesus Christ as Lord. Many believers will confess that the lordship of Christ has been a progressive experience, and that what once seemed to them to be a state of true lordship was in truth quite immature and undeveloped. Let the judgment therefore be with God, the only one capable of knowing the thoughts and intents of our hearts.

Let us recognize, then, that the visible church will always be a mixed body. Since the visible church includes both sheep and wolves in sheep's clothing, and since the sheep themselves are not yet everything their Lord intends them to be, the visible church cannot help but be an embarrassment to itself and to its Lord. It is not always the creature of "splendor, without a spot or wrinkle or anything of the kind" (Ephesians 5:27) it is meant to be. But the church is a wonderfully hopeful body, and one for which Christ died. Within its sometimes confused company, the members of the church visible find fellowship and eternal sustenance.

The concept of the church as visible and invisible reminds us that God is the final arbiter on membership in the church. Over the centuries most communions have had some set of requirements for those who would become part of the membership. This requirement is proper enough in its own right; organizations need such structures if they are to serve any significant purpose. But churches always ought to treat their own requirements with a kind of holy diffidence, recognizing that we see through a glass darkly and that only God can know the true state of a human soul. Our judgments are always influenced by our own limitations and even by our defensiveness. No doubt our greatest obligation to the church visible is to be, ourselves, as worthy as possible of belonging.

Another frequent description of the church is similar in some sense to the church visible and invisible—*church militant* and *church triumphant*. "The church militant" refers to the church on earth, busy in its task. The term is at times maligned because of its apparent military motif, but it is consistent with both Scripture and tradition in recognizing we are engaged in warfare against evil. The term is meant to describe spiritual conflict. "The church triumphant" describes those believers who have died and are now in the presence of God; their warfare is ended, their conflict ceased.

The idea of the church triumphant has classical expression in the Apostles' Creed—"the communion of saints." From the beginning, believers have insisted the church is made up of all who believe in Christ, whether living or dead. This belief gives a grand sense of a community that overarches time and the grave. The believer exists not only in the flesh but in Christ. In the flesh, a believer is separated from those who have died, but in Christ the community remains.

The communion of saints is most vivid in the sacrament of Holy Communion. Worship leaders sometimes remind communicants that the Table of the Lord reaches around the world, so they are kneeling with persons of every tribe, tongue, and nation. This statement is proper. We can also say we take Communion, as the ancient liturgies say, "with all the company of heaven"—that is, with all the people of God who have ever lived.

Such claims of the church lift it out of the company of what would otherwise seem to be similar organizations. The relationship of its members over the ages is mystical, because the community is divinely ordained, and because its unity is not in any contemporary leader or even ultimately in the definitions of a creed but in its Lord, Jesus Christ. Thus, we can be members of the community even if a local branch of the community refuses us membership. The ultimate decision is with the Lord of the church. Indeed, even if we judge ourselves unworthy, we can be overruled by the Lord of the church, who welcomes us when we do not welcome ourselves.

To be invited to become part of such a body, whether by baptism, confirmation, or adult decision, is a divine compliment. Having received, by grace, membership in the church invisible, we ought never be casual about membership in the church visible. Whatever its limitations and problems (to which each of us, by our joining, adds), it is the best earthly vehicle for the purposes of God. The church is, audacious as the claim may seem, the body of Christ in our world.

BECAUSE WE THE CHURCH BELIEVE the church is the body of Christ in the world, I will try as a member of that body to be worthy of this high calling.

BELIEVING AND LIVING

All of us should know the church at two levels. Inevitably, we know it as we have experienced it in some local body of worshipers. This experience colors our theology of the church, making it either easy or difficult to believe in the holiness of the community as the body of Christ. In our study, we learn about the church at another level—its place in the plan and purpose of God.

As you review your own experience in one or more local church communities, how would you compare them with the biblical expectations of the church as the body of Christ?

We have defined the church as the body of persons who profess faith in Jesus Christ. Should that definition be enlarged in any way, and if so, how would you change it?

Where have you experienced the church at its best, and what about that particular community so impressed you?

If you could do one thing to make your own Christian community more true to its calling, what would it be?

SEEKING MORE UNDERSTANDING

You may wish to do further study of terms used to describe the church—*one, holy, catholic, apostolic, visible* and *invisible, militant, triumphant*—and to locate additional descriptive terms. A theological word book and/or a dictionary of the Christian church would provide such information. Check your church or public library, local bookstore, or the internet.

PRAYER

"O God, we pray for thy Church, which is set today amid the perplexities of a changing order, and face to face with new tasks. Baptize her afresh in the life-giving spirit of Jesus! Bestow upon her a great responsiveness to duty, a swifter compassion with suffering, and an utter loyalty to the will of God. Put upon her lips the ancient Gospel of her Lord. Fill her with the prophets' scorn of tyranny, and with a Christ-like tenderness for the heavy-laden and downtrodden. Bid her cease from seeking her own life, lest she lose it. Make her valiant to give up her life to humanity, that, like her crucified Lord, she may mount by the path of the cross to a higher glory; through the name of Jesus Christ our Lord. Amen."

—*Walter Rauschenbusch, 1861–1918*

22

Sacraments

Baptism   **Eucharist**

New   **Holy Communion**   **Means**
covenant   Repentance   **of grace**

Physical elements   Spiritual truths

Washing of regeneration

Salvation and forgiveness of sins

Outward signs of an inward grace

Mystery and physical reality

Signs of Sacred Things

"The cup of blessing that we bless, is it not a sharing in the blood of Christ? The bread that we break, is it not a sharing in the body of Christ?"

—*1 Corinthians 10:16*

LIFE QUESTIONS

We humans are spiritual creatures, but we are also physical. For that reason we look for physical carriers of the spiritual realities that mean so much to us. Such a physical element also provides a form to which we can return when we want at other times to have the same kind of spiritual experience.

What shall these physical forms or rituals be? Are some more significant than others? Why should forms or rituals that came into existence centuries ago be preferable to something we might develop in our own time? Indeed, isn't it possible a contemporary sacrament might convey meaning to us more effectively than something from the past? What authority do the sacraments of the church have? Which sacraments ought to be observed, and why?

ASSIGNMENT

Our Scripture passages will lead us through several ritualistic observances, beginning with altar-building in the early chapters of Genesis and including the Passover rites. Major emphasis will be on Baptism and Holy Communion, since these sacraments are most widely observed in the vari-ous branches of Christendom and because they are the most frequently referred to in the Scriptures. Look for ties between the first altar-builders and contemporary worshipers, and between the Passover and Holy Communion.

Day 1   Genesis 8:20-22 (pleasing odor); 12:1-9 (an altar to the Lord)
Introduction and Readings 231, 232, and 233

Day 2   Exodus 12:1-28, 43-51 (festival of Passover)
Readings 234 and 235

Day 3   Matthew 3 (baptism for repentance); 28:16-20 (baptism for all nations); Mark 14:12-26 (loaf and cup)
Readings 236 and 237

Day 4   John 6:25-59 (food of eternal life); Acts 8:26-40 (Ethiopian baptized)
Readings 238 and 239

Day 5   1 Corinthians 10:1-22 (sacraments no guarantee of salvation); 11:17-34 (proper conduct)
Readings 240 and 241

Day 6   Read and respond to "The Church Teaching and Believing" and "Believing and Living."

Day 7   Rest and prayer

DAILY PRAYER

Pray for the persons and situations on your Prayer Concerns list and about issues or concerns emerging from your daily reading and study.

SACRAMENTS

SCRIPTURE	READINGS

DAY 1

Genesis 8:20-22; 12:1-9	Introduction and Readings 231, 232, and 233

DAY 2

Exodus 12:1-28, 43-51	Readings 234 and 235

DAY 3

Matthew 3; 28:16-20; Mark 14:12-26	Readings 236 and 237

SCRIPTURE	READINGS

DAY 4

John 6:25-59; Acts 8:26-40	Readings 238 and 239

DAY 5

1 Corinthians 10:1-22; 11:17-34	Readings 240 and 241

DAY 6 STUDY MANUAL	PRAYER CONCERNS
"The Church Teaching and Believing" and "Believing and Living"	

THE CHURCH TEACHING AND BELIEVING

For as long as we human beings have reached toward God, we have sought physical expressions that will make the reality of God more accessible. Some of these expressions have come to be known in the church as *sacraments*. And often in the process of celebrating sacraments, worshipers receive a new sense of divine grace. Thus, we speak of the sacraments as "means of grace."

The word *sacrament* itself is instructive. The Latin root, *sacramentum,* means literally "oath." The word *oath* conveys the idea of the binding quality of the sacraments, reminding us that religion means "to bind back." The Greek word, however is *mysterion,* "mystery" (the term still used in the Orthodox Church). Mystery is a powerful factor in any experience of God. Because God is Spirit, our relationship to God involves elements quite beyond our grasp. Thus the importance of sacraments: They provide the physical reality, available to our senses, to help us objectify the greater realities beyond our reach.

The Beginning of Sacraments

The word *sacrament* is not found in the Bible, but its practice is there from early in the book of Genesis. Early church theologians, including especially Augustine (A.D. 354–430), taught that the Old Testament includes many sacraments. Circumcision, as the covenant mark for Israel, was seen by the theologians as a sacrament, and reasonably so. Here was physical evidence, for the male members of the community, that they were bound in covenant with God. In a sense, the idea of grace was present, since circumcision was ordinarily performed when the child was only a few days old and so was received into the covenant without any personal merit. Early Christians had good reason to see circumcision as a sacramental act for the Jews, since the writer of Colossians extended its symbolic significance to Christian believers when he spoke of "spiritual circumcision," the "putting off the body of the flesh" through new life in Christ (Colossians 2:11).

The Passover celebration also had all the qualities of a sacrament. Its ritual provided physical elements that represented spiritual truths: unleavened bread, lamb bone, bitter herbs, wine. The Christian sacrament of Holy Communion works with some of the same ideas; and where Passover was celebrated with the death of a lamb, Christians gave reverence to the body and blood of the Lamb of God, Jesus Christ. As the Gospels report it, the first celebration of Communion was in the context of the Passover meal (Mark 14:12-25).

Indeed, the first Christians found a kind of sacramental significance in virtually every ritual of Judaism. We might say that because most of the first Christians were Jews, it would be natural for such persons to find a tie with the faith in which they were born. But the believers of the first century understood that the Hebrew Scriptures had, almost from the beginning, anticipated messiah. For that reason, they saw the practices of Judaism as replete with features that would preview the messiah. For them, it was not by chance that so many elements in Judaism found fulfillment in Jesus Christ. As they saw it, it could not have been otherwise.

Jesus made such an identification when he reminded his hearers their ancestors had eaten manna in the wilderness but now there was "bread that comes down from heaven, so that one may eat of it and not die. I am the living bread that came down from heaven. Whoever eats of this bread will live forever; and the bread that I will give for the life of the world is my flesh" (John 6:50-51).

The History of Sacraments

Over the centuries of church history, the church has looked upon several practices as sacraments. Augustine identified as a sacrament, or a mystery, anything that signified one thing at the level of reason and another at the level of faith. With a grand flourish, he saw all creation as a sacramental system. But Augustine also identified particular actions as sacraments, actions specifically recognized as sacraments in the New Testament.

Two sacraments are recognized and practiced by almost all of Christendom—Baptism and Holy Communion. Their wide acceptance rests on the fact they both were clearly authorized by Jesus Christ and both practiced by the New Testament church. Nevertheless, both have been subjects of continuing controversy. The several bodies of Christendom have different opinions about who may receive the sacraments (including issues of both physical maturity and spiritual readiness), and about the nature of the effect on persons receiving them.

The Sacrament of Baptism

Christian baptism had its nearest roots in the ministry of John the Baptist, but its symbolic roots go further back in Judaism. The process of ordaining Aaron and his sons for their ministry as priests began with a washing with water (Leviticus 8:6). Israel's tabernacle in the wilderness included a bronze basin in which the priests were to wash their hands and feet before going to the altar to minister; "they shall wash with water, so that they may not die" (Exodus 30:20).

The water needs little explanation as a symbol. It is, quite simply, a picture of cleansing. But we can miss the solemnity of the ritual. The cleansing is so serious a matter that the several rituals are hedged about with details, and in the case of the priestly cleansing, with a life-and-death warning. All these instructions emphasize both the peril of unworthy conduct and the power of the ritual. Such seriousness is far removed from an attitude that sees baptism as only a formality, or in the case of an infant, only a lovely and sentimental act.

John the Baptist caught the seriousness of water-cleansing in his preaching and the baptisms that followed. He "appeared in the wilderness, proclaiming a baptism of repentance for the forgiveness of sins" (Mark 1:4). This baptismal cleansing was, sacramental; the ritual act declared physically what had happened spiritually. Seekers came "confessing their sins" (1:5), an inward act, then received the outward sacrament of water cleansing.

The importance of baptism in the life of the church is clear. As Jesus bid farewell to his disciples, he first declared his authority and then said, "Go therefore and make disciples of all nations, baptizing them in the name of the Father and of the Son and of the Holy Spirit, and teaching them to obey everything that I have commanded you" (Matthew 28:19-20). His instructions indicate baptism was to be a rite of initiation into discipleship, with teaching following.

Obviously, the disciples took Jesus at his word. When Peter finished his sermon on the Day of Pentecost, those who were "cut to the heart" by his message asked what they now should do. Peter answered, "Repent, and be baptized every one of you in the name of Jesus Christ so that your sins may be forgiven" (Acts 2:38). Peter used the same sacramental order John the Baptist had used: Repent (inward); then be baptized (outward). But clearly, this baptism was no incidental matter; it was closely linked with the forgiveness of their sins.

We might wonder why the ritual would be necessary if the inner change—by way of repentance—has occurred. Is it merely a formality? By no means. Baptism is an act of obedience, substantiating what has happened within. It is also a public affiliation. By this act, community is both acknowledged and celebrated, and spiritual independence is rejected.

Being baptized has another crucial value for the person . By identifying the inner decision and change with an outward act, and by this act's involving a community, a ponderable strength

The water and chalice symbolize the two sacraments most widely celebrated in Christendom, Baptism and Holy Communion—the bath and the meal. The chalice is referred to as both the cup of suffering and the cup of blessing—suffering, the blood of Christ; blessing, our salvation. Water signifies cleansing and regeneration, and dying to sin and being raised to new life—a reflection of Christ's death and resurrection.

enters the life of the convert. We cannot always hold in memory the quality of a moment of decision or of experience. Indeed, even the most vivid experience can be nullified by changing mood or changing circumstance. In some instances, memory may succeed in wiping out not only the importance of an experience but even its very existence. Such is the fleeting quality of decisions and experiences. But the sacrament is a physical event, marked by specific words and actions. So Martin Luther, tempted to doubt the state of his soul before God, would remind himself he was baptized.

So while a sacrament does, indeed, partake of mystery, it also claims a certain physical reality. A sacrament is a recognition that humans are both spirit and body. And although the experience of the spirit is the primary factor in our relationship to God, physical symbols of our spiritual realities are essential to our humanness.

Various issues have surrounded both Baptism and Holy Communion. In the case of Baptism, three matters should be mentioned. One is the mode of baptism. It is variously administered by sprinkling, pouring, and immersion. The importance of these differences should not be minimized, because—as the whole subject of sacraments makes clear—physical and ritual procedures are vehicles of grace and experience. But basically, all modes of baptism are intended to convey the concept of cleansing. Beyond doubt, immersion provides the most vivid picture, and historical theologians probably would agree immersion was the earliest form of baptism. This fact does not, however, invalidate or discredit other forms, all of which are nearly as old as the Christian church.

A second issue of baptism is more crucial, the relationship between baptism and salvation. Within this issue is the further question of infant baptism, that is, whether one should be baptized until one is consciously able to accept the grace for oneself. The New Testament largely assumes a missionary situation where only believers (and their households) are baptized. The Catholic and Orthodox traditions, and numbers of Protestant bodies, believe that through baptism a person is born again in Christ; that the act itself is salvific. Some groups accept this idea but also contend persons may experience a new birth independent of baptism. Still other bodies, including especially Baptists, Disciples, and Churches of Christ, believe baptism should not be performed until after a person has consciously accepted Jesus Christ as Savior.

A third issue involves the baptismal formula. Nearly all Christian bodies use the phrase commanded by Jesus—"baptizing them in the name of the Father and of the Son and of the Holy Spirit" (Matthew 28:19). In the early twentieth century, however, some Pentecostal bodies observed that in baptisms reported in the book of Acts, the formula was "in the name of Jesus Christ" (Acts 2:38; 10:48). They believe baptism can be correctly administered only in Jesus' name.

The Sacrament of Holy Communion

As indicated earlier, the sacrament of Holy Communion has roots in the Jewish celebration of the Passover. But on the night Jesus celebrated his last Passover, he introduced a decidedly new element: The host became the sacrifice. Jesus "took a loaf of bread, and when he had given thanks, he broke it and said, 'This is my body that is for you. Do this in remembrance of me.' In the same way he took the cup also, after supper, saying, 'This cup is the new covenant in my blood. Do this, as often as you drink it, in remembrance of me'" (1 Corinthians 11:23-25).

Though the words of institution vary among Christian bodies, each service of Holy Communion is a reenactment of that evening event and also a recalling of Calvary. Believers remember the sacrificial death of Christ. During early generations of church history, the Communion service was part of a congregational meal. In First Corinthians Paul indicates, on one hand, that early Christians were already beginning to trivialize the ceremony (1 Corinthians 11:17-34), and on the other hand, that Paul was filled with awe and respect for the sacredness and the inherent power of the event. The sacrament was more than simply a memorial service; Christ was present, with the potential for both healing and judgment.

Holy Communion is also referred to as the *Eucharist*. The word comes from a Greek word meaning "to give thanks," and it refers to Jesus' giving thanks for the bread and the wine. Catholics refer to the service as the "Mass"; Protestants speak of "the Lord's Supper" or "the Last Supper"; Orthodox churches use the term "the Divine Liturgy."

Nearly all contemporary Christian bodies follow essentially the same patterns in their sacrament of Communion but have distinct differences of opinion about what is happening. The major issue is the nature of Christ's presence in the sacrament. The Orthodox, Roman Catholics, Lutherans, and many Anglicans believe Christ is bodily present in the elements of bread and wine. However, Lutherans traditionally believe the substance of the bread and wine are not changed into the body and blood of Christ, but that they only coexist with one another, so that bread is joined together with body and wine with blood. This view is known as *consubstantiation*. The traditional Catholic view, *transubstantiation*, is that at the point in the Mass when the elements are consecrated, the substance of the bread and wine is transformed into the substance of Christ's body and blood, even while the appearances of bread and wine remain.

Many Protestant bodies believe the power of Christ is present in the Eucharist for those who receive it with faith. The "presence" is real but not in the sense of either consubstantiation or transubstantiation. Other Protestants insist the service is an event honoring Christ and remembering his sacrifice, but not identifying his presence in a distinctive way.

Because of these differences of belief (and in some instances, because of other doctrinal distinctives) many bodies in Christendom do not welcome to the sacrament persons of other Christian denominations. Where anyone is welcome to participate in the sacrament, the practice is commonly referred to as "open Communion"; and where only persons of a particular Christian body, or even of a particular congregation, may commune, "closed Communion."

Holy Communion is sometimes described as a "saving ordinance" because of the grace present to redeem and to restore. Some people find this service a setting for emotional or physical healing, perceiving that in taking the bread and the wine, they are taking to themselves the health of Jesus Christ.

Seven Sacraments

Both the Roman Catholic and Eastern Orthodox bodies recognize seven sacraments, including Baptism and Holy Communion. *Confirmation* is a personal affirmation of the vows taken for one at baptism and is commonly offered to children or youth. Adults also are often confirmed. Confirmation is usually preceded by a period of intensive training. *Reconciliation* (or *penance*) is a ritual for contrition, or sorrow for sin. The liturgy of reconciliation has four parts—contrition, confession, act of penance, and absolution.

Anointing of the sick is frequently referred to as *extreme unction*, because from the Middle Ages until rather recently it was a ritual used when someone was thought to be dying. Now the sacrament is being returned to its original meaning, as an anointing with oil for purposes of healing through prayer. This ritual is practiced in one form or another by many Protestant churches but is not considered a sacrament by Protestants.

Marriage is held sacred in all Christian bodies but recognized as a sacrament in the Catholic and Orthodox traditions. Marriage as sacrament emphasizes the spiritual as well as the physical union of wife and husband. From a pragmatic perspective, viewing marriage as a sacrament quite possibly elevates the union in the minds of spiritually sensitive persons. Protestant communions believe marriage is holy but do not believe it is portrayed in Scripture as a sacrament.

Ordination, the seventh sacrament of the Catholic and Orthodox communities, is the setting apart of persons for service under the auspices of the church. In Catholicism, ordination is known formally as "the sacrament of holy orders." Although Protestantism teaches the "priesthood of all believers," it nevertheless acknowledges that certain persons have a more particular calling. Most Protestant bodies practice ordination, though they do not consider it a sacrament. In a large number of communions, including Catholicism, ordination is performed by the laying on of hands (1 Timothy 4:14).

Other Sacramental Observances

In several Protestant bodies, *foot-washing* is observed as a sacrament. They base their teaching on Jesus' words to the dis-

An *ordinance* of the church is an established practice or ceremony carried out as a memorial or an act of obedience. The sacraments are ordinances, but not all ordinances are sacraments. Different modern Christian denominations use the term to designate different specific practices. In nonsacramental traditions, Baptism and Holy Communion are called ordinances because they were "ordained" by Jesus. Some church traditions view the elements of the sacraments as having saving power of their own and call these practices *saving ordinances.*

223

ciples after he had washed their feet on the night before his crucifixion: "So if I, your Lord and Teacher, have washed your
feet, you also ought to wash one another's feet" (John 13:14).
While Roman Catholicism does not consider foot-washing a
sacrament, the Pope by tradition washes the feet of twelve
priests, or even prisoners or poor persons, on Maundy Thursday.
Some bishops of the Roman Catholic Church follow the same
example. Individual congregations of different communions
sometimes include such an observance during Holy Week.

The *love feast,* particularly as observed by Moravians and the
Church of the Brethren, is not identified as a sacrament but is
treated in much the same fashion. It is a worship service built
around a common meal—usually a simple one—and intended
to bring to mind the fellowship of the earliest Christians.

Some Christian bodies, notably the Friends (Quakers) and
the Salvation Army, do not observe any sacraments. George
Fox, the founder of the Society of Friends, taught that the only
true baptism is baptism in the Spirit, and the only true communion is inward communion with God. The Salvation Army also
emphasizes the baptism of the Holy Spirit, teaching that Christ
never intended Baptism or Communion to be repeated continually. Like some other Protestant bodies, Salvationists dedicate
their infants to God in an act that is in its own way an equiva-
lent of infant baptism.

What then is a sacrament? Granted, many forms and rituals
have blessed the life of the church and the lives of individual
believers over the centuries. What makes some of these sacraments while others are not?

Above all, they must have been ordained by Christ himself.
This definition holds true across Christendom, including those
Protestant bodies that prefer to speak of such observances as
"ordinances" rather than as sacraments, because they are acts
"ordained" by Christ. The Council of Florence, in the fifteenth
century, defined the seven sacraments practiced by Catholicism
and clarified the three elements necessary for a sacrament—a
form of words, material things (such as bread and wine in Communion) that are the "matter" of the sacrament, and intention to
do what the church does in celebrating the sacrament. Although
the Catholic and Orthodox communions have seven sacraments,
they nevertheless identify Baptism and Eucharist as "the two
great sacraments of the gospel."

For the believer, the heart of the matter would surely be the
desire to do whatever our Lord has commanded, to do it in
faith, and in the process, to recognize the grace that can be conveyed to the believer in faithfully receiving the sacraments.

BECAUSE WE THE CHURCH BELIEVE Christ has
ordained special means of conveying grace, I will
faithfully observe these ordinances, to the glory of
God and to the nurture of my Christian life.

224

BELIEVING AND LIVING

Few matters of doctrine affect the typical believer more intimately than the sacraments. Because they are visible, they are more comprehensible to us than such doctrines as the Holy Spirit or the Trinity. But because they are visible and physical, they may also be trivialized or taken for granted.

What about Holy Communion, as you have experienced it, most surely conveys faith and grace to you?

_____

_____

If you have observed both immersion and sprinkling as forms of baptism, what has impressed you in each instance as especially meaningful?

_____

_____

We sometimes hear of Communion services in various settings where other elements are substituted for the bread and wine. Are other elements ever adequate for a true celebration of the Eucharist? Explain. What minimal elements would you need, personally, for an adequate celebration of Communion?

_____

_____

What merits do you find in the view that recognizes marriage and ordination as sacraments? Why might you not so recognize them?

_____

_____

If your church background did not include emphasis on the sacraments, what meaning do they have for you now?

_____

_____

SEEKING MORE UNDERSTANDING

To remind yourself of the language and actions related to the sacraments, locate a hymnal or book of worship that includes the rituals for the sacraments of Baptism and Holy Communion and read the several forms of the rituals. Notice what teachings of the church are affirmed and what is professed through word and act by all participants in the celebrations. Think about how these sacraments are for you signs of sacred things.

PRAYER

"We do not presume to come to this thy table, O merciful Lord, trusting in our own righteousness, but in thy manifold and great mercies. We are not worthy so much as to gather up the crumbs under thy table. But thou art the same Lord, whose property is always to have mercy. Grant us therefore, gracious Lord, so to partake of this Sacrament of thy Son Jesus Christ, that we may walk in newness of life, may grow into his likeness, and may evermore dwell in him, and he in us. Amen."

—*Book of Worship, The Methodist Church*

23

Adoration
of God

Worship

Confession
of sins

Communion
with God

Praise

Prayer

Private worship   Public worship

Offer of ourselves to God

Worship in spirit and truth

Hearing the Word

In Spirit and Truth

"God is spirit, and those who worship him must worship in spirit and truth."

—John 4:24

LIFE QUESTIONS

Humans are worshiping creatures who reach beyond themselves, realizing something more exists than our physical senses can apprehend. At its worst, our worship is self-seeking, a means to benefit ourselves by winning the favor of whatever gods there may be. At our best, we are God-adoring, seeking after God simply because God deserves such adoration.

But what is worship, and why is worship so essential to us? How do we worship best? Have I worshiped when I have not felt God's presence? What is the relative importance of public and private worship? And how does prayer fit into our lives, our service to humanity, and our relationship to God?

ASSIGNMENT

In a sense, we could take the whole book of Psalms as our Scripture for this week. But we may be surprised to discover that, other than the directions given in the Pentateuch for the Tabernacle, the Bible offers few specific commands or suggestions about how we should worship. Perhaps especially we need to know the importance of righteousness in worship, that is, of our being right with the God we seek to adore.

Here is a lesson as close to us as table grace or our daily devotional reading and as sublime as Isaiah's vision in the Temple. Our Scriptures call for intelligent, excited involvement.

Day 1   Exodus 19:9-25 (people prepare for covenant ceremony); 2 Chronicles 6 (prayer of dedication); Psalm 24 (entering the sanctuary)
Introduction and Readings 242 and 243

Day 2   Psalms 148 (all creatures to praise the Lord); 150 (hymn of praise)
Readings 244 and 245

Day 3   Isaiah 1:8-20 (justice rather than sacrifice); 6 (vision of the Holy God)
Readings 246 and 247

Day 4   Matthew 6:5-18 (response to God not for show); John 4:1-26 (worship in spirit and truth)
Readings 248 and 249

Day 5   Luke 18:1-8 (persistence in prayer); Revelation 5 (worthy is the Lamb)
Readings 250, 251, and 252

Day 6   Read and respond to "The Church Teaching and Believing" and "Believing and Living."

Day 7   Rest and prayer

DAILY PRAYER

Pray for the persons and situations on your Prayer Concerns list and about issues or concerns emerging from your daily reading and study.

WORSHIP

SCRIPTURE	READINGS
DAY 1	
Exodus 19:9-25; 2 Chronicles 6; Psalm 24	Introduction and Readings 242 and 243
DAY 2	
Psalms 148; 150	Readings 244 and 245
DAY 3	
Isaiah 1:8-20; 6	Readings 246 and 247

SCRIPTURE	READINGS
DAY 4	
Matthew 6:5-18; John 4:1-26	Readings 248 and 249
DAY 5	
Luke 18:1-8; Revelation 5	Readings 250, 251, and 252

DAY 6 STUDY MANUAL	PRAYER CONCERNS
"The Church Teaching and Believing" and "Believing and Living"	

THE CHURCH TEACHING AND BELIEVING

The primary calling of believers is to worship God; the primary business of the church is worship. Our gospel is earthbound if we declare "good news" that fails to find its ultimate reach in the adoration of God. Our service efforts will in time run dry for lack of inner impulse, and we will become less than we were created to be. But when we truly worship, we regain the finest part of what we are, the image of the divine.

Worship is more than one of the activities of the church; it is the heart from which all else flows. Without it, the rest of life loses its impelling quality. Even the poorest worship makes us reach beyond ourselves. The best worship brings us into the presence of God and then restores us to passionate service on earth.

Earliest Pictures of Worship

Genesis pictures the human race, in its earliest scenes, in unspoiled communion with God. We are made in God's image, and the breath of God is in us (Genesis 1:27; 2:7). Under such circumstances, what could be more normal than to commune with God? Such is the mood until the relationship is marred by sin.

Then, with no word of explanation and no suggestion as to how it has come to pass, the practice of worship becomes part of the human story. In one sense, it is a disastrous introduction, as Cain becomes jealous of his brother Abel at the time of their offerings to God and then murders him. On the other hand, Abel's offering is effective; it pleases God. Human groping after God is not in vain, nor is pleasing God beyond human reach.

Still another element comes into the worship story when Noah "built an altar to the LORD" (Genesis 8:20). Now there is a particular place, and with it a more obvious ritual. When Abraham and Sarah become the central characters in the biblical record, the altar becomes central with them. Each phase of Abraham's spiritual journey is marked by the building of an altar and the worship of God.

The next notable step in the structuring of worship comes with the organizing of the people of God, Israel. Exodus gives us both the political foundation of the nation, in the Law—particularly, the Ten Commandments—and the spiritual foundation of the nation, in the plans for the Tabernacle and the orders of worship. Exodus envisioned an order built on the substantial base of Law and worship.

But the intricate system of worship had its pitfalls. Time and again prophets and psalmists pointed that out. Samuel told King Saul,

"Surely, to obey is better than sacrifice,
and to heed than the fat of rams" (1 Samuel 15:22).

The prophet Amos, speaking for the Lord, made the same point fiercely in a cry to his generation:

"I hate, I despise your festivals,
and I take no delight in your solemn assemblies. . . .
Take away from me the noise of your songs;
I will not listen to the melody of your harps.
But let justice roll down like waters,
and righteousness like an ever-flowing stream" (Amos 5:21-24).

The psalmist, pleading passionately for forgiveness, recognizes that God has "no delight in sacrifice" or a burnt offering:

"O Lord, open my lips,
and my mouth will declare your praise. . . .
The sacrifice acceptable to God is a broken spirit;
a broken and contrite heart, O God, you will not despise" (Psalm 51:15-17).

The prophets and the psalmists knew ritual, important as it might be as a conveyor of worship, was meaningless if not marked by a commitment to lead a righteous, godly life. The quality of worship was measured by interior matters—sincerity, integrity, purity of heart—and exterior matters—justice.

But this lesson worshipers in every generation find difficult to learn. Rituals are easier to manage than the thoughts and intents of the heart and the demand for justice. And humans always look for shortcuts; we want rituals that work like magic. But biblical religion has nothing to do with magic. It is a matter of heart worship and ethical conduct.

Jesus Defines Worship

Jesus made this point in any number of ways. For instance, when he gave his disciples a pattern for prayer, he encouraged them to address God in the intimate language of relationship: "Our Father" (Matthew 6:9). When you fast, he said, don't do it so people will recognize that you're being religious; "put oil on your head and wash your face" (6:17). When you pray, "do not heap up empty phrases" (6:7).

But Jesus put the matter of worship into the most succinct terms in a conversation with the woman of Samaria. She worshiped on the mountain traditional to her people, Mount Gerizim; and since Jews centered their public worship in Jerusalem, she wanted a definitive answer: Which was the right place to worship? Jesus answered, "The hour is coming when you will worship the Father neither on this mountain nor in Jerusalem. . . . But the hour is coming, and is now here, when the true worshipers will worship the Father in spirit and truth, for the Father seeks such as these to worship him. God is spirit, and those who worship him must worship in spirit and truth" (John 4:21-24).

Most believers will agree worship in spirit and truth is the goal of their worship, but most will confess they do not regularly attain it. The more thoughtful also will confess some uncertainty about the meaning of "spirit and truth." Worship ought never to be simply a formula; so we seek for truth in the inward parts. The ancient poet asked who could stand in God's holy place, then answered,

"Those who have clean hands and pure hearts,
who do not lift up their souls to what is false,
and do not swear deceitfully" (Psalm 24:4).

To worship in the spirit suggests that the breath, or spirit, of God in us should reach out to God's Spirit. The deepest reality in us cries out to the surest reality in all the universe, God.

But worship is pursued with quite ordinary means. And this fact is both its peril and its wonder. Because worship is channeled through our human emotions, the worshiper can easily confuse the spiritual with attitudes and feelings that have nothing to do with God. We approach God with a range of emotions nearly as wide as the whole emotional catalog. Proper worship can be silent (Habakkuk 2:20) or wildly exuberant (Psalm 150). The worshiper may be awestruck or jubilant. We may be so impressed with God's holiness and otherness that we cry with Isaiah, "Woe is me!" (Isaiah 6:5), or so struck by God's nearness that we say with Paul, "Abba! Father!" (Galatians 4:6).

Because biblical worship involves the whole person, all of the senses are called into play. Obviously sound is a factor, through both music and whatever words are employed, both liturgical and sermonic. Even though Israel could not use graven images, sight was a factor in worship, in the beauty invested in their Tabernacle and their Temple. Smell came into worship for Israel and for several Christian communions in their offering of incense. Touch is experienced in the anointings with oil or water in both the Hebrew and Christian liturgies. Even taste is experienced in most Christian traditions, in the sacrament of Holy Communion, or in love feasts—and surely in Israel, in their festive occasions centered in the Temple or synagogue and later in the home.

"Because your steadfast love is better than life,
   my lips will praise you.
So I will bless you as long as I live;
   I will lift up my hands and call on your name."
—Psalm 63:3-4

Continuing Elements of Worship

Although contemporary Jewish worship might seem quite different from Christian practice, several basic elements are common to both. This situation isn't surprising, since Christianity has its roots in Judaism. Our first picture of Peter and John after the Day of Pentecost and the birth of the church is of their "going up to the temple at the hour of prayer" (Acts 3:1). Paul began most of his churches by meetings in the synagogue. The worship most natural to the first Christians was the worship they had known as Jews. Though Temple sacrifices continued in Jerusalem until the destruction of the Temple in A.D. 70, the earliest Christians were synagogue-oriented rather than Temple-oriented. And since Christ's sacrifice was a "once for all" sacrifice (Hebrews 9:12), they no longer had need of the sacrificial system.

But other elements of their experience in Judaism were as important as ever—prayers, exposition of the Scriptures, and singing. Their exposition of Scripture took on a new quality because now they read their Hebrew Scriptures through the lens of their experience in Jesus Christ. As Matthew put it so often in his Gospel, "All this took place to fulfill what had been spoken by the Lord through the prophet" (Matthew 1:22). As for singing, the Psalms that had been their mainstay in worship continued to be important, but now there was more: "Be filled with the Spirit, as you sing psalms and hymns and spiritual songs among yourselves, singing and making melody to the Lord in your hearts" (Ephesians 5:18-19).

Worship in contemporary Christianity ranges all the way from Quaker services, where at times not a word is spoken except the dismissal, to Pentecostal services, where individual, vocal prayer—including speaking in tongues—may seem confusion to an outsider. Yet each of these bodies, and all others between, understand their practices as true to Scripture and based in Scripture. The ultimate test of all worship, contemporary or ancient, traditional or unstructured, is the one Jesus gave to the woman of Samaria—that it be "in spirit and truth" (John 4:24).

Private Worship: Prayer

Important as is public worship of God, it is not a substitute for private worship, especially worship through prayer. Without a doubt more people pray than engage in public worship. Prayer is so instinctive to human beings, and so essential, that many pray who do not think of themselves as being religious. In some instances, even people who do not believe in God pray. Logic may rule out a divine being, but longing for communion with the eternal insists on ignoring logic.

What, exactly, is prayer? The dictionary reminds us the word *prayer* comes from the Latin *precari*, which means "to entreat." But as soon as that definition is given, those who have studied prayer in even modest fashion will insist prayer is much more than entreating. Prayer is also adoration and giving thanks; it is

From the beginning of the church Christians celebrated the Resurrection weekly with Sunday worship services and annually at Easter, often called the Christian Passover. When Constantine gave Christianity official status in the fourth century, the main festivals of the Christian year were Easter and Pentecost. The celebration of the birth of Jesus at Christmas seems to have started in the fourth century, though East and West at first celebrated different dates. Gradually the church began to include a period of preparation for the main festivals—Advent before Christmas, Lent before Easter, and the seven weeks after Easter as preparation for Pentecost. The modern church year begins with Advent and includes Epiphany, Lent, Holy Week, Easter, Pentecost, and Kingdomtide, though terms designating the seasons and holy days may vary.

confession of sins and lifting the heart in praise. Prayer may be a petition for one's own welfare or selfless intercession for the needs of another. Prayer may be as simple as the prayer, "Lord Jesus Christ, Son of God, have mercy upon me, a sinner," or it may be as eloquent as the biblical psalms.

But varied as our prayer practices may be, the Christian tradition establishes some boundaries on what constitutes prayer. To say with the poet, "Prayer is the soul's sincere desire, / Uttered or unexpressed," is not quite enough. Many of the soul's desires, including some very sincere ones, are profane and utterly wicked. Also, for a prayer to be biblical, the desire must be directed to God. Eloquence or form does not define prayer; it must have God as its considered destination. Prayer must be more than aimless meditation, and certainly more than talking to oneself.

That is, prayer is conversation with God—an unequal conversation, of course, since God is God and we are human. Thus it has elements and emphases not likely found in our conversations with fellow human beings. Adoration, confession, and petition (even to the point of intercession) appear only occasionally in ordinary conversation, but they are significant parts of the conversation we call prayer. Also, the more a person prays, the more prayer will have a conversational quality; and the divine-human friendship will become increasingly significant in the prayer experience.

Jesus and Prayer

When one of the disciples asked Jesus to teach them to pray, he told them, "When you pray, say," and proceeded to give them a short prayer (Luke 11:1-4). Clearly, it wasn't meant to be an incantation, though sometimes believers have reduced it to that. As a pattern, it offers intimacy (addressing God as "Father"), reverence ("hallowed be your name"), a prayer for God's purposes to be done ("Your kingdom come"), an appeal for the common necessities of life ("Give us each day our daily bread"), an acknowledgment of sin with an appeal for forgiveness ("And forgive us our sins"), and a plea to be saved from trial and temptation. In a sense this pattern makes prayer seem simple, and in a sense it is. Perhaps Jesus meant to give only a primer of prayer, expecting those who learned the lesson well to go further on their own.

So what more can we learn about prayer from Jesus? We can see from his own practice that prayer was utterly essential in Jesus' life. As strong as was Jesus' sense of mission and his compassion for the needs of the multitudes, he chose at intervals to leave the people and their needs in order to commune with God. For those who understand the enormity of life's issues, prayer means survival. We cannot function rightly without it. Jesus knew this, and his example teaches us.

Jesus also made clear prayer is a relationship, and an intimate one. Some practices of prayer work from a base of fear. A

232

great deal of common prayer is only petition: God is seen as a dispenser of favors who must be solicited. Many popular forms of meditation are simply communing with one's own soul. None of these catch the quality that most characterized Jesus' prayers. His form of address to God was a relational word, *Father*. He used it not only as the opening of his model prayer but in the prayer at Gethsemane, when intimacy was at its zenith (Matthew 26:39), and again at his crucifixion, when he prayed for his tormentors and as he breathed his last (Luke 23:34, 46). Jesus' prayers were never shoutings at a distant God. Indeed, when Jesus prayed at the tomb of Lazarus, just before raising him from the dead, there is even a kind of playful quality: "Father, I thank you for having heard me. I knew that you always hear me, but I have said this for the sake of the crowd standing here" (John 11:41-42).

Is such intimacy in prayer intended for all believers, or is it restricted to Jesus alone? Surely Jesus was setting a pattern for a high quality of relationship in prayer when he used intimate relational terms, and surely the Gospel writers intended the material they transmitted should be an example for the generations of believers.

Jesus' practice of prayer also teaches prayer is action. Some perceive prayer to be valuable only for the effect prayer has on the person who prays. But when Jesus sent out the seventy on their mission, he said the task to be done was too big for the group going out. Strangely, however, he did not suggest they try to enlist other laborers. Rather, he said, "The harvest is plentiful, but the laborers are few; therefore ask the Lord of the harvest to send out laborers into his harvest" (Luke 10:2).

Does this suggest God must be persuaded to help in the divine enterprise? Not at all. It simply underlines what is inferred in all our saying of the Lord's prayer:

"Your kingdom come.

Your will be done,

on earth as it is in heaven" (Matthew 6:10).

Through prayer, we participate in bringing the will of God to pass. This idea is not surprising, since by our deeds we also hope to assist in bringing God's will to pass. But because of our inadequate view of prayer—our spiritualizing it—we hesitate to approach prayer as we approach our service for God. Jesus made no such distinction.

In something of the same mood, Jesus taught persistence in prayer. In his parables of the man who seeks bread from his neighbor at midnight (Luke 11:5-8) and of the widow seeking justice from an unjust judge (18:2-8), Jesus taught his followers "to pray always and not to lose heart" (18:1). He made clear there is no reluctance on God's part, but for reasons not necessarily clear to us, we must persevere in prayer. Perhaps it is for the same reason we must persevere in the work of the Kingdom—because the good we (and God) wish to see accomplished faces opposition.

Worship and Prayer: The Reach to God

Students of world religions often emphasize that all humans seek after the eternal; and being human, they seek in somewhat similar ways. They practice some form of prayer, because they instinctively sense God can be approached. They are likely to look up when they think of God, not because they think the world is flat but because in a psychological sense, to think of God is to think loftily, to think up. On the other hand, worship usually includes bowing or even prostration, out of a sense of the difference between humans and God, including a sense of human unworthiness.

Worship patterns are affected by changing times and changing culture patterns. Take music, for instance. Israel worshiped with trumpet, lute, harp, tambourine, and cymbals. The organ, with more than two thousand years of history, has been the major worship instrument for most churches for several hundred years. Recently, drums, guitars, and synthesizers have appealed to many. So too with structures of ritual. Many basic elements of worship have remained since the first century, and the use of the Psalms goes back to pre-Christian worship. But some groups, like the Society of Friends (Quakers), have chosen silence as a dominant element, while revivalist groups have concentrated on singing, lengthy preaching, and informal prayers. African-American worship has had lengthier services and more vigorous congregational involvement.

So great variety exists even within the common human reach to God. But some factors are basic to Christian worship. Worship must focus on God; human pleasure and fulfillment almost always follow, but they are not the point of worship. Second, ritual is helpful, but it is not the final criterion for worship. Jesus answered that issue in his conversation with the woman of Samaria. God seeks those who worship "in spirit and truth," because God is spirit (and indeed, God is truth); so God "seeks such as these to worship him" (John 4:23-24). Certain rituals may appeal to us aesthetically, emotionally, or nostalgically—all evidences we may easily mistake for spirit. But spirit and truth are the issue, not the rituals we use.

No doubt the most earnest believers will seek for excellence in their practices of worship, both public and private. They will conclude that while God receives the humble and contrite heart, whether that heart comes crudely or elegantly, the heart that loves God best will want to approach God with as much excellence and beauty as possible, knowing always, however, that the greatest beauty in worship and in prayer is the worship characterized by sincerity and love.

BECAUSE WE THE CHURCH BELIEVE God desires our worship and prayer, I will seek God earnestly, in spirit and truth.

BELIEVING AND LIVING

Nothing about the Christian life is more familiar to the believer than prayer, and few things more familiar than public worship. And yet most of us will confess we don't think much about what we believe concerning worship or prayer. Perhaps we reason that worship and prayer are so much a matter of the heart it is somehow inappropriate to analyze them. And yet, because they are so important, they deserve intelligent, consecrated thought. What have you learned about prayer that is most important to you in your own walk as a believer?

_____

_____

As you think about your own experiences of public worship, how much of what you prefer in worship has to do with nostalgia, emotion, or aesthetics? How do you separate these elements from the primary issue of worshiping God "in spirit and truth"?

_____

_____

Think about the worship services in your church. What about the services would make worshipers aware that praise of God is the purpose of worship?

_____

_____

What is the most fulfilling element in your own prayer life? What is most frustrating?

_____

_____

If you could plan the worship service for your church, what would it look like? Why would you plan it this way?

_____

_____

SEEKING MORE UNDERSTANDING

If grace before meals is not a pattern in your own life or in the life of your family, consider beginning the practice. Talk it over with others in your household and come to some agreement so others do not feel coerced. To overcome any shyness or awkwardness, you might use silent prayer for a while or locate a book of graces to be read aloud. As you and others become comfortable, take turns praying grace.

PRAYER

"Enable me, O God, to collect and compose my thoughts before an immediate approach to Thee in prayer. May I be careful to have my mind in order when I take upon myself the honor to speak to the sovereign Lord of the universe, remembering that upon the temper of my soul depends, in very great measure, my success.

Thou are infinitely too great to be trifled with; too wise to be imposed on by a mock devotion and dost abhor a sacrifice without a heart. Help me to entertain an habitual sense of Thy perfections, as an admirable help against cold and formal performances. Save me from engaging in rash and precipitate prayers and from abrupt breaking away to follow business or pleasure, as though I had never prayed. _Amen_."

—_Susanna Wesley, 1670–1742_

24

Christian life
Discipleship
Belief in action

Belong to Christ
Serve God and neighbor
Deny self
Ethical living

Life in community

Cross-bearing
Inward and outward goodness
Obedience

Empowered by the Holy Spirit

Living the Christian Life

"If any want to become my followers, let them deny themselves and take up their cross daily and follow me."

—*Luke 9:23*

LIFE QUESTIONS

In some ways, the Christian life is like fine art: We may not be able to define it, but we know it when we see it. Of course we're cautious about defining it lest we seem to be drawing boundaries where the Scriptures have not. And since we're saved by faith, isn't it dangerous to set up standards that would tend toward works? And yet, it seems the Christian life ought to be open to some kind of definition.

So how ought a person to live who has received the name *Christian?* What is expected of us after we become part of the community of faith? Are there standards a Christian can be expected to meet? And if so, who sets them? Or are we all free-lancers, living as we wish?

ASSIGNMENT

Although the specific elements of the Christian life are found primarily in the New Testament, we have preliminary patterns of ethics and conduct in the writings of the Old Testament. After all, the first generation of believers had no other document to go on. We will notice, as we read, that the biblical description of the Christian way of life is wide-ranging. It has to do with both the interior and exterior life, with our relationship to God and to our fellow humans, and with matters ranging from our daily work to our entertainment, our thoughts, and our conversation. Indeed, to do full justice to this lesson, we could well reason we'd have to read the entire Bible.

Day 1 Psalm 1 (the way of the righteous); Micah 6:1-8 (what the Lord requires)
Introduction and Readings 253 and 254
Day 2 Matthew 5 (life in the new age); 6 (practical piety)
Readings 255 and 256
Day 3 Matthew 7 (meaning of Jesus' message); Mark 8:34-38 (take up the cross)
Readings 257 and 258
Day 4 Matthew 25:14-26 (wise stewardship); 1 Corinthians 13 (the gift of love)
Readings 259 and 260
Day 5 Ephesians 4:17–5:21 (living the new life); James 2:14–3:12 (faith and works, wisdom from God)
Readings 261 and 262
Day 6 Read and respond to "The Church Teaching and Believing" and "Believing and Living."
Day 7 Rest and prayer

DAILY PRAYER

Pray for the persons and situations on your Prayer Concerns list and about issues or concerns emerging from your daily reading and study.

DISCIPLESHIP

SCRIPTURE	READINGS
DAY 1	
Psalm 1; Micah 6:1-8	Introduction and Readings 253 and 254
DAY 2	
Matthew 5; 6	Readings 255 and 256
DAY 3	
Matthew 7; Mark 8:34-38	Readings 257 and 258

SCRIPTURE	READINGS

DAY 4

Matthew 25:14-26; 1 Corinthians 13	Readings 259 and 260

DAY 5

Ephesians 4:17–5:21; James 2:14–3:12	Readings 261 and 262

DAY 6 STUDY MANUAL	PRAYER CONCERNS
"The Church Teaching and Believing" and "Believing and Living"	

THE CHURCH TEACHING AND BELIEVING

Nothing is closer to the heart of Christian faith, as we experience it, than discipleship. Yet discipleship isn't mentioned in either the Apostles' Creed or the Nicene Creed. Three modern creeds address the subject. The faith statement from the United Church of Canada declares,
"We are called to be the church:
to celebrate God's presence,
to love and serve others,
to seek justice and resist evil,
to proclaim Jesus, crucified and risen."
The Korean statement of faith speaks of the church as
"those who are united in the living Lord
for the purpose of worship and service."
A Modern Affirmation states that our faith "should manifest itself
in the service of love
as set forth in the example of our blessed Lord,
to the end
that the kingdom of God may come upon
the earth."
The absence of any such definition in the ancient creeds does not tell us the early church had no doctrine of the Christian life; nor does the presence of such themes in modern creeds prove the contemporary church is more effective in these matters.

Some people would say we need nothing more than Jesus' words: "If any want to become my followers, let them deny themselves and take up their cross and follow me" (Mark 8:34). Others would remind us a disciple is, by definition, nothing other than a *learner,* a pupil who follows his or her teacher.

We might ask if a description of the Christian life really belongs to a study of doctrine. In a sense, the topic seems more like material for a manual of Christian conduct. This would be true if Christian discipleship were only a body of beliefs. But Christianity requires its beliefs be put into action. For this reason no word for a Christian is more feared than *hypocrite.* On the other hand, we are also uneasy lest Christianity become nothing but a collection of legalisms. A faith whose Lord said the whole of teaching could be summed up in two commandments, love God with all your being and love your neighbor as yourself, should never be reduced to a list of rules.

But of course there is a middle ground between license and detailed rules. And yes, the Christian life is essential to doctrine, if doctrine is to be more than an intellectual curiosity. Perhaps our generation especially needs instruction in conduct, since we are conditioned to give undue emphasis to the rights of the individual. Discipleship promises no such right. To the contrary, it says we have accepted the sovereignty of a Lord.

Old Testament Standards
The only written guide for the first generation of Christians was the Old Testament, the Hebrew Scriptures. So the early Christians built their lives and their ethical systems rather largely on the documents they had inherited, the Law and the Prophets.

All through the Old Testament is a call for ethical conduct. This theme in Israel's religion largely marked them off from their neighbors. Israel's major bond to their God was their Law, and the covenant that required them to fulfill the demands of the Law.

So for them, life came down to being godly or ungodly, righteous or wicked. They understood God abhorred evil and evil conduct would therefore cut them off from God. Their standard of ethical conduct was far-reaching enough that, applied to our own times, we still find it demanding. It covered every imaginable human relationship and insisted also on "pure hearts" (Psalm 24:4). The Law and the Prophets called for both inward and outward goodness. Granted, in practice many of the people probably settled for ritual offerings they hoped would qualify them before God. But their Law, Prophets, and Writings all held up a strong ethical standard.

And those who were willing to settle for ritual religion were soundly rebuked by the prophets:
"He has told you, O mortal, what is good;
and what does the LORD require of you
but to do justice, and to love kindness,
and to walk humbly with your God?"
(Micah 6:8).

The New Testament Standard
Jesus asked for even more. When he said, "You have heard that it was said. . . . But I say to you" (Matthew 5:21-22), it was to make the commandments more demanding, not less. His was no comfortable religion. He welcomed sinners gladly, but he called for a new commitment to righteousness.

Jesus' epic statement comes to us in what is popularly called the Sermon on the Mount (Matthew 5–7). Scholars over the centuries have disagreed as to the application of this sermon. Some say the sermon is a rule for the accomplished kingdom of God but quite impossible for life in our present culture. Others contend it is the standard for believers in every century and our obligation is to come as close as possible to fulfilling its requirements.

In any event, the believer accepts it as a challenge to a better way. Without doubt it calls for a way of life that is beyond our ordinary ability. But this does not excuse the believer from striving to approach its standard. No attitude is more inappropriate to a disciple than cutting the call to fit convenience. A disciple may justifiably fall short of the calling, but a disciple is never allowed to revise the master's standards.

As Paul tried to delineate the Christian life for his converts, he never compromised the standards set by his Lord. He insisted they be "blameless on the day of our Lord Jesus Christ" (1 Corinthians 1:8). When the apostle called for a blameless life, he was speaking of a complete turnaround. It was a bold faith declaration when he wrote, "So if anyone is in Christ, there is a new creation: everything old has passed away; see, everything has become new!" (2 Corinthians 5:17).

But what stands out most, both in the teachings of Jesus and in the way of life spelled out in the letters, is a quality best described as toughness. We are startled by the difference between the openness shown the sinner and the stringency set upon the disciple. Jesus said, "Come to me, all you that are weary and are carrying heavy burdens, and I will give you rest. ...For my yoke is easy, and my burden is light" (Matthew 11:28-30). But when a disciple said, "Lord, first let me go and bury my father," Jesus answered, "Follow me, and let the dead bury their own dead" (8:21-22). He promised the Twelve, "You will be hated by all because of my name" (10:22). The apostle warned the young preacher, Timothy, "Indeed, all who want to live a godly life in Christ Jesus will be persecuted" (2 Timothy 3:12). As we review the centuries of church history, we see an ebb and a flow in persecution; some Christians live in an era of peace, while other generations and localities are always on the edge of martyrdom. But the standard and the expectation remain the same for every generation. The call to discipleship is a call to heroic living. The specifics are spelled out differently from one time or place to the next, but the commitment is the same; and it is demanding.

Elements in the Christian Life: Communion With God

A proper definition of the Christian life begins with right relationship with God. This is not to say the spiritual life is more important than service or ethical conduct; but it is an acknowledgment that service and ethical conduct, as faith measures them, cannot long be maintained without substantial inner resources.

The towel and basin symbolize humble service, the measure of discipleship in God's kingdom. After washing the disciples' feet, Jesus said, "I have set you an example, that you also should do as I have done to you" (John 13:15). The disciple picks up the towel and basin Jesus put down and follows his example.

The disciple is inseparable from the Master. Many persons who admire the ethical teachings of the Christian faith nevertheless look upon communion with God as mystical and impractical. They may admit it is enriching for a certain type of "spiritual" person, but they think of it as having limited importance.

But communion with God is the essence of the Christian life and the Christian community. The believer belongs to the Lord. Christian commitment is to a Person, not simply to a body of belief. Therefore nothing about this way of life is so important as maintaining a proper relationship to that Person. All else stems from this relationship.

The disciple therefore maintains an intentional devotional life. Everyone prays when in trouble, including many who will not pray again until the next occasion of trouble. A disciple prays, not because of trouble but because of a desire to be in communion with the Master. Many people read the Bible, perhaps even study it, because they know it is a superb piece of literature. The disciple recognizes the Bible's literary value but reads it out of love for the Lord from whom it has come. Great numbers of persons go to a house of worship on special occasions, perhaps a funeral service or a wedding. The disciple looks upon attendance at a church as being at least as inviolable as attendance at work. The motivation is simple: The place of worship is a special, ordained place of meeting with God, and a disciple knows nothing is more important than meeting regularly with God in the company of the community of God.

And yet, a logical issue arises. We have described devotion as an expression of love. But on the other hand, we list this devotion as one of the requirements of discipleship, as if it were commanded of us, or as if devotion can be organized. But can a relationship be organized? Can love have rules?

By all means. Love does, in fact, have rules; and the best relationships have structures. Love makes the rules—in marriage, on fidelity from the partner; in a parent, on care for the child; in a child, on honor and respect for the parent. Rules do not limit love; they provide love with channels for greater effectiveness. Love will still burst forth with ecstatic moments, but it is far more likely to have those moments if it has been preserved by the disciplines of the journey.

So disciples maintain a faithful devotional life, not because they always feel like it but because love requires it. Love asks for disciplines because love wants to devote itself to the beloved. The disciplines may not necessarily feel rewarding, but they provide the setting in which the rewards occur.

Elements in the Christian Life: Ethical Living

Early Christians were popularly known as "the people of the Way." They had taken upon themselves a way of life that distinguished them from the culture around them.

This distinction may have been easier to draw in the first century than in our time and place. Once Christianity moved out of Galilee and Judea and into the broader Roman world, it was in a culture where gods were a marketplace commodity and where morality and ethics were as malleable as the gods. When Paul said, "There is no longer Jew or Greek, there is no longer slave or free, there is no longer male and female; for all of you are one in Christ Jesus" (Galatians 3:28), he was flying in the face of all established order. And when the writer of Ephesians told Christian slaves, "Slaves, obey your earthly masters with fear and trembling, in singleness of heart, as you obey Christ" (Ephesians 6:5), the culture would have given assent to the counsel even though they didn't grasp the reason. But when he continued, "And, masters, do the same to them . . . for you know that both of you have the same Master in heaven, and with him there is no partiality" (6:9), he was challenging ideas about social status in the culture.

But in many ways our times are not that different from the world in which the Christian faith was first lived out. Unfortunately, the church has become more accommodating of the prevailing culture. First-century Christians understood what Paul meant when he wrote, "Do not be conformed to this world, but be transformed by the renewing of your minds, so that you may discern what is the will of God—what is good and acceptable and perfect" (Romans 12:2). We are not so sure, because we have blurred the boundaries too long.

Then too the complexity of modern life has made many ethical decisions extremely complex, and perhaps some moral decisions as well. Theft was easier to define in a basically agricultural economy than it is in a world of corporations, public lotteries, commodity shares, and currency markets. Mutual funds have made it easier for an investor to diversify; they have also made it more difficult for a conscientious investor to know if money is invested in truly ethical enterprises.

Some earnest believers cope with complex ethical problems by concentrating on specific issues. They deal with rampant materialism by doing all of their buying at garage sales, or they respond to television's invasion of life by selling their television set. Others, troubled by the corrupting quality of much entertainment, withdraw entirely from secular movies, plays, or books. The exponential growth of Christian bookstores, Christian radio, Christian television, and Christian schools has provided believers with new choices. It has also raised the possibility believers may become so isolated from their culture they can no longer be effective salt or leaven. Being "the people of the Way" is not simple in our contemporary society. But of course it never has been and never will be.

Believers need to keep a protest in their souls. Because culture patterns *are* culture patterns, we often slip into them unknowingly. A believer can easily mouth common cultural assumptions as if they were Scripture. Say something often enough, and people will believe it. The influence of negative cultural mores is an immediate and persistent issue.

242

Is it possible to live a truly godly, holy, ethical life in the modern or post-modern world? Not only is it possible; it is absolutely essential. Living such a life is a mark of a true disciple, as it always has been and always will be.

Elements in the Christian Life: Service to God and Others

Christians follow one who commanded them to take up a cross daily and follow him. *Cross* is a term difficult to define. But if we draw the definition from the example of Jesus, the cross is a burden that belongs to another and that we choose to take up in the other's stead. That is, when one follows Jesus, one enters a life of service. Jesus dramatized the point by taking the role of a slave, washing his disciples' feet. "So if I, your Lord and Teacher, have washed your feet, you also ought to wash one another's feet. For I have set you an example, that you also should do as I have done to you" (John 13:14-15).

Service has become hard to define. Now that a nation's economy has become known as a service economy, the concept of service has been blurred with the idea of profit. Self-help literature, and some preaching too, has encouraged service on the basis of the benefits received by serving. Without doubt, we usually feel better after we have served others, but feeling better should not be a motive for serving. "Service is good business" may be true, but such a slogan isn't the basis on which Jesus called his disciples to serve. We serve because it is the right thing to do, because Jesus commanded it, and because in serving we are following the example of our Lord.

Service must never become calculating; the two words together make an oxymoron. Jesus healed the sick and fed the multitudes without discrimination. We have no way of knowing if any followed Jesus permanently because of the miracles he performed for them. He didn't ask the intentions or the sincerity of those who came to him for healing. His task, he seemed to say, was to serve. What others did with his service was their concern. If we judge what Jesus did on the basis of the returns he received, we must conclude he served unwisely, since such a small number chose ultimately to follow him. But that, again, was their choice. His calling was to serve. He has committed that calling to those who are his disciples.

The disciple can, and should, serve at any time, in any place, in any way. We can serve our own families or strangers we will never meet again. We can serve physically, mentally, or psychologically—by cleaning a house, explaining a lesson, or encouraging the discouraged. We can serve by our money, our hospitality, or our good will. The possibilities are endless, as are the needs. What is generally in short supply is our sensitivity to need and our readiness to inconvenience ourselves in order to take up the other's cross.

But service is a mark of the Christian disciple, and it ought to be performed in a spirit that honors the disciple's Lord. If disciples are to be known by their love, that love will most often demonstrate itself in service.

The Meaning of Life

Humans believe life must have meaning, and are on a quest for that meaning. Paul found that meaning: "For to me, living is Christ" (Philippians 1:21). Life is to be lived to the glory of God. And as someone has said, living to God's glory cannot be just "moderately important"; it must be the grand passion of life.

But what of those believers for whom it is not the grand passion, for whom following Christ is, at best, only moderately important? Come to think of it, doesn't that description fit most believers? Indeed, is it perhaps uncomfortably close to describing my own life? If so, where do I fit into Christ's kingdom?

Clearly, disciples of Jesus are always in the process of becoming what they ought to be. The original twelve disciples were often characterized by self-seeking. Often they seemed to miss entirely what Jesus was trying to accomplish. The second generation of believers—those to whom the letters were originally addressed—were just as prone to ordinariness. As a matter of fact, the letters would be quite short if these believers hadn't provided the apostles with so many issues needing correction.

Our Lord works with what is available. By careful nurturing, moderate disciples become passionate ones, but it is usually a long process. We can hardly expect otherwise, considering the standard of excellence to which ultimately we aspire. Whatever the present limitations of any disciple, the commitment should be the same: "I press on to make it [the goal] my own, because Christ Jesus has made me his own" (Philippians 3:12). Because our Lord has seen in us the potential for greatness, we strive unceasingly to fulfill his divine expectations. A disciple can do no less.

> BECAUSE WE THE CHURCH BELIEVE a distinctive way of living is demanded of followers of Jesus Christ, I dedicate myself to being a disciple of whom my Lord never need be ashamed.

BELIEVING AND LIVING

Theologically, a Christian is easy to define; a Christian is a person who has accepted Jesus Christ as Lord and Savior. But defining the Christian life isn't so easy. In a sense, we spend all our years growing into the definition. But at this point in your understanding and your aspirations, how would you describe the life of discipleship?

_____

_____

We say the Christian way of life is a distinctive way of life. Consider that persons of other faiths demonstrate their love of God and neighbor through caring service to others. What then makes the Christian way distinctive?

_____

_____

What particular guidance do you take from the Sermon on the Mount for your life?

_____

_____

Look again at the prayer of Mustafah the tailor. Consider your occupation, your community, and write your version of Mustafah's prayer.

_____

_____

_____

_____

_____

_____

SEEKING MORE UNDERSTANDING

Review the week's assigned Scriptures, readings, and study manual commentary to see what clues are there to answer the question, As a Christian, how am I to serve God? Make a list or write a summary paragraph as a personal reminder.

PRAYER

"O God, I am Mustafah the tailor and I work at the shop of Muhammad Ali. The whole day long I sit and pull the needle and the thread through the cloth. O God, you are the needle and I am the thread. I am attached to you and I follow you. When the thread tries to slip away from the needle it becomes tangled and must be cut so that it can be put back in the right place. O God, help me to follow you wherever you may lead me. For I am really only Mustafah the tailor, and I work at the shop of Muhammad Ali on the great square."

—*A Muslim's first prayer as a Christian*

25

Sanctification

Perfect love · **Called to be holy** **A holy people**

Second work of grace

Set-apart life **Gift of God**

Holiness expressed in love

Maturity

Purity of heart and life Perfect as God is perfect

A Life Pleasing to God

"For I am the LORD your God; sanctify yourselves therefore, and be holy, for I am holy."
—*Leviticus 11:44*

LIFE QUESTIONS

Holiness, a true sacredness of life, has through the ages been a passionate pursuit of a few. To all the rest, it is a matter of almost total indifference.

After all, why should it matter? What difference does holiness make in our everyday world of jobs, taxes, mortgages, and success? If our goal in life is to be canonized, holiness would of course be important. But for the average person, holiness is beset with questions: What does holiness really mean? What difference does it make? Why would we want to be holy? And even if we want holiness, how do we become holy?

ASSIGNMENT

Holiness is a word found all through both the Old and the New Testaments. In the Old Testament, it is associated almost entirely with God. But because we are God's people, it becomes an issue for us too.

As you read, you will notice that at first the call for sanctification is largely by way of ritual. In time there is more emphasis on purity of heart. In the New Testament, conduct is emphasized, but vital holiness is also seen as a gift of God.

Day 1 Exodus 19 (a holy nation); Leviticus 11:24-47 ("be holy, for I am holy") Introduction and Readings 263 and 264

Day 2 Psalm 24 (clean and pure); Ezekiel 36:22-38 (restored for the sake of God's holy name) Readings 265 and 266

Day 3 Romans 6 (sanctification result of justification and righteousness); 1 Corinthians 3 (God's temple) Readings 267, 268, and 269

Day 4 Philippians 3:7-21 (reach for maturity); 2 Peter 1:1-11 (holy living); 1 Thessalonians 4:1-12 (purity of life through the Holy Spirit) Readings 270 and 271

Day 5 Ephesians 1:3-23 (chosen to be holy and blameless); 4:1—5:2 (clothed with a new self) Readings 272 and 273

Day 6 Read and respond to "The Church Teaching and Believing" and "Believing and Living."

Day 7 Rest and prayer

DAILY PRAYER

Pray for the persons and situations on your Prayer Concerns list and about issues or concerns emerging from your daily reading and study.

SANCTIFICATION

SCRIPTURE	READINGS
DAY 1	
Exodus 19; Leviticus 11:24-47	Introduction and Readings 263 and 264
DAY 2	
Psalm 24; Ezekiel 36:22-38	Readings 265 and 266
DAY 3	
Romans 6; 1 Corinthians 3	Readings 267, 268, and 269

SCRIPTURE	READINGS
DAY 4	
Philippians 3:7-21; 2 Peter 1:1-11; 1 Thessalonians 4:1-12	**Readings 270 and 271**
DAY 5	
Ephesians 1:3-23; 4:1–5:2	**Readings 272 and 273**

DAY 6 STUDY MANUAL	PRAYER CONCERNS
"The Church Teaching and Believing" and "Believing and Living"	

THE CHURCH TEACHING AND BELIEVING

Our purpose in turning to God is that we should be saved. God's purpose is that we should be holy. God, being gracious, seems to accept us on our terms, in that he saves us even though we show neither inclination toward nor hunger for holiness. But we disappoint the divine love if we settle for less than our ultimate sanctification.

The writer of Ephesians was so convinced of God's desire for our holiness that he put it in extravagant terms—extravagant, that is, unless we are equally caught up in the hunger for sanctification. God, he said, "chose us in Christ before the foundation of the world to be holy and blameless before him in love" (Ephesians 1:4). Our holiness has been in the mind of God for a long time; the very point of our choosing in Christ is that we should be "holy and blameless"; and the measure of this quality is that it is lived out in love.

This brings us to a fascinating observation. The quality of holiness, or sanctification, is of course the quality of godliness. And yet it was the desire to "be like God" (Genesis 3:5) that got Adam and Eve in trouble. Theirs was an unholy quest; they sought, by disobedience, what God desired to give them through their obedience. And they sought not God's character but God's power.

Sanctification comes from the Latin word *sanctus,* which means "holy." In the most basic sense, then, to be sanctified is to be made holy. Most Christian communions understand holiness to be the goal of the Christian life. But, most believers do not consider holiness to be supremely important. Throughout the Scriptures and the history of the Christian community, sanctification has been the less-than-understood goal, and spiritual mediocrity has been the norm.

Sanctification in the Old Testament

Probably no word is more prominent in the Pentateuch—the five books of the Law with which the Old Testament begins—than the word *holy*. It dominates, both in frequency and significance, both Exodus and Leviticus. As Israel approaches Sinai and the giving of the Law, God tells them, "Indeed, the whole earth is mine, but you shall be for me a priestly kingdom and a holy nation" (Exodus 19:5-6). A profound sense of holiness was to characterize their preparation: They would wash their clothes (an outward sign of their inward

cleansing), they were to abstain from sexual union during the preparatory days, and they were to "be careful not to go up to the mountain or to touch the edge of it" (19:12). Such was their sense of the holiness of God, and such their context for understanding themselves as God's "holy nation."

What to a modern reader may seem unnecessarily intricate laws in Exodus and Leviticus were to the purpose of becoming a holy people. The levitical laws dealt with matters believed to pollute life. Holiness and wholeness were more than a play on words; they were seen as fact. To be holy was to be whole and complete, orderly as God intended the creation to be. Whatever was ritually "unclean" was a violation of this order. Holiness implies a sharp distinction between the sacred and the profane.

Holiness, as Leviticus presents it, is a cooperative action between humans and God. "Consecrate yourselves [or, sanctify yourselves, as older translations put it] therefore, and be holy; for I am the LORD your God. Keep my statutes, and observe them; I am the LORD; I sanctify you" (Leviticus 20:7-8). The people were to sanctify themselves by keeping the laws God had given them, and God in turn would sanctify them. This basic pattern of divine and human interaction also characterizes the New Testament teachings on sanctification. Believers make themselves available to the purposes of God by their human consecration, and God in turn acts upon the dedicated soul.

The Old Testament perceived holiness as an issue for all of life. The meticulous regulations regarding bodily functions, cleanliness, unclean animals, and ritual observances emphasized that all of life was being lived out in God's sight. Holiness was not a sabbath event; it was a factor in everything a person did. And it affected everything they did. So the prophet Ezekiel complained that when Israel had "lived on their own soil, they defiled it with their ways and their deeds" (Ezekiel 36:17). Not only were they unclean; they had made the land unclean.

Sanctification in the New Testament

Jesus added a special dimension to the issue of holiness in the Sermon on the Mount. Having challenged his followers with new standards regarding murder, adultery, oaths, and retaliation, he then extended the boundaries of love. Jesus said, "Love your enemies and pray for those who persecute you, so that you may be children of your

Father in heaven" (Matthew 5:44-45). And what was the style of their Father in heaven? Indiscriminate love. Anybody, Jesus said, can love those who love them. He summed up the matter quite simply: "Be perfect, therefore, as your heavenly Father is perfect" (5:48). The goal was holiness of the most demanding kind, holiness that was perfect as God is perfect—a holiness that would express itself in love.

This holiness went beyond what they had previously known as holiness or perfection. Stringent as were their levitical laws, they were largely matters of measurable conduct. So too with the admirable standards set forth by the psalmist who called for "clean hands and pure hearts," from people who

> "do not lift up their souls to what is false,
> and do not swear deceitfully" (Psalm 24:4).

The psalmist was calling for high ethical conduct. But Jesus was asking for more—love that knew no boundaries. Here was a standard that could not be fulfilled by even the most meticulous religiosity or the most ethical conduct. It called for hearts that looked with love upon everyone, regardless of their connections or their deserving. A love, that is, such as God demonstrated daily through the gracious beneficence of nature.

But in his abrupt challenge, Jesus was only reflecting what the writer of Leviticus had said generations earlier: "You shall be holy, for I am holy" (Leviticus 11:45). These words are startlingly matter-of-fact, as if on one hand anyone would realize that being part of the divine community would of course entail holiness such as God embodies, and on the other hand, as if this level of holiness were to be achieved simply by announcing it as one of the requirements of community life.

But whether in Old Testament or New Testament, holiness is clearly expected of God's community—a taken-for-granted in this community. Holiness was expected in Israel and expected in the church. To be the people of God is to be a holy people. Holiness is not an elective course.

Nor is being holy easy. Paul reasons that in our natural state, we are slaves to sin and that we are made free only by dying with Christ and becoming "alive to God in Christ Jesus" (Romans 6:6-11). But then the secret is to "become slaves of righteousness," to achieve sanctification (6:18-19). Clearly, this righteousness is hard to define. Paul explains that it is not "a righteousness of my own that comes from the law, but one that comes through faith in Christ, the righteousness from God based on faith" (Philippians 3:9). We might wish such righteousness could be attained by keeping certain laws, even fairly stringent ones. Instead, it is a righteousness "based on faith" and expressing itself in love.

No wonder Paul says he has not yet obtained this; rather, "forgetting what lies behind and straining forward to what lies ahead, I press on toward the goal for the prize of the heavenly call of God in Christ Jesus" (3:13-14). If Paul acknowledged he was "straining" in order to reach the standard, we should hardly

The nine-pointed star represents the fruit of the Spirit in the lives of those who live by the Spirit—love, joy, peace, patience, kindness, generosity, faithfulness, gentleness, self-control (Galatians 5:22-23). Depictions of this symbol sometimes have the first initial or name of each fruit in the points of the star. The nine points might also bring to mind the nine gifts for service by Christians in 1 Corinthians 12:4-11. Whether fruit or services, the Holy Spirit is the source.

be surprised continuing generations find holiness a goal often out of our reach.

Unfortunately, most of us don't seem to think of sanctification as a goal. In this we are different from the New Testament world, where almost without fail the community of believers was addressed as *saints*—from the same word as sanctification. The New Testament knew of one kind of Christian: people engaged in the pursuit of an ideal—holiness. Probably the world around them, like ours, thought it an impossible dream.

The ideal is sharply defined in Ephesians as a life of "maturity, to the measure of the full stature of Christ" (Ephesians 4:13). The goal was to become like the Master. So it isn't surprising that before long believers came to be known as *Christians*, since at their best they were like Christ, and at their least they were committed in that direction. Here was sanctification, indeed—a life of such quality it was not blasphemous to call the person Christlike.

Nor is it surprising that, historically, those who have exhibited a level of holiness are usually those who have a profound sense of the divine sacrifice. To take seriously the death of Christ for human salvation yet be content with spiritual mediocrity seems nearly impossible. If indeed we understand we have been saved by the sacrifice of Christ, we are compelled to live with excellence that strives to honor such a sacrifice.

The Holiness of Seclusion

Because holiness is difficult to transfer from paper to practice, one of the continuing paths of pursuit has been the way of seclusion. In its earliest form, seclusion took shape in monasticism. Of course the principle of seeking God in social isolation is as old as human experience; those who have longed to grow in faith have always sought brief periods of aloneness. Jesus was alone in the wilderness for forty days before beginning his public ministry (Matthew 4:1-11), and Paul went into the deserts of Arabia for three years shortly after his conversion (Galatians 1:15-19).

But this kind of isolation became a movement early in Christianity. Emperor Constantine's endorsement of the Christian faith after his conversion in the fourth century not only put an end to persecution; it made Christianity so much a part of the establishment that many of the devout felt they must separate themselves in order to keep the purity of their faith. Some of them chose a completely solitary life, as hermits, while others entered monasteries or convents.

In either case, they sought to abstain from the things of the world—specifically meat, strong drink, sexual activity and marriage, and cosmetics or self-glorifying dress. They gave themselves to prayer, spiritual exercises, and acts of charity. With passing time, they came to be seen as persons of particular virtue, so that others came to them for prayer or blessing. The monastic form of seclusion continues to the present day, espe-

Christian monasticism as a practice is the oldest form of religious life. Christians who felt called to seek God through a life of denial and solitude characterized by praise, prayer, study, and work withdrew from public life. During the late third century and early fourth century individual Christians retreated to the desert in Egypt and Syria seeking the pure Christian life they thought unattainable in the existing churches. Communal monasticism began in 320 with Pachomius's community in Egypt. During the intellectual darkness of the Middle Ages, monks and nuns helped keep the Christian faith alive by preserving the early documents and teachings of the church.

cially in the Orthodox and Catholic communions. The degree of isolation and the severity of life vary widely among the several religious orders.

Protestantism has had its own form of seclusion. Several movements that have eventually become denominations prided themselves, at some early point in their history, at being "peculiar people." The Quakers (Society of Friends) observed particular forms of address, wore particular costumes, and abstained from any reading material or entertainment judged to be harmful to their spiritual life.

While these movements did not isolate themselves physically as the desert monks and monastic orders did, they sought to be "in the world but not of the world." They hoped by their cultural isolation to keep themselves free from the sins of the world, and also to be a witness to a decadent society, and with it all, to be a holy people.

The Holiness of Involvement

As surely as some have sought to achieve holiness by isolating themselves, either physically or culturally, others have seen the way of holiness in the world of action. Among organizations, the best example would be the Salvation Army, a movement that, not incidentally, has a strong doctrine of holiness. But their holiness is pursued in service to humanity altogether as much as in prayer and in certain cultural restraints.

Among individuals, many names stand out. One of the most notable would be Mother Teresa (1910–1998), founder of the Missionaries of Charity, a nun of great sanctity. She was known throughout the world for the active quality of her holiness. Her order has had a particular impact through its work with lepers, orphanages, and the dying poor.

Can one way to holiness—seclusion or involvement—be praised over the other? Probably not. Jesus himself was an activist, condemned by his enemies for his sociability. He taught, healed the sick, cast out demons, and engaged in vigorous public debate. Yet he also withdrew frequently from even his closest disciples in order to be alone with God. Jesus began his ministry with forty days of utter isolation; it is not beyond imagination that he isolated himself at other times during his adult years prior to the record of the Gospels. But certainly his basic pattern was one of constant engagement in human need. Most of his holiness, in the three years of his ministry, was carried out in the arena of action.

Both ways have hidden perils. Those who pursue holiness by seclusion may be trying, unconsciously, to escape the world in which they live. They may even develop an antagonism toward the culture, thus isolating their witness as well as their person. The activist, on the other hand, can easily become so involved in the swirl of human need as to lose the sense of the divine. And in either case, the end of holiness—a true and utter commitment to God—may be lost in the paraphernalia of the means.

Doctrines of Sanctification

The Eastern Orthodox Church has a strong emphasis on holiness. Their term is *divinization,* which means the recovery of the likeness to God invested in humans at their creation. This likeness was lost through sin. But as Athanasius of Alexandria (293–373) put it, Christ "was made human that we might be made divine." The true goal of the human life is that we might become godly.

In the Orthodox tradition it is seen as a process: A person, seeking to follow Christ, lives less and less for the usual matters of this world and more and more for the world to come. Constant, frequent prayers are a means to this end, as is sacrificial living. The sacraments (or "mysteries," as the Orthodox church refers to them) also play a major part by their conveying of grace. Good works are a factor, but these good works are a product of the goodness of God working in the individual and not a result of human goodness. The final goal is to recover the divine likeness, or to attain perfection. According to Orthodox teaching, when persons gain this perfection, they not only recover the holiness and immortality lost at the Fall, but they actually come to a state higher than that Adam and Eve enjoyed.

Sanctification does not have as central a place in Roman Catholic teaching as it does in Orthodox teaching. Catholicism teaches that grace leads believers to good works and these good works are themselves marks of holiness. The sacraments are also a vehicle for the work of God in the Christian life. But while sanctification is not as clearly taught in the Catholic tradition, many Catholics demonstrate lives of holiness. Some are in service orders or in ministries of prayer. But vast numbers are Catholic laypersons who, in their hunger for piety and in their love of Christ, attend mass every day.

The Reformed and Lutheran churches generally teach sanctification is part of the justification process and therefore part of the act of salvation. They reject the teaching that persons can attain perfection through sanctification. Perfection, they teach, is ours only through the justification that is in Christ; and that justification is the righteousness of God in Christ, and thus perfect. This perfection is a limited perfection since it always reflects our human weaknesses. No doubt this point of view is in part a reaction to the earlier Catholic emphasis on works, which was one of the issues of the Reformation. The Reformation position, which made sanctification part of the original experience of justification, also gave the emphasis on grace that so stirred the thinking of the first reformers.

Within the Protestant communions, the strongest doctrinal emphasis on sanctification has come through the Wesleyan movements. These bodies have their roots in two eighteenth-century Anglican priests, John and Charles Wesley. The Wesley brothers sought to bring renewal to the Church of England without thought of starting an independent religious body. But eventually—mainly after their deaths—a variety of Wesleyan and Methodist bodies came into existence.

At first the Wesleys sought holiness by a severe regimen of prayers, study, fasting, and service. Their doctrine and their practice drew upon a number of Orthodox and Catholic mystics, as well as several Puritan writers. Although they continued to be very disciplined believers, in time their teaching of sanctification gave equal place to a sanctifying experience, often referred to as "a second definite work of grace."

John Wesley, the primary founder of the Wesleyan movement, was cautious about claims regarding such an experience. He said it should be expected at the moment of a believer's death. Nevertheless, he insisted it was possible in this life to come to a perfect love for God and that it could happen instantaneously. In any event, he and his followers taught that God intended for every believer to love God perfectly and that what God intended, God was able to accomplish.

The holiness groups that grew out of the Methodist movement encouraged their people to seek an experience of holiness and to consider their salvation not truly complete unless they had moved on to this further experience.

Sanctification's Common Goal

Although the various bodies of Christendom have different views of sanctification, all agree Christians should seek purity of life. To put it directly, God's purpose for believers is not spiritual mediocrity. If we take seriously the teaching that Christ suffered and died for human salvation, we can hardly be content with casual religiosity.

And although the range of beliefs among Orthodox, Catholic, and various Protestant believers varies greatly, all communions agree that believers should grow in their faith and be influenced by faith in their conduct. Unfortunately, such growth seems always hard to come by. Even in the earliest days of the church, the apostle Paul confessed his frustration with the progress of his converts. He observed that because they were still "infants in Christ," he had to feed them "with milk, not solid food, for you were not ready for solid food" (1 Corinthians 3:1-2).

Nevertheless, every generation of believers has had its core of earnest seekers. And in spite of the varying doctrinal positions, the basic ground is surprisingly inclusive. All agree God wills believers to be holy: "For I am the LORD your God; sanctify yourselves therefore, and be holy, for I am holy" (Leviticus 11:44). And though some communions fear the pursuit of perfection may lead to "works righteousness," all Christian bodies urge their members to seek constantly a higher standard of Christian living. No communion urges its adherents to be content with their present spiritual state.

And although few contemporary Christian movements teach that sanctification occurs in an instantaneous experience, all of them acknowledge growth in grace comes at least partly through the avenue of Christian experience. These experiences during prayer, worship, service, or the sacraments are, in some real measure, sanctifying moments.

The Christian life is a high and holy calling. Anything less is a disappointment to God. And to the believer too.

> BECAUSE WE THE CHURCH BELIEVE God has called us to a life of holiness, I will seek daily to grow into the fullness of the stature of Jesus Christ.

BELIEVING AND LIVING

Some paths to holiness appeal to some, others to others. Persons who pursue holiness by picketing for or against a cause can hardly imagine moving into a desert monastery for the rest of their lives; but the desert monastic would be equally put off at the thought of the picket's role. As you ponder your own relationship with God, which path to holiness seems most compatible to you—and why?

_____

_____

When have you had an experience (or several) you might call a sanctifying moment, when you felt your life had made a significant move toward holiness?

_____

_____

Reflect on these questions and respond: What are some ways I can move closer to perfection or holiness? What behaviors might be hindering my growth? How will I change them?

_____

_____

What is it about holiness that appeals to you? Why do you think more believers don't pursue a deeper walk of faith?

_____

_____

SEEKING MORE UNDERSTANDING

To clarify your own understanding of holiness or sanctification and its importance in your life, write a definition of what holiness includes in terms of what you believe and how you live. On the basis of this work, how would you characterize your desire for and growth toward perfection or holiness?

PRAYER

"Lord, more and more
I pray Thee, or by wind or fire,
Make pure my inmost heart's desire,
And purge the clinging chaff from
    off the floor.

I wish Thy way,
But when in me myself would rise
And long for something otherwise,
Then, Holy One, take sword and
    spear, and slay.

Oh, stay near by,
Most patient Love, till, by Thy grace,
In this poor silver, Thy bright face
Shows forth in clearness and serenity.

What will it be
When, like the lily or the rose
That in my flowery garden blows,
I shall be flawless, perfect, Lord,
    to Thee?"

—*Amy Carmichael, 20th century*

26

Second Coming   Christian hope   Kingdom of God
Nature redeemed
Righteousness and justice
An unexpected hour   Signs of the time
Be ready   Hope in the face of death   Parousia
Only God knows end of time
Assured expectation
Sovereign over world and history

Ending With a Beginning

"Beloved, we are God's children now; what we will be has not yet been revealed. What we do know is this: when he is revealed, we will be like him, for we will see him as he is. And all who have this hope in him purify themselves, just as he is pure."

—*1 John 3:2-3*

LIFE QUESTIONS

Once a subject has become a center of attention for the extreme, it can easily lose its place in the realm of thoughtful discussion. Such a situation is unfortunate under any circumstances, since it means the debasing of human discussion, but tragic if the subject is an important and beautiful one.

The Christian hope is such a subject. Here is a topic with the power to sustain persons through the direst of circumstances and to give them the strength to live triumphantly. But because it is so vital, it is also easily abused.

What, in fact, is the Christian hope? What are its sources in the Scriptures and in the classic teachings of the church? How do we determine the real from the extreme? And is there, in truth, a Christian hope for our time and for all time, or is this only a kind of pious fantasy?

ASSIGNMENT

The Christian hope is based, ultimately, on the character of God, and on God's intentions for the creation—especially, God's intentions for the human creature. Therefore, our readings will begin with the Creation story and will include some of the magnificent visions of the Hebrew poets and prophets. The New Testament writers spell out this hope in more specific terms, and yet, always with a certain enigmatic quality that compels the believer to leave the details to God. Obviously, that's where the details belong.

Day 1   Genesis 1:1–2:3 (God's good creation);
Psalm 62:5-8 (confidence in God)
Introduction and Readings 274 and 275

Day 2   Isaiah 11 (coming rule of Messiah); 60 (God the glory of Zion)
Readings 276 and 277

Day 3   Matthew 24:1-44 (end of the age); John 14:1-14 (the way, the truth, the life)
Readings 278 and 279

Day 4   1 Thessalonians 4:1-11 (live to please God); 2 Peter 3 (promised Lord's coming)
Readings 280 and 281

Day 5   1 John 2:18–3:3 (the true faith); Revelation 22 (coming soon)
Readings 282 and 283

Day 6   Read and respond to "The Church Teaching and Believing" and "Believing and Living."

Day 7   Rest and prayer

DAILY PRAYER

Pray for the persons and situations on your Prayer Concerns list and about issues or concerns emerging from your daily reading and study.

CHRISTIAN HOPE

SCRIPTURE	READINGS
DAY 1	
Genesis 1:1–2:3; Psalm 62:5-8	Introduction and Readings 274 and 275
DAY 2	
Isaiah 11; 60	Readings 276 and 277
DAY 3	
Matthew 24:1-44; John 14:1-14	Readings 278 and 279

SCRIPTURE	READINGS
DAY 4	
1 Thessalonians 4:1-11; 2 Peter 3	**Readings 280 and 281**

SCRIPTURE	READINGS
DAY 5	
1 John 2:18–3:3; Revelation 22	**Readings 282 and 283**

DAY 6 STUDY MANUAL	PRAYER CONCERNS
"The Church Teaching and Believing" and "Believing and Living"	

CHRISTIAN HOPE

THE CHURCH TEACHING AND BELIEVING

We know there has to be an end, sometime, somewhere. The question is this: What kind of end will it be? The mind that shuts out God may be inclined to view the end with despair. Thus the popular phrase, in common discussion, "the end of the world," is understood negatively.

But believers are impelled by hope, a hope as old as creation, and one grounded in the character of God. The reasoning is quite simple, and in its own way, quite beyond refutation. The recurring motif in the Genesis story of Creation is this: "And God saw that it was good" (Genesis 1:10, 12, 18).

That's how the world began. If the universe has any logic at all, this beginning must shed some light on the world's end, which is to say that the very term *end* refers more to purpose than to finality. What end did the Creator have in mind as the creation unfolded? If the end is to be consistent with the beginning, the end will be *good*—a setting of divine pleasure.

At its beginning, the universe was a place of harmony. Nature was fruitful but not exploited. Humans were pictured by the Genesis writer as being in the image of God, and thus in open communion with the divine. But something happened—the coming of sin, specifically, disobedience to God. Harmony was replaced by discord.

The rest of the biblical story is the record of the struggle to regain the potential present at Creation. Here is the essence of the Christian hope. And it is both significant and wonderful that the believer's hope came to birth as soon as the human story went wrong.

Through much of the Old Testament, struggle and hope are intertwined. Now and again the biblical writers—especially the prophets—envisioned a perfect day. They saw this hope in the coming of God's chosen ruler, from the family of David. The prophet Isaiah spoke of a "shoot [that] shall come out from the stump of Jesse [David's father]" (Isaiah 11:1). Blessed with gifts of leadership from the spirit of the Lord, and with a heart whose "delight shall be in the fear of the LORD" (11:2-3), his reign, the prophet said, would offer righteousness to the poor and "equity for the meek of the earth" but sharp judgment on the wicked (11:3-4).

Centuries later, Christian writers connected Isaiah's prophecy with a millennial period described in Revelation 20:1-6, a period of perfect peace. Just as the biblical writers claimed many Old Testament passages as descriptive of Jesus Christ, they and the early church theologians and preachers saw many of the most idyllic prophetic writings as referring to the Christian hope. This view was consistent with their basic conception that the church was now heir to the ancient promises. They understood there was a continuing community of God, made up of Israel and the church; thus any Old Testament prophecies not yet fulfilled in Israel would now be fulfilled in and through the church, or at the end.

Several points are notable about the Old Testament visions of a perfect day. They perceived a world so peaceful even nature would be redeemed; the enmities that normally characterize its inhabitants would come to an end (11:6-9). They recognized nature had been victimized by human sin, so they believed nature would be restored when humans returned to the will of the Creator. They envisioned a world of prosperity, not in gaudy, materialistic terms but in charming pastoral prospects:

"They shall all sit under their own vines
and under their own fig trees,
and no one shall make them afraid"
(Micah 4:4).

And it would be a world where

"nation shall not lift up sword against nation,
neither shall they learn war any more" (4:3).

Especially notable, the prophet measured the glory of the perfect time by the righteousness of the ruler and by the justice with which all persons would be treated. The prophetic sense of justice and equity carried over into the perfect day. The prophetic vision was never simply of peace or prosperity, but always one with justice for all and care for the most helpless.

Although the prophetic descriptions are so beautiful they sound like Eden revisited, there is never any doubt they are visions of this earth. The New Testament portrayal of the Christian hope envisions a world beyond this world, a heaven; but the prophetic visions of the Old Testament were of perfect government and perfect peace and prosperity on this earth.

What Jesus Taught

The disciples expected Jesus to set up a kingdom on this earth. This expectation was so deeply imbedded in their thinking they held to it even after

259

the Resurrection. Just before Jesus' ascension, they asked him, "Lord, is this the time when you will restore the kingdom to Israel" (Acts 1:6)? Like all other humans, the disciples were curious about the future. But their curiosity was more deeply rooted. The Jews had long been subject to foreign powers and had believed that when their messiah came, they would be delivered. The disciples believed this was Jesus' role. No wonder they asked him about the future of Israel.

Furthermore, John the Baptist had prepared the way for Jesus with the message, "Repent, for the kingdom of heaven has come near" (Matthew 3:2). Matthew's Gospel reports that after Jesus had been baptized and had passed through a period of prayer and testing in the wilderness, he "began to proclaim" the same succinct message (4:17).

For us, "the kingdom of heaven" has a spiritual sound; but for first-century Jews, it sounded political. They had waited for most of six centuries; now they wanted a kingdom that would deliver them from their enemies. Jesus seemed to feed this hope by his frequent references to the kingdom of heaven. But his references to the Kingdom must also have left the thoughtful wondering. What, for example, did he mean when he said, "Blessed are those who are persecuted for righteousness' sake, for theirs is the kingdom of heaven" (5:10)? Or when he warned his followers that unless their righteousness exceeded that of the scribes and Pharisees, they would "never enter the kingdom of heaven" (5:20)? What sort of kingdom would this be, that the righteousness of the most scrupulous keepers of the Law, the Pharisees, could not qualify?

So many of Jesus' parables were about the kingdom of heaven, but they too had a puzzling quality. The Kingdom, Jesus said, is like a mustard seed that is small but becomes "the greatest of shrubs" (13:31-32), like yeast that leavens a whole lump (13:33), a treasure hidden in a field (13:44), or a pearl a merchant sells all to obtain (13:45-46). How must the disciples have understood these parables at the time they heard them?

In any event, the disciples maintained an undiminished hope of Jesus' becoming their king. So much so that when Jesus began to tell them he must go to Jerusalem, to suffer and be killed, and then to rise again, Peter "began to rebuke him" for saying such things (16:21-22). Their dreams of the future did not include suffering and dying.

But in Jerusalem, the disciples had their opportunity to raise the questions so important to them. When Jesus said the time was coming when not one stone of the Temple would be left on another, it gave the disciples a basis for a question no doubt more complex than they realized. "Tell us, when will this be, and what will be the sign of your coming and of the end of the age?" (24:3). Whether they knew it or not, they were asking three questions that were not necessarily related to one another; and Jesus' answer seems to weave through those questions in

Speaking of Jesus, Hebrews 6:19 says, "We have this hope, a sure and steadfast anchor of the soul." When the top of the anchor is in the shape of a cross, it is called an anchor cross; and its message of hope is twofold—salvation from sin and eternal life through the death and resurrection of Jesus Christ. Christians in the catacombs used the anchor to symbolize hope in Jesus Christ. They could look at the anchor and see hope, while non-Christians saw only an anchor.

such a way that succeeding generations struggle to find the logical order they desire.

Some of Jesus' words applied to the destruction of Jerusalem, including the dismantling of the Temple in A.D. 70, just a generation later. A reference to the Temple had brought about the whole discussion. Also, in the years following Jesus' crucifixion there were several instances of false messiahs (24:4-5). It is difficult to say whether Matthew 24:9-28 applied to that tragic era or to some later time yet to come. Every generation, from Jesus' day to our own, has been inclined to apply the "signs" to its own time.

Obviously Matthew 24 and 25 are important. For sheer length, they are nearly as long as the Sermon on the Mount (5–7). Their significance is heightened by the fact that they report events that come only days before Jesus' crucifixion, as if their content were integrally bound up with Jesus' whole mission and purpose. So what lessons might we gain from them today? What, if anything, do they say to our time?

To begin with, we need to realize how vast is the stretch of time. Science should help us do this, since it speaks about thousands and millions of years; but we are still like children returning from a long trip, asking every five minutes, "Are we almost home?" From a biblical point of view, we are living in the end times, in the last days. But this has been true since the birth of Jesus in Bethlehem; his coming signaled the beginning of the end. We need therefore to live with a healthy sense of expectancy. We should know full well both the value and the mystery of each day so we live our days with a kind of holy awe.

We also ought to realize the "signs of the times" are more general than specific. Recognizing this takes much of the fun out of the game of predicting, but it is true to what Jesus said. After warning that no one knows the day or the hour, Jesus explained that it will be as it was in the days of Noah. "For as in those days before the flood they were eating and drinking, marrying and giving in marriage, until the day Noah entered the ark, and they knew nothing until the flood came and swept them all away" (24:38-39). No better description could be given of life as "normal" than to say it is a time when people eat, drink, marry, and give their children in marriage. This is life in its most routine terms. Even the "wars and rumors of wars" and the "famines and earthquakes in various places" (24:6-7) do not offer a timetable; they are "but the beginning of the birth pangs" (24:8). That is, they are part of the usual pattern of crises. Those who find signs of the return of our Lord in each new conflict or natural disaster only embarrass the gospel and its larger message.

A third teaching from these chapters is so emphatic, yet many persist in missing it. Who knows when the end will come? Jesus answered, "But about that day and hour no one knows, neither the angels of heaven, nor the Son, but only the Father" (24:36). Such matters are God's business, and God's alone.

But what of Jesus' saying we should learn a lesson from the fig tree—that its show of leaves is a sign summer is near? Once again we must keep in mind that time is an indefinite quality in the Scriptures, especially as it has to do with the working out of the purposes of God. A thousand years are, indeed, like a day with God; heaven has time for its purposes. We also need to appreciate the vagueness of the figure of speech: Yes, we know that when the fig tree comes to a certain point, "summer is near"; but all sorts of things can happen to speed up or delay that process, as *The Farmer's Almanac* and every meteorologist know. God knows the eternal calendar, and for those who have faith, that ought to be enough.

The fourth issue is the most important of all, since it has to do with our response to the divine plan. As Jesus put it, "Therefore you also must be ready, for the Son of Man is coming at an unexpected hour" (24:44). Jesus then proceeded to tell a parable of an unfaithful slave who thought his master had delayed his coming, and the vivid story of the ten bridesmaids, five who were ready for their event and five who were not. Then, again, the warning: "Keep awake therefore, for you know neither the day nor the hour" (25:13).

The believer has a very specific assignment—not to draw up the divine calendar but to be ready for whatever might happen. The believer is to be busy about the Master's business.

Some Special Terms

Before we go further in our study of the Christian hope, several terms you may have heard ought to be defined. Some of them appear frequently in books and sermons about end times. The most common is the *Second Coming,* also referred to as the Second Advent, or by the Greek word *Parousia,* which means "coming." It speaks of the return of Jesus Christ to the earth in power and glory.

When Christ returns, it is believed he will lift from the earth those who are his, both living and dead (1 Thessalonians 4:13-18). This event is referred to as the *rapture,* from a Latin word meaning "to carry off." But when this rapture will take place is a matter of disagreement among those who especially emphasize the Second Coming. Some believe the rapture will occur before what is often called "the great tribulation." Others believe it will take place midway in the tribulation; that is, after three and a half years. Still others believe the body of believers will not be raptured until the end of the tribulation period. Then, there are those who believe some will be raptured sooner and others later, depending on the state of their souls.

Some who believe that the church will be raptured at the beginning of the tribulation believe there will be another coming of Christ at the conclusion of the tribulation, which they call the *revelation.* They use this term to say this later coming will be a revealing of the full glory of Christ so all will know the greatness of his power.

The *great tribulation* is the name given to the seven-year period of severe suffering that is to come upon the earth (Matthew 24:21-30, and possible sections of Revelation). This period is when the *antichrist* will exercise his full power. The antichrist is, as the name implies, a person in opposition to Christ. The Scriptures speak of the antichrist both as a spirit always at work in the world and as a particular person at a particular time.

The reign of evil in the tribulation period also includes the *beast,* who will have authority for three and a half years, and another beast who will institute a mark that will be required if one is to buy or sell. This *mark of the beast* will be given on the right hand or the forehead, the number 666 (Revelation 13).

The *millennium* is a thousand-year reign of perfect peace. Those with a *premillennial* view believe Christ will return prior to this period, in order to reign during the millennium; those with a *postmillennial* view believe that Christ will return following this millennium (Revelation 20:1-7). A third position, the *amillennial,* teaches that the thousand years of Christ's reign should be interpreted symbolically rather than literally. Some believe that after the millennium there will be a battle between two world powers, *Gog* and *Magog* (Ezekiel 38; Revelation 20:8). A more familiar term, the *battle of Armageddon,* refers to a final battle between the forces of evil and God, occurring at Megiddo in Palestine. Some believe this battle will be literal: others see it as symbolic.

The Christian Hope

Study of the end times captivates many people. Its importance should not be minimized, but we need also to realize all the details of the rapture, the tribulation, the millennium, Armageddon, and Gog and Magog are speculative and can never be finally proved. Which events are symbolic and which are literal is unclear. Nor can we know for sure the chronological order of events. For that reason, discussion can easily become not only nonproductive but sometimes disrupting and unkind.

Such a situation is especially unfortunate when it casts a pall over the whole doctrine of the Christian hope, because this hope is one of the grand teachings of the church. To be a Christian is to be a person of hope; and while that quality of hope marks all the life of a Christian, its highest expression is in its serene expectations regarding those matters the secular mind looks upon as endings. The Christian hope understands all such endings are only beginnings. This hope is centered in Jesus Christ, and it represents the crowning demonstration of Christ's power.

Many elements might be included in a discussion of the Christian hope, but three deserve special consideration. Perhaps the most intimate and personally important element is the hope individual believers have as they face death. Christians believe that because Christ lives, they shall live also. Christian burial services are characterized by the words of Jesus to Martha, the sister of Lazarus: "I am the resurrection and the life. Those who believe in me, even though they die, will live, and everyone who lives and believes in me will never die" (John 11:25-26).

Logically, it is inconceivable for a Christian to die in despair, though it is possible that some believers, failing to grasp the teachings of their faith, might do so. The Christian hope rests in the character of Christ, his death for our sins, his assurance of our salvation, and his resurrection from the dead. As John Wesley said, believers "die well," because their hope is secure.

A second expression of the Christian hope is in the return of Jesus Christ. This hope is as old as the church. When the first disciples saw their Lord ascend, they were assured by two men in white robes, "This Jesus, who has been taken up from you into heaven, will come in the same way as you saw him go into heaven" (Acts 1:11). Many rituals of Holy Communion include a reference to this hope with the words "Christ has died; Christ is risen; Christ will come again." Some have believed that the return of Christ occurs only at the death of the believer, and others that it is symbolic rather than literal. But a substantial portion of the church, through all the centuries of its history, has believed Christ will return in bodily form to receive his believers, both living and dead, and to begin the consummation of all things. This belief is rightly termed "the blessed hope." This hope has sustained millions of believers through all varieties of physical, economic, and emotional distress.

A third form of the Christian hope is belief in the kingdom of God, or as it is termed in Matthew's Gospel, the kingdom of heaven. This Kingdom was the focus of John the Baptist's ministry as he prepared the way for Jesus and the focus of many of Jesus' parables. Like other concepts, it too has been interpreted in a variety of ways. Some believe the kingdom of heaven is fulfilled simply in the conversion of individuals. Some have understood it to be a physical kingdom that will someday—perhaps in the millennium, or in eternity—operate in our world. Still others have understood the kingdom of God as a kingdom of righteousness —a reign of justice and peace brought about by the faithful work and witness of God's people.

Whatever form the Christian hope takes, our conception of it will no doubt be less than the fulfillment that one day will come to pass. Even the most extravagant dreams of secular visionaries and of godly prophets cannot perceive the fullness of God's vision for the universe and for the human race.

Will the Christian hope ever fully come to pass? Without a doubt. We must leave with God the nature and particulars of the hope, but we can be assured of its accomplishment. Over the centuries, no prayer has been raised more frequently than
    "Your kingdom come.
    Your will be done,
        on earth as it is in heaven" (Matthew 6:10).
Speaking of the coming of his kingdom, Jesus once asked, "Will not God grant justice to his chosen ones who cry to him

day and night?" And he answered his own question, "I tell you, he will quickly grant justice to them" (Luke 18:7-8). Believers rest secure in that good word. Their prayers, labors, and trust will in time be fulfilled.

> BECAUSE WE THE CHURCH BELIEVE in the certainty of the Christian hope, I will pursue God's kingdom on this earth, and I will rest secure in my contemplation of the future.

BELIEVING AND LIVING

The teaching of the Christian hope seems sometimes to have been wounded in the house of its friends. Sometimes those who have loved this hope the most and who have defended it most vigorously have also raised it to question. What do you question or find most difficult to believe about the second coming of Christ? Why?

_____

_____

When have you seen someone face death with true Christian hope? From your knowledge, what gave that person such hope?

_____

_____

If persons told you they find it impossible to see any hope in our world because of all the tragedy they have seen or experienced, how would you respond to them?

_____

_____

What hope do you personally see for the kingdom of God to come on our earth? In what ways can you or I contribute to the coming of the Kingdom?

_____

_____

SEEKING MORE UNDERSTANDING

You may want to do further study on some of the difficult subjects related to the Christian hope. For example, use some Bible commentaries to gain insight into the discussion of the end of the age in Matthew 24. Or if your interest is in the book of Revelation, read _Breaking the Code: Understanding the Book of Revelation,_ by Bruce M. Metzger (Abingdon Press, 1993). Check availability from your church library or a religious bookstore.

PRAYER

"And when grim Death doth take me
     by the throat,
Thou wilt have pity on thy handiwork;
Thou wilt not let him on my
     suffering gloat,
But draw my soul out—gladder than
     man or boy,
When thy saved creatures from the
     narrow ark
Rushed out, and leaped and laughed
     and cried for joy,
And the great rainbow strode across
     the dark."

— Diary of an Old Soul,
George MacDonald, 1824–1905

27

Jesus Christ the judge

Judgment

Eternal separation

Day of the Lord

Heaven

Hell

Acceptance or rejection of Christ

Judgment Day

Eternal fellowship with Christ

Judge also advocate

Accounting for lives lived deeds done

A Time of Reckoning

"Shall not the Judge of all the earth do what is just?"

—*Genesis 18:25*

LIFE QUESTIONS

Judgment is a pendulum subject. We swing from one side to another, depending on our most recent experience or on what event is currently in the news.

The Bible, however, has no such wavering. From Genesis 2 to Revelation 22 it lets us know, in straightforward fashion, that judgment is, will be, and ought to be. Then, however, numbers of questions come to our minds. If God is a forgiving God, then why does God judge us? When will judgment be, and how will it be carried out? Who will make the judgment, and by what standard? And since we all face judgment, how might we prepare?

ASSIGNMENT

Finding Scripture passages on judgment isn't difficult. It is difficult, however, to read them intelligently and with emotional balance. Before we know it, our feelings come into our doctrine of judgment, whether those feelings are negative or positive. That's why it's good that judgment ultimately rests with God.

Meanwhile, we need to seek some understanding of the meaning of judgment and the principles involved, because our understanding of judgment plays an important part in our attitude toward God, life, our fellow creatures, and what people sometimes call "fate."

Day 1 Genesis 2:4-17 (man, a living being); 3:1-19 (with sin comes death) Introduction and Readings 284 and 285

Day 2 Psalm 96 (the Lord coming to judge); Jeremiah 25:15-38 (the cup of God's judgment); Amos 5:18–6:14 (day of the Lord) Readings 286 and 287

Day 3 Matthew 11:20-24 (woe to the unrepentant); 12:35-42 (judgment an accounting); 25:14-46 (judged according to our actions) Readings 288 and 289

Day 4 Romans 2:1-16 (God's righteous judgment); 2 Corinthians 5 (confidence in facing death) Readings 290 and 291

Day 5 2 Peter 2:4–3:13 (final coming and judgment); Revelation 20 (opening of the books) Readings 292 and 293

Day 6 Read and respond to "The Church Teaching and Believing" and "Believing and Living."

Day 7 Rest and prayer

DAILY PRAYER

Pray for the persons and situations on your Prayer Concerns list and about issues or concerns emerging from your daily reading and study.

SCRIPTURE	READINGS
DAY 1	
Genesis 2:4-17; 3:1-19	Introduction and Readings 284 and 285
DAY 2	
Psalm 96; Jeremiah 25:15-38; Amos 5:18–6:14	Readings 286 and 287
DAY 3	
Matthew 11:20-24; 12:35-42; 25:14-46	Readings 288 and 289

SCRIPTURE	READINGS

DAY 4

Romans 2:1-16; 2 Corinthians 5	Readings 290 and 291

DAY 5

2 Peter 2:4–3:13; Revelation 20	Readings 292 and 293

DAY 6 STUDY MANUAL	PRAYER CONCERNS
"The Church Teaching and Believing" and "Believing and Living"	

THE CHURCH TEACHING AND BELIEVING

Like it or not, judgment is. Not just in the Bible, or in religious documents, but in life. Nothing could be more certain. Because judgment is not necessarily precise in its action, we fail at times to take it seriously. But it is certain.

We testify to that certainty in some of our common phrases. Someone says, "Just wait and see: He'll get his one of these days." And again, "What goes around comes around." No one has said it better than the seventeenth-century German poet, Friedrich Von Logau:

"Though the mills of God grind slowly,
    yet they grind exceeding small;
Though with patience he stands waiting,
    with exactness grinds he all."

We believe in judgment—sometimes gladly, sometimes with fear, sometimes with anger. But we believe in it, because we believe in justice. Very few prospects are quite so offensive to us as life without justice, and no cry is angrier—whatever the age of the person speaking—than the simple lament, "It's just not fair!" But there is no justice without judgment. Justice comes to pass through the process of judgment.

Perhaps, however, this is the point at which we become most uneasy, this point where justice and judgment meet. We're afraid judgment might fall without justice, that judgment might be as unjust as all the matters that make us think judgment is necessary. So any thought of judgment demands faith—faith that the Judge will indeed give justice. Abraham's ancient cry is apt for every human soul: "Shall not the Judge of all the earth do what is just?" (Genesis 18:25). Only one answer can be given, and we hope desperately that our faith is well-founded.

Old Testament Views of Judgment

Judgment is introduced in the book of Genesis by way of warning, or more correctly, by way of a commandment with a warning. As Adam is introduced to the wonders of the garden, he is commanded not to eat of the tree of the knowledge of good and evil, "for in the day that you eat of it you shall die" (Genesis 2:17). In time Adam and Eve violate the warning, and judgment is passed. The worst of the judgment is written into the event itself, except of course for the factor of death. That comes too, perhaps in several ways—by a quality

of death that entered into the rest of life, by eventual physical death, and by the mystery of judgmental death.

The emphasis in judgment throughout the Old Testament is on judgment in this life. Often these judgments are delayed; that is, in judgments that fall upon nations, the judgment doesn't necessarily fall on the generation that initiates the sin. The people of Israel are told that the nations that had inhabited Canaan before them had "defiled themselves" so that "the land became defiled," so defiled that it "vomited out its inhabitants" (Leviticus 18:24-25). But such a judgment might be a long time in coming. Abraham is told that he will die in peace but that his descendants will eventually, generations later, wipe out the Amorites. But this is a long way off, because "the iniquity of the Amorites is not yet complete" (Genesis 15:15-16). No wonder, then, that the Old Testament writers so often speak of the iniquity of parents being visited on the children to the third and fourth generation (Exodus 20:5).

There is in this understanding a kind of inexorable quality. When the writer of Leviticus speaks of the land vomiting out its inhabitants, it is as if the land itself cannot bear the sins of the people. A modern conservationist might use such language to describe what has happened to the soil in the millions of acres people have abused. The biblical writer believes that the land itself has a kind of moral quality, and that it will not always endure immoral inhabitants. So too with the philosophy of the sins of parents being visited on the children for coming generations. It sounds like a sentence being passed; but in truth it is a sober statement of fact, not unlike an economist telling the present generation that if we use up the financial reserves, future generations will be left without protection.

Much of the biblical warning of judgment is just that simple. It doesn't call for divine wrath (though the biblical writer may make such a reference). Often it is little more than what can be expected when the laws of good sense and morality, so often the same, are flouted. So many instances of judgment—biblical, historical, and personal—are as clear as fourth-grade arithmetic. We do wrong, and we suffer. Life adds up.

Justice is one of a few dominant themes in the Old Testament. The people of Israel believed passionately that goodness is rewarded and evil is punished, and they expected it to happen on this earth. When judgment was delayed, suggesting that justice might not happen, the Old Testament saints grew impatient. When the tide of history was running against Israel, the psalmist cried out, "Rouse yourself! Why do you sleep, O Lord?" (Psalm 44:23). The psalmist seems more distressed over what appears to be a lapse in justice than over the immediate suffering he is experiencing. This isn't surprising; after all, if God failed to be just, what hope or order did the universe hold?

Human nature is such that we think of judgment primarily as falling on other people or other nations. Some of the Hebrew prophets, however, dared to pronounce judgment on their own people. Jeremiah is the most notable example. He had to tell his people that their sufferings were God's will; they had broken the covenant, and now God was using the Babylonians to punish them. Amos preached to a complacent and self-satisfied people who were confident that when judgment came, it would be on their enemies. The prophet answered,

"Why do you want the day of the LORD?
It is darkness, not light;
   as if someone fled from a lion,
   and was met by a bear;
or went into the house and rested a hand against the wall,
   and was bitten by a snake" (Amos 5:18-19).

Judgment in the New Testament

People often naively assume that the Old Testament is a severe book while the New Testament is a book of love. This surely cannot be said of the subject of judgment. Jesus taught that his very coming was itself a judgment. The cities that had received his ministry but had failed to respond were in the greater danger. "For if the deeds of power done in you had been done in Tyre and Sidon [Gentile cities], they would have repented long ago in sackcloth and ashes. But I tell you, on the day of judgment it will be more tolerable for Tyre and Sidon than for you" (Matthew 11:21-22). Jesus' language is shocking when he warns, "I tell you, on the day of judgment you will have to give an account for every careless word you utter" (12:36). This is not a gentle Jesus but a highly demanding one.

These statements from Jesus also suggested a specific time of judgment. The Old Testament writers usually seemed to see judgment in an unfolding of history; but now Jesus was speaking of a particular "day of judgment," something set up in the calendar of God. The same idea is suggested in Jesus' parable of the talents, though the phrase *day of judgment* is not used. But the judgment is portrayed as a specific time of reckoning when "the master of those slaves came and settled accounts with them" (25:19). So too with the judgment of the nations; it is described as happening "when the Son of Man comes in his glory" and is seated on his throne. Then "all the nations will be gathered before him" (25:31-32). This scene has all the quality

Judgment and justice go together. A pair of balances symbolizes the justice we can be sure of at the last judgment because Jesus our Savior will be our judge. Saint Michael the archangel is often pictured carrying a pair of balances to weigh the souls of people at the last day, though there is no Scripture basis for Michael in this role.

In the Old Testament "the day of the Lord" defines the time God will triumph over God's enemies (Jeremiah 46:10). The people of Israel identified themselves with God, so they saw it as a day of victory over their enemies too. But the prophets did not see the people as being on God's side, so "the day of the Lord" became a day of wrath and judgment for Israel as well as for other nations (Joel 2:1-2). In the New Testament "the day of our Lord Jesus Christ" is the day of final judgment, implying victory for those who are aligned with Christ and wrath for his enemies.

of a particular occasion; certainly it does not in any sense convey the feeling of the gradual unfolding of history.

Paul uses the same specific language when he speaks of "the day" when God "will judge the secret thoughts of all" (Romans 2:16). The final judgment described in Revelation also is portrayed as an event—a time when "books were opened," including "the book of life," and "the dead were judged according to their works, as recorded in the books" (Revelation 20:12). Everything about the language of the New Testament indicates a specific occasion of judgment.

What Kind of Judgment Will It Be?

The standard by which the judgment will be carried out is—or ought to be—a matter of primary concern to everyone. Salvation, we learned earlier, is by the gift of God. We are saved by faith in Christ, and we trust in the merit of his death at Calvary. Nevertheless, the several descriptions of the judgment speak almost exclusively of the deeds persons have done. The book of Revelation says "the dead were judged according to their works, as recorded in the books" (Revelation 20:12). But it speaks also of the book of life and says "anyone whose name was not found written in the book of life was thrown into the lake of fire" (20:15).

Jesus' parable of the talents (Matthew 25:14-30) and his description of the time when "all the nations will be gathered before him" (25:32) both speak of life lived or of deeds done. In the parable of the talents, a man of substance entrusts portions of his holdings to his servants while he is away for an extended period. When he returns, he brings the stewards together for an accounting. Those who had fulfilled their responsibility well were praised, and were told to "enter into the joy of your master" (25:21). But a worker who did nothing to increase what had been trusted to him was severely condemned. Even his original holding was taken from him, and the master said, "As for this worthless slave, throw him into the outer darkness, where there will be weeping and gnashing of teeth" (25:30).

Two things surely stand out. First, judgment will be on the basis of what persons do with those possibilities entrusted to them; and second, the stakes are high. Taken simply in the context of the story, both the rewards and the punishments seem out of proportion to the successes and failures of the participants. It sounds as if our lives on this earth are significant to a degree we simply do not comprehend.

The second story is more specific. Jesus said the Son of Man "will separate people one from another as a shepherd separates the sheep from the goats" (25:32). The worthy ones are invited to "inherit the kingdom" that has been prepared for them "from the foundation of the world" (25:34). Why? Because when Jesus was hungry, thirsty, a stranger, naked, sick, or in prison, these people cared for him. The recipients themselves are surprised, because they don't remember ever helping Jesus in such a way. But Jesus explains that when they did such kindnesses for "the least of these," they did it for him (25:40).

By striking contrast, when he sends the other group "into the eternal fire prepared for the devil and his angels" (25:41), it is by the same standard of judgment. These persons neglected Jesus when he was hungry, thirsty, a stranger, naked, sick, or in prison; and they had done so by their inattention to "the least of these" (25:45). A modern reader finds the repetition tedious, as Jesus speaks the same list of human pain four consecutive times. But this is the Middle Eastern way of emphasizing a point. It is a drumbeat of clarity: At the judgment, our standing will be determined by our treatment of those who are rejected not only by society but in some ways by life itself.

How do Jesus' stories of the judgment square with our understanding of salvation by grace alone? If the teaching of the New Testament is consistent, we must conclude we cannot in any way win our eternal salvation by works of human righteousness. But it is just as surely true that Christ's sacrifice at Calvary does not endorse spiritual laziness on the part of those who claim to have accepted that sacrifice. In some fashion, the atoning work of Christ and our poor human works meet. The apostle Paul seemed content to live with some such ambivalence: "Work out your own salvation with fear and trembling," he wrote, "for it is God who is at work in you, enabling you both to will and to work for his good pleasure" (Philippians 2:12-13).

In truth, this need not bother us at all. We have the opportunity first to accept the gracious gift of God; then, empowered by this new life, we work in the spirit of Christ to fulfill God's purposes. How God chooses, finally, to measure such matters in the judgment is, obviously, God's prerogative. We can be sure that God is just; we can also be sure of our own standing by our acceptance of our Lord's sacrifice and by our faithfulness in following his command and example.

One of the most significant points at which faith and works intersect has to do with the spirit in which we do our work. Paul addressed the issue graphically. Jesus Christ, he said, is the foundation of God's eternal building, and believers build upon that foundation. But what materials do we bring to the building process? It could be "gold, silver, precious stones, wood, hay, straw"; and in time, "the work of each builder will become visible, for the Day [that is, the Day of Judgment] will disclose it, because it will be revealed with fire, and the fire will test what sort of work each has done" (1 Corinthians 3:11-13). It is possible, the apostle said, that the work we have done will be "burned up." This will not affect the salvation of the builder, but "the builder will suffer loss." On the other hand, if good materials have been used, the work will survive and "the builder will receive a reward" (3:14-15).

Paul does not explain what he means by gold, silver, precious stones, wood, hay, and straw. He must have reasoned the people at Corinth would know what he meant, and so should we. The works that survive will be those that spring from faith and that seek the glory of God. Clearly enough, works that are self-seeking will not stand the test of fire. It is not enough that we be busy with good works; we must do the works of goodness in a spirit that pleases God. And that is a faith issue.

The Fires of Hell?

Dramatic terms appear again and again in these judgment passages. In the Scripture we have just read, we are told "the fire will test what sort of work each has done" (1 Corinthians 3:13). In Jesus' story of the rich man and Lazarus, we read that the rich man was in Hades and that he asked for Lazarus "to dip the tip of his finger in water and cool my tongue; for I am in agony in these flames" (Luke 16:24). The one who was condemned in Jesus' parable of the talents was sent "into the outer darkness, where there will be weeping and gnashing of teeth" (Matthew 25:30). Those at the judgment who are found to have neglected the needy are sent away "into eternal punishment" (25:46). The writer of Revelation says that "anyone whose name was not found written in the book of life was thrown into the lake of fire" (Revelation 20:15). And again, "But as for the cowardly, the faithless, the polluted, the murderers, the fornicators, the sorcerers, the idolaters, and all liars, their place will be in the lake that burns with fire and sulfur, which is the second death" (21:8).

These statements are strong and insistent. They don't appeal to our sensibilities, but that has nothing to do with an intelligent discussion of the subject. Nor is it satisfactory to discount their severity by noting that they come from a different time. This is to assume that our times are wiser than any other; and while this is a common assumption in every generation—perhaps especially in ours—it is a subjective assumption. Indeed, one might well argue that our times, with their permissiveness and flight from responsibility, are particularly unreliable in their thinking.

Might the references to fire, flames, and outer darkness be symbolic or figurative? Possibly. But this does not by any means diminish the severity being described. Figures of speech are often used to make real something that a person could not otherwise conceive of. If authors want you to picture beauty, shock, joy, or fear in a matter outside your experience, they will find an analogy within your experience to help you get the picture. Without a doubt the most fearful prospect of divine judgment is God's displeasure and separation from God. But our minds fail to grasp something as profound as God's disappointment and displeasure, or utter isolation from God. Fire, flame, and darkness, on the other hand, are within the realm of our experience and of our sensibilities. Come to think of it, perhaps the offense of our sensibilities at descriptions of hell is the point of the matter. The descriptions are meant to be offensive.

Several matters are clear. For one, the reality and the nature of hell will not be settled by a vote, not even a vote of scholars and theologians. Further, we should be properly cautious of a

The word *hell* is used in some English Bibles to translate the Hebrew *Sheol*, the place of the dead in the Old Testament, and the Greek words *Hades* and *Gehenna*, the place of punishment for the dead. In Christian theology hell is the final state of unrepentant sinners after the final judgment, and heaven is the state of the redeemed. In the Catholic tradition, souls who have died in a state of grace go to *Purgatory*, where they undergo purification until they are admitted to heaven after the final judgment.

person who thinks, talks, or preaches about hell constantly, and also of those for whom hell never enters the mind. Each is, in its own right, a spiritual pathology; the one, of excess, and the other of neglect. We should also be cautious of anyone who pretends to have a complete description of God's plan of judgment. Judgment is one of many things that should be left to the divine intelligence. At the same time, we should remember there is no particular value in the statement, "I just can't believe God would be like that." Our personal opinions about God don't really carry much weight.

One thing, however, is sure. We ought to live and place our faith in such a way that we do not fear divine judgment. A true love of God ought to motivate every element of our living, and that perfect love should cast out fear (1 John 4:18). But the fact of an ultimate judgment should constantly remind us of the sublime wonder and gravity of being human. Our lives have consequence. Our deeds, our words, and our thoughts are profoundly and eternally significant.

The Lord of Judgment

In Christian theology, the whole issue of judgment is to be viewed through one supreme fact—the person of the Judge. The New Testament makes clear that Jesus Christ will be the Lord of Judgment Day. Some theologians remind us that because Jesus became flesh and lived a human life, he can be trusted to understand us. From a biblical point of view, we remind ourselves that Jesus Christ is described as our "advocate with the Father" (1 John 2:1). It is an intriguing mix of roles; we appear before a judge who is also our advocate.

Certainly it is significant that both the Nicene Creed and the Apostles' Creed include judgment as part of the doctrine of Christ. Judgment does not appear in these creeds where we might expect it, in the portion about the resurrection and the life of the world to come. Rather, as the creeds unfold the doctrine of Christ, they conclude with his role of judgment. Thus the Apostles' Creed speaks of our Lord's being "at the right hand of God," and then, "from thence he shall come to judge the quick [the living] and the dead." The Nicene Creed follows the same continuity. After describing Christ "seated at the right of the Father," it continues,

"He will come again in glory
to judge the living and the dead,
and his kingdom will have no end."

As these ancient creeds present it, the judgment is primarily an issue of Jesus' role and ministry.

Judgment is an awesome concept. And our feelings about judgment fluctuate with our state of being and with the nature of the times. But the fact of judgment is inescapable. To expect something less is to reduce ourselves to meaninglessness. To be human is to be responsible. Anything less is an affront to our worth and to the God who invested divine breath in us.

BECAUSE WE THE CHURCH BELIEVE in divine judgment, I will remember that the God who judges us is the same God who loves us, and I will live a life motivated by that love.

BELIEVING AND LIVING

Because we live in a culture that says, "No one's going to tell me what to do," or that challenges, "Who made you my judge?" we are disposed against the idea of judgment. It is a philosophical hurdle for us. And yet, all of us know judgment is a necessity for an orderly universe. How would you explain the meaning and purpose of judgment in general to a person who objects to the doctrine of a final judgment?

In your own mind, how do you picture hell?

How does the idea of a final judgment play a part in your decisions of conduct?

When, if ever, have you experienced consequences in daily living that caused you to reorder your life?

If you, as clergy or as layperson, were asked to preach a sermon on judgment, what elements and insights would you include in the sermon?

SEEKING MORE UNDERSTANDING

Stories of judgment are found throughout the Bible. Read some of these and identify common themes, situations, and attitudes that provide insight into the nature and meaning of judgment: Genesis 6:5–8:22; 11:1-9; 2 Samuel 12:1-25; Daniel 5; Acts 5:1-11. Summarize your findings.

PRAYER

"Throw away Thy rod,
Throw away Thy wrath.
Oh my God,
Take the gentle path.

For my heart's desire
Unto Thine is bent;
I aspire
To a full consent. . . .

Though I fail, I weep;
Though I halt in pace,
Yet I creep
To the throne of grace. . . .

Throw away Thy rod;
Though man frailties hath,
Thou art God.
Throw away Thy wrath."

—Selected stanzas from " "Discipline,"
by George Herbert, 1593–1633

28

Spiritual body

Temple of the Holy Spirit

Wholeness of soul and body

Resurrection

Bought with a price

Resurrection of the body

Dead raised to new life

Death destroyed

Physical body

Perishable becomes imperishable

Jesus Christ the first fruits

Creator God redeems creation

Resurrection of the Body

"So it is with the resurrection of the dead. What is sown is perishable, what is raised is imperishable. It is sown in dishonor, it is raised in glory. It is sown in weakness, it is raised in power. It is sown a physical body, it is raised a spiritual body."
—*1 Corinthians 15:42-44*

LIFE QUESTIONS

By this time we have noticed that some things we think ought to be in the classic creeds of the church are not there. On the other hand, some things that surprise us are there—like the statement, "I believe in the resurrection of the body."

Why is that idea in the Apostles' Creed, and what does it mean? Does it really mean the physical body? And if so, why? What makes the body that important? Aren't we, above all else, spiritual creatures? Why is a phrase like this in the creed, and why does it really matter?

ASSIGNMENT

The Bible's unique attitude toward the body begins with the story of Creation in Genesis 1 and 2 and continues to the book of Revelation. The biblical attitude toward the body reaches full expression in the teaching on the resurrection of the body but only after a long preliminary case has been established—including lessons in the care of the body in the Old Testament Law, the danger of sins particularly related to the body, and the bodily

resurrection of our Lord. The journey is longer and more impressive than we might readily anticipate.

Day 1   Genesis 1:24–2:9 (Creation, breath of life); Psalm 25:4-10 (trust in God's power to save) Introduction and Readings 294 and 295

Day 2   Job 14 (mortal humans); 19:21-27 (faith in a redeemer) Readings 296 and 297

Day 3   Matthew 6:25-34 (assurance that God cares); John 1:1-18 (God took on human nature) Readings 298 and 299

Day 4   John 5:16-30 (the Son gives life); 1 Corinthians 6:9-20 (our bodies members of Christ); 2 Corinthians 4 (God will raise us also) Readings 300 and 301

Day 5   1 Corinthians 15:1-57 (resurrection of the body); 2 Corinthians 5:1-10 (a building from God) Readings 302 and 303

Day 6   Read and respond to "The Church Teaching and Believing" and "Believing and Living."

Day 7   Rest and prayer

DAILY PRAYER

Pray for the persons and situations on your Prayer Concerns list and about issues or concerns emerging from your daily reading and study.

276

RESURRECTION

SCRIPTURE	READINGS
DAY 1	
Genesis 1:24–2:9; Psalm 25:4-10	Introduction and Readings 294 and 295
DAY 2	
Job 14; 19:21-27	Readings 296 and 297
DAY 3	
Matthew 6:25-34; John 1:1-18	Readings 298 and 299

SCRIPTURE	READINGS
DAY 4	
John 5:16-30; 1 Corinthians 6:9-20; **2 Corinthians 4**	**Readings 300 and 301**
DAY 5	
1 Corinthians 15:1-57; 2 Corinthians 5:1-10	**Readings 302 and 303**

DAY 6 STUDY MANUAL	PRAYER CONCERNS
"The Church Teaching and Believing" **and "Believing and Living"**	

THE CHURCH TEACHING AND BELIEVING

How strange that the early church, in all the struggles of putting together a creed, would say, "I believe in the resurrection of the body." It seems so unspiritual, so unlikely, and so out of place. "Creator of heaven and earth" is majestic, and "communion of saints" is strangely mystical; but "resurrection of the body" is somewhere between the mundane and the impossible. We aren't sure the body should matter enough to get into the creed; and as we consider the principles of physics and chemistry, we don't know that we can believe the body can be resurrected—nor for that matter, that we want it to be.

But the early church knew what it believed, and it based its commitments in the Scriptures. What it believed about the resurrection of the body expressed both its conviction about the worth of the body and its confidence in the completeness of the divine triumph. The consummation of all things would include the body. Anything less and the divine victory would be incomplete.

The Old Testament and the Body

Genesis declares humanity is made in the image of God (Genesis 1:26-27). Then, in vivid and instructive imagery, the writer says God made humankind "from the dust of the ground, and breathed into his nostrils the breath of life; and the man became a living being" (2:7). The elements of human creation are strikingly diverse—the dust of the earth and the divine breath. The writer goes on to say the animals too were formed "out of the ground" (2:19), but no reference is made to the divine breath.

The human body is given a distinctive role. Dust it may be, but it is the carrier of the breath of God. The task sanctifies the vessel.

The Old Testament writers hold faithfully to this sacredness of the human body. When Cain kills his brother Abel, his brother's blood cries out to God from the ground (4:10). It is from the ground that Cain is cursed. It is the ground that "opened its mouth" to receive Abel's blood, and it is the ground that "will no longer yield to you [Cain] its strength" (4:11-12). Cain has several fears as he faces God's judgment for what he has done, and the first is that God has driven him "away from the soil" (4:13-14). This fear is more than a fear of losing his livelihood; his body has

been cut off from its physical (and mystical) source. Everything about the death and punishment that follows speaks of the unique relationship between the body and the earth. The murder of Abel is a violation of the very planet. We are inclined to see in this murder a violation of the divine breath, but the Genesis writer concentrates more on the body and the soil from which it came.

We are not surprised, then, that when the earth is judged to be so corrupt that a flood must come, the writer says "all flesh had corrupted its ways upon the earth," and that God declared he would "destroy them along with the earth" (6:12-13).

Nor is it surprising that the laws of Exodus and Leviticus make so much of matters having to do with the body. When the priests are ordained to their office, they are first of all washed with water. Then sacramental blood is put on the right ear, the right thumb, and the right big toe (Exodus 29:4, 20). The Israelites considered bodily discharges as making them "ceremonially unclean" (Leviticus 15:2), so they were to bathe in water. This act was not simply a matter of physical cleanliness but of ritual purity, and it had to do with the significance of the body and its life functions.

Recall that Job makes an especially notable witness regarding the worth of his body. He does so at a time when his body has become a reproach to him; he acknowledges that he

"wastes away like a rotten thing,
    like a garment that is moth-eaten" (Job 13:28).
His body is ravaged by disease, with "loathsome sores . . . from the sole of his foot to the crown of his head" (2:7). In such a state, Job might justifiably want to be rid of his body. His "breath is repulsive" to his wife, and he is "loathsome" to his family (19:17). Yet with all of that, he dares to say,

"and after my skin has been thus destroyed,
    then in my flesh I shall see God" (19:26).
No one can say what Job had in mind in this extraordinary witness. At the least, it was a moment of ecstatic faith. But from the point of view of our immediate interest, his statement demonstrates the importance Job gave to his body. Even in its tragic state, it was his habitation, and he cherished the possibility of its restoration. Perhaps we can hear in Job's words an early testimony to "the resurrection of the body." Scholarly restraint reminds us not to read too much into his words; faith, on the other hand, reminds us not to read too little.

The New Testament and the Body

The most powerful New Testament statement about the body is in God's act in Jesus Christ. The Gospel of John tells of the Word—that is, Jesus Christ—who "was with God," and who "was God," through whom "all things came into being" (John 1:1-3). This Word, John continues, "became flesh and lived among us, and we have seen his glory, the glory as of a father's only son, full of grace and truth" (1:14). If one would ask, What is the most striking evidence of the dignity and worth of the human body? the answer would have to be that God chose to become flesh in a normal human body. If the Word can accommodate itself to this housing, then the body deserves immensely more respect than we give it. Let this be forever the estimate of our physical dignity, that God lived in human flesh for more than thirty years.

But in earlier centuries the body had been under significant philosophical attack. The eminent Greek philosopher Plato (427–347 B.C.) taught that the body was temporal, material, and changeable while the soul was eternal, lacking substance, and unchangeable. This teaching, of course, led to the idea that the soul had kinship to the divine while the body was alien to it. Thus as a practical person would see it, the soul was the best of the human creature and the body was a burden to be borne, a kind of necessary evil.

Such an idea had a certain natural appeal. It corresponded with typical human experience. With our minds we want to do what is right, but our bodies won't cooperate. Plato's theory, or the conclusions others drew from it, fit well with human experience; so the body became a kind of villain. If it weren't for the encumbrance of the body, what noble creatures we would be!

Nor is it surprising, then, that some people in the church became attracted to a point of view that looked upon the body as a burden. They might well have reasoned that Paul himself seemed to suggest that flesh and mind were at odds with each other: "So then, with my mind I am a slave to the law of God, but with my flesh I am a slave to the law of sin" (Romans 7:25). In any event, a heresy developed that is known as *gnosticism*. Basically gnosticism was a belief that life is made up of the spiritual and the material, and that the spiritual is good while the material is evil.

The gnostics were *docetists,* or *seemists.* They taught that Jesus, as the spiritual Son of God, couldn't have had a real human body, since the body is material and therefore evil. Thus, their "seemist" name, since they said Jesus could only have "seemed" to be in a body.

Several heresies developed from this docetic thinking, but for our purposes, the most important is this: It saw the body as being evil. In the face of that heresy, the early church declared unhesitatingly, "I believe in the resurrection of the body." Not only was the body not evil; it was so good, so divinely ordained that it would survive death itself.

The phoenix is a mythical bird of pre-Christian origin that came into Christianity in the first century as a symbol of Christ's resurrection and the resurrection of those who die in Christ. According to legend, the phoenix is said to live for five hundred years in the Arabian desert and at its death bursts into flames but rises again fresh and new from its ashes. The phoenix and the date palm tree are often used together. The Greek word for the date palm is *phoenix,* and the ashes of the date palm are used as fertilizer for new date palm seedlings.

In this, the Christian gospel was, indeed, good news. It was a step beyond the teaching of the Old Testament Scriptures, which, except for rare passages, did not offer hope of a personal, physical resurrection. Even though everything about Old Testament teachings gave reverence to the body, those teachings fell short of declaring its physical resurrection.

The very truth of God's coming in the flesh in the person of Jesus Christ is the most dramatic statement for the sacredness of the body. Jesus' earthly ministry underlined that conviction in practical ways. His feeding of the multitudes and his response to their physical needs were a tacit witness to the body's worth. He never told the hungry to spiritualize their needs in lofty thinking. Each time Jesus healed the sick, he endorsed the worth of the body. And while he was emphasizing God's care when he said, "And even the hairs of your head are all counted" (Matthew 10:30), it is worth noticing that he made his point by reference to the most disposable part of the human body.

Jesus' Resurrection and Ours

Of course any belief in the resurrection of the body is closely tied to Jesus' resurrection from the dead. Paul insists that the two are inseparable. Some persons in the church at Corinth had come to believe there was no resurrection of the dead. But Paul answered, "If there is no resurrection of the dead, then Christ has not been raised" (1 Corinthians 15:13), and all the rest of the structure of belief falls too. The issue of the resurrection was its physical reality, as Paul's continuing arguments indicate. If the resurrection were simply spiritual or philosophical, no sizable controversy would have developed. Such ideas leave room for logical maneuvering and for variable positions. Physical resurrection, on the other hand, is substantial—in fact, its issue is *substance*. For a believer, it is a challenging idea to believe, but a wondrous lift to the spirit if fully accepted.

It was the bodily quality of Jesus' resurrection that was an issue for the disciples. The New Testament is clear and forthright about this. The disciples were no more susceptible to hopeful imagining than we are. They recognized they might be too ready to raise their own hopes. Thus when Jesus appeared among them after his resurrection, he dealt immediately with their unspoken concern: Was he real? That is, did he represent reality as they knew it, by being physical? So as soon as Jesus had greeted the disciples, "he showed them his hands and his side" (John 20:20). Thomas, whom we call the doubter, and who had not been with the disciples at that time, wanted the very evidence the others said they had already received: "Unless I see the mark of the nails in his hands, and put my finger in the mark of the nails and my hand in his side, I will not believe" (20:25). Thomas wanted absolute physical evidence.

The Gospel of Luke adds still another dimension to the physical quality of Jesus' resurrection body. Luke reports that when Jesus appeared among the disciples, they "thought that they were seeing a ghost" (Luke 24:37). Jesus met their concern head on: "Touch me and see; for a ghost does not have flesh and bones as you see that I have" (24:39); and with this, he showed them his hands and his feet. But "in their joy they were disbelieving and still wondering" (24:41).They thought what they were seeing was too good to be true; perhaps they reasoned within themselves that they were creating a vision out of their own hungry joy. So Jesus did the most common of human deeds. Asking them for something to eat, he received from them "a piece of broiled fish, and he took it and ate in their presence" (24:42-43). Now they knew the Resurrection was physical; a piece of broiled fish proved it.

Nagging Questions

Granted, there is something wonderfully reassuring about the physical nature of our Lord's resurrection, and granted, this physical element demonstrates dramatically the worth and importance of our human bodies. Nevertheless, numbers of questions remain. Not all may be important, but they nag for answers.

Such questions arose in the earliest days of the church. Paul dealt with some of them in his first letter to the church at Corinth. Some are quite ordinary, but we sense that such questions evoked the larger, theological questions about the viability of physical resurrection.

The Corinthians wanted to know what kind of body the resurrected persons would have. Paul was both direct and impatient in his answer: "Fool! What you sow does not come to life unless it dies" (1 Corinthians 15:36). He proceeded to draw analogies from nature. "As for what you sow, you do not sow the body that is to be, but a bare seed, perhaps of wheat or of some other grain. But God gives it a body as he has chosen, and to each kind of seed its own body" (15:37-38). The seed that is sown is a tiny, perhaps even a shriveled, thing; we don't expect that it will reappear in this form. Rather, we look for a fresh, green plant, a burst of promise.

"So it is," Paul continued, "with the resurrection of the dead. What is sown [the dead, human body] is perishable, what is raised is imperishable" (15:42). Paul then slipped into the style of Hebrew poetry. It is surprising that our translators don't present it as such; certainly the mood is song:

"Sown in dishonor, . . . raised in glory."

"Sown in weakness, . . . raised in power."

"Sown a physical body, . . . raised a spiritual body" (15:43-44).

The server at the restaurant or the guest at your dinner party is likely to raise questions similar to those Paul dealt with. And the questions are real to those who raise them. What happens to those who have been cremated? What about the person who has suffered an amputation, or whose body has been eaten by several wild beasts? Others wonder if those who have died as infants will be infants through all eternity. And what about those whose bodies are in some way deformed or unattractive—will they carry such a body into eternity? Paul might well answer that the new plant will not carry the burdens of the seed that has been sown.

But all these questions, including those that seem absurd or inconsequential to some, demonstrate the importance of "the resurrection of the body." And while a philosophical person might reason that bodies—even glorified ones—aren't really necessary in the world to come, Christian doctrine insists that the body and soul need each other. And of course Paul would have us understand that the eternal body will be inestimably better than the earthly one it replaces. Any imaginings in this detail, no matter how exotic, will fall short of eventual reality.

Practical Implications

But if the promise of resurrection be true, what manner of persons ought we to be? Does the resurrection of the body carry some ethical implications? Scripture would answer yes. The essence of stewardship is that we think of ourselves as persons in trust, and certainly no trust is more immediate and more accessible than the body. There is a lapse in logic when we speak respectfully of the gifts and talents endowed by God but neglect the body in which those gifts and talents reside and are expressed.

Of course, the qualities and capacities that make the body so remarkable make it equally vulnerable to evil. The eye that sees, the ear that hears, the drive that compels are as capable of error as of greatness.

Paul confronted this issue at one level in the church at Corinth. In Corinth, where prostitution was a matter of course, some believers slipped easily into sexual immorality. Paul pleaded, "Shun fornication" (1 Corinthians 6:18). He explained that "the fornicator sins against the body itself." How serious is this? Paul's answer deals specifically with the issue of the body and what it is: "Do you not know that your body is a temple of the Holy Spirit within you, which you have from God, and that you are not your own? For you were bought with a price; therefore glorify God in your body" (6:19-20).

When Paul speaks of the body as "a temple of the Holy Spirit," he brings a new dimension to an Old Testament picture. At Creation, humans received the breath, or spirit, of God. But now, as believers, they have received the Holy Spirit in their lives in a new and more tangible measure. They are *temples* of God's Spirit, places of worship for the Eternal. In Romans, Paul brings further light to the role of the body, urging believers "to present your bodies as a living sacrifice, holy and acceptable to God" (Romans 12:1). Once more he uses the language of worship, and once more he draws upon the imagery of his Jewish heritage. This time Paul portrays the believer's body as part of the church's corporate "living sacrifice," in contrast to sacrifices a levitical priest would have offered. Those sacrifices were dead; this one is living, ready to fulfill the purposes of God.

The worth of the body, as expressed especially in the promised resurrection of the body, had profound repercussions for human life and conduct. It meant that whatever one did with the body had potentially eternal significance. Since the Holy Spirit dwelt in the body, and the body was of such quality as to escape death's grasp, then the body was decidedly more than a receptacle for the soul. The body had honor in its own right, and extraordinary worth through the value of the soul dwelling within it. Not only did the soul dwell there; the soul and body were united by the Creator. To touch one is to touch the other.

No wonder the early church included in its declaration of faith "I believe in the resurrection of the body." By doing so, they not only affirmed their expectations about eternal life; they also reaffirmed their belief in supreme human worth. Where the gnostic philosophy of the first-century world saw the body as an impediment or evil, Christianity saw it as a temple of God's Spirit. And where first-century philosophy anticipated our being rid of the body at death, Christian teachers declared that God would resurrect it.

So, "when this perishable body puts on imperishability, and this mortal body puts on immortality, then the saying that is written will be fulfilled:

'Death has been swallowed up in victory'" (1 Corinthians 15:54).

BECAUSE WE THE CHURCH BELIEVE in the resurrection of the body, I will treat my body as a sacred gift of God and as a dwelling place of the Holy Spirit.

BELIEVING AND LIVING

The Christian doctrine of the body, as drawn from its belief in bodily resurrection, has peculiar points of intersection with contemporary thinking. This generation is as attentive to the body and its well-being as any in history. Medical advances have extended life expectancy and have reduced pain. The media give a constant stream of advice about health and nutrition.

But while in many ways our contemporary culture seems almost to worship the body, it fails to see the body's sacredness; and of course it isn't likely to subscribe to the idea of a bodily resurrection. How would you explain to a nonbelieving friend the Christian idea of the sacredness of the body?

_____

_____

People in biblical times lived so close to the soil that they were better equipped than we are to sense their own mystical tie to the earth. How can a contemporary city dweller have any such feeling?

_____

_____

    As you read Job's faith cry that someday "in my flesh I shall see God," what do you think he meant?

_____

_____

    What contemporary religious and cultural philosophies seem to you to be similar to gnosticism?

_____

_____

    As you contemplate issues related to the resurrection of the body, what questions trouble you? What in the doctrine is reassuring to you?

_____

_____

SEEKING MORE UNDERSTANDING

    C. S. Lewis's novel *The Great Divorce* (Touchstone Books, 1996) challenges one's thinking about the world to come and our place in it, and like everything else by Lewis, it is very readable. You might enjoy reading it for the subject matter but also to experience Lewis's ability to handle profound ideas in simple language. Most bookstores and libraries would have Lewis's books.

PRAYER

"Sing with all the saints in glory,
sing the resurrection song!
Death and sorrow, earth's dark story,
to the former days belong.
All around the clouds are breaking,
soon the storms of time shall cease;
in God's likeness we, awaking,
know the everlasting peace. . . .

Life eternal! heaven rejoices:
Jesus lives, who once was dead.
Join we now the deathless voices;
child of God, lift up your head!
Patriarchs from the distant ages,
saints all longing for their heaven,
prophets, psalmists, seers, and sages,
all await the glory given."
      —"Sing With All the Saints in Glory,"
      William J. Irons, 1812–1883

29

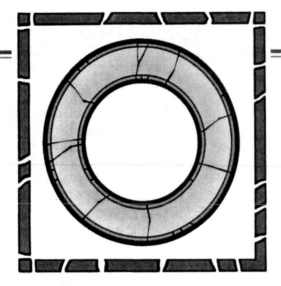

Death conquered | Eternal life | Worship constant

Life everlasting

Eternal communion with God

Sorrow gone | New heaven and new earth | Love supreme

Life in perfect relationship with God | | Death through Adam life through Christ

Begins when Christ becomes Lord of one's life | Future life life now

World and Life Without End

"For God so loved the world that he gave his only Son, so that everyone who believes in him may not perish but may have eternal life."
—John 3:16

LIFE QUESTIONS

So what is the end of it all? Are we simply candles, waiting to be snuffed out? Will each of our human stories end with our becoming little more than a contribution to the earth's compost pile? And if that be true of us individually, can we expect much more of history in its totality?

And yet, if God has made us, as the Scriptures declare, can our story end in such a meaningless way? What is the end of it all—for the individual, and for the human story?

ASSIGNMENT

The Scripture passages for this week follow an uneven course through the Old Testament. Certainly the Creation story gives an exalted view of our human worth, but then the emphasis through most of the Old Testament is on our mortality. This feeling reaches something like despair in the book of Ecclesiastes. But in Daniel we see for the first time a reference to resurrection.

The New Testament moves to a mood of hope. This hope finds its basis in Jesus Christ, with a grand consummation in the book of Revelation.

As you read, watch for any continuing thread of human significance, even in those passages that cannot affirm such a hope.

Day 1 Genesis 1:26–2:25 (God's image, God's breath); Psalm 16 (joy in God's presence) Introduction and Readings 304 and 305

Day 2 Psalm 49 (life and wealth fleeting); Ecclesiastes 1 (repetition in life); 2:12-26 (one fate for all); Daniel 12:1-4 (resurrection) Readings 306 and 307

Day 3 Matthew 19:16-30 (how receive eternal life); John 11:1-44 (Jesus the resurrection and life) Readings 308 and 309

Day 4 Romans 6 (eternal life God's free gift); 2 Corinthians 4:7–5:10 (God who raised Jesus will raise us) Reading 310

Day 5 Revelation 21 (renewal of creation); 22 (God the Lamb) Readings 311 and 312

Day 6 Read and respond to "The Church Teaching and Believing" and "Believing and Living."

Day 7 Rest and prayer

DAILY PRAYER

Pray for the persons and situations on your Prayer Concerns list and about issues or concerns emerging from your daily reading and study.

ETERNAL LIFE

SCRIPTURE	READINGS
DAY 1	
Genesis 1:26–2:25; Psalm 16	Introduction and Readings 304 and 305
DAY 2	
Psalm 49; Ecclesiastes 1; 2:12-26; Daniel 12:1-4	Readings 306 and 307
DAY 3	
Matthew 19:16-30; John 11:1-44	Readings 308 and 309

SCRIPTURE	READINGS
DAY 4	
Romans 6; 2 Corinthians 4:7–5:10	Reading 310
DAY 5	
Revelation 21; 22	Readings 311 and 312

DAY 6 STUDY MANUAL	PRAYER CONCERNS
"The Church Teaching and Believing" and "Believing and Living"	

THE CHURCH TEACHING AND BELIEVING

We humans were built for eternal life. Everlastingness is our native state. That's the message of the first two chapters of Genesis. But we went wrong; that's the bad news of Genesis 3. And with our going wrong, we became hostage to death. The inhabitants of Eden are told that if they disobey, in that day they will die. Physically, they don't die that day, but they are now beholden to death. The human story has taken on a different tone.

But we humans don't give up easily on the idea of eternal life. Perhaps it is a kind of memory of Eden, so that like a person with a severed limb, we still have sensations of feeling for a possibility of what once was. With almost no assurance of personal life beyond the grave, the writers of the Old Testament placed their hope in the next generation. Children gained importance of a special kind. As in all ancient cultures they were, of course, economic security. Thus the psalmist would say that sons are

"Like arrows in the hand of a warrior. . . .
Happy is the man who has
    his quiver full of them" (Psalm 127:4-5).
But for the devout, children were far more than financial provision. They carried on the family name, and with it the family dreams. When King Ahab tried to buy Naboth's vineyard, even offering "a better vineyard for it," Naboth refused: "The LORD forbid that I should give you my ancestral inheritance" (1 Kings 21:2-3).

But ancestral inheritance wasn't enough for the human soul. The psalmist was in an especially grateful mood when he looked at the "boundary lines" that had fallen for him "in pleasant places." So he wrote,

"For you do not give me up to Sheol,
    or let your faithful one see the Pit.
You show me the path of life.
    In your presence there is fullness of joy;
    in your right hand are pleasures forevermore"
        (Psalm 16:10-11).
Was the psalmist speaking of eternal life, or was he simply rejoicing that his death was being postponed? The language seems more ecstatic than a simple expression of gratitude for extra years. The references to "the path of life," "fullness of joy," and "pleasures forevermore" at God's "right hand" seem to reach beyond this present planet. Whether it was a faith statement, an occasion of exultant gratitude, or a doctrinal position before its time, it is a bright place in the book of Psalms.

On another occasion a psalmist declares the same kind of hope, although springing from a different mood. He is reflecting on "times of trouble," when his persecutors seem to prosper. He observes that for all of their pomp, "they are like the animals that perish" (49:12). But he sees a contrast:

"Death shall be their shepherd;
straight to the grave they descend,
    and their form shall waste away;
    Sheol shall be their home.
But God will ransom my soul from the power
    of Sheol,
    for he will receive me" (49:14-15).
One ought not to make too much of such a statement. But at the least, it shows the hunger for life (and vindication) beyond the grave, and surely also some measure of expectation.

Even the most dismal of Old Testament books, Ecclesiastes, is a peculiar tribute to the vigor of hope. The writer is seriously disillusioned because he thinks life should be more than it is proving to be. He is sure people should gain more

"from all the toil
    at which they toil under the sun" (Ecclesiastes
        1:3).
And while he finds futility in almost everything, he is especially distressed that

"The people of long ago are not remembered,
    nor will there be any remembrance
of people yet to come
    by those who come after them" (1:11).
He is troubled by the futility of accumulating for the next generation, because "who knows whether they will be wise or foolish?" (2:19). He observes that "the fate of humans and the fate of animals is the same; as one dies, so dies the other," and he fears that "humans have no advantage over the animals; for all is vanity. . . . Who knows whether the human spirit goes upward and the spirit of animals goes downward to the earth?" (3:19-21).

But he doesn't like it this way, and he doesn't think this is the way it should be. And while he doesn't have faith enough to expect anything more, he has faith enough to be troubled by the way it is. Something in his soul is certain that life ought to hold more significance. Call him a pessimist, but understand that his pessimism springs from his high expectations. Say again, a kind of memory of Eden.

The New Testament View

But a new quality of hope comes in the New Testament. Sometimes it springs in the soil of human searching. When a rich young man came to Jesus, he came with the question, "Teacher, what good deed must I do to have eternal life?" (Matthew 19:16). We cannot say for sure what the inquirer had in mind by the term *eternal life,* but certainly it was more than mere earthly gains, because he already had those. His question came from his realization that there must be more, and he addressed his question to Jesus because he recognized he would get the answer from him.

And certainly Jesus' comments on the incident in the conversation that followed with his disciples indicated more. Jesus spoke of a time "when the Son of Man is seated on the throne of his glory" and his followers with him; and he assured his disciples they "will inherit eternal life" (19:28-29).

The concept of eternal life should not be limited, on one hand, to life after death. But neither should it be limited to a higher quality of life on this earth. Eternal life is rightly perceived as a life that begins when Christ becomes Lord of an individual's life and continues into eternity. The quality is eternal on this earth, thus demonstrating Jesus' words, "I came that they may have life, and have it abundantly" (John 10:10). The length too is eternal, in this world and to world without end.

Jesus made a particular claim to conquest of death in the raising of Lazarus, the brother of Martha and Mary. In his conversation with Martha, Jesus said, "I am the resurrection and the life. Those who believe in me, even though they die, will live, and everyone who lives and believes in me will never die" (11:25-26). Here was an all-encompassing claim; it was a promise not only for Lazarus but for any who believe in Christ. With such a declaration, Jesus abolished the death penalty of Genesis. Paul made such an association in his teaching about the resurrection of Jesus. "For since death came through a human being [Adam], the resurrection of the dead has also come through a human being; for as all die in Adam, so all will be made alive in Christ" (1 Corinthians 15:21-22).

No wonder, then, that Paul described Jesus as "the first fruits of those who have died" (15:20). For believers with a knowledge of Judaism, that phrase was a vivid picture. Faithful Jews had for centuries brought the first produce of harvest, flock, or herd to the place of worship as a symbol of what belonged to God and in celebration of the full harvest that would soon follow. So Jesus came before God as the first harvest of human victory over death, with the tacit promise that a continuing harvest would follow.

So it is that baptism was a symbol of death and resurrection. All who were baptized into Christ Jesus, Paul explained, "were baptized into his death"; and "therefore we have been buried with him by baptism into death, so that, just as Christ was raised from the dead by the glory of the Father, so we too might

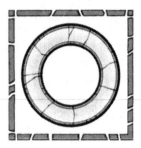

The continuous circle with no beginning and no ending symbolizes eternal, everlasting life with the one God in three persons whose nature and existence is perfect, complete, and eternal.

walk in newness of life" (Romans 6:3-4). To be baptized into Christ is to participate in the one person who has been raised from the dead (6:8-9). The spiritually alert could see in every baptism the announcement of eternal life in Christ.

The Larger Picture

Christian belief in eternal life is always more than simply a personal victory, no matter how magnificent those personal victories might be. The biblical view of life always includes the community of God's people, and beyond that, the grand scope of history.

The biblical story pictures the whole creation out of joint as a result of human sin. If God's will is to be done, the whole creation must be brought back to order. This is the essence of Jesus' petition,

"Your kingdom come.
Your will be done,
    on earth as it is in heaven" (Matthew 6:10).
And this, of course, is the mood of the book of Revelation. Whatever else may be said of this often confusing book, Revelation makes clear that God's purposes are now being finally and completely done. So loud voices in heaven are heard saying,

"The kingdom of the world has become
    the kingdom of our Lord
    and of his Messiah [Christ],
and he will reign forever and ever" (Revelation 11:15).
The triumph is not simply that of a minority, nor is it purely spiritual; the very "kingdom of the world" has become at last "the kingdom of our Lord." The battles described in Revelation are also conflicts involving the powers of history. While the visions of Revelation may well be symbolic in many details, the principle is clear: God's victory is ultimate and complete.

This message is consistent with the whole biblical story. The kingdoms of this world often are pictured as being at enmity with the people of God and the purposes of God. Whether it is the massive wickedness of Sodom and Gomorrah, the enslaving power of Egypt's pharaoh, the brutality of Nineveh, or the high-handedness of Babylon, the particular victims are God's people—because they represent the purposes of God, which are contrary to the worldly plans of humanity. Revelation portrays a dramatic reversal of this story. The kingdoms of this world are now to become the kingdom of our Lord and of his Christ.

But that isn't all. Since the Bible perceives nature itself as out of tune with the divine plan, this too must be corrected as eternal life is finally established. After all, eternal life could not be true in either practice or spirit if nature itself were still unredeemed. The Hebrew prophets anticipated this day:

"They will not hurt or destroy
    on all my holy mountain;
for the earth will be full of the knowledge of the LORD
    as the waters cover the sea" (Isaiah 11:9).

Paul pictured nature as longing for such a time. "For the creation," he said, "waits with eager longing for the revealing of the children of God," longs to "be set free from its bondage to decay" (Romans 8:19-21). Appropriately, when the heavenly scene opens in Revelation 4, the throne of God is surrounded not only by twenty-four elders (representing Israel and the church, the twelve tribes and twelve apostles), but also "four living creatures" (Revelation 4:6-8). These living creatures, representing the animal kingdom and humanity, sing; "day and night without ceasing they sing,

'Holy, holy, holy,

the Lord God the Almighty,

who was and is and is to come" (4:8).

The final victory of God, eternal life to the full, includes a return of nature to its original role of glorifying God, and of sublime peace in all of its parts.

But still, that is not all. Humanity's greatest distress is not in nature or in the realm of war and politics, but within. Nature and world affairs can surely add to the measure of distress; but the most profound and insistent expressions of distress are, in a large sense, homegrown. There is, therefore, a poignant beauty in the song of Revelation:

"See, the home of God is among mortals.

He will dwell with them;

they will be his peoples,

and God himself will be with them;

he will wipe every tear from their eyes.

Death will be no more;

mourning and crying and pain will be no more,

for the first things have passed away" (21:3-4).

This is indeed a new age, with a definition of eternal life that is as wide as the mercy of God. After all, endless life would be a sentence rather than a promise if it included the pain, crying, death, and tears we normally think of as part of living. In truth, however, tears, pain, and mourning are features of death, because they take from us either life or our ability to enjoy and possess life fully. They must go if eternal life is to have breadth and depth as well as length.

Perhaps this is why the Scriptures declare that there will be "a new heaven and a new earth" (21:1). Our present earth is corrupted by sin and all of sin's associates. As for heaven, we must enter into the perception of the first-century biblical world to understand the problem. Ephesians explains the nature of the conflict in which we humans are engaged. "Our struggle is not against enemies of blood and flesh, but against the rulers, against the authorities, against the cosmic powers of this present darkness, against the spiritual forces of evil in the heavenly places" (Ephesians 6:12).

The apostle was saying what all of us know, that there is more to evil than munitions and pornography. We realize that behind all the measurable evils of our world—murder, rape, theft, injustice—are matters almost impossible to quantify—greed, prejudice, anger, lust, to name a few. Matters that must be called, for lack of a better term, spiritual. Negative spiritual.

The writer of Ephesians described such powers as "the spiritual forces of evil in the heavenly places." He meant us to understand that these forces are real—something humans experience daily. If the apostle's language seems simplistic, realize he is seeking to make the concepts accessible to our understanding. But don't think of him as naive.

Quite likely, this corruption of the "heavenly places" by the spiritual struggle makes essential "a new heaven" as well as a new earth. At the least, the writer of Revelation is portraying an ultimate cleansing of the entire universe, to provide a new start. Eternal life deserves no less.

And What of Heaven?

Public opinion surveys reveal that a vast majority of persons believe there is a heaven and that most of them believe they are going there. But what is heaven? Jesus promised the repentant criminal who died beside him, "Truly I tell you, today you will be with me in Paradise" (Luke 23:43). The night before, Jesus had told his disciples there are "many dwelling places" in the Father's house and that he was going "to prepare a place" for them (John 14:2). A number of verses in Revelation, especially in the last two chapters, describe some elements of what this dwelling place will be.

From a relatively few biblical descriptions, popular culture through the ages has constructed elaborate images of heaven. Scholars sometimes say these popular descriptions trivialize heaven, reducing it to the level of cartoon and sentiment and innocent humor. Probably so. And yet, these pictures have their own merit in that they give form to some of the longings of the human heart. Who is to say that Emily Dickinson or William Blake is more qualified to imagine heaven than the child saying bedtime prayers or the nearly illiterate person who painfully spells out John 14:2, then dreams from that base?

Because of course heaven is beyond us in every way. We find a lift in the poets, artists, and composers who provide images of beauty for our edification; but we also remember with Paul that
"no eye has seen, nor ear heard,
    nor the human heart conceived,
what God has prepared for those who love him"
        (1 Corinthians 2:9).
Whatever heaven may be, it is certainly beyond the grasp of our present physical and mental equipment. If we could conceive the totality of heaven, it would cease to be heaven, since it would be within the management of earthly perception.

But what general statements can we make from what the Scriptures say? Above all, heaven will be "the home of God ... among mortals" (Revelation 21:3)—the ultimate restoration of what was lost by sin. Because God is the very ground of our being, to be separated from God in any measure is to be distorted. And only when our relationship with God is perfect will we be truly, utterly fulfilled. Every other measure of heaven rests on this, that in heaven God makes home with us mortals. Obviously, we can't imagine this being the measure of happiness except as we have come to love God with all of our being. Heaven can be heaven only to those who have turned their beings toward God.

For them, heaven is the end and goal of all things. It is not so much a reward at the end of life as it is the completion of life; that is, in heaven, life is *complete*.

Many other matters are clear from the Scripture. Heaven is portrayed as having values dramatically different from our earth, so that the matters for which people spend their lives here will there be part of the pavement and masonry. Sorrow will be gone. Love will be supreme. Worship will be constant. These ideas presuppose we will be quite different persons. That is, we will have a capacity for goodness, beauty, love, worship, and for levels of fulfillment beyond our imagining.

Each person can imagine much more. This is our privilege, perhaps a lovely faith-activity; but it is not appropriate to a doctrinal statement. The only caution is that our imagining of heaven ought to have a biblical pattern and be worthy of such an exalted theme.

The End of the Matter

The Bible is the story of God's relationship to the human race. As such, it is a love story. But it is also a story of conflict. The characters have barely settled into their roles when the struggle between good and evil is engaged. That conflict continues through the story of Cain and Abel, the Flood, the tower of Babel, the faith-struggle of Abraham and Sarah, and the establishing of the nation of Israel. The story finds music and prayers in the Psalms and magnificent exhortations in the prophets, then takes a decisive turn at the crucifixion of our Lord. On occasion, according to the prophets, the struggle has taken place on the broad field of the nations; but every day and every hour it goes on in the minds, affections, and spirits of individual human beings.

Often during the centuries, the saints of God have cried, "How long, O LORD?" Sometimes even the most hopeful have wondered in despair if the battle might be lost. But ten millions of times, in settings both mundane and breath-taking, believers have declared their ultimate expectation: "We look for the resurrection of the dead, / and the life of the world to come," in the words of the Nicene Creed; and "I believe in . . . the resurrection of the body, / and the life everlasting" in the Apostles' Creed.

And always, then, amen. World without end, amen!

BECAUSE WE THE CHURCH BELIEVE in eternal life, I will live, love, work, and pray each day with eternity in my soul.

BELIEVING AND LIVING

Our lesson says we humans are made for everlastingness, so that against all odds we believe in something beyond the grave for the individual and look for a happy ending for our human story. In what ways have you sensed that quality of hopefulness in your own life? Where have you seen evidences of it in others?

_____

_____

What difference does it make in your own outlook on life and conduct if you believe there is life beyond the grave?

_____

_____

Suppose you find yourself in a conversation with someone who does not believe the Bible; what kind of logical case can you make regarding the eventual victory of God, goodness, and righteousness, and the defeat of death?

_____

_____

If eternal life begins here on earth, how is it experienced in daily living?

_____

_____

When you think of heaven, what ideas and pictures come to your mind? Why do you think you picture heaven this way?

_____

_____

SEEKING MORE UNDERSTANDING

We occasionally hear sermons about heaven, though not often. Even less often do we hear of a scholarly book about heaven. But historian Jeffrey Burton Russell has written a book he has titled *A History of Heaven: The Singing Silence* (Princeton University Press, 1997), a panoramic view of what has been written about heaven. Check availability at your public library or a bookstore.

PRAYER

"Unto him who is gone hence, O my Saviour, open thou, we beseech thee, the door of thy mercy, O Christ; that he may rejoice in glory, as he partaketh of the joys of thy kingdom.

What pleasure in this life remains unmarked by sorrow? What glory can endure upon this earth unchanged? All is feebler than a shadow, more deceptive than a dream; for death in a single moment takes all things away. But in the light of thy countenance, O Christ, and in the joy of thy beauty, give rest to those whom thou hast chosen, for thou lovest humankind."

— *Eastern Orthodox Prayers for the Dead*

30

New life in Christ   Living   Serving humanity

Growth in righteousness   **Christs to one another**   Transformed by beliefs

Salt   Light

Beliefs shape attitudes and conduct

Right teaching   **Company of believers**   Right practice

The Difference Believing Makes

"And he [Abram] believed the LORD; and the LORD reckoned it to him as righteousness."
—Genesis 15:6

LIFE QUESTIONS

Beliefs have consequences because beliefs inform conduct. Rarely is the link between beliefs and conduct an immediate cause-and-effect experience. We can prove it only long after the fact. Sometimes, in fact, people profess beliefs all their lives without those beliefs seeming to make much difference, for good or ill, in the way they live. Which means believing is a more complex process than we usually realize. Sometimes it seems there is a long stretch between what we believe and how we live. Or perhaps we don't really know what we believe, so that our conduct is being shaped by what we truly but unconsciously believe rather than by what we think we believe.

By now we have spent nearly a year discussing specific beliefs. If we accept these beliefs as something more than abstract theories, what difference will they make in our lives? In what ways will we be more Christian, more useful, more fulfilled? Or should we even expect to be? What difference will these beliefs make in the life of the church?

ASSIGNMENT

Some of our Scripture passages make specific reference to believing; others have to do more with the nature of the godly life. In the latter instances, the inference is that such living is springing from beliefs. If you look up *believe* and its several cognate forms in a concordance, you will discover a wide variety of results of believing, either promised or experienced.

Such Scriptures are both a challenge and an encouragement. As we read, we ought (even more than usual) to ask ourselves how best to apply these passages in our daily living.

Day 1   Psalm 15 (walk blamelessly); Proverbs 4 (the way of wisdom)
Introduction and Readings 313 and 314
Day 2   Habakkuk 3 (rejoice in the Lord); Matthew 5:1-20 (living under God's rule)
Readings 315, 316, and 317
Day 3   Matthew 9:35–10:42 (discipleship); Galatians 6:1-10 (for the good of all)
Readings 318 and 319
Day 4   1 Thessalonians 1 (an example to all); John 3:1-21 (whoever believes, eternal life)
Readings 320 and 321
Day 5   Hebrews 11:32–12:13 (perseverance in the race); James 1:2-18 (endurance through testing); 2:14-26 (faith and works)
Readings 322 and 323
Day 6   Read and respond to "The Church Teaching and Believing" and "Believing and Living."
Day 7   Rest and prayer

DAILY PRAYER

Pray for the persons and situations on your Prayer Concerns list and about issues or concerns emerging from your daily reading and study.

LIVING

SCRIPTURE	READINGS
DAY 1	
Psalm 15; Proverbs 4	Introduction and Readings 313 and 314
DAY 2	
Habakkuk 3; Matthew 5:1-20	Readings 315, 316, and 317
DAY 3	
Matthew 9:35–10:42; Galatians 6:1-10	Readings 318 and 319

SCRIPTURE	READINGS

DAY 4

1 Thessalonians 1; John 3:1-21	Readings 320 and 321

DAY 5

Hebrews 11:32–12:13; James 1:2-18; 2:14-26	Readings 322 and 323

DAY 6 STUDY MANUAL	PRAYER CONCERNS
"The Church Teaching and Believing" and "Believing and Living"	

THE CHURCH TEACHING AND BELIEVING

The creeds end as we expect them to: *Amen.* We see the *Amen* as a period to the declaration and look to our church bulletin or prayer book to see what comes next.

But the *Amen* signals what's to come next. This hurried word, this "so be it," is now ours to implement. If indeed the creeds are to mean anything more than a quaint historical statement, if they are to be truly, dynamically relevant, there will need to be an *Amen,* a *so-be-it.* And it is the business of believers to deliver that *so-be-it* to our world. The creeds fulfill themselves as believers walk out into society as the transformed persons implicit in the creeds. We have said, "I believe," and we have listed our believings. Now we say, "Amen," not simply because the statement is complete but because we want the creed to come to pass; we want it to be so.

The Scriptures encourage us to examine our lives in order that we may grow in righteousness, and to examine is to judge whether we have grown. So what difference has my study made, or what difference should I expect my believing to make?

The Bible assumes, from beginning to end, that what we believe makes a difference, and a great one. At a time when for most people "every inclination of the thoughts of their hearts was only evil continually," Noah stood out because he was "a righteous man, blameless in his generation" (Genesis 6:5-9). The majority of people were evil because of what they thought. Noah was righteous because when God spoke, Noah "respected the warning" (Hebrews 11:7).

So too with Abraham, who is pictured as the ancestor of all who live by faith. Genesis says he "believed the LORD; and the LORD reckoned it to him as righteousness" (Genesis 15:6). We know nothing about Abraham's character or achievements prior to his act of believing; we know only that at a certain point, "Abram went, as the LORD had told him" (12:4). Those who have brought God's will to pass are those who have *believed,* and believing, have acted upon their beliefs.

The Divine Expectation

Those who believed God were expected to be different. In the case of Noah, the difference was dramatic. In a world almost unbelievably corrupt, he was righteous. Most of the time, of course, the lines between good and evil are not so sharply drawn. In a sense, serving God effectively may be more difficult in such times, since the boundaries are harder to distinguish. Still, this is the mark of believers, that they have the spiritual acumen to see such boundaries. Where the culture at large sees only a vague neutral territory, the person with belief sensibilities sees a line of decision.

For God's covenant people, Israel, the belief system was drawn up in an intricate legal code. Seen from other than a faith perspective, that legal code may appear overly detailed and without any particular logic. In truth, it has a dominant operating principle—to help Israel maintain its differentness, its holiness, so it could fulfill its divine task.

Believer must have become a defining term early in the life of the church. In the Old Testament, the distinction was between Jews and non-Jews; but in the New Testament, where the church was a mixture of ethnic groups, the distinction was between believers and unbelievers.

So Paul explains to the church at Corinth, "Tongues, then, are a sign not for believers but for unbelievers, while prophecy is not for unbelievers but for believers" (1 Corinthians 14:22). Paul praises the church at Thessalonica because its people have become "an example to all the believers in Macedonia and in Achaia" (1 Thessalonians 1:7). The Thessalonians do not know and probably will never see these persons, but they are bound up with them in the company of "believers." When the apostle encourages young Timothy to fulfill his potential, he tells him to "set the believers an example" (1 Timothy 4:12). It sounds as if the first Christians identified themselves within their own conversations as *believers*—and likewise, their shorthand term for the rest of the world was *unbelievers.*

This use of language is powerful and instructive. The first Christians identified themselves by their common beliefs. When Paul spoke to the Thessalonians about the believers in Achaia, he assumed they felt a kinship with these people. After all, they were all bound together by a common body of belief; and although these bonds were invisible, they were powerful beyond description. Indeed, perhaps no bonds are more powerful than beliefs held in common. It is easy to clasp the hand of such a person and say, "Brother, Sister."

And might it be that one of the greatest weaknesses in Christendom today is the absence of such a bond of believing? The beliefs are there. The church has the same grand deposit of belief that has sustained it through centuries of persecution and change. Nor can we blame heresies or potential heresies of our time. Every period of church history has had to cope with questioning and controversies. The problem may be that those who presumably belong in the company of believers do believe with so little intensity, and probably with so little knowledge.

Assumedly, then, we who have been studying doctrine for months, and discussing it with other believers, should be different from when our study began. But how? In what ways should we be changed? The best place to seek an answer is in the record of the original body of Christian believers, as recorded in the New Testament.

Conduct

Without a doubt, the first-generation Christians understood their conduct was to be transformed by their beliefs. Jesus had planted this seed with his disciples in the Sermon on the Mount. "You are the salt of the earth," he said. "You are the light of the world" (Matthew 5:13-14). The disciples were to bring flavor and light to the earth, and they would do so by their example. They were to be people of "good works," and these good works would bring glory to God.

The letters—the oldest portion of the New Testament—are packed full of counsel for daily Christian conduct. From a theological point of view, we might say they are made up almost entirely of *orthodoxy* and *orthopraxis*—that is, right teaching and right practice. The apostolic writers could not imagine the two being separated.

But it was not easy. Most of us can hardly imagine the difficulty of developing an ethical code for believers in the first-century world. The first of those believers had a good start because they were Jews and as such possessed a magnificent code of conduct in the Torah. But the Gentile believers came from every imaginable heritage, some of which endorsed the kind of conduct believers knew to be wrong and destructive.

Sometimes, ironically, people used the teachings of the faith to justify unchristian conduct. They took Paul's preaching about the grace of God to argue that the more evil they did, the more opportunity for grace to work (Romans 3:8; 6:1-2). Then, it seems some believers in Thessalonica were so caught up in expectation of Christ's return that they were neglecting their work. Paul not only instructs such persons to work; he points out they have forsaken "the tradition that they received from us" (2 Thessalonians 3:6). "Now such persons we command and exhort in the Lord Jesus Christ to do their work quietly and

The vine is the most widely used plant form in Christian art. Its meaning may be understood on two levels. First, as a symbol of the new relationship between God and human beings in Jesus Christ. Jesus is the vine, his followers the branches. The necessity of the connection between the vine and branches is expressed in Jesus' words: "Those who abide in me and I in them bear much fruit, because apart from me you can do nothing" (John 15:5). The vine and the branches may also represent the church, which is made up of believers who abide in the Lord Jesus.

to earn their own living" (3:12). The basis of Paul's appeal is a doctrinal one in that he urges them "in the Lord Jesus Christ."

In at least one instance Paul uses a sublime doctrine to make what seems to be a pedestrian point. In appealing for humility among the members at Philippi, he reminds them that though Christ Jesus "was in the form of God," he "emptied himself, / taking the form of a slave" (Philippians 2:6-7). Paul's argument not only gives us a magnificent statement of the preexistence of Christ; it also indicates the importance Paul gave to conduct. He related the doctrine of Christology to something as prosaic as humility versus human conceit. One could hardly ask for more convincing evidence that in the early church conduct mattered and that it was directly related to doctrine.

Mission

Their beliefs informed and drove their sense of mission. They were people with a purpose in living, and that purpose related directly to what they believed.

We know Paul's story best because of the letters and because the latter half of the book of Acts concentrates on his story. But clearly the same sense of mission compelled all in the early church, whatever their role. To be a Christian was to be in mission, and much of the time the mission was carried on at the peril of livelihood and life. When the New Testament reports a local congregation was meeting in a particular person's home, we think of theology, church structure, and small group ministry; but in the first century it also meant ostracism and the possibility of violent persecution. Yet by such house meetings the mission of the church was fulfilled.

Their Lord had said, "You will be my witnesses in Jerusalem, in all Judea and Samaria, and to the ends of the earth" (Acts 1:8). Those who first heard that message had, in the main, traveled no more than a day's journey from their homes. To go through Samaria was to suffer cultural and religious shock. But now their Lord had told them to go "to the ends of the earth." They could hardly have imagined what that might mean, but they set out to do as they had been told. They believed, and that belief left them with a mission.

A Different Kind of Life

If believers take seriously the creeds of the church, they find a symmetry and a cohesiveness in life. Life holds together, with purpose and significance. The Scriptures make no guarantee believers will escape such common disruptions of life as sickness, bereavement, and natural disasters. But they do assure a capacity to cope effectively and triumphantly with life's varying fortunes. Believers expect to be "more than conquerors" (Romans 8:37), which is to say that while believers cannot control the circumstances of life, neither are they victims of those circumstances. This understanding makes for a different attitude toward life.

Greatness in Living

Jesus said he had come so that people might "have life, and have it abundantly" (John 10:10). A people who profess to have received eternal life ought obviously to live life in a demonstrably superior way. This greatness in living begins with new life in Christ, but its development is built on the framework of beliefs.

The quality of this continuing structure depends almost entirely on the quality of the framework. We cannot fully judge the efficacy of a baptism or a conversion on the basis of the believer's life. In the language of analogy, the health of a baby at birth does not guarantee its health at adolescence or adulthood; nurture in the intervening period will make all the difference.

And so it is with believers. The regenerative act is of God. We can therefore reasonably conclude it is effective in every instance, not only for life in eternity but for new life on earth. The divine elements must be the same in every case, since regeneration is the work of the Holy Spirit and since the Holy Spirit is not inconsistent in quality or performance.

But what happens after the regenerative act depends heavily on human agents. The teaching persons receive and the nurture setting in which they live can be used of God, but only to the degree human agents cooperate with God. A number of factors contribute to the quality of this nurture. Doctrine is one of the most important because it provides the framework on which the spiritual growth occurs.

But teaching in doctrine tends to be a missing—or seriously neglected—factor. In at least some measure, this omission reflects the intellectual climate of the time. Few judgments frighten people more than that they should be called narrow-minded. *Doctrinaire,* on one hand, is seen as a pejorative term, while no goal is more esteemed than to be "open-minded." But of course the purpose of an open mind, as someone has said, is eventually to close it. But inconclusiveness in thought is seen by many as a virtue; so they are reluctant to say, "This I believe."

Also, modern and post-modern minds tend to be skeptical of the wisdom of the past. They see tradition as an impediment rather than an endorsement, and the proceedings of church councils carry little weight. Nothing so handicaps our interest in doctrine as a misperception of the nature of doctrine. We think of it as theories to be learned and reasoning to be remembered, and of course doctrine includes these elements. But doctrine is also a song to be sung. Indeed, it is literally thousands of songs. Any hymn of substance is a declaration of some doctrine of the church, and the best hymns are profound theological statements. When carolers sing,

"Mild he lays his glory by,
born that we no more may die,"

they have touched upon Christology, atonement, and salvation. Sung thoughtfully, such words are enough to lift a believer to ecstatic heights.

And the hymns of the many Christian communions are full

of such statements. The gospel hymn "I Love to Tell the Story" might well be paraphrased "I Love to Sing the Doctrine." Our failure is twofold: On one hand, we don't realize doctrine is a song to be sung; and on the other, when we sing doctrine, we rarely recognize the wonder of which we are singing.

Doctrine is also a primary source of comfort and strength. We know this implicitly, but we don't comprehend what we know. The bereaved are often sustained by their knowledge of the doctrine of eternal life, but they wouldn't think of expressing it that way. The lonely find strength in the continuing presence of God without realizing they are implementing the doctrine of the Holy Spirit. When thoughtful students of history expect justice will eventually show itself in the affairs of nations, they are invoking the doctrine of judgment, know it or not.

Doctrine is, of course, an intellectual pursuit. Little need to make that point to persons who have spent months studying the subject! But knowledge of doctrine is much more than a cerebral enterprise. Doctrine engages the whole person.

The Wonder of What We Believe

So what shall we say when we ponder the doctrine of revelation? At the least, we will stand in awe that God has chosen to reveal what is often beyond physical perception, and that persons have conveyed these insights from one generation to the next. The doctrine of the Scriptures? Who can read this story without marveling that such a book has been preserved over millennia and still speaks with undiminished power?

We say we believe in God, but we say it with exultation rather than with groveling fear, because God has been revealed to us not only as Creator—a source of wonder, indeed!—but also as Redeemer; for as Christians we understand God most fully as the divine is revealed to us in Jesus Christ. And we take a deep breath as we declare our belief in Jesus Christ, because we have gone beyond simple sentiments about a fine teacher or a profound moral example and have acknowledged he is the preexistent Son of God. The Holy Spirit, God with us? Yes, and empowering us to become all God has intended the daughters and sons of earth to be.

The wonder never ceases. The person in the next automobile is made in the divine image, a creature for whom Christ died, and with the potential for saintliness. The luncheon roll at the restaurant reminds us of the Body we receive at Holy Communion, and the storefront church on a back street declares Christ has established the church and the gates of hell cannot prevail against it.

We call ourselves Christian believers. Such identification doesn't mean we will never again have questions. Rather, when we question, it will be with more perception, more depth, and more fortitude. In a world where so many are passionate about trivial matters, we have chosen deliberately to be passionate about those things that matter most. We are not ashamed to say we believe. We are only astonished that we can belong to such a company as this—the community of believers.

> BECAUSE WE THE CHURCH BELIEVE the church is made up of believers, I gladly count myself in that sacred company.

BELIEVING AND LIVING

In popular perception, the word *believer* is often caught somewhere between naiveté on one hand and fanaticism on the other. What was your perception of the word *believer* when you began this study, and how do you perceive it today?

_____

_____

Without looking at previous lessons, write a personal *credo* ("I believe" statement), building it entirely on the matters that currently stand out in your mind as the most important elements of your believing:

_____

_____

_____

_____

How close is this personal creed to either the Apostles' Creed or the Nicene Creed? Explain the differences.

_____

_____

How has your personal creed changed from what it was when you began this study?

_____

_____

SEEKING MORE UNDERSTANDING

The hymns of the church have carried the doctrines of the church. Using a church hymnal, look carefully to see what doctrines you find conveyed in the hymns. Read slowly enough to get beyond familiar rhythms. Consider which hymns and hymn writers are especially effective at conveying doctrinal truth. Notice the era in which the writers lived, and see if you can find a pattern of emphasis at different points in church history.

PRAYER

"Incline us O God! to think humbly of ourselves, to be saved only in the examination of our own conduct, to consider our fellow-creatures with kindness, and to judge of all they say and do with the charity which we would desire from them ourselves."

—*Jane Austen, 1775–1817*

304

CPSIA information can be obtained at www.ICGtesting.com
Printed in the USA
LVOW09s0029130614

389842LV00002B/2/P

9 780687 075638